The Cuban Connection

Eduardo Sáenz Rovner

THE CUBAN

A book in the series Latin
America in Translation /
en Traducción / em Tradução

Sponsored by the Consortium
in Latin American Studies
at the University of North
Carolina at Chapel Hill and
Duke University

CONNECTION

Drug Trafficking, Smuggling,
and Gambling in Cuba from
the 1920s to the Revolution

Translated by Russ Davidson

The University of North Carolina Press
Chapel Hill

Translation of the books in the series Latin America in Translation / en Traducción / em Tradução, a collaboration between the Consortium in Latin American Studies at the University of North Carolina at Chapel Hill and Duke University and the university presses of the University of North Carolina and Duke, is supported by a grant from the Andrew W. Mellon Foundation.

Designed by April Leidig-Higgins
Set in MinionPro by Copperline Book Services, Inc.
Manufactured in the United States of America

Originally published in Spanish by Universidad Nacional de Colombia Colección CES as *La conexión cubana: narcotráfico, contrabando y juego en Cuba entre los años 20 y comienzos de la Revolución*, © 2005 Eduardo Sáenz Rovner

The paper in this book meets the guidelines for permanence and durability of the Committee on Production Guidelines for Book Longevity of the Council on Library Resources.

The University of North Carolina Press has been a member of the Green Press Initiative since 2003.

Library of Congress Cataloging-in-Publication Data
Sáenz Rovner, Eduardo.
  [Conexión cubana. English]
The Cuban connection : drug trafficking, smuggling, and gambling in Cuba from the 1920s to the Revolution / Eduardo Sáenz Rovner ; translated by Russ Davidson.
  p. cm. — (Latin America in translation/en traducción/em tradução)
Includes bibliographical references and index.
ISBN 978-0-8078-3175-5 (cloth : alk. paper)
  1. Drug traffic — Cuba — History — 20th century.
2. Organized crime — Cuba — History — 20th century.
3. Gambling — Cuba — History — 20th century.
4. United States — Foreign relations — Cuba.
5. Cuba — Foreign relations — United States.   I. Title.
HV5840.C85S2413   2008
364.1'0609729109041 — dc22   2008020373

12 11 10 09 08   5 4 3 2 1

To my mother

Havana is rather a smoldering volcano of life, of Kaffir politics, of race and class struggles; it is brutal, realistic, palpitating with vitality as few cities in Latin America—the new, violent stridency of a culture and a way of life still unfulfilled, its contours still undetermined.

—Carleton Beals, *The Crime of Cuba* (1933)

Contents

Acknowledgments xi

Introduction 1

1 U.S. Prohibition and Smuggling from Cuba 17

2 Drug Trafficking and Political Anarchy during the 1930s 31

3 The Chinese and Opium Consumption in Cuba 45

4 Corruption and Drug Trafficking in Cuba during the
   Second World War and the Early Postwar Years 57

5 Lucky Luciano in Cuba 65

6 The Prío Socarrás Government and Drug Trafficking 75

7 Gambling in Cuba 81

8 The Andean Connection 95

9 Contacts in France 103

10 The Batista Dictatorship and Drug Trafficking 113

11 Revolution 123

12 The Diplomacy of Drug Trafficking at the Beginning
    of the Revolution 135

Epilogue 147

Notes 153

Bibliography 211

Index 237

Acknowledgments

I am indebted to the scholars who read drafts of the book and offered valuable suggestions at various stages: Charles W. Bergquist (University of Washington), José C. Moya (UCLA and Barnard College), Bernardo Parra (Universidad Nacional de Colombia), and Francisco E. Thoumi (Universidad del Rosario, Bogotá).

I also thank my colleagues at the Center for Social Studies and the School of Economic Sciences, both located at Colombia's National University, for their assistance to my research. I likewise extend appreciation to the late Robert Levine, Elena Sabogal, and Steve Stein, all affiliated with the Center for Latin American Studies at the University of Miami. I also benefited greatly from assistance given by the staff of the Cuban Heritage Collection — a truly outstanding resource — and the Pan American Airways Archive, both of which are located at the University of Miami's Richter Library.

Others who offered valuable assistance are Fred Romanski of the U.S. National Archives and Records Administration, College Park, Maryland, branch, and the staff of the following archives: Cuba's Archivo Nacional, Havana (with thanks in particular to Julio López Valdés); Colombia's Archivo General de la Nación (Bogotá); the U.S. National Archives and Records Administration, Southeast Region in Atlanta and Northeast Region in New York City (special mention to Richard Gelbke); and the Federal District Court for Miami, Florida.

I am also grateful to the following individuals for their friendship and assistance while this book was being researched and written: Orlando Acosta, María Hericinda Barahona de Sandoval, Luis Carlos Barriga, Susana Mabel Cabanillas, Amparo Caicedo, Enrique Córdoba, Thomas Fischer, João Gonçalves, Myriam Jimeno, Abel Ricardo López, Gerardo Reyes, Alvaro Román, Jorge Sanguinetty, Ernesto Sierra, and Víctor Uribe Urán.

While my research was under way, I presented working papers both at the University of Miami and at several scholarly conferences and events: the

Cátedra Anual de Historia held at Colombia's National Museum; the Cátedra Unesco (by invitation of Professor Luis Astorga) conducted by Mexico's National Autonomous University; and a seminar organized regularly by the School of Economic Sciences at Colombia's National University, where at various points in my research I also engaged in discussions with my students.

To Professor Luis A. Pérez Jr., who suggested that I submit the manuscript to the University of North Carolina Press, I owe a special debt of gratitude, as I do to Elaine Maisner, senior editor at UNC Press, and to the two anonymous readers who critiqued the manuscript.

I made my first visit to Havana in November 2002 in the company of my brother, Mario; since then, he has steadily followed the course of my research. During my repeated visits to the University of Miami, my mother, Marta Rovner de Sáenz, allowed me to turn her Miami Beach apartment into a study overflowing with books and documents about Cuba, into a place where one conversed only about Cuban history and listened only to Cuban music. I dedicate this book to her.

The Cuban Connection

Introduction

A t the end of December 1956, two Colombian brothers, Rafael and Tomás Herrán Olózaga, were apprehended in Havana while holding a shipment of heroin valued at sixteen thousand dollars. The brothers, a chemist and pilot, respectively, were twins who hailed from elite families in Bogotá and Medellín. Their paternal great-great-grandfather, Tomás Cipriano de Mosquera, and great-grandfather, Pedro Alcántara Herrán, had served as presidents of Colombia during the nineteenth century. On their mother's side, they were closely related to the Echavarría Olózaga family, which formed part of Medellín's leading industrial clan.[1]

The brothers had arrived in Havana on 1 November 1956, from Colombia, passing first through Jamaica. Arrested with them were two Colombian women, one of whom had helped bring the drugs into Cuba. The other, Tomás's wife, functioned as a courier, smuggling the drugs into the United States using her status as a university student in Philadelphia. A Cuban was also arrested along with the four Colombians.

The Herrán Olózaga brothers confessed that they had brought drugs into Cuba before. After their arrest, all of the parties except Tomás were released on bail and traveled to Mérida, Mexico. Tomás, evidently the gang's leader, remained imprisoned in Cuba for a year. After gaining his freedom, he returned to Medellín. In February 1957, however, agents of the Colombian Intelligence Service, backed by an official of the U.S. Federal Bureau of Narcotics, raided the brothers' laboratory in a Medellín suburb, where they had been processing cocaine since at least 1952. In the wake of this action, officials learned that the brothers had previously trafficked in Ecuadorian opium. As early as 1939, in fact, both the Colombian and German police had suspected that Rafael was a drug trafficker, suspicions created when they learned of his attempt to get a German drug manufacturer to sell cocaine and morphine in amounts greater than one kilogram to the Union Pharmacy he operated in Medellín.[2]

THE CASE OF THE Herrán Olózaga brothers demonstrates that cross-border drug trafficking in Latin America was anything but an enterprise of the poor.[3] On the contrary, it demanded a certain know-how as well as financial capital and international connections. In view of such requirements, it is little wonder that a considerable number of drug traffickers who operated in the region during these years were of immigrant origin. Furthermore, the incident involving the Herrán Olózaga brothers assumes added significance precisely because it did not represent an isolated event in mid-twentieth-century Cuba. All through the era of Prohibition in the United States, from 1920 until the mid-1930s, the island served as a source of contraband alcohol for its northern neighbor, and illegal drugs were sent from Cuba to be processed in European laboratories. Furthermore, in addition to serving as a transmission zone for drugs, Cuba became a country in which a variety of prohibited substances were consumed, from the opium used by members of the immigrant Chinese community (the largest such community in Latin America), to the marijuana used by those of more humble origin, to cocaine, the drug of choice among members of the country's elite.

Over the first decades of the twentieth century, Cuba's economy became closely tied both to international commerce and to successive waves of migration. Already possessing one of the richest economies in the Americas during the colonial period, Cuba experienced a growth boom led by sugar beginning in the early years of the nineteenth century. Moreover, by 1900, Cuba ranked as the second-most-urbanized country in Latin America, after Uruguay and a little ahead of Argentina.[4] Cuba's development during these decades was highlighted by the continued growth of the sugar sector, which reached its zenith in 1925 and persisted at high levels until 1930, when the Great Depression dealt a severe blow to demand. By the outset of the 1920s, Cuba commanded 65 percent of the U.S. market for sugar; the island, in turn, became the principal market for boxcars and the second-biggest market (after Japan) for train tracks produced in North America. Cuba also served as a major outlet for other machinery and durable goods manufactured in the United States and, along with Canada and Mexico, constituted one of the three largest markets for North American investment in the Americas. Such robust economic growth yielded positive social outcomes: by 1930, Cuba had attained the second-highest life expectancy in Latin America, trailing only wealthier Argentina, and its population boasted a literacy rate of 70 percent.[5] Even Cuba's nonwhite population exceeded the Latin American average for literacy; in 1919, for example, the literacy rate among Afro-Cubans stood at

53 percent.[6] In 1934, Cuba possessed no fewer than fifty-one radio stations (half of them located in Havana), a figure exceeded worldwide by only three countries — the United States, Canada, and the Soviet Union.[7] Even during the 1950s, when Cuba felt the effects of an unstable sugar market and slackening economic growth, it remained among the hemisphere's elite countries in terms of social and economic indicators. In this period, many middle-class residents of Havana enjoyed a high standard of living and benefited from the fruits of a consumption boom. Simultaneously, however, and equally significant, the gains registered by the country's construction and industrial sectors worsened the economic gap between Havana and the rest of the country, paralleling the inequalities that divided Cuba's urban and rural sectors more generally.[8]

Cuba's population and Cuban society had been formed by different waves of migration. One such wave occurred in the early nineteenth century, when a considerable number of French fled the chaos that engulfed Haiti after its triumphant slave rebellion. Escapees from the former French colony established themselves primarily on Cuba's eastern end, and in lesser numbers around Havana and Matanzas, and contributed to the modernization of Cuba's sugar and coffee production.[9] In 1819, another contingent of French arriving from another former colony, Louisiana, founded a settlement that eleven years later would be rechristened Cienfuegos.[10] The second major wave of migration, a massive one that endured for several decades, involved the Spanish. During the first half of the nineteenth century, some 60,000 Spaniards immigrated to Cuba, more than the total number of Spanish immigrants to all of the remaining countries of the Americas over the same period.[11] Then, between 1868 and 1898, Cuba witnessed the arrival of 1,000,000 Spaniards — 464,503 civilians and 535,495 soldiers. Even discounting both the soldiers who died during the wars of independence and the civilians and soldiers who returned from the island to Spain, this high level of migration means that until 1902 Cuba served as the principal destination of Spanish immigrants. In addition, substantial numbers of Chinese, Jamaicans, Haitians, Middle Easterners, and other Europeans immigrated to Cuba. The North American community was likewise numerous.[12] The stream of North American migrants into Cuba began in the last years of the nineteenth century and included speculators, fortune hunters, prostitutes, and entire families. These colonists found their way into Cuba from all parts of the United States and purchased tracts of rural property where they could work the land. In this respect, they were particularly drawn to the provinces of Camagüey and Oriente and to the Isle of Pines. So strong, in fact, was the immigrants' attachment to the Isle of Pines that certain elements among them exerted great pressure to have it annexed to the United States.[13] Furthermore, nearly eighty of the American agricultural colonies established in Cuba contained immigrants of other nationalities — British, Canadian, German, and Scandinavian.[14] Japanese immigrants founded an agricultural cooperative on the Isle of Pines, shipping much of the cooperative's products to the North American market.[15] In 1931, Cuba's foreign population included Spaniards (59 percent), Haitians (18 percent), Jamaicans (6.5 percent), Chinese (5.8 percent), and North Americans (1.6 percent), with other nationalities and ethnicities accounting for the remainder.[16]

Although the Spanish immigrants had fanned out across the island, almost half of them made their home in the province of Havana.[17] Similarly, the city of Havana served as the main port of entrance, though a substantial number of immigrants disembarked at Santiago de Cuba.[18] With the exception of the Canary Islanders, who set themselves up on family farms to grow tobacco, the Spanish immigrants generally elected to settle in Cuba's cities. Such decided preference for urban living conformed to the pattern exhibited elsewhere — for example, among their compatriots who had taken up residence in Argentina.[19]

Of course, obtaining a firmer idea of the true, or net, number of Spanish immigrants to Cuba requires taking into account how many returned to Spain and how many made multiple entries into Cuba. As late as 1933, the majority of the children of these immigrants kept their Spanish citizenship, thereby inflating the number of Spaniards counted within the island's total population. Yet even in light of these factors, the size of Cuba's Spanish colony far exceeded that of all the country's other immigrant communities combined.[20] In addition, most Spanish immigrants to Cuba were male; the country's Spanish immigrant colony had the lowest proportion of women of any such colony in Latin America.[21]

In 1900, as a consequence of the great influx of immigrants into Cuba, the island's U.S. military governor, Leonard Wood, established a temporary settlement for them, Camp Triscornia. This camp, which served many of the same purposes as New York's Ellis Island or Buenos Aires's Hotel for Immigrants, was located off the Bay of Havana, on the shore across from the district known as Old Havana. Immigrants were required to stay in this collection of buildings surrounded by countryside until either the government could guarantee them work or some friend, relative, or organization was willing to accept responsibility for them. The camp also housed foreigners undergoing the deportation process.[22]

By and large, the Spanish immigrants to Cuba prospered economically; indeed, by 1932, they ran an estimated nearly forty-three thousand businesses, dispersed across multiple areas of service, commerce, and industry. Above all, however, Spanish immigrants dominated the island's trade and commerce. In 1899, for example, more than half of Cuba's shopkeepers were Spanish. A generation later, more than half of the island's stores and corner businesses, known as *bodegas*, still remained owned by Spanish immigrants.[23] Furthermore, the most successful Spanish merchants had since the nineteenth century operated as middlemen and lenders of capital to the sugar refineries, and a considerable number had become plantation owners.

The first decades of the twentieth century were also strongly tinged by the Cuban wars of independence and their aftermath and by the island's stronger integration with the U.S. economy as well as the burgeoning influence of North American cultural values. Moreover, the destruction and disorder wrought by the wars had left the old creole bourgeoisie in a battered and weakened state. In the wake of the Ten Years' War (1868–78), the properties of wealthy creole *independentistas*, or those fighting for independence from Spain, were expropriated. The war of 1895–98 subsequently brought the new middle-class leadership of the independence movement into direct confrontation with both the Spanish imperial authorities and the Cuban elite. To these developments were added new economic opportunities and patterns of consumption stemming from the expansion of the U.S. economy and its influence on the island's rapid growth at the outset of the twentieth century, along with a newfound belief in the ethic of the self-made man. This belief, quickly adopted and assimilated by a growing number of Cubans, was accompanied by widespread social mobility and the rise of a new stratum of merchants, businessmen, and managers.[24] Similarly, communications — both on the island itself and with the outside world — also experienced rapid improvement. Impressive strides occurred in both shipping and air transport; the Havana airport, in fact, claimed the distinction of being among the first of the world's airports to handle international flights.[25] In the economic sphere, trade between North America and the island increased from $27 million in 1877 to $430 million in 1917.[26] Finally, direct U.S. investment in Cuba climbed from $215 million in 1914 to $1.3 billion in 1924.[27]

This climate of social fluidity and economic growth and of openness not only to the United States but also to international flows of goods and capital, aligned with the practice of accepting immigrants from other countries, contributed to the growth of Cuba's underground economy. In his analysis of recent patterns of drug trafficking, such as those found in Colombia, Christian M. Allen has noted that as a "trans-national industry," drug trafficking flourishes when those countries that harbor and export it effect strong linkages to streams of legal goods and services. Thus empowered, drug traffickers avail themselves of the "commercial and technological advances in licit industries" and deeper "economic ties to the U.S."[28] The conditions identified by Allen apply to Cuba during the first six decades of the twentieth century.

In light of Havana's cosmopolitan character, dynamic economy, and privileged geographic position, those inhabitants who trafficked in goods and people were not just Cuban but were of various nationalities and included North Americans, Europeans, and Middle Easterners.[29] Moreover, in cosmopolitan societies, to take up Francisco Thoumi's line of argument, "ethnic minorities who lack strong loyalties to the main currents of society have formed the nucleus of the trafficking networks" for illicit goods.[30] In keeping with this dynamic and reflecting their multinational character, the drug traffickers developed networks in Europe, the Middle East, South America, and the United States. Thus, Cuba was not a simple victim of drug trafficking, as contemporary writers on the island have argued,[31] but instead played a very active, forward role in the operation of the business. Indeed, with regard to the trade in both illegal drugs in particular and legal products in general, Latin American businessmen, as a recent work on South American commodity chains makes clear, "were much more than simple marionettes set to dance by overseas commands and demands. They were not simply passive victims. Often they played enterprising, defining, and even controlling roles."[32]

Furthermore, the international trade in illegal drugs is ultimately a matter of supply and demand, with demand coming from consuming countries and supply from producers and traffickers. A country or region does not become a base of operations for drug traffickers and their networks simply by virtue of its geographic proximity to markets. Rather, the economic, political, social, and even judicial conditions governing regions and countries play a role, as do producers and exporters.

Contraband and smuggling had a long history in Cuba, and the country suffered both from an inefficient system of justice and from rampant and widespread corruption.[33] Between 1902 and 1958, "not a year went by without conspiracies, revolts, or political assassinations." Such chronic instability fostered an environment that lacked any clear rules for maintaining civic peace, an environment in which corruption, although constantly denounced, was never punished.[34] Taking the diagnosis one step further, the climate of political anarchy and pervasive corruption, combined with the close ties between Cuba and especially Havana and international currents of trade and migration, facilitated the consolidation of drug trafficking on the island. Thoumi is therefore correct in asserting that "beyond yielding profits, illegal economic activity requires the existence of both weak state and social mechanisms for controlling individuals' behavior."[35] Kathryn Meyer and Terry Parssinen are similarly correct in stating that "narcotics traffickers thrive in areas of political tension and instability."[36]

The events described and analyzed in this book cover nearly half a century, from the time of U.S. Prohibition in the 1920s to the first years of the Cuban Revolution, when the subject of drug trafficking became one more weapon in the Cold War and one of the U.S. government's key pressure points in attacking Fidel Castro's regime. The volume thus examines not only Cuban history but also the perceptions and fears that underlay U.S. domestic and international politics. To significant effect, the period studied in this book coincides with what another work has called "the classic period of narcotic control" in the United States — "classic in the sense of simple, consistent, and rigid."[37] This history therefore transcends the limits of national borders, not only because it concerns the movement of goods and people across such borders but because the problems it confronts were seen to reflect not only local issues but matters pertaining to other societies as well. That the narrative I trace, furthermore, necessarily occurs within the larger framework of transnational history is really beyond question, since Cuba, in the words of Damián J. Fernández, "was born transnational."[38] In equal measure, a transnational focus that emphasizes international connections — both material and cultural — within the context of the economic expansion of the West also underlines this work.[39]

The book also reveals information, for the most part heretofore unpublished, about drug trafficking networks in Cuba and about the traffic of drugs between the island and other regions of the world, including not just the United States but also the Andean countries, Mexico, the Middle East, and France. Through the pages of this work pass a procession of people of varying nationalities, including Spaniards, Chinese, French of Corsican origin, Middle Easterners, Latin Americans, and members of the U.S. mafia — as well as Cubans, of course. As documents from Cuban and North American archives demonstrate, the mafia concentrated its business ventures in Cuba

mainly on casinos and the hotel industry, not, as Cuban writer Enrique Cirules has asserted, on drug trafficking.[40] Following the trail of Cirules's argument, other scholars have maintained that before the Cuban Revolution, "the
North American mafia had made plans to fully develop drug trafficking and
drug consumption in Cuba."[41] However, the mafia's commitment to such a
plan was not at all certain.

Casinos were legal in Cuba, and when they were joined with hotels, the
resulting businesses yielded very high profits. During the 1950s, moreover, the
government subsidized these ventures through the extension of generous loans.
Conversely, despite the complex structure of the drug trafficking networks
— a function of their global scale — the business itself remained relatively
small (though dangerous as a result of the application of constant pressure, especially from the United States). Shipments and confiscations were measured
in grams, ounces, pounds, and kilos, not in tons, as has recently been the case.
During the decades that form the principal period of this study, the economic
and political power of drug trafficking was limited to bribing middle-range
functionaries and police; now, however, the drug trade has permeated the
highest levels of the state, weakening it and allowing drug traffickers to wield
extensive political power.[42]

U.S. authorities also used the problems associated with drug trafficking
as a device to combat communism during the Cold War. The central role in
this effort was played by the Federal Bureau of Narcotics (FBN), a U.S. government agency founded in 1930 and directed since its inception by the obsessive
Harry J. Anslinger. Anslinger viewed drug trafficking and drug consumption
as purely a police problem; he characterized drug traffickers as "murderers"
and drug addicts as "criminals first and addicts afterwards."[43] Furthermore,
Anslinger brooked no opposition to his ideas, regardless of whether such
opposition originated from abroad or from within the United States.[44] He
also embodied a political tradition that came out of the Progressive Era, a
time of "profound [U.S.] social transformations resulting from industrialization, urbanization, and new patterns of immigration" when reform-minded
zealots sought to condemn and prohibit any type of conduct that might be
considered "deviant," such as the consumption of alcohol and drugs, gambling, prostitution, and homosexuality.[45] Reformism of this type, promoted
by persons of Anglo-Saxon and Protestant background, sought especially to
control immigrants who came from the southern and eastern parts of Europe
(Catholics and Jews) and who generally lived in urban working-class neigh-
borhoods.[46] In the view of David T. Courtwright, "Industrialization created

influential groups for whom unregulated commerce in intoxicating drugs was not profitable, and these groups acted as a counterweight to those for whom it was still lucrative. . . . As the social environment changed, becoming more rationalized, bureaucratized, and mechanized, the distribution of cheap intoxicants became more troublesome and divisive."[47] Hence, certain pleasures and practices that people in the United States had fancied at the beginning of the century now offended reformers, who sought to oppose and proscribe such vices.[48] David Musto thus correctly concludes that the narcotics problem in the United States was more political than medical and legal.[49] Equally valid is Dwight B. Heath's assertion that "many of the problems associated with drugs and alcohol, significantly, can best be viewed as social constructs."[50]

As a result of all of these factors, Cuba became in one sense an escape valve, a place in which North American visitors could have free rein to explore areas of experience unchecked by the norms and strictures of their own society. At the same time, their pursuit of such experience does not mean that they "corrupted" the island. North Americans did not introduce gambling, drinking, or even drug consumption to Cuba. Cuban society was unmistakably one of options, options that included a host of decadent pleasures. Ironically, after Fidel Castro gained power in 1959, his campaigns, complete with moralizing overtones, to reform society smacked of the same type of anxiety and concern that had sparked similar campaigns in the United States decades earlier.

I strongly disagree with the assertion that drug trafficking in prerevolutionary Cuba "functioned as a type of genocide" and "as a business protected by the government" in which "the dominant class, the agents of imperialism, poisoned Cuban youth with drugs and narcotics."[51] In reality, marijuana and opium use resulted in arrests and prosecution, with justice meted out, such as it was, along class and even racial lines: jail sentences for selling and consuming drugs went to the poor — small-time traffickers or consumers — who generally dealt in marijuana or to Chinese immigrants accused of smoking opium. Persons of means and members of the elite also "poisoned" themselves by taking drugs such as cocaine, but their wealth or privileged place in society generally afforded them protection from the law. And although many Cubans saw holding power and governing as meaning little more than enriching oneself at the cost of the state, successive governments on the island did not necessarily protect large-scale drug dealers; on occasion, the government even went after them — for example, during Fulgencio Batista's dictatorial second administration in the 1950s.

Recent work published in Cuba concerning drug trafficking, such as the studies by Enrique Cirules and Francisco Arias Fernández, portrays the island prior to 1959 as a haven of official corruption fueled by drug trafficking while claiming that Batista personally supported the drug traffickers. Again, however, no empirical evidence has come to light to sustain the notion that Batista offered such support during the 1950s.[52] Just as Cirules and Arias Fernández attempt to picture the Cuba of this era as a den of corruption, other Cuban authors, equally lacking empirical evidence but citing "official" figures, claim that before the triumph of the revolution, the "Bordello of the Caribbean" or the "Brothel of America," with a population of just over 6 million, had between 100,000 and 150,000 prostitutes and 20,000 brothels.[53] According to Amir Valle, following the line of Cirules's argument, "it clearly emerges [that] one of the root causes of the increase in prostitution on the island [was] the penetration by North American mafia bosses of the secret world where the relationship between government and social and economic power gets fleshed out, above all at the beginning of the last years of the 1920s." Valle adds that in Havana, "whorehouses sprang up in every imaginable location, each one having more than ten prostitutes, and no important place in the city could be found where drugs did not circulate. Huge amounts of money were gambled away, and thousands of prostitutes were at immediate beck and call."[54]

Regarding these works, Louis A. Pérez Jr. observes that "public policy and historical constructs fused as Havana sought purposefully to discredit the prerevolutionary past. Indeed, revolutionary policy and revisionist historiography early arrived at a consensus which affirmed the turpitude of the old order. The past was characterized as a vice-laden age in which oppression, corruption, and exploitation flourished under the enforced sanction of the United States."[55]

In analogous fashion, after the Second World War, the same North American tourists perceived Miami and Miami Beach as a combination of "sun, sand, and sea; of sex, sport, and sin. Part Montecarlo and part Babylon," an environment in which visitors from the northern United States could frolic and take liberties while enjoying anonymity. In 1950, Florida counted 4.5 million visitors, and southern Florida alone was visited by 2 million tourists, including middle-class Cubans who chose to come to Miami in the summer, when low-season rates prevailed.[56] Yet despite the presence of thousands of these tourists, no one would advance the theory that the Cubans were corrupting Miami.

Of course, to demonize and castigate foreigners for the imperfections of one's own country is not a tendency unique to revolutionary Cuba. The Chinese, too, blamed foreign elements for drugs, gambling, and prostitution in their land.[57] Timothy Brook and Bob Tadashi Wakabayashi have elucidated how "a popular historiography targets foreigners as morally culpable for having used opium to intoxicate, impoverish, and demoralize the Chinese people — deploying what Chinese in the twentieth century have dubbed 'policies to empoison.'"[58] The popularity of such a view notwithstanding, scholarly study has cast doubt on the idea of seeing China "as a victim of the opium plague" or, conversely, of contending that opium was "merely imposed by imperialism."[59] Another scholar, William O. Walker III, quite rightly notes that "the history of drug control plays an essential part in our understanding the United States–Latin American relations in much of the twentieth century."[60] Walker emphasizes culture's defining role in the diplomacy of drug trafficking between the two Americas, arguing that "there exist side by side a producing culture, a culture of consumption, a culture of violence on the part of traffickers, and a bureaucratic culture that has as its object the destruction of the other three. What is at stake in this clash of cultures is how the members of each culture understand the world around them."[61] For Walker, coca leaf chewing in the Andes, as with pulque, marijuana, and peyote consumption in Mexico, have been "traditions, simply put, . . . part of Indian and Latin American culture."[62] Moreover, he adds, "The use of substances such as coca leaves and marijuana had become tacitly accepted activities in several countries. As a result, drugs, inseparable from the cultural expression of countless people in Latin America, would not be readily controlled there."[63] In Walker's estimation, respect neither for the law nor for U.S. antidrug policies has permeated the "producer cultures,"[64] and he thus concludes that the study of drugs "necessarily becomes a study of cultures in competition."[65] Walker's thesis, based fundamentally on Mexico, Peru, and Bolivia, does not apply (or at best applies only marginally) to the Cuban case. The "millenarian" practices in those countries are a world apart from twentieth-century drug trafficking, a phenomenon that falls within the orbit of transnational business dealings. Furthermore, over the first half of the twentieth century, a high percentage of drug traffickers in Cuba as well as in South America were foreigners or immigrants. In short, drug traffickers were the product not of the "culture of drugs" but of criminal "cultures" whose members set their sights on amassing wealth. In characterizing Latin American drug trafficking in general and the Cuban variant in particular, it is more appropriate to use the term "entrepreneurial crime," an expression employed by Humbert S. Nelli in his book on organized crime in the United States.[66] In the case of

Cuba, three groups — Cuban whites, Spanish immigrants, and French *contra-bandistas* — developed relatively sophisticated networks through which to supply Cubans with cocaine and heroin. These networks operated in a manner that paralleled the island's trade in legal goods, under the umbrella of an economy tied closely to international commerce and to the infusion of people from abroad.

According to Ivelaw L. Griffith, the islands of the Caribbean serve as a bridge for drug trafficking, connecting the source, South America, to the biggest market, the United States.[67] Nevertheless, for all its persuasive simplicity, Griffith's argument does not provide very much information about Cuba in particular, where events transpired differently from those on other islands between the 1920s and 1960.[68] During these years, drugs moved across approved maritime and air routes that implied a certain level of economic development and sophistication in communications. (The drugs were not carried on illicit flights that landed on illegal airstrips, phenomena of more recent decades that constitute central factors in Griffith's analysis.) Furthermore, if simple geographic proximity provides the underlying explanation for Cuba's development, why did drug trafficking have no great importance either in the Dominican Republic and Haiti or in Jamaica during these years? Haiti became important to the drug trade only at the beginning of the 1980s, when Haitian military officials formed alliances with Colombian drug traffickers, who used Haiti as a transshipment point for drugs.[69] Moreover, although arrests of people for marijuana use had occurred in the Dominican Republic since the middle of the 1960s, the country did not assume importance as a venue for drug shipments until the beginning of the 1980s, when groups engaged in organized crime arrived.[70] An international traffic in cocaine in Jamaica dates back only to the 1970s.[71]

Finally, the scholarly literature makes only limited reference to drug trafficking and drug consumption in Cuba. Walker's pioneering study focuses on Mexico and South America. Paul Gootenberg's book includes chapters on Peru and Mexico; the chapter on Peru mentions Cuba's importance for drug trafficking. In his chapter on Mexico, Luis Astorga underscores the important role of Cuban drug traffickers after 1960.[72] Meyer and Parssinen note in passing drug trafficking and consumption's importance in Cuba during the 1920s and 1930s.[73] In her book on tourism in Cuba, Rosalie Schwartz alludes in places to drug traffic and to the use of drugs on the island.[74] Douglas Valentine cites examples of drug trafficking in Cuba in his book about the Federal Bureau of Narcotics.[75] Finally, Cirules's writings on Cuba are full of assertions and arguments relative to drug trafficking and narcotics that lack any empirical foundation and derive ultimately from subjective political judgments. To date no scholar has published a systematic work dealing with the diplomacy of drugs, drug trafficking, and drug use in Cuba during the decades preceding the revolution.

This volume offers a number of specific points and arguments:

- Drug trafficking cannot be tied directly to poverty; on the contrary, it required international connections, a particular kind of know-how, and access to a certain amount of capital.
- The dynamism of the Cuban economy, the consolidation of its close ties to international trade and migration, and the development of the country's network of international communications during the first decades of the twentieth century facilitated drug trafficking, which ultimately became a business that reached across the globe.
- Cuba's physical proximity to the United States does not in itself explain the drug trafficking networks that existed between the two countries. The island's close ties with the North American economy and the role of both legitimate trade and contraband must also be taken into account.
- Conditions internal to Cuba, such as political instability, a climate of permissiveness, and judicial impunity are also key to understanding the drug trade and the consumption of illegal drugs.
- During the period under study, a significant number of drug traffickers both in Cuba and in South America were immigrants who had settled in the region.
- In Cuba, patterns of illegal drug consumption were related to ethnicity and class.
- Cuba cannot be considered a "victim" of drug trafficking. Native Cubans as well as immigrants living on the island played a very active role in the development of international drug trafficking networks.
- The expansion of casinos in Cuba in the years before the revolution did not derive from the simple presence of the U.S. mafia. Casino construction accorded with Cuban government policies to stimulate tourism and to compensate for the fluctuations in sugar prices on the international market; gambling, furthermore, was a deeply rooted tradition throughout Cuban society.
- The subject of drug trafficking advanced political ends during the Cold War. During the first years of the revolution, the FBN accused Castro of

heading up drug trafficking from the island; by the same token, Cubans accused North Americans of having corrupted the island country by engaging in various illicit activities, among them drug trafficking.

- The U.S. mafia was not involved in the drug business in Cuba. The FBN's political perceptions (as in the Luciano Affair) and those of contemporary Cuban authors are alike in being wrong on this point.

Although this book focuses on the subject of drug trafficking, it also includes chapters that deal with smuggling and gambling as part of a wider trajectory of vice. The first chapter takes up the topic of U.S. Prohibition during the 1920s and 1930s and the related problem of smuggling from Cuba. Chapter 2 considers two other issues critical to the 1930s — the Cuban political backdrop and drug trafficking. Chapter 3 deals with Chinese immigration to Cuba and the related issue of opium consumption. Chapter 4 analyzes the 1940s, while chapter 5 ties these years to a critical discussion of the Luciano Affair, the controversy surrounding the several months that Salvatore Lucania, alias Lucky Luciano, spent in Cuba during 1946–47. Chapter 6 considers the problem of drug trafficking under the government of Carlos Prío Socarrás. Chapter 7 covers gambling in Cuba, emphasizing that the practice was not "imposed" by the U.S. mafia but sprang from traditions deeply rooted on the island. Chapters 8 and 9 discuss the connections forged by drug traffickers between Cuba and the Andean countries, France, and the Middle East after the Second World War. Chapter 10 deals with the matter of drug trafficking during the second government of Fulgencio Batista (1952–58), and chapters 11 and 12 examine the first years of the revolution. Continuities existed between the antidrug policies of Batista's second administration and those pursued by Fidel Castro during the early years of his rule; the two *caudillos* were as one (though for different reasons) in their efforts to capture and contain drug traffickers, a finding that runs contrary to accusations that they collaborated and participated in the drug trade. Finally, the epilogue traces the activities of drug traffickers who had to leave Cuba after the revolution and transfer their business elsewhere in the Americas and in Europe to continue supplying the North American market. The epilogue also discusses how Miami became a center for both contraband and drug distribution beginning in the 1960s.

I offer a clarification regarding the use of the term "narcotics." I use the word generically in this book to refer to a variety of prohibited drugs. Strictly speaking, of course, "narcotics" applies to opium and its derivatives. The term was used on the international level when opiates were seen as the major problem.

Methodological Note on Archival Sources

This work is based principally on research carried out in different sections of two archives, Cuba's National Archive in Havana and the U.S. National Archives and Records Administration in College Park, Maryland. At Cuba's National Archive, I consulted nine collections that included both documents from Cuban government agencies and private papers donated to the archive. The information covered such topics as drug trafficking, smuggling, crime, immigration, international relations, and Cuban domestic politics. At the U.S. National Archives and Records Administration, I consulted as exhaustively as possible the rich documentation found in Record Group 170, which contains records of the Drug Enforcement Administration, the successor to the FBN. The FBN documents that I consulted include correspondence pertaining not only to Cuba but also to Mexico, Central America, Colombia, Ecuador, Peru, Bolivia, Chile, Europe, and the Middle East, all of which were directly connected to drug trafficking into and out of Cuba. I also consulted Record Group 59, which contains a large quantity of State Department information covering such pertinent topics as relations between the United States and Cuba, drug trafficking, smuggling, and Cuban internal affairs.

I also conducted research in several other archives, including the Pan American World Airway Archives at the University of Miami, which contains documentation on the development and modernization of Cuba's air-based communications; the Cuban Heritage Collection, also at the University of Miami, which contains materials relating to the history of Cuban social and political life; Colombia's Archivo General de la Nación, in Bogotá, which yielded more information about the Herrán Olózaga brothers; two regional branches of the U.S. National Archives and Records Administration (the Southeast Region, in Atlanta, and the Northeast Region, in New York City), which house judicial records for Florida and New York, respectively; and the criminal docket records of the U.S. District Court in Miami. Information garnered from these archival materials has been supplemented by information derived from published primary materials and newspapers.

Chapter 1

U.S. Prohibition and Smuggling from Cuba

In 1914, the U.S. Congress received a flood of petitions, signed by 6 million people, urging it to ban alcoholic beverages.[1] Six years later, a constitutional amendment prohibiting the manufacture and sale of alcoholic beverages across the United States went into effect. With these actions, the era of Prohibition had arrived in the United States; it lasted for nearly a decade and a half.

Yet civic and religious campaigns against alcohol consumption were hardly new to the country. They had flared sporadically since the beginning of the nineteenth century, when Protestant ministers began to preach against the practice of imbibing liquor. The first national group to take up the call was the Woman's Christian Temperance Union.[2] Workers and labor leaders alike also condemned the consumption of alcohol when it was carried to the extreme.[3] On the state level, Michigan approved an amendment to its constitution in November 1916 that prohibited the sale of liquor, an action that half of the state's counties had already taken some five years earlier. Prohibition's early success in Michigan resulted from well-orchestrated campaigns carried out by civic and religious leaders, supported by the region's major business figures — most notably, Henry Ford. Ford supported Prohibition in the interest of efficiency and profits (alcohol consumption lowered workers' productivity), and his company featured a department responsible for overseeing workers' family lives and controlling their drinking habits.[4] Ford's crusade against alcohol spread to other groups of business leaders.[5]

The idea of regulating the lives of human beings both at work and at home to create an abstemious, more productive workforce thus gained strength among U.S. business owners during the first decades of the twentieth century.[6] As a consequence of the country's entrance into the First World War, the federal government accrued greater powers, and the nation developed an outlook that emphasized austerity and unleashed feelings against whatever sounded German, including most of the country's large breweries.[7] A further source of support for Prohibition came from Big Tobacco. Cigarette manufacturers with well-known brands and national markets found that Prohibition worked to their advantage, since the sale of tobacco and cigarettes manufactured on a local scale by small companies generally took place in bars and saloons.[8]

Michigan's implementation of Prohibition immediately fueled a very lucrative trade in contraband alcohol from neighboring Ohio.[9] When Prohibition subsequently went into effect across the United States in January 1920, however, Canada became the principal source of contraband liquor in the United States, and the city of Detroit, strategically located on the border between Michigan and Canada, emerged as the focal point for the illicit trade. The business of smuggling liquor attracted a wide range of participants — entire families; secretaries who crossed the Detroit River between Windsor, Ontario, and Detroit, every day on their way to work; elements of organized crime, often operating with official complicity. Boats and ferries of every type crossed the river with contraband aboard, and during the winter, when the river froze over, caravans of automobiles made their way across. To transport the contraband liquor, cables were even extended from one bank of the river to the other. Indeed, contraband alcohol and its distribution (including the thousands of illegal distilleries and home stills that sprang up to help serve the trade) trailed only the automobile industry in importance among businesses in Detroit and its environs.[10]

Similarly, other entrepreneurs set up plants in the Mexican border cities of Piedras Negras and Ciudad Juárez to manufacture whiskey for shipment to the United States. The owners of the Ciudad Juárez distillery were in fact natives of Colorado. An island near the Yucatán Peninsula and the port of Ensenada in Baja California functioned as transit points for shipping liquor to Florida and to the U.S. West Coast, respectively.[11] Alcohol was also funneled into the United States through the Bahamas, where it was legally imported from Great Britain.[12]

Although the United States and Canada signed an agreement to clamp down on contraband liquor, the document had little practical effect. U.S. officials wanted a total embargo on the export of alcohol from Canada, but Canadian leaders were not inclined to shut down all distilleries and breweries, particularly in Ottawa, where the industry had become a major pillar of the local economy. Moreover, as the Canadians hastened to point out, Americans comprised the great majority of smugglers.[13] A group of gangsters of Jewish origin known as the Purple Gang controlled much of the business of importing and distributing Canadian whiskey through Detroit. The gang's most notorious clients included Al Capone's crime syndicate in Chicago.[14] Other bands of smugglers, generally of immigrant origin, also operated out of Canada, exporting both liquor that was legally produced and liquor that came out of home stills to buyers and markets in New York and Chicago.[15] In time, the violation of the law of Prohibition reached such proportions in the United States that journalist and social critic H. L. Mencken commented, "The business of evading [Prohibition] and making a mock of it has ceased to wear any aspects of crime, and has become a kind of national sport."[16]

Prohibition also meant that bartenders and other workers in U.S. saloons and taverns abruptly found themselves unemployed, and many consequently sought work in Havana, where the number of bars was growing prodigiously. Furthermore, several North American liquor manufacturers responded to the ban by shifting operations and opening plants — completely legal — in Cuba.[17] Entrepreneurs in other fields also seized opportunities to open businesses on the island. For example, John Bowman, a leading New York–based hotelier, purchased Havana's Hotel Sevilla just a few months after Prohibition went into force.[18]

Thus aided by Prohibition and its ripple effects, Cuba evolved into a country in which North Americans could act freely and openly, liberated from the moral pieties of their own society.[19] As historian Louis A. Pérez has observed, "It was not merely the availability of alcoholic beverages. . . . The opportunity to drink carried a subtext of individual freedom and indulgence." Moreover, "Cuba was constructed intrinsically as a place to flaunt conventions, to indulge unabashedly . . . in bars and brothels, at the racetrack and the roulette table, to experiment with forbidden alcohol, drugs, and sex."[20] Two other authors have made a similar point: by the 1920s, "Cuba had become a haven for revelers who escaped U.S. prohibitions against alcohol, horseracing, boxing, gambling and other indulgences. Cuba was freedom personified, close enough for easy access, yet beyond the reach of North American authority."[21] When their teams traveled to Cuba during the winter, American Major League baseball players frequently had difficulty playing because they had overindulged in alcoholic beverages the night before.[22]

Yet Havana was not the world's only city where the norms and restrictions imposed by Western bourgeois society were routinely violated. Since the early years of the twentieth century, London's West End had enjoyed a similar status. With its mixture of theaters, nightclubs, and other attractions, the district lured a variety of types — top-hatted aristocrats, tricksters and petty criminals, professional artists of both sexes, all of them unhampered by either the strict schedules of the working world or the constraints of Victorian morality and thus free in their own way to experiment with every type of enticement, including drugs.[23] Buenos Aires, too, featured a West End–like district whose racy offerings included, in the words of one visitor, "cinematographic shows . . . which for indecency cannot be outdone either in Port Said or Havana."[24] Buenos Aires's brothels and nightclubs also offered their patrons drugs: indeed, the consumption of illegal drugs in Argentina during the first decades of the twentieth century was reflected in the dialogue of stage plays and in the lyrics of the tango *Tiempos viejos* ("Do you recall, brother, what times those were? . . . Nothing was known of cocaine or morphine").[25]

Cuban writer Fernando Ortiz described early-twentieth-century Havana as a "port — then the busiest and best-known in the New World — where Spain's fleets and navy were docked for months at a time, giving rise to the corrupt and criminal environment that typifies all of the world's great ports, through which parade a robust and steady collection of cosmopolites and adventure seekers."[26] Building on this heritage, Prohibition helped to solidify Havana as one of the brightest stars in the world's firmament of vice, at least in the eyes of visiting Americans.

North American visitors to the island learned to sample the delights not only of Cuban rum but also of a wide variety of European liqueurs and spirits that were advertised in a series of English-language publications produced for the North American tourist trade.[27] Not surprisingly, many tourists jumped at the opportunity to acquire all kinds of liquor, intending to smuggle it back into the United States. U.S. customs agents, fully aware of this practice, searched all passengers returning from cruises for contraband. Those caught not only lost the illicit liquor but were slapped with fines.[28] The advent of air travel opened another channel for transporting contraband. In the 1920s, Areomarine West Indies Airways began to fly passengers from New York to Havana, with stops in New Jersey, South Carolina, Miami, and Key West; the return trip became known as the Hi-Ball Express, since many passengers brought bootleg liquor.[29]

Pan American Airways began operations in October 1927 with a flight that carried mail between Key West and Havana.[30] A year later, the airline initiated its Miami-Havana passenger flights, and for a number of years, Havana remained the most popular foreign destination for U.S. passengers.[31] In 1928,

Pan American inaugurated a flight between Havana and Puerto Rico, with stopovers in the Cuban cities of Camagüey and Santiago. The 1920s also saw impressive growth in the amount of maritime traffic between the United States and Cuba. A score of passenger ships plied weekly between U.S. ports and Havana, while a considerable number of automobile travelers took ferries between Key West and Havana. During the winter months, five trains made daily runs from Chicago to New Orleans, where travelers embarked on ships for Havana; another rail route connected Chicago and St. Louis with Key West.[32]

Throughout the twentieth century, Cuban officials of varying ideological orientations actively promoted tourism, which they saw as potentially the country's second-most-lucrative source of revenue after sugar. During the early part of the century, Havana was spruced up and modernized not only to make life more comfortable for its residents but also to increase its appeal for the North American tourist trade. The government spent significant sums of money between 1907 and 1919 to improve and upgrade highways, bridges, ports, city streets, and sewer systems throughout Cuba, and the end of the First World War helped ignite a construction boom in Havana.[33] This program built on efforts begun just after the Spanish-American War, when the American occupation force, as much to further North American interests as to help Cubans, expanded the network of paved roads and improved the telephone and public health services.[34] In short, Havana's evolution into a prime tourist spot resulted from the interplay of several factors: geographic proximity to the U.S. mainland, the alternative that it provided to a society constrained by Prohibition, and the city's rapid modernization and beautification, which took place within the broader framework of solid islandwide economic growth.

IN MID-DECEMBER 1924, the U.S. consul general in Havana reported that the city "has become the main base for smuggling operations. . . . Cuba is the base not only for contraband alcohol but for drug trafficking and the movement of illegal immigrants as well." To confront the problem, U.S. State Department officials suggested that the country negotiate a treaty with Cuba, modeling it on the formal agreement concluded with Canada six months earlier and on the treaty currently being negotiated with Mexico. The agreement with Cuba, proponents further suggested, should incorporate an extradition clause applicable in drug-related cases.[35] Canada and the United States signed such an extradition agreement at the beginning of January 1925.[36]

U.S. Department of Justice officials also believed that the passage of both drugs and illegal foreigners through Havana "had grown by staggering proportions."[37] The U.S. secretary of the treasury added to the chorus, observing that Cuba had become a ground zero for the export of alcohol and narcotics.[38] To bolster their case, Treasury Department agents collected information about the various types of contraband (liquor, drugs, and illegal immigrants) smuggled out of Cuba.[39] The illegal flow of immigrants, alcohol, and narcotics between Cuba and the United States was not just the subject of diplomatic communiqués; a good many people noticed how contraband trade permeated the texture of everyday life. It acquired a literary dimension, too, providing material for two fictional works of the late 1930s, Ernest Hemingway's *To Have and Have Not* and Cuban journalist Enrique Serpa's *Contrabando*.[40]

Prohibition had led to the steady smuggling of rum into the United States by ship, but some confusion existed about who was running the contraband rum. One point of view held that it came in on ships operating under the flags of various countries. Department of State officials believed, however, that the majority of ships hauling rum operated under the Cuban flag.[41] Others pointed out that numerous Cuban ships were registered in Honduras.[42] The Department of State also claimed to have evidence that the captains of rum-smuggling ships presented counterfeit embarkation orders to high-level Cuban authorities such as the governor of Havana and Cuba's secretary of state, who evidenced "indifference . . . to the presentation of false documents."[43]

Smuggling between Cuba and North America had a rich and long history dating back to at least the eighteenth century. Moreover, until the island achieved independence from Spain at the end of the nineteenth century, much of Cuba's trade occurred clandestinely.[44] As early as the seventeenth century, smugglers coming from Jamaica set up "veritable trading fairs" along the Cuban coastline.[45] After Spain succumbed to intense British pressure and signed an 1817 treaty prohibiting the slave trade, even slaves — in massive numbers — were smuggled in.[46]

Manuel Moreno Fraginals has noted that from the sixteenth and seventeenth centuries on, smuggling did not bear "a criminal connotation" either for many of the colony's inhabitants or for its Spanish administrators; during this period, in fact, several of the island's cities owed their prosperity precisely to smuggling and illicit trade.[47] Another scholar, Ramiro Guerra y Sánchez, has observed that "the practice of smuggling was widespread. . . . The indulgent complicity of the island's governors and other Crown officials was achieved by their sharing in the take and their ready understanding that the trade in clandestine goods was the principal source of wealth for the colony."[48] In *Contrabando*, one of the book's central characters tellingly "exuded a naive admiration for the smugglers, failing to discern any difference, by way of right and wrong, in their actions."[49]

In 1925, as the United States labored to stem the influx of contraband liquor and other goods, its ambassador to Cuba requested an audience with President Gerardo Machado to discuss "the activities of the so-called *Flota del Ron* (Rum Fleet) that's operating between Havana's port and areas not far from it along the coast of the United States."[50] In the negotiations to sign a treaty prohibiting smuggling, the Americans requested the right to inspect and confiscate goods on Cuban ships but sought to deny Cubans the same right with regard to U.S. ships, claiming that "ships leaving U.S. ports have not contravened Cuban laws with respect to the importation of illicit goods." In addition, any attempt to grant such reciprocity would encounter stiff opposition in the U.S. Senate as a consequence of pressure brought by lobbyists for the country's merchant marine.[51] Nevertheless, Cuban negotiators insisted that this clause be eliminated or that reciprocity be granted. A legal adviser to the Cuban government expressed the feeling, widely shared among his countrymen, that such negotiations had to defend and uphold the national interest: "Cuba, by virtue of its weakness and small size, has to be very careful in its actions, since, as [José] Martí reflected, the country's ability to command respect from the membership of the international juridical community depends on its carrying out such actions with a high measure of dignity."[52]

The United States had already signed parallel agreements aimed at stopping the smuggling of alcohol with Great Britain, Norway, Denmark, Germany, Sweden, Italy, Panama, and the Netherlands.[53] All of these agreements included the clause rejected by the Cubans. Nonetheless, Cuban officials insisted that the right to board ships on the high seas was reciprocal in nature and that justifiable and well-founded reasons, not merely suspicions or "reasonable cause," must exist before a ship could be detained.[54]

Because American officials believed the proposed series of agreements with Cuba to be extremely important, they compromised and agreed to the clauses as reworked by the Cubans. In early 1926, Cuba and the United States signed three treaties. The first, the Additional Extradition Treaty, was signed on 14 January and supplemented a 1904 treaty by incorporating clauses pertaining to "crimes against the laws for the suppression of the traffic in narcotic products" and to "infractions of the customs laws or ordinances which may constitute crimes." The second treaty, signed on 4 March, addressed mutually agreed-upon mechanisms for suppressing the smuggling of intoxicating liquors. The final treaty, signed on 11 March, covered not only drug and alcohol smuggling but also traffic in illegal immigrants and the smuggling of goods and products in general.[55]

During the period of negotiations over the Rum Treaty, as Cubans referred to the convention that sought to further suppress the smuggling of liquor, Cuban rum manufacturers tried unsuccessfully to prevent their government from signing the agreement.[56] The newspaper *Heraldo de Cuba* editorialized against the treaty, emphasizing the economic losses that distillers would incur and describing the proposed document as "a humiliating blow to Cuban sovereignty." Furthermore, the newspaper reported, Gustavo Gutiérrez, a lawyer within Cuba's State Department, had, as a gesture of protest, resigned his post.[57] Press coverage, however, was not uniformly negative. A progovernment editorial in the newspaper *El Mundo* asserted that the three 1926 treaties constituted "a new success for our diplomacy, . . . a brilliant campaign on behalf of our sovereignty," and insisted that in return for "our demonstration of friendship," the United States should accede to Cuba's request to revise the current commercial treaty between the two nations.[58] In spite of both the pressures that Cuban liquor manufacturers brought against the treaty and the rumors that circulated from time to time, especially in the pages of the *Heraldo de Cuba*, that the government was going to renounce it, the treaty remained in force throughout the period of Prohibition in the United States.[59]

Although the Cubans had the support of Americans with a direct stake in the island's economy (businessmen who exported goods manufactured in the United States to Cuba and the owners of sugar plantations and refineries), the island government failed to obtain the adoption of a new treaty carrying reciprocal terms of trade to protect the country's sugar market in the United States. The U.S. sugar beet lobby was instrumental in thwarting the proposal and in pushing through an accompanying increase in the tariff on Cuban sugar during the 1920s. The tariff increase led Machado and the Cuban ambassador to the United States, Orestes Ferrara, to declare that Cuba would find itself obliged to embark on a policy of economic self-sufficiency and industrialization.[60] Despite Cuba's objections, the United States would not deign to negotiate a new commercial treaty until the beginning of the 1930s, when the Great Depression was already under way and U.S. policymakers had turned to signing bilateral treaties as a method of stimulating international trade.

At the beginning of 1929, an American diplomat serving as liaison between the U.S. embassy and the Department of Treasury's agent in Havana wrote that the smuggling of alcohol "presents the greatest problem" and complained that "Cuban authorities as a whole are corrupt, weak, and indifferent when it comes to cooperating in trying to halt this traffic."[61] A State Department official expressed a very different view, however, declaring that "Cuba has been all but eliminated as a base of operations for those smuggling liquor."[62] American opinion on the subject clearly was far from uniform. Such discrepancies, added to the complaints and pressures brought by Cuban rum manufacturers and even government officials, suggest that rum smuggling had at least become more difficult.[63]

Perceptions aside, however, documents and official correspondence from the period indicate numerous instances in which ships departed Cuban ports for the United States carrying large quantities of contraband alcohol.[64] The smuggled liquor comprised primarily different brands of rum but also included wines and other spirits, and the ships were captained and crewed by men of various nationalities, including North Americans, Cubans, Spaniards, and Britons. The smugglers loaded the liquor legally in Cuba (generally in Havana), with manifests declaring ports in Honduras or occasionally Belize, Guatemala, the Bahamas, or Mexico as the destinations. However, the ships would ultimately head for ports in Florida, Louisiana, Georgia, and New York. Most of the vessels were registered under the U.S., British, Cuban, or Honduran flags. The Honduran registration was a pure front, a disguise: ships bearing it belonged to other countries. Vessels registered to Honduras theoretically had no reason not to transport liquor from Cuba to countries where it was legal. But all but the most naive observers must have realized that the ships could not have had ports in Guatemala or Honduras (many of them primitive fishing villages) as their terminal points, since neither country had markets sophisticated enough to absorb the cargos supposedly being imported. Still another disembarkation point for the ships was the sparsely populated archipelago of Saint Pierre and Miquelon, a French settlement situated to the south of Canada's Newfoundland coast. Saint Pierre, popularly dubbed the Champagne Island, was known to be one of the drop points visited by rum smugglers.[65] When circumstances required them to do so, the ships' captains fell back on the same excuses: they had lost their manifests or had drifted off course because of bad weather or because of damage to the vessel suffered when leaving port. In Havana, the captains' contacts were either

Cubans or Americans operating under cover of legal companies or occasionally even customs agents.

In addition to liquor, the smuggling routes between Cuba and the United States were also used to transport other contraband goods such as Cuban fruit and American cigarettes to Florida and Cuba, respectively. In particular, cigarettes were smuggled onto the U.S. military base at Guantánamo.[66] Drugs brought into the United States from Cuba, a relatively important problem in their own right, also traveled the same routes.[67]

In many cases, despite American diplomats' complaints to the contrary, Cuban authorities cooperated in suppressing smuggling. Indeed, American officials at times credited their Cuban counterparts for detaining and capturing smugglers.[68] And although numerous ships steamed out of Havana Harbor loaded with contraband, Cuban bureaucrats often made careful inspections of ships awaiting embarkation, coming on board to verify cargos, manifests, and compass settings. In some cases, when smugglers refused to allow or sought to evade inspections, Cuban authorities fired shots.[69]

As one U.S. observer pointed out, while Americans as a whole may have embraced Prohibition with enthusiasm when it was first adopted, they soon lost their taste for it, and the federal government compounded the problem by failing to invest the necessary resources to seal the country's land and sea borders and prevent contraband from entering.[70] Prohibition not only failed but brought violence in its wake by strengthening the hand of organized crime in the United States. Faced with a shrinking number of supporters and a growing number of critics, Prohibition became a central theme in the 1932 U.S. presidential race, with Democratic candidate Franklin D. Roosevelt promising to repeal the ban if elected. Both Republicans and Democrats seemed more interested in discussing Prohibition than in offering programmatic solutions to the Great Depression, a state of affairs that caused renowned educator and social philosopher John Dewey to remark, "Here we are in the midst of the greatest crisis since the Civil War and the only thing the two national parties seem to want to debate is booze."[71] In 1931, while serving as governor of New York, Roosevelt had supported the anti-Prohibition campaign.[72] After he assumed the presidency, Congress repealed Prohibition, with some supporters of the measure chanting, "Vote, vote! We want beer!" during the debate leading up to the vote.[73] Business magnates such as brothers Pierre and Irénée Du Pont threw their support behind the move to end Prohibition. Their motives were not entirely divorced from economic self-interest. While many business leaders clearly believed that Prohibition infringed on individual freedom, they also hoped that the federal income tax would be replaced by a tax on alcohol consumption.[74]

The end of Prohibition, however, did not spell the end of the trade in contraband liquor. Smuggling from Cuba continued because it offered a way to evade taxes. Consequently, a great flotilla of ships, registered variously to Honduras, Guatemala, and Great Britain and marked by their manifests to sink anchor in Central American and Canadian ports, continued to head for the United States bearing cargos of illicit liquor.[75] The liquor thus shipped had been legally manufactured and included such labels as Mill Creek, Isidoro Jaureguizar, La Campana, Ceferino Lavín, and even Bacardi Rum.[76]

Predictably, American officials voiced their displeasure over this renewed wave of smuggling. High officials of the Cuban government were very sensitive to such complaints, especially in light of the efforts then under way to negotiate a new treaty governing commercial relations between the two countries, a treaty in which the Cubans were seeking reciprocal terms of trade.[77] The Cuban government, like those of many other Latin American countries, reacted to the Great Depression by signing commercial treaties to protect the country's primary exports at the expense of nascent industrial interests. The Roosevelt administration was receptive to signing such bilateral agreements, which it viewed as a way to help rebuild and widen the country's share of international trade. To this end, the United States negotiated and signed a total of thirty-seven commercial agreements, many of them with Latin American countries, including Cuba. A bilateral treaty meant that Cubans could defend their sugar market in the United States without having to weaken or sacrifice a corresponding strength in their local economy, although more industrialized Latin American countries could not avoid doing so.[78] Between 1927 and 1933, Cuba also concluded commercial treaties with Spain, Canada, France, Japan, Portugal, and Chile, among other countries.[79]

Cuban officials also believed that "illegal conduct and bribery" undermined the country's "moral order."[80] At the same time, however, Cuba's secretary of the treasury emphasized that the trade in smuggled goods between Cuba and the United States cut both ways:

All of the smugglers operate out of bases in Florida, and, eager to learn about the system of contraband, its organization, and inner workings, I arranged for two inspectors to move to Tampa and Key West, tasking them to give me a report explaining just how the smugglers operate in the United States. . . . At bottom, the effective and final stamping out of contraband goods will be impossible as long as American cigarettes are taxed at such a prohibitive level in Cuba and the United States maintains its tariff on liquor. Both policies make smuggling a productive business.[81]

The secretary's skepticism was grounded in a realistic assessment of the environment. All the same, the Cuban authorities launched a campaign to break up the operation that was smuggling liquor out of the country from the ports of El Mariel and Bahía Honda. In so doing, they discovered that numerous customs agents were caught up in the illegal activity. The government responded by firing the customs administrator in El Mariel and expelling from the country several Americans involved in the smuggling operations.[82] The investigations and resulting dismissal of various government employees directly affected the country's liquor manufacturers, who in protest threatened to shut down Cuba's twenty-six operating distilleries.[83]

TRAFFIC IN ILLEGAL immigrants particularly involved the Chinese, who were regularly smuggled out of Cuba to the United States. U.S. authorities periodically rounded up illegal Chinese aliens and sent them back to Cuba, straining relations between the two countries.[84] Chinese persons also entered the United States illegally from western Canada; in fact, the U.S. vice consul in Vancouver issued false documents that enabled Chinese immigrants to enter the country.[85] Although the traffic in illegal aliens may have centered on the Chinese, numerous cases were reported involving Spanish, Greek, and Armenian immigrants, among other nationalities.[86] As might be expected, a brisk market existed for false papers, passports, and Cuban birth certificates and for American naturalization papers. Foreigners eager to settle in the United States could buy the documents on the streets of Havana. Not coincidentally, Tampa, Florida, served simultaneously as one of the main sources for false birth certificates and as home to a considerable colony of Cuban expatriates.[87]

Yet another channel of illegal immigration involved Haitians, who were ferried over and deposited on Cuba's coasts before dispersing to work as field hands on the island's plantations.[88] Jamaicans and Haitians combined to form the second-largest immigrant bloc on the island, trailing only the Spanish. The large number of immigrants from Jamaica and Haiti resulted in part from a 1912 Cuban governmental decree promoted by the country's sugar industry, which had been searching for a source of cheap manual labor.[89] Cubans outside the sugar sector had opposed this initiative, arguing that Cuba already had too many blacks and that further immigration from the Antilles would lead inexorably to the island's "Africanization." Nonetheless, the sugar barons prevailed.[90]

The smuggling of both alcohol and illegal immigrants ultimately was driven by political and social circumstances within the United States as well as by the close ties that had developed between the Cuban and U.S. economies. Conversely, drug trafficking in Cuba flourished not only because of these external factors but also because of conditions that were internal to the island, including Cuba's plunge into political anarchy, leading to a state of impunity that fostered a broad range of criminal conduct.

Chapter 2

Drug Trafficking and Political Anarchy during the 1930s

I n 1933 and 1934, Cuba underwent revolutions, creating a climate of political anarchy. The situation, coupled with a legal system of dubious integrity, intensified the country's high level of illegal activity in general and its drug trafficking problem in particular.[1] In opposing the government of President Gerardo Machado, the group known as ABC resorted to sabotage, terrorism, and political assassination.[2] Beginning in 1930, ABC and other groups opposed to Machado created an atmosphere of terror in Havana by exploding bombs and assassinating political enemies.[3] According to Frank Argote-Freyre, "The secret societies initiated an extensive campaign of urban warfare and terror . . . to destabilize the government and to show the United States that the Machado Administration could no longer protect the extensive business holdings of US companies and individuals. It was the first time that urban warfare was unleashed on a large scale in Cuba. . . . Urban warfare became a staple of Cuban politics."[4] As the political crisis deepened, the price of sugar also fell steeply, causing a rapid decline of Cuba's agricultural sector. Conditions in the countryside deteriorated to such an extent that in September 1933, two hundred thousand agricultural workers took possession of nearly 120 sugar mills, retaining control for several weeks.[5]

The instability overtaking Cuba posed a problem for the United States. President Franklin D. Roosevelt responded to the challenge by naming Sumner Welles, then serving as an assistant secretary of state, as ambassador to Cuba. Roosevelt hoped that Welles, a veteran of diplomatic missions to Latin America, would mediate and defuse the conflict between Machado and his opponents. Events, however, outran the ambassador. A general strike called by disaffected elements ended with Machado's resignation, and although Welles quickly gave his support to provisional president Carlos Manuel de Céspedes, civil and military factions opposed to Céspedes would not be placated. Their continued opposition led to Ramón Grau San Martín's ascendancy to power.[6] The United States did not recognize the new Cuban government, nationalistic in tone and committed to a program of economic, social, and political reform; indeed, only a handful of countries were bold enough to establish diplomatic relations with the Grau administration.[7] The U.S. president's representative in Havana, who found little to like in Grau's predecessor, was even more critical of Grau's government, characterizing it as "inefficient, inept, and unpopular with all the better classes in the country."[8]

Scholars have offered differing interpretations of the changes taking place in Cuba at this time. In Robert Whitney's eyes, the 1933 revolution resulted from the mobilization of the masses and "undermined the institutions and coercive structures" of the "oligarchic state."[9] In contrast, Louis A. Pérez Jr. believes that the deliberate, calculated opposition of the U.S. government helped intensify the widening political anarchy:

> Unable to overthrow the government from without, [Welles] sought to undermine it from within. Nothing was as central to this policy as promoting the continuation of instability and disorder. . . . Nonrecognition [of Grau's government] also served to prolong political turmoil in Cuba. It was a deliberate effort to foster instability, designed to maintain pressure on both the government and the opposition. Nonrecognition obstructed government efforts at reconciliation with its opponents precisely because it offered the opposition incentive to resist the government. Those who otherwise might have supported the government demurred; those who opposed the government were encouraged to conspire and resist.[10]

In the brief time before Grau's government fell, bombs exploded from one end of the island to the other. A bomb was lobbed through the window of the home of Colonel Carlos Mendieta, and the leader of the ABC group, Joaquín Martínez Sáenz, sought asylum in Miami after shots were fired at his automobile.[11] Officers of the armed forces barricaded themselves inside Havana's Hotel Nacional, from where they were brought out "by nothing less than cannon shot" by soldiers loyal to a group of noncommissioned officers headed by Sergeant Fulgencio Batista, according to the account given by his brother-in-law years later.[12]

Lack of support from the armed forces, then under Batista's direction, complemented by pressure from the United States, forced Grau to resign the presidency on 15 January 1934. He was succeeded by his secretary of agriculture, Carlos Hevia, who stepped down in the face of opposition from different groups. A few days later, Mendieta assumed the post of provisional president. The United States immediately recognized the Batista-backed Mendieta.[13] Further diplomatic action soon followed, as on 29 May, Cuba and the United States signed a new treaty that not only abrogated the existing treaty between the two countries, which dated back to 22 May 1903, but also eliminated the Platt Amendment, which had been attached to the Cuban Constitution and had made Cuba a virtual protectorate of the United States.[14]

Although Grau's resignation temporarily stabilized the political situation, the opposition continued to employ the tactic of terrorism. It became the modus operandi of Joven Cuba, a group created by Antonio Guiteras Holmes, who had served as secretary of the interior, war, and the navy under Grau. Guiteras was no stranger to the use of illegal force, having earlier organized an armed insurrection against Machado in Oriente province.[15] In addition, the number of strikes afflicting the country continued to multiply, and the government reacted by forcefully suppressing them.[16]

Conditions continued to deteriorate, and the violence escalated. On 27 May 1934, several shots were fired from an automobile at the Havana residence of the American ambassador. On 15 June, opponents used a bomb in an assassination attempt on President Mendieta during a luncheon in his honor. Two days later, shots again rang out, this time at a march by ABC activists along Havana's seafront. Fourteen people were killed and more than sixty others wounded.[17]

On the night of 5 July 1934, five bombs exploded in Havana, while three others were defused. British officials speculated that "student agitation may be partly responsible for the recrudescence" of violence in the capital.[18] On the afternoon of 18 August, a pair of bombs exploded in El Encanto, one of Havana's main department stores, while it was full of customers. Several people were killed, and many others were wounded.[19] Three days later, the government frustrated an attempted military coup. According to official accounts, the leader of the conspiracy, an army colonel, was killed while resisting arrest. Two of his co-conspirators were placed under arrest and subjected to court-martial.[20]

The coup may have failed, but the restiveness and political violence persisted. On 31 August, two students captured in the act of placing a bomb were facing trial in a Havana courtroom when a group of men stormed into the chamber, guns blazing, and freed them. The police recaptured the students a short time later and apparently executed them in cold blood. Such events could only exacerbate tensions.[21] Only a few days later, on 3 September, a group of workers striking the Cuban Telephone Company exchanged shots with company employees who had not joined the walkout.[22] The same week, fifty bombs exploded in Havana; at the end of the month, authorities confiscated three tons of dynamite from a yacht anchored in the bay near Havana. Rumors circulated that even greater quantities of explosives had been smuggled into Cuba from Florida.[23] The unrest spread beyond Havana, with outbreaks of violence reported in Camagüey, Santiago, and the port of Nuevitas.[24]

As the months wore on, the breakdown in civic order worsened. In November 1934, the government was rattled by an armed rebellion. Camp Columbia, Cuba's main military garrison, was the target of several bombs, one of which was flung against Batista's house.[25] On 17–18 December, a total of thirty-two bombs exploded in Havana. The following day, seventeen packages containing bombs were discovered at Havana High School, adjacent to the University of Havana.[26] On 17 February 1935, during Havana's Carnival celebrations, edgy revelers panicked when firecrackers exploded; seven people suffered injuries in the ensuing stampede.[27]

The agitation gradually spread. In the middle of February 1935, public school teachers, high school students, and students at the University of Havana went on strike, hoping to topple the government. The strikers initially received support from teachers and students in other parts of Cuba, and over the next month a broad range of government employees joined. Workers and protesters in the country's interior took control of several sugar mills and industrial plants. With militancy on the rise, the army struck back on 6–7 March, raiding the University of Havana and unearthing weapons and a large supply of munitions. With the support of Batista and the army, Mendieta's government survived.[28]

On 8 May 1935, the armed forced apprehended and killed Joven Cuba's Guiteras during a confrontation at El Morrillo, located on the coast near Matanzas, as he and several companions were attempting to flee to Mexico on a yacht. A Cuba-based Honduran diplomat was subsequently arrested on the charge of collaborating with Guiteras and his group, while members of Joven Cuba later assassinated the naval official who had revealed Guiteras's location.[29]

The British ambassador to Cuba reported on the anarchy that had taken hold in Havana and the transgressions that flowed from the chaos:

What is so astonishing . . . is the facility with which anybody with a grievance can obtain a bomb and place it in the house of the enemy. . . . All idea of restraint and discipline is vanishing. The police are either indifferent or helpless. . . . Acts of violence are carried out daily and no arrests are made. The police do not even investigate the crimes. . . . The judges are frightened to condemn [the terrorists], and so terrorism continues. . . . The present Government are so totally lacking in authority that even the simplest administrative acts cannot be carried out. . . . The weakness of the Administration has led to many abuses, and it is said on all sides that the corruption in the Government Departments is more flagrant than it has ever been before. The ministers seem to have no control over their Departments, and no knowledge of what their subordinates are doing. . . . I do not suppose that Cuba has ever had an honest government, but the corruption at present is regarded by tolerant Cubans as worse than usual.[30]

NOT SURPRISINGLY, in such a climate of political violence and instability, the problem of drugs persisted. In 1932, the Havana newspaper *El País* inveighed against "the authorized and enormously scandalous importation of narcotic products," especially opium.[31] The newspaper also reported that formulas for concocting mixtures of narcotics were freely passed around and that thirty-one offices of the public health service in interior provinces had "stopped remitting quarterly reports regarding the use of these kinds of products."[32] Buttressing *El País*'s claims, U.S. diplomats in Cuba reported that "narcotics are imported illegally into Cuba in great quantities, [according to] store owners who deal in those products legally."[33] Such drugs frequently were reexported to the United States.[34]

U.S. diplomats reported to Washington that two ships belonging to the Compañía Transatlántica Española (the *Marqués de Comillas* and the *Habana*) regularly transported narcotics.[35] The company, founded in 1881 and headquartered in Barcelona, had for years carried goods and Spanish immigrants on its ships, calling at the Spanish ports of Bilbao, Santander, Gijón, La Coruña, Barcelona, Valencia, Málaga, and Cádiz before arriving in the New World.[36] Drugs were also being carried by sailors on vessels operated by a number of other shipping lines and companies, including an Italian firm, Navegazione Libera Tristina, whose ships called at Marseille, Havana, Veracruz, and Tampico on their way to New Orleans; the North German Lloyd company, whose vessels docked at Havana and at Mexican ports before reaching Texas; the Ward Line and the United Fruit Company, whose ships arrived in Cuba from Costa Rica; and German ships from which drugs were off-loaded in Santiago de Cuba. The narcotics brought into Cuba came out of European laboratories,[37] and the smuggling obeyed a larger, international dynamic. In these years, much of the drug traffic between Europe and the rest of the world was carried out by sailors who operated on their own, buying small amounts of drugs in the bars of European port cities and selling the contraband when their ships reached ports in the United States or other countries.[38]

In 1937, Antonio Gil Carballo, a subinspector with Cuba's secret police and onetime chief of the organization's narcotics squadron, noted the tremendous difference that existed between the price of cocaine in Barcelona and in Cuba as well as the exceptionally high sums of money opium fetched in Cuba.[39] Moreover, when Cuban drug prices exceeded those in the United States, as happened on occasion, Cubans responded by importing narcotics from their neighbor to the north.[40] Ships operating under the U.S. flag and crewed by Americans systematically smuggled illegal drugs as well as numerous other products into Cuba from the United States.[41]

Morphine, heroin, and cocaine were originally produced in legitimate, licensed European laboratories, primarily in Germany, Great Britain, France, Switzerland, and the Netherlands. The drugs then entered a pipeline that led to illegal markets. In 1931, the League of Nations attempted to curb this practice by placing stricter controls on production in the laboratories and on companies' subsequent efforts at marketing and sales. Controls imposed in Europe were of limited value, however, as drug traffickers simply set up illegal laboratories in other parts of the world.[42] One of the prime new locations was Turkey, where poppies that had traditionally been supplied to European laboratories were grown and where European and Japanese interests had established laboratories to do the front-end work of producing narcotics.[43]

In a lengthy 1943 report on the illegal drug situation in Cuba, Claude Follmer, an agent of the U.S. Federal Bureau of Narcotics (FBN), observed,

> The narcotic traffic in Cuba, and the activities of Cuban narcotic smugglers supplying illicit drug traffickers in the United States, reached a peak during the period between the repeal of the National Prohibition Act on December 5, 1933, and the date of Italy's entrance into the present war as an Axis Power on June 10, 1940. During this period, steamships of the Italian and German lines brought large quantities of illicit narcotics into Cuba for local consumption and foreign distribution. Individuals, who had long been classified as major violators of the Narcotics Laws in the United States

by the U.S. Bureau of Narcotics, including such notorious persons as Salvatore Zappoli and Larry Gordon, made business trips to Cuba ostensibly [*sic*] for the purchase of illicit narcotic drugs. Cuban liquor smugglers, who had previously enjoyed an extremely lucrative liquor trade and with whom the smuggling of narcotic drugs had formerly been only a side line, now concentrated their efforts on illicit narcotic smuggling and established new contacts for their contraband in the coastal cities of the Southeastern section of the United States.[44]

Although Cuba's delegate to the League of Nations had admitted as early as 1928 that "the issue of limiting the production of narcotic drugs is of such magnitude that no government devoted to the health of its people can ignore it,"[45] Cuban officials generally downplayed drug trafficking and even argued that it was diminishing.[46] In 1935, A. Cañas Perdomo, director of public health on the island, reported, "illicit trafficking continues to shrink considerably."[47] Cañas's successor drew the same conclusion, stating that in 1936 and 1937, drug trafficking in Cuba "was clearly in the process of decline."[48] Another public health official, Dr. Domingo F. Ramos, blithely declared on 20 April 1937, "In our Republic, all activity associated with the importation, distribution, trafficking, and use of narcotic products, as well as their confiscation, is under seamless control — impeded, or regulated, or subject to punishment — such that no further measures need be taken."[49] According to a British diplomatic report, Ramos, a successful physician educated in Paris and Havana and at Cornell University, was "completely subservient to Colonel Batista, to whom he owes his post."[50]

Cuba incurred new international obligations when its delegate ratified a League of Nations convention on narcotics that resulted from a conference in Geneva in June 1936. Each signatory to the convention agreed to establish a specialized police force dedicated to suppressing drug trafficking and consumption, though Cuban officials took the position that they already had such a force.[51] Ratifying the convention in Geneva was one thing, but winning support for it in Cuba was another. Although the country's secretary of health and welfare backed the convention and the president introduced it to the Senate for consideration and approval, ratification stalled.[52] The convention encountered more success elsewhere: between 1936 and 1938, a great many countries, including Brazil, Colombia, and Guatemala, ratified it.[53] In August 1947, a high Cuban government official wrote that the convention had been sent to the Senate ten years earlier, "and the Senate has yet to move ahead and consider it, nor has the Executive branch pushed it to do so. It would be very good if the Ministry of Public Health used its influence in the Senate to help get the convention approved."[54] At around the same time, the secretary-general of the United Nations urged Cuba and other countries that had failed to ratify the convention to take action "with a view toward assuring the speedy ratification."[55]

Although the convention languished in the Cuban Senate, Cuba's penal code still mandated that any pharmacist convicted of violating the law regarding controlled substances pay a fine and serve between one and six months in jail. If the violation resulted in a death, the amount of the fine increased substantially and the violator's jail term was extended to between twenty-eight and seventy-two months. The code of social protection instituted at the beginning of October 1938 not only strengthened the penalties for drug trafficking but criminalized possession of drugs by anyone who was not found to be a "habitual drug addict." A local commission thus concluded categorically that "Cuban legislation prevents and punishes all activity related to the importation, distribution, and use of narcotics."[56]

A wide gap existed between such high-flown legal rhetoric and the reality of day-to-day life. Reports published in the journal of Cuba's secret police confirmed the widespread use of opium on the island among those of Chinese origin and noted that cocaine was a favorite accompaniment to parties attended by the country's wealthier set and that the use of marijuana, though only "newly popular" in Cuba, had already spread across the entire country.[57] José Sobrado López, chief of the secret police's drug bureau, warned that cocaine "was a privilege reserved for people of wealth, because of its extremely high cost."[58]

In contrast, marijuana was believed to be popular among "thugs and ruffians of color" — that is, blacks and mestizos — "coming out of the lower elements of society."[59] However, statistics collected by Sobrado López showed that of 867 persons convicted of selling marijuana between 1935 and 1940, 469 (54 percent) were classified as white. Almost 95 percent of those guilty of selling marijuana were male, although use of the drug was common among prostitutes, and *chulos* (pimps) smoked as well as sold it.[60] The "harmful herb" came to Cuba "from Mexico [and was] smuggled onto [Cuba's] coasts in considerable quantity."[61] Eventually, however, Cuba began to produce marijuana for local consumption.[62]

In the mid-1930s, President Carlos Mendieta had asked the Foreign Policy Association, an organization located in New York, to analyze social and economic conditions on the island. In response, the association set up a special study group, the Commission on Cuban Affairs, which issued its report in 1935. The commission found that Cuban crime in general had racial and socioeconomic dimensions: "Occupying the bottom of the social scale, and with little opportunity for social and economic advancement, the Negroes provide numerous recruits for the Cuban under-world. According to the 1932 statistics, a racial group containing 27 per cent of the population was responsible for about 50 per cent of the serious crime. . . . In this year 7,655 whites committed offenses in comparison with 4,284 Negros and 2,867 mulattoes."[63]

In other Latin American countries, marijuana was typically used by underworld types—that is, prostitutes and sailors in port cities and persons incarcerated in jails and prisons.[64] In the United States, conversely, marijuana use was not considered a public health problem until the 1930s. Policymakers previously saw pot smoking as merely a vice in which only ethnic minorities, bohemians, jazz musicians, sailors, and others who lived on the margins of society indulged. A 1929 FBN report pointedly stated that marijuana use in the United States "is noted particularly among the Latin Americans or Spanish-speaking population. The sale of *cannabis* cigarettes occurs to a considerable degree in states along the Mexican border and in cities of the southwest and west, as well as in New York City and in fact wherever there are settlements of Latin Americans."[65] When studies began to discover that Anglo youth were using marijuana, church and educational groups began to exert pressure to have the substance declared illegal. The FBN supported such efforts, stigmatizing marijuana as a drug that induced violent behavior by its users. The U.S. Congress responded to the mounting pressure by passing the Marijuana Tax Act, and President Franklin D. Roosevelt affixed his signature to the legislation in August 1937, thereby making the sale of marijuana a federal crime.[66]

Perhaps reflecting the strength of the U.S. campaigns against marijuana, its effects were represented as being more harmful that those of more powerful drugs.[67] According to FBN director Harry J. Anslinger, "The prolonged use of marijuana . . . usually leads to insanity, as well as to crime."[68] One Cuban author dubbed the drug "the most evil of vices," claiming that marijuana users "suffer violent delusions [and commit] not only a great number of the most atrocious sexual offenses, but also crimes of remarkable violence and ferocity."[69] Sobrado López equally melodramatically proclaimed that marijuana produced an "unbridled eroticism" and turned those who smoked it "into dangerous criminals . . . aggressive and violent." Marijuana, he concluded, was "the drug that has victimized Cuban society, provoking a huge number of crimes and tragedies."[70] The notion that persons under its influence became completely irrational was reflected in a trial involving two Cuban soldiers who attacked and killed a Spanish businessman. The military tribunal hearing the case accepted the reasoning offered by the lawyer for the soldiers that since his clients had been acting under the effects of marijuana, they could be tried only for voluntary manslaughter, not for first-degree murder.[71] Another writer echoed the idea that marijuana use bore the blame for numerous ills in Cuban society, inveighing against the "cursed herb" that "above all works its intoxicating effect on youth" and constituted "a misfortune for our country." He saw marijuana as one of the country's chief vices, in company with alcohol, homosexuality, and "pleasuring oneself."[72]

GIVEN CUBA'S cosmopolitanism, it is not surprising that a large number of the island's drug traffickers were foreigners, many of them long established in Cuba. One typical example was César Hernández Márquez, a thirty-eight-year-old Palestinian who adopted a Spanish name and pursued a life of crime, trafficking in drugs, liquor, and illegal immigrants.[73] His business took him between Cuba and the United States, and he was captured in Miami in February 1933 and deported back to Cuba the following May. In December 1933, Hernández Márquez took two bullets from an assassin's gun. According to his brother and another witness, the alleged killer, a Spaniard, Alvaro García y García, had targeted Hernández because the two men had argued about a shipment of sixty pounds of drugs worth twenty-two thousand dollars. In the opinion of U.S. authorities, "The death of César Hernández Márquez eliminates one of the leading smugglers in Cuba."[74] Another case involved two Egyptians, José Louza and Ismail Towfie Ibrahim, whom the secret police arrested along with a Cuban companion, Epifanio Álvarez, in May 1938. The three were in possession of four hundred pounds of unprocessed opium that had been stored in Álvarez's house in Güines, in the province of Havana. Although the three traffickers had been caught red-handed, the ensuing investigation stalled when they bribed high-level agents and officials in the secret police as well as the judge assigned the case.[75]

Undercover work was an effective way of gathering intelligence about drug trafficking activity. For example, two FBN agents, Sarro Vaccaro and Samuel L. Rakusin, infiltrated a gang headed by Dave Simpson (a.k.a. David Myers) of Chester, Pennsylvania. Pretending to be traffickers, Vaccaro and Rakusin made their way to Havana, where they met with a known U.S. drug trafficker,

Frank Johnson. Johnson referred them to a forty-two-year-old bar owner and Spanish immigrant, Manuel Lozada y González, who in turn confided that he received drugs from South America and Europe primarily through two individuals, the first officer and the physician on the Spanish steamer *Alfonso XIII*. Vaccaro and Rakusin learned that the drugs were off-loaded in Havana by Rafael Esmori y Rodríguez, a sergeant in the White Fleet Police Guard and a friend of Lozada, and by José Francisco (Tomás) de la Peña y Rodríguez, an employee of the Port of Havana Docks steamship company. Following instructions from Lozada, the two FBN agents headed to a boat owned by José Quiñones Campos, with whom they negotiated the purchase of drugs held on Quiñones's vessel. The drugs in question — thirteen pounds of opium suitable for smoking and thirty-one tubes, each containing between twenty-five and fifty grams of cocaine — had a value of fifteen thousand dollars and were packed in a tin can, which was soldered shut and taken to the *Carmina*, a schooner owned by Victoriano Bengochea and Manuel Fernández, who had outfitted their boats to carry not only drugs and liquor but also fugitives from justice. The *Carmina* was supposedly headed toward the Yucatán on a fishing expedition but actually set course, with its load of contraband, for the United States. At Boca Grande, near Tampa, the U.S. Coast Guard, alerted by Vaccaro and Rakusin, stopped the boat. Skipper Miguel Estévez Infante and a deckhand, Benedicto Mauriz, each received prison sentences of five years. In Cuba, a total of nineteen members of the gang, most of them Spanish but also including some Americans and Cubans, were rounded up and put on trial.[76]

One Spanish immigrant who prospered via drug trafficking was José Antonio Fernández y Fernández.[77] Fernández arrived in Cuba in 1920, at around the age of twenty. Despite being from the Spanish region of Asturias, Fernández was known as El Gallego, a designation bestowed generically on all Spanish immigrants in Cuba regardless of their regional origins. After reaching Cuba, Fernández spent two years working as a bartender before he and an associate purchased a restaurant near the Havana docks. Through the restaurant, Fernández became friends with Spanish sailors who worked on the ships that brought drugs from Barcelona, and he eventually became a distributor for the drugs that his countrymen were smuggling into Cuba. In 1927, Fernández sold his business and traveled to the United States and to several Latin American countries, where he established contacts with members of the criminal underworld. He returned to Cuba at the end of 1927 and was arrested when customs agents found several vials of cocaine concealed in his clothes. He was subsequently freed on bail. The advent of the Spanish Civil War interrupted

Spain's maritime traffic, so Fernández developed connections with sailors on two Italian ships, the *Istria* and *Aras*, both of which belonged to the Compagnia Italiana di Navigazione. The vessels called at the Francoist-controlled ports of Vigo and Cádiz, where they took on shipments of drugs.

In October 1936, a Havana pharmacist, Ernesto Álvarez Digat, agreed to process opium paste provided by Fernández. Álvarez Digat refined part of the opium into five kilos of heroin before being arrested; in 1938, he was sentenced to one year in prison. Although Fernández was also arrested, he again eluded justice, this time as a consequence of lack of evidence.

Fernández again attracted police attention, and in April 1940 police detectives obtained a warrant and raided his house, where they found seven pounds of cocaine and eight pounds of morphine. Fernández's status as a major figure in the distribution of illegal drugs in Havana was demonstrated by the immediate and severe reduction in the availability of such drugs in Havana and the corresponding increase in the number of addicts who asked to be admitted to the Lazareto del Mariel clinic because they could no longer obtain drugs on the street.

Fernández was arrested after the raid, but his lawyer got the case postponed, keeping Fernández outside the clutches of the law. In 1943, after at least a dozen additional postponements, and because of pressure exerted on witnesses to testify against him, Fernández was finally sentenced to a year in prison. He appealed the verdict, however, and remained free after posting five thousand dollars in bail money. Facing the prospect of deportation, Fernández used his lawyer's family connections to clear bureaucratic obstacles and obtain Cuban citizenship despite the looming prison sentence. By 1945, however, Fernández's rope had temporarily played out as the Supreme Court rejected his appeal and confirmed his one-year prison sentence. Pleading ill health, however, the wily Fernández served his time in the Quinta Covadonga, a combination hospital and vacation retreat frequented by immigrants from the Asturias region of Spain.

Moreover, Fernández was not about to be rehabilitated. Five years later, in 1950, El Gallego was importing morphine from Spain and maintaining connections with other key Cuban drug figures, including Abelardo Martínez del Rey, known as El Teniente, and Octavio Jordán Pereira, alias El Cubano Loco, both of whom trafficked in drugs from Peru and Spain to supply the Cuban and U.S. markets. By this time, Fernández had amassed a considerable fortune. He owned a store that specialized in glassware and pottery and another that sold furniture, was a partner in a factory that manufactured dominoes, and possessed abundant real estate — an apartment building, four houses in Havana, and a getaway home at the beach. Fernández exemplified the hardworking and successful Spanish merchant common in Cuban business circles, except that his line of work was illegal

Fernández and other Spanish immigrants to Cuba generally were rapidly absorbed into the island's mainstream. The Chinese, who constituted Cuba's second-largest overseas immigrant community, did not receive the same reception or enjoy the same treatment as immigrants of European origin. Furthermore, the fact that a significant number of them used opium made the Chinese a much easier target for rejection.

Chapter 3
. . . .

The Chinese and Opium
Consumption in Cuba

O pium had been used in China as a medicinal drug since the ninth century, hundreds of years before the European empires established colonial beachheads there. In the sixteenth century, the Portuguese began to use opium as well as precious metals, tobacco, and spirits such as brandy to obtain Chinese silk, tea, and spices. By the advent of the nineteenth century, opium use had become very common in China as a consequence of the deliberate dissemination of the drug by both Western interlopers and the Chinese themselves. The former included the British East India Company as well as French, Dutch, and American business agents. When the Chinese government later sought to stop the opium traffic, the British kept it going by instigating what became known in the West as the Opium Wars of 1839–42 and 1856–58. The continued trade in opium, forced on China by the victorious Western powers, yielded enormous profits for the British Crown and for U.S. and British business interests. The British used some of the profits to help finance the export of Chinese tea to Great Britain. The merchants who cultivated poppies in India also reaped great profits. Chinese opium use steadily expanded, and in the middle of the nineteenth century, when massive numbers of Chinese began to migrate to other parts of the world, including Cuba, they took the habit of smoking opium with them.[1]

While the number of Chinese who used opium may have grown ever higher during the nineteenth century, most users apparently did so in moderation, often for social reasons, without becoming addicted or harming their health.[2] Those who smoked the drug in China did not sit slumped in seedy opium dens, with eyes glazed over, as popularly depicted in the Western press. On the contrary, users came together in social and fraternal halls that scarcely differed in any way from other well-ordered and respectable venues of leisure activity and social intermingling.[3] The Chinese living in London at the end of the nineteenth century gathered in similar establishments to smoke opium.[4] Moreover, an 1895 British royal commission charged with studying the use of opium in India also concluded that the practice was quite common but caused little harm.[5] In the United States, too, opium was used in moderate amounts to treat a variety of medical conditions without creating patterns of addiction.[6] Nevertheless, the fact that a considerable number of Chinese immigrants in Cuba used opium heightened xenophobia and contributed to their adverse treatment, such as frequent arrests and other run-ins with the law. Also contributing to the negative sentiment was the fact that Cuba received the highest number of Chinese immigrants of any Latin American country — according to one study, published immigration data show that 114,232 Chinese entered the island between 1847 and 1874.[7] According to Manuel Moreno Fraginals, approximately 160,000 Chinese migrated to Cuba between the beginning of the nineteenth century and the first decades of the twentieth century.[8] Many Chinese workers, known as coolies, were brought in to help fill the demand for manual labor on the island's sugar plantations.[9] A substantial number of others were imported to help lay track for Cuba's rapidly expanding railway network.[10] Chinese traffickers in human labor all but kidnapped their countrymen or enticed them to leave China with false or deceptive information. Such coercive practices had few differences from the African slave trade. Indeed, the coolies embarked at the Portuguese colony of Macao and were transported by companies with firsthand experience in the black slave trade. As with the Middle Passage, coolies endured subhuman conditions onboard ship, and many died at sea; others used opium to help them survive the long crossing.[11] Furthermore, after arriving in Cuba, the Chinese discovered that they were obligated to work for eight years to compensate the traffickers for the supposed costs of the voyage. In practice, these coolie laborers were sold into service as if they were slaves.[12]

Many of the migrants fared scarcely better on land than they had at sea. As a rule, living conditions on Cuban haciendas were horrific during the nineteenth century. Although the Chinese looked down on black slaves, the two groups lived in roughly the same conditions and in close proximity to each other. The punishments meted out to slaves and coolies also differed little. Slaves who refused to work received twenty-five lashes of the whip; under the same circumstances, coolies received twelve. Such treatment not only was cruel but also was a direct violation of Cuban law, which had expressly prohibited such punishments since 1854.[13] Medical care was all but nonexistent, and the mortality rate was extremely high. The coolies were plagued by chronic illness and physical abuse, and they committed suicide in large numbers. As many as one-third of all Chinese workers on Cuban haciendas died by taking their own lives, either individually or as part of a collective pact.[14]

In 1887, just one year after the emancipation of the slaves in Cuba, blacks and mulattos on the island founded the Directorio Central de las Sociedades de la Raza de Color (Central Board of Associations of Colored People), which sought to achieve equality among all Cubans both on the basis of race and before the law. To further these objectives, the group sued not only whites but also Chinese on the grounds of discrimination.[15] The owners of estates and plantations in Cuba were accustomed to treating their laborers, even natives of Spain, as if they were slaves. As a result, in the words of one nineteenth-century immigrant from the Canary Islands, on Cuban sugar plantations, "Canary Islanders were treated like Africans, and not like Spaniards; they were treated like serfs, like outcasts; exploited miserably, subjected to abuse and punishment; robbed of what little they made from their backbreaking work in the sugar mills; even the honor of their women and daughters was violated."[16]

The first Chinese diplomatic mission visited Cuba in 1874. Its members planned to travel the length of the island to investigate and document mistreatment of their countrymen. After returning to China, the members of the mission issued a report in which they indicted Cuban landowners for systematically mistreating coolie workers.[17] The landowners apparently condoned Chinese laborers' use of opium because it helped to ensure social control by making the Chinese more amenable to accepting the work demands imposed on them.[18]

Despite concerted opposition from Cuban *hacendados*, the Chinese and Spanish governments signed a treaty to end the traffic in coolie labor. The fact that many coolies had joined the rebel forces during Cuba's 1868–78 Ten Years' War (Guerra de los Diez Años) contributed to the sense of unease felt by the Spanish Crown.[19] Chinese persons who had come to Cuba of their own volition or who had fulfilled the eight-year service obligation took up all types of occupations, working as artisans, storekeepers, and cooks in towns and cities across the island. By 1858, they formed a large enough community in Havana that the center of the city began to see the development of a distinct Chinese quarter.[20] During the nineteenth century, "all of the highly mechanized sugar mills were replete with Chinese" workers, and some Chinese even became sugar mill owners.[21] Another element in the mix was "a not inconsiderable stream of Chinese who arrived via the United States with a small amount of capital and a keen entrepreneurial spirit."[22] These immigrants established themselves in the cities, including Havana, and gave rise to subsequent groups of Chinese businessmen.[23] The Chinese also worked in a wide variety of urban trades — as craftsmen, day laborers, longshoremen, and workers in cigarette and cigar manufacturing plants.[24]

A number of similarities existed in the patterns of nineteenth-century Chinese migration to the United States and to Cuba. Most Chinese who settled in the United States came from the Canton region, which for decades had been associated with the opium trade. Furthermore, almost all of the migrants were male, and while the majority were married, they undertook the voyage by themselves, motivated by the idea of accumulating savings and returning to China. To finance both their trip and the initial costs of settling down in a foreign country, the migrants indebted themselves to Chinese merchants, who in turn took steps to block the men's return to China until all debts had been liquidated. As in Cuba, Chinese immigrants to the United States experienced stinging racial discrimination, including periodic instances of mob violence and bloody demonstrations involving mutilation and decapitation as well as murders and lynchings in Los Angeles; San Francisco; Denver; Seattle; Tacoma, Washington; and Rock Springs, Wyoming. Moreover, these men were prevented from bringing their spouses to the United States, a systematic denial that constituted the first case in which an entire ethnic group was refused the right of immigration into the country. Unlike in Cuba, where the Chinese could and did marry black and mulatto women, U.S. laws against race mixture as well as the day-to-day realities of racial discrimination prevented Chinese immigrant men from establishing any kind of enduring relationships with women. Only the massive migration of Chinese women after the Second World War equalized the number of Chinese men and women living in communities in the United States.

Estimates show that one-quarter of Chinese immigrant workers in the United States smoked opium during the nineteenth century. The sale of opium was a lucrative business, and the struggle to control the trade resulted in violence between groups organized into secret societies. Between 1850 and 1870, those who smoked opium in the United States were exclusively Chinese; subsequently, however, whites — generally persons who lived on the fringes of society — began to use the drug. Its use was also a byproduct of war, as many soldiers who had been wounded during the U.S. Civil War became drug addicts and began to frequent opium dens in the Chinese districts of San Francisco and New York. As these opium dens gained popularity and as the habit of using opium spread among white men and women, countermeasures were not long in coming.[25]

A 1902 publication coauthored by Samuel Gompers, the founder and president of the American Federation of Labor, reflects the virulent U.S. racism against Chinese immigrants:

> The racial differences between American whites and Asiatics would never be overcome. The superior whites had to exclude the inferior Asiatics by law, or if necessary, by force of arms. . . . The Yellow Man found it natural to lie, cheat, and murder, and 99 out of every 100 Chinese are gamblers.
>
> The Chinese entice children to become opium fiends. What other crimes were committed in those dark fetid places when these little innocent victims of the Chinamen's wiles were under the influence of the drug, are almost too horrible to imagine. . . . There are hundreds, aye, thousands of our American girls and boys who have acquired this deathly habit.[26]

Numerically, the Chinese migration to Great Britain was less important than its counterpart in the United States. In 1911, for example, only 1,319 people of Chinese origin (90 percent of them male) arrived in Great Britain. For the British, the Chinese predilection for setting up opium dens and engaging in gambling was not a source of concern, at least not immediately. In fact, during the last decades of the nineteenth century, many Britons visited these establishments, eager to drink in their supposedly exotic atmosphere. The British had actively promoted the opium trade and had greatly enriched themselves in the process, thereby developing what may have been a more sophisticated — or cynical — outlook. Their attitude was also softened by the Royal Commission's study, which found that opium taken in moderate amounts was medically beneficial. Yet even British tolerance had its limits. After 1914, British women, freed from the Victorian ethos, began to rub shoulders with the Chinese immigrants, creating fears of a "yellow threat" stemming from opium use and racial intermingling. British society also began to see the games of chance favored by the Chinese not as pleasant diversions but as evil habits capable of corrupting both women and children. Reflecting the rising sense of alarm, one religious figure warned of the alleged risks that women "would become infatuated with colored men . . . a danger in regard to which girls should be warned." He concluded, "the morals and civilization of the Yellow man and the European are fundamentally different."[27]

Between 1903 and 1929, Cuba experienced a second wave of Chinese immigration that included twenty thousand people.[28] Although the new immigrants differed from their predecessors in that they were free of any service obligations, almost all were male: in 1931, barely 1 percent of Cuba's total Chinese population was female.[29] While Chinese immigrants were found throughout Cuba, they gravitated in large numbers to Havana, which eventually became home to the third-largest concentration of Chinese in the Americas behind San Francisco and New York.[30] Moreover, although the Chinese lived and operated businesses in different sections of Havana, they concentrated in the city's growing Chinatown.[31] Like other immigrant groups, the Chinese drew strength from clustering together, but they also acknowledged and assimilated certain local customs and traditions — for example, the Chinese contributed to Havana's Carnival celebrations with an impressive float that sported paper dragons and other ethnic ornamentation.[32] A 1932 travel bulletin estimated the population of Havana's Chinatown at thirty-five thousand and noted that the Chinese controlled the city's fruit and vegetable distribution business.[33] The Chinese also opened laundries and sold low-priced meals, establishing inexpensive restaurants and fried-food stands.[34] According to Moreno Fraginals, "The records for commercial permits granted by the Havana city council for the years 1880–1895 . . . indicate that for new laundries, the Chinese share came to 83 out of 100; for fruit and vegetable businesses, 77 out of 100; for low-cost restaurants, 14 out of 100; and for retail nurseries, 9 out of 100."[35] The Cuban census of 1907 reveals that many Chinese immigrants had ceased to be salaried employees and had become business owners in their own right.[36] As late as 1958, nearly half of the small-business owners who appeared in the yellow pages of the Havana telephone directory under the "fruits, foodstuffs, and vegetables" heading were of Chinese origin.[37] Havana supported three Chinese newspapers, while another Chinese newspaper of leftist orientation was published in Santiago until Batista shut down its operations during his second administration.[38]

Unlike the trafficking in other drugs, for which Cuba served as a pipeline into the U.S. market, opium was by and large introduced for local consumption by the Chinese and thus remained on the island.[39] Government statistics for the twentieth century indicate that a large number of the arrests made in Cuba for drug use involved people of Chinese origin.[40] Antonio Gil Carballo noted that of the 2,255 drug addicts admitted to the Lazareto del Mariel facility prior to 1936, half were Chinese, a statistic that supported his assertion that "those smoking and hooked on opium are almost all Chinese."[41] Nevertheless, opium use was not the exclusive preserve of the Chinese. Between

1910 and 1920, young adults from well-off white families gathered to smoke opium in one of the social clubs located on one of Havana's most exclusive boulevards, the Paseo del Prado.[42] The heavy concentration of opium use within the Chinese community, however, drew unwelcome attention. In 1931, Havana's newspapers ran articles denouncing a drug trafficking gang that operated openly along Dragones, a street in the heart of Chinatown.[43] In 1934, several Chinese immigrants in Camagüey were convicted of maintaining an opium den in a private residence.[44] In 1936–37, a series of "intensive raids" were carried out against opium dens throughout the island.[45]

For several decades, Cuban officials used El Lazareto del Mariel, a seaside hospital about fifty kilometers west of Havana, as a facility for quarantining and treating drug addicts.[46] In 1927, the secretary of public health had ordered the addicts then housed in one of the wings of Havana's Calixto García Hospital moved "provisionally" to the Mariel hospital. The move proved long-lasting, however, and drug addicts were still housed there during the 1950s.[47] Moreover, the Lazareto also served as a detention center, and some of the inmates escaped at the slightest opportunity.[48]

A number of individuals, all of Asian background, peddled drugs in Havana's Chinese district.[49] According to Gil Carballo, one of them, known as El Chinito Lima, enjoyed "some of the most influential contacts in Cuba, enabling him to get around the authorities."[50] The district retained its notoriety into the 1950s: wrote one foreign journalist, "Like most New World Chinatowns, the one in Havana has its morbidly secretive side, its dens where opium is smoked and other vices practiced."[51] Overall, however, the Chinese distinguished themselves as a law-abiding group, posting "the lowest crime rate of any population group in Cuba."[52]

Several bloody incidents took place within Havana's Chinese community in 1926, however. The violence stemmed largely from political feuding between local Chinese associations, feuding that mirrored political loyalties and vendettas imported from China. Members of the rival associations accused each other of trafficking in opium, and the seriousness of the confrontations spurred the local press to suggest that the Chinese district be broken up "for reasons of public hygiene and safety."[53] At the beginning of September 1926, concerns regarding the situation spread to the national level when Cuba's secretary of the interior requested that authorities in each of the country's provinces prepare a report on local Chinese associations, paying particular attention to their political and criminal activities.[54] The reports indicated that while some of the associations devoted themselves to gambling and opium consumption, the majority were bona fide community organizations whose members were industrious and respectful of the law.[55] Two reports from the city of Cárdenas illustrated the larger dynamic. The first document noted that Cárdenas had two Chinese associations, both of them entirely legitimate and aboveboard. The second report, however, alerted the interior department that an opium den had been discovered in the city, resulting in the detention of a dozen Chinese men. The writer concluded that "with regard to illegal gambling . . . I can provide assurance that the majority of houses designated as gambling dens belong to Asians, these people are given to promoting and indulging in the vice wherever they turn up."[56] Authorities also investigated particular individuals considered dangerous and, reflecting the wider climate of prejudice and suspicion, were only too willing to listen to accusations of wrongdoing brought, fairly or not, against Chinese immigrants.[57]

The president of Havana's Chinese Community Association launched a two-pronged defense of his group's members: on the one hand, he stressed that they were upright and patriotic; on the other hand, he protested the reports printed in the city's newspapers that the government of Gerardo Machado "intends to undertake an intensive campaign against Chinese citizens living in this country."[58] His concerns regarding witch hunts were not unfounded. Machado's ten-point platform for the 1925 presidential election included the promotion of "good immigration."[59] Responding to the association's complaint, the secretary of the interior wrote that although the group itself was well regarded by the public, the government needed to take action "against those wayward elements, dangerous and disruptive, that unfortunately abound within the capital's Chinese community."[60] Although the government may have intended to confine its police actions to documented lawbreakers, the campaign entailed so many abuses that the Chinese government's diplomatic representative in Havana protested "the manner under which, in practice," Chinese accused of opium smuggling were being deported.[61] The representative's objections, however, carried little or no weight: just a few days later, the Cuban government deported to Hong Kong a group of Chinese immigrants considered "undesirable aliens."[62]

Cuba also had specifically prohibited Chinese immigration since the early 1900s. In 1902, just prior to official U.S. recognition of Cuban sovereignty, the U.S. military governor on the island severely restricted Chinese entry into Cuba, and this resolution remained in effect until 1919. In 1904, Tomás Estrada Palma, Cuba's first president, issued a decree requiring that all Chinese traveling through Cuba deposit large sums of money with the government.

The threat of forfeiture, officials reasoned, would discourage these travelers from remaining in the country.[63] In 1926, the Cuban government limited Chinese entry to diplomatic representatives and individuals who fell within highly restricted categories.[64]

The complaints heard in Cuba about immigration in general and about Chinese immigrants in particular were common in societies experiencing varied and large-scale waves of migration. Manuel Barroso, a physician and adviser to the homicide bureau of Cuba's secret police, wrote in that organization's magazine, "Despite existing laws and in defiance of those laws, our country is the recipient of undesirable immigration. Such immigration serves the special interests of gangs that, from their niche in foreign ports, disperse corruption and death to the far corners of the earth. . . . Our law must be reformed so that penalties are made more severe and foreign riff-raff and traffickers are expelled without any hesitation whatsoever."[65] Following this same anti-immigrant line, a newspaper published in Sancti Spíritus, a town in central Cuba, asserted in a 1917 editorial,

> The most distinguished of our scientific bodies, the Havana Academy of Sciences, has now joined the protest, voiced by so many for so long, against immigration by certain elements that exacts such a heavy price on the social and political development of the Cuban nation. Adding the Academy of Sciences to this collective voice removes any doubt that people of certain races, above all Chinese, Jamaicans, and Haitians, represent a clear danger to the health and well-being of Cuba's citizens; they carry the germs of diseases and parasitical infections as yet unknown to this country, raising the prospect of planting and spreading them among our countrymen.[66]

Such fears and prejudices made their way even into scholarly circles. For example, on the occasion of his induction into the Cuban Academy of History, Colonel Francisco López Leiva wrote that Cuba was the victim of an "invasion of foreign criminals": "This criminal rabble, this anonymous mass of drug addicts, thugs, thieves and murderers, these dregs of other societies, make their way here, to Cuba, to try their luck." He suggested that "this burdensome filth that is infesting new generations of Cubans with its vices and impurities" be expelled wholesale from the country and emphasized that it was "necessary . . . to attract by all possible means desirable immigration (whites and families)."[67]

In recommending ways for Cuba to deal with the problems of vice and crime, Gil Carballo, too, yielded to chauvinistic sentiments: "We are many fewer in number than during the time of the Spanish Empire, and we have a distinctly superior culture to that created by the yellow-complected, slant-eyed man; we must therefore quickly arrest the damage in order to avoid deleterious consequences down the road."[68] Anti-Chinese feeling was so strong that even scholar Fernando Ortiz, writing in the second decade of the twentieth century, could not detach himself from its influence: "Through opium, homosexual practices, and other highly developed corruptions of its secular civilization, the yellow race weakened [Cuba's] moral fiber."[69]

OTHER LATIN AMERICAN countries with substantial Chinese communities also experienced opium trafficking and use. The first wave of Chinese immigrants to Mexico arrived in 1864 to help construct a railway line running south from Ciudad Juárez. In 1871, a second group of Chinese immigrants arrived in the port city of Veracruz and were soon linked with the use of opium.[70] Official records indicate that just over fourteen thousand Chinese immigrated to Mexico between 1895 and 1949; as in Cuba, almost all — just under 98 percent in this case — were male. Not until 1930 did significant numbers of Chinese women begin to enter Mexico.[71]

The opium trade also infiltrated Mexican government circles and was co-opted by unscrupulous officials. One of the most flagrant opportunists was the governor of Baja California, Colonel Esteban Cantú. During the 1910s, Cantú enriched himself by permitting Chinese traffickers to import and distribute opium. Cantú sold opium brought from Europe directly to members of Los Angeles's Chinese community. In addition, Cantú and his father-in-law profited from the deposits his government required companies that imported Chinese immigrants to post.[72] Between 1922 and 1933 in Baja California, out of 418 arrests made for opium use and 141 for opium trafficking, 32 percent and 38 percent, respectively, involved individuals of Chinese origin.[73] During the 1920s, furthermore, members of a Chinese gang in both Sinaloa and Durango were charged with growing poppies.[74]

Two decades later, Chinese traffickers had become a major factor along the border between Ciudad Juárez and El Paso, Texas and in Tijuana, astride the border between Mexico and California.[75] The drug trade had also moved further south in Mexico: several Chinese were arrested in Guadalajara, which had turned into a focal point for the distribution of opium and housed laboratories for processing both opium and heroin.[76] Between October 1944 and March 1945, the Tijuana police arrested nearly one hundred people, approximately half of them of Chinese origin, for selling and using drugs.[77] The cutoff in the supply of drugs from Asia during the Second World War significantly increased the opium traffic between Mexico and the United States, which in turn led to an increase in the production of poppies in Mexico, an enterprise that involved both the Chinese and Mexicans, including a general in the Mexican army.[78] Mexico thus became the principal source of opium for the U.S. market.[79]

Following the Second World War, this flow of opium, at times managed by Chinese operating on both sides of the U.S.-Mexican border, ballooned to include multiple points in Mexico.[80] The Mexicans and the Chinese (many of them naturalized Mexicans) organized and oversaw the opium traffic between the two countries, relying on the willing collaboration of political figures and selected government officials, including most notably the long-standing chief of the Ministry of Public Health and Sanitation's Drug Enforcement Bureau.[81]

Historian Gabriela Recio points out that in Mexico, as in the United States and Cuba, "the Chinese were accused of contaminating society with their vices."[82] From 1910 on, the Chinese periodically faced calls for their expulsion from Mexican territory. In 1925, an expressly anti-Chinese assembly, held in Nogales, tied the Chinese to the opium traffic and asked that they be brought to account. In 1921, two Chinese associations in Baja California tangled with each other for business reasons, carrying the animosity against Asian immigrants to new heights.[83] Among the politicians who harbored anti-Chinese feelings was the future president of the country, Plutarco Elías Calles.[84] Alarmed by the outpouring of anti-Chinese sentiment, the Chinese community's benevolent society condemned drug traffickers of Chinese origin as "harmful elements," trying, as in Cuba, to counter the popular impression that the Chinese as a whole were disposed toward criminal conduct.[85] Indeed, many Chinese transplants in Mexico became successful businessmen and distinguished themselves by their modesty and work ethic.[86] Nevertheless, resentful of competition, politicians, labor unions, and members of the business community launched anti-Chinese campaigns that culminated during the depression with the expulsion of the Chinese from the state of Sonora. Anti-Chinese agitation also resulted in the murder of various immigrants and in the adoption of prohibitions against marriages between Chinese immigrants and Mexican women.[87]

Peru was the third node on the triangle of Latin American nations having large colonies of Chinese. Roughly eighty-seven thousand Chinese immigrants entered Peru between 1859 and 1874, the majority recruited as re-placements for freed black slaves on the country's sugar plantations.[88] Opium dens began to appear in Peru.[89] However, the government, seeking revenue, established a monopoly on the importation of opium beginning in 1887. The opium, which entered the country through the port of El Callao, was imported from Germany and Holland as well as from China and Persia. The commercialization of opium in Peru took the form of concessions awarded to private-sector merchants on the basis of public auctions. The merchants, who were of Chinese as well as Peruvian and European origin, wholesaled the drug to Chinese small-business owners, who in turn sold it in their stores to consumers.[90] Although Peru's laws governing the opium business stipulated that the drug could be sold only to persons of Chinese origin, Peruvians inev-itably flaunted the law and acquired opium for their personal use.[91] Until the middle of the twentieth century, when Peru joined wider antidrug campaigns, the Ministry of Public Health's narcotics enforcement section limited its ef-forts basically to controlling pharmacy transactions and to cracking down on Chinese opium dens.[92] The situation, however, was more complicated and re-quired greater vigilance. From time to time in Peru, traffickers of Chinese ori-gin also engaged in the illegal sale of such opiates as morphine and heroin.[93]

In sum, then, Chinese immigrants throughout Latin America brought with them the custom of using opium, most prominently in Cuba, Mexico, and Peru. Furthermore, while Chinese immigrants to Latin America did not suffer the same degree of violence as in certain parts of the United States, they none-theless remained the object of discrimination and xenophobia. In attempt-ing to assimilate, immigrants in Latin America—especially those who were poor and from radically different cultures—clearly became a lightning rod for conflict. Serious as it was, such conflict lacked the intensity of the disputes that inflamed the political landscape in Cuba during the middle decades of the twentieth century, when competing interests fought to control power and use it illicitly for their private enrichment. In the shadow of this struggle, as the Second World War disrupted the flow of illegal drugs from Europe and Asia, the drug trafficking networks that existed in Cuba and the United States developed further.

Chapter 4

. . . .

Corruption and Drug Trafficking in Cuba during the Second World War and the Early Postwar Years

A t the end of 1942, as the United States marked the first anniversary of its entrance into the Second World War, agents of the Federal Bureau of Narcotics (FBN) found a quantity of morphine and cocaine from Cuba in Kansas City. The drugs had been siphoned from legally imported quotas and then brought back clandestinely into the United States.[1] Based on this case, the FBN decided that it would no longer grant permits for the export of legal shipments of drugs from the United States to Cuba. Such a policy presumably would prevent the drugs from being diverted to illegal channels.[2] The case, however, did not stop there, as the U.S. embassy in Cuba requested that an FBN agent be designated to assist the Cuban ministry of health in reconstructing how the drugs had been diverted. Bureau officials chose a lead agent, Claude Follmer, who had been in charge of the initial investigation in Kansas City.[3] In turn, the Cuban Department of State authorized Eduardo Palacios Planas, commissioner of drugs in the health ministry, to exchange information about his country's narcotics situation with U.S. officials.[4] Perhaps the least surprising element of the case was that the drugs had turned up in Kansas City, at the time a hotbed of corruption and organized crime: "If Chicago was the most corrupt city in the country, Kansas City was a close second, with its municipal police department run by a former Capone gangster."[5]

In his lengthy report, Follmer blamed the episode squarely on Cuba's police force: "As the result of inefficiency and corruption, past and present, in the national police, all of the vices known to modern civilization have prospered for many years in Cuba. At present, just as in the recent past, the major criminal conduct in Cuba revolves around assassination, gambling, prostitution, and an extensive traffic in marijuana and narcotic drugs."[6] Follmer drew attention to a new channel through which narcotics were smuggled into Cuba. With the outbreak of the Second World War, drugs previously imported from Europe had been replaced by Peruvian cocaine, brought to the island on Chilean ships. In 1943, he noted, "the Republic of Cuba is literally inundated with Peruvian cocaine, which in the case of Havana is sold to several thousand of the city's cocaine addicts." Follmer concluded that the Cuban authorities would not take any important countermeasures and that illegal drugs would continue openly to be sold.[7]

British diplomats believed that Cuban corruption and its entanglements with gambling and the drug trade originated within the highest circles of government and the military. Army commander Colonel José A. Pedraza was "a big gambler and spender," and both Pedraza and Colonel Angel González had personal stakes in the gambling business; moreover, the head of the Cuban navy had enriched himself through smuggling.[8] In early 1941, Pedraza and González plotted unsuccessfully to overthrow Fulgencio Batista, resulting in the arrest and exile of the two men.[9]

At the end of 1942, British diplomats in Washington, D.C., strengthened their criticisms of Cuban corruption:

> Both the State Department and the American ambassador are very worried about the corruption existing in the Cuban government, a corruption which, though endemic, apparently now exceeds anything which had gone on previously. . . . Before President Batista's arrival [in Washington], it had been discussed in the State Department whether the subject of the venal atmosphere of his government should be broached to him. However, it was decided that little could be done about it at the moment and the nearest approach was a suggestion by President [Franklin D.] Roosevelt that American experts be sent to Cuba to assist in reforming the Civil Service. This suggestion was completely ignored by Batista.[10]

The British chancery, undoubtedly influenced by the reports from its diplomatic mission in Havana, strongly criticized Batista's first administration (1940–44): "His regime, has been remarkable, even in Cuba, for its corruption and inefficiency. . . . Cuban participation in the war is a farce. Its chief consequence is that it has afforded the president an excuse for imposing additional taxes, the proceeds of which have gone into the pockets of himself and his friends."[11]

The U.S. ambassador to Cuba, Spruille Braden, expressed similar sentiments: "Illicit dealings and corruption in all its forms are fully operative in

Cuba and involve both low and high-level individuals. Even those in the president's immediate circle, and some members of the cabinet . . . have a direct interest in the profits realized from such practices."[12] Some months later, Braden reiterated, "Corruption has never before been so rampant, so organized, or so profitable for those at the top."[13]

Wilson Beers, the U.S. Treasury Department's representative at the Havana embassy, also reported on the spreading corruption in Cuba and the key role played in it by military officials and police close to Batista, whom Beers dubbed the Palace Gang. Beers concluded, "Cuba has a huge number of drug addicts among people with money to burn, theater people, professionals and businessmen, elements within the entertainment world and night clubs, prostitutes, etc., those who are reaping the benefits of the current era of prosperity in Cuba and are willing and able to pay extraordinary sums" for drugs.[14]

One of the high-level officials who fit Braden's profile of corruption was General Manuel Benítez, chief of Cuba's secret police during Batista's first administration. Benítez, who was also suspected of assassination and embezzlement, apparently had a personal interest in the gambling that took place in Havana's most prominent nightclub, the Tropicana, and used his influence to protect the cabaret when its neighbors, including the Belén School, an elite Jesuit-run institution, complained about the gambling and excessive noise.[15] In October 1944, Ramón Grau San Martín returned to power under the standard of the Cuban Revolutionary Party (also known as the Auténticos), but he failed to rein in the country's corruption, and the situation may indeed have worsened: "Embezzlement, graft, corruption, and malfeasance of public office permeated every branch of national, provincial, and municipal government."[16]

Although U.S. diplomats stationed in Cuba had scarcely shied away from protesting their hosts' criminal corruption, some Americans living on the island also took part in illegal activities, as U.S. officials well knew. In the communities bordering the Guantánamo military base, for example, U.S. Marines regularly visited prostitutes, took drugs, and gambled.[17] The U.S. embassy also acknowledged that American workers and officials took advantage of lax conditions to import contraband cigarettes through the port of Havana.[18] More seriously, Americans transported drugs between Cuba and Miami. For example, Winthrop Gardiner used his legitimate position with a U.S. company in Cuba as cover to carry drugs between Florida and the island.[19]

Despite the possibility that Americans in Cuba exaggerated their criticisms and despite the fact that widespread corruption there was not a new phenomenon (in the country's 1922 elections, for example, a fifth of the candidates had criminal records), the country's levels of corruption undeniably rose during and after the Second World War.[20] Some authors blame this increase on the rapid expansion of North American investment in Cuba after the First World War, which excluded Cubans from managerial roles in the broader economy and limited them to the work and rewards offered in the public sector.[21]

Historian Jules R. Benjamin, conversely, has argued that Cuba's corruption problems resulted from the combination "of the colonial [Hispanic] heritage of Cuban politics," "the increasing stream of dollars" flowing out of Washington, D.C., through lend-lease programs, and favorable international sugar prices.[22] Along broadly similar lines, Louis A. Pérez has written, "World War II created new opportunities for Cuban economic development, few of which, however, were fully realized. . . . Funds were used irrationally. Corruption and graft increased and contributed in no small part to missed opportunities, but so did mismanagement and miscalculation."[23] For his part, Carlos Alberto Montaner has argued that from the outset of the twentieth century, Cubans and residents elsewhere in Hispanic America saw the state "as the primordial means of enrichment and as a source of jobs" governed by "favoritism and *compadrazgo*," a system of family-based relationships and social bonds.[24]

Presidents Grau (1944–48), Carlos Prío Socarrás (1948–52), and Batista (1940–44, 1952–58) enriched themselves during their years in office. Both Grau and Prío Socarrás followed a well-trod path, building palatial homes and living luxuriously. Grau, furthermore, disillusioned a great many people because of the extreme gulf between his reformist rhetoric on the one hand and the absolutely corrupt practices of his second administration on the other. When officials began to investigate charges of embezzlement against Grau, gunmen stole the records of the inquiry in 1949. Nothing symbolized the corruption that flourished under Grau's presidency better than his minister of education, José Manuel Alemán, who in 1948 escaped to the United States with millions of dollars, which he supposedly personally carried in several suitcases. The members of Batista's inner circle likewise enriched themselves, but Batista himself, a former sergeant of humble background, surpassed all others in amassing wealth. In 1959, his personal fortune was estimated at $300 million. Batista's investments spanned a number of businesses and industries, including sugarcane, rice plantations, land transport, cement plants, radio stations, publishing houses, real estate, and public services.[25]

Although the Cuban variant may have had distinctive features, it was also part of a larger dynamic, since corruption as a whole increased across Latin

America during and immediately after the Second World War as a consequence of a wide variety of factors: price controls, rationing, Export-Import Bank and lend-lease loans and initiatives, economic speculation, blacklists of businessmen from the Axis powers, nepotism, the uncontrolled rotation of jobs between the public and private sectors, insecurity brought on by cycles of rapid expansion followed by sudden crises, rapid growth of the state sector, the substantial number of large-scale contracts awarded, excessive presidential power and executive branch legal impunity, the exploitation of development plans and budgets, the participation of politicians and military officials at all levels in economic development programs as well as in business ventures that erased the boundaries between public and private interest, the concession of monopolies, the growth of cities in which local governments traded favors for votes, and the protection of certain economic groups and sectors to the detriment of other groups and of society in general. Furthermore, not just local businessmen and political figures grabbed at the opportunity to enrich themselves; American citizens did so, too, capitalizing on the growing U.S. influence in Latin America.[26]

The Cuban government's official assessments of the country's drug situation differed sharply from those of British and U.S. representatives. Eduardo Palacios Planas, for example, took issue with Follmer's statements, claiming, based on reports prepared by the judicial police, that the illegal use of drugs in Cuba had declined by at least half between the first six months of 1942 and of 1943.[27] Palacios Planas also protested the FBN's decision to include Cuba on its 1942 list of the principal countries from which illegal drugs were sent abroad.[28] In line with this position, the Cuban government's 1940 and 1941 reports to the League of Nations contended that the illegal use of narcotics "is not significant in Cuba."[29]

Privately, however, Palacios Planas sounded a much different note. In September 1930, he wrote to FBN director Harry J. Anslinger to express his concerns and frustrations regarding the illegal sale and use of drugs on the island. Palacios also expressed his pessimism that the government would follow through with a pending decree that would enable Cuba to fulfill its obligation under Article 15 of the 1931 League of Nations convention to create a special agency to "regulate, supervise, and control the sale and purchase of drugs" and to "organize a campaign against drug addiction, taking such steps as are necessary to prevent it and to suppress illegal trafficking."[30] Palacios Planas gave Anslinger an unflinchingly honest assessment of the situation:

Until now, I've been able to control the import, export, preparation, and distribution of narcotics, but their use as well as the suppression of illegal trafficking have been outside my hands. If our government decides to promulgate this decree, then I assure you that there will be no problems with trafficking. Unfortunately, though, our authorities have other countrywide concerns — politics. As a Cuban, I feel a sense of shame over the attitude adopted here, but over and above that, my own position as a responsible person obliges me to suggest the following to you: you should write to our government to insist that it establish and fund a department to centralize the authority to control drug trafficking in all its aspects. It would be advisable for you to stress that in the absence of such action, all permits to export drugs into Cuba will be suspended.[31]

Officials in the U.S. State Department agreed that Cuba had not created an agency in accordance with the terms of the 1931 League of Nations convention but nevertheless refrained from taking any measures as extreme as those proposed by Palacios Planas. Instead, they recommended that Ambassador Braden express to the Cuban chancery the U.S. government's desire that Cuba stop dithering and fulfill its commitments.[32]

On 24 January 1944, Palacios Planas visited the U.S. embassy in Havana and reported that the decree would be promulgated within a matter of days.[33] Two months later, however, the matter was still pending. Embassy officials contacted Cuba's new health minister, Alberto Recio, and its minister of state, Jorge Mañach, to insist that the office be established.[34] Recio declared that although he believed that the Cuban government had controlled the legitimate sale and purchase of drugs, he agreed that an office to control the illegal drug trade should be established "without delay."[35] Palacios Planas then stated that he would have nothing to do with the new office, promptly causing Recio to ask for the drug commissioner's resignation on the grounds that he had stated his opinions to the press.[36] Palacios Planas saw the matter differently, explaining to Anslinger that "given the impossibility of getting my government to comply with Article XV of the Convention, I find myself obliged to resign the office of Drug Commissioner."[37] Although the decree was ostensibly ready for President Batista's signature, he never signed it, and the creation of an office to centralize the control and regulation of drugs was postponed indefinitely.[38]

When Grau assumed the presidency at the end of 1944, however, the United States again began to exert pressure for the creation of the office.[39] In July 1945, the government finally issued a decree creating the Departamento General de

Control de Drogas Estupefacientes (General Department for the Control of Narcotic Drugs). The new department was attached to the Ministry of Health and Social Welfare, which received an augmented budget.[40] After almost fifteen years of stubborn procrastination, Cuba finally was in formal compliance with the terms of Article 15.

In the magazine *Bohemia*, Antonio Gil Carballo asserted that "as a consumer nation of hard drugs, Cuba occupies first place." He further denounced "the reprehensible intervention of certain high-level authorities" in the outgoing Batista government, placed his hopes on the new administration and its "postulates" of "moral regeneration," and declared that Grau "has been the one chosen to effect the moral liberation of our youth."[41] For his part, Wilson Beers strongly endorsed the appointment of Benito Herrera as Cuba's new director of the secret police, a position in which he would be in charge of cracking down on drug traffic and illegal drug use. According to Beers, Herrera was "the one honest person" available.[42]

When the secret police contracted with Gil Carballo to instruct and train twenty-five antinarcotics agents, Beers's predictions seemed to be borne out.[43] Gil Carballo's optimism soon faded, and a few months later he complained that the time allotted to him for instructing the new agents had been cut by several months. He also emphasized that marijuana trafficking was on the rise but that only petty dealers were being arrested. Substantial cocaine supplies remained available on Cuba's black market, brought into the country via Chilean ships and likely on Argentine vessels as well. According to Gil Carballo, the central figure in the trafficking of cocaine in Cuba was Angelito Cañal, who lived in Havana's Chinatown and operated under the protection of Inocente Álvarez, Cuba's minister of state. Gil Carballo also believed that while the chief of the secret police's antinarcotics bureau, José Sobrado López, was personally honest, he lacked the power to resist pressures applied from above and therefore confined himself to pursuing minor offenders.[44]

A report issued by Sobrado López's antinarcotics unit seemed to bear out Gil Carballo's gloomy assessment, indicating that most of the 363 people arrested for drug-related offenses during 1946 were drug addicts (who were generally sent to the Lazareto hospital in Mariel) or small-time peddlers — Gil Carballo's "little fish." Furthermore, almost all of the arrests and confiscations involved either marijuana or morphine (including opium). About half of the marijuana dealers and users were white, while three-quarters of the morphine addicts were of Chinese origin. Over the same year, the government had confiscated a mere one gram of cocaine, the drug of choice among wealthier users, and that had come from a black dealer.[45] Cuba's reports to the United Nations Economic and Social Council also demonstrate that the prosecution of marijuana cases focused on the lower classes. Of forty-five drug cases prosecuted in Cuba during 1946, for example, thirty-three involved marijuana, while the remaining twelve involved "unspecified" drugs.[46]

If Beers's high hopes for Herrera's appointment as chief of the secret police were largely dashed by internal Cuban realities, the situation was soon complicated even further by a new, external development — the arrival in Havana near the end of 1946 of Italian-American mafia don Salvatore Lucania, popularly known as Lucky Luciano. Luciano remained in Havana for several months, and his presence on the island marked a new point of conflict in U.S.-Cuban drug policy diplomacy.

Chapter 5

Lucky Luciano in Cuba

I n 1936, Salvatore Lucania, better known as Lucky Luciano, was convicted on charges of running a prostitution ring in New York City and sentenced to between thirty and fifty years in prison. Luciano had been born in Sicily but in 1906 moved with his family to the United States, where he climbed through the ranks of organized crime to become the head of the New York syndicate. The man who prosecuted the case against Luciano and fifteen of his mobster associates was Thomas E. Dewey, then serving as New York City's district attorney, and the long sentences the men received were intended to cripple the mob by removing some of its top overlords. In early 1946, however, Dewey, now the governor of the state of New York, agreed to commute Luciano's sentence on the condition that he be deported immediately to Italy. According to two members of the U.S. armed forces, Murray I. Gurfein and Charles R. Haffenden, Luciano had in effect bargained for his freedom by lending support to the American war effort against Germany and Italy. Though imprisoned, the mafia boss still controlled the New York city waterfront, and he had used his influence and underworld contacts to obtain and share with U.S. officials information about potential American collaborators in the German campaign to sink ships crossing the Atlantic. Luciano also used his contacts in Italy to obtain information that would help the U.S. Navy coordinate the logistics of landing Allied troops in Sicily. Dewey maintained, however, that the commutation of Luciano's sentence was purely a routine matter, in keeping with the state's established policy of deporting foreign-born prisoners as a way to save money. The governor, in fact, had done nothing more than follow the recommendation of the state parole board.[1]

After Luciano's deportation, rumors began to circulate that he wanted to leave Italy and return to the Western Hemisphere to coordinate and maintain control over his U.S. business interests. Cuba and Mexico were among the countries reported as possibilities, while another story stated that Luciano had obtained an Argentine passport and moved to Buenos Aires.[2]

Although U.S. authorities warned their Cuban counterparts about Luciano's intentions, the gangster nonetheless entered Cuba quietly and uneventfully, arriving by air in Camagüey on 29 October 1946.[3] His passport was stamped with visas for Cuba, Brazil, Bolivia, Colombia, and Venezuela.[4]

Prior to his incarceration, Luciano had lived a life of glittering opulence in New York. He spent his winter vacations in Miami and summered in Saratoga, rubbing shoulders with personalities from the entertainment world and members of the social and political elite.[5] In Havana, Luciano resumed his grand lifestyle, living openly with a young New York heiress at his side and frequenting racetracks and the Casino Nacional. As in New York and Miami, he not only fraternized with American celebrities such as Frank Sinatra who vacationed on the island but also mingled with Cuban political figures.[6]

Indalecio Pertierra, a representative in the Cuban legislature and the manager of Havana's Jockey Club, used his influence to help Luciano obtain legal residency in Cuba. He was also on close terms with two members of the Cuban Senate, Francisco Prío Socarrás (brother of Prime Minister Carlos Prío Socarrás) and Eduardo Suárez Rivas (president of the Senate in 1944 and 1945), and with Paulina Alsina, the widow of President Ramón Grau San Martín's brother, Francisco. Luciano rented and had an option to buy a house in Havana's Miramar district, an area of expensive and luxurious homes. According to a U.S. antinarcotics agent, the house belonged to General Genovevo Pérez Dámera, chief of the Cuban general staff. Luciano collaborated with a group of men including Pertierra and Suárez Rivas to set up a new airline, Aerovías Q, that operated flights between Havana and Key West, Florida, and Pérez Dámera saw to it that its planes were allowed to land on the military runway in Camp Columbia, on the outskirts of Havana, thereby bypassing immigration and customs controls. In addition, the government granted the airline special tax exemptions. Luciano's privileges did not end there, however. After a failed attempt on his life at the end of December 1946, Pertierra arranged to have two members of the Presidential Palace Police assigned to Luciano as bodyguards. His cozy relationships with high-level Cubans enabled him to bring in a dozen gangsters from the United States to help him manage his interests in the Casino Nacional. Luciano remained in frequent contact with fellow mobster Meyer Lansky, a friend and partner since childhood, and two notorious fixtures of American organized crime, Frank Costello and Benjamin "Bugsy" Siegel, visited Luciano on the island. Even Jack Dempsey, the former world heavyweight boxing champion, had business dealings with Luciano in the form of a fifty-thousand-dollar investment in the Gran Casino Nacional. Ralph Capone, brother of Al Capone, was also rumored to have met with Luciano in Havana.[7] Moreover, an official of the Federal Bureau of Narcotics (FBN) reported that members of the New York mob carried money to Havana to give to Luciano.[8] Lansky reportedly worked "to pull all the strings he could to keep his friend [Luciano] in Cuba," even interceding personally with Batista to remind the dictator of the "enormous bribes they had been paying him over the years and demanding his cooperation."[9] Alsina may have played a role in this connection, as she was well known for taking bribes in return for arranging contacts and facilitating various business dealings.[10] Furthermore, since Grau was a bachelor, Alsina acted as First Lady, a position that gave her considerable power.[11] Within the British embassy, in fact, she was considered to be "the power behind the throne."[12] According to Herminio Portell-Vilá, Grau's administration was characterized by rampant favoritism and nepotism: "he permitted members of his immediate family, in particular his sister-in-law, as well as his cronies and protégés, to exercise a pernicious influence on his government."[13] In addition to Alsina, Grau named various other relatives to official posts.[14]

Two days before Christmas 1946, the most powerful leaders of the U.S. mafia met in Havana's Hotel Nacional to discuss how to divide the profits from their casinos. The crime bosses also took up a related matter, the construction of the Flamingo Hotel and Casino in Las Vegas and their concerns that Siegel and his girlfriend, Virginia Hill, were skimming off part of the construction money for themselves. Sinatra provided the entertainment for this underworld summit.[15]

In December 1946, when Harry J. Anslinger, director of the FBN since its founding in 1930, learned of Luciano's presence in Cuba, the FBN put several Hotel Nacional employees on its payroll as informants, including a telephone operator and an elevator attendant.[16] Cuban authorities did not take an interest in the matter until the mafia kingpin was seen at the racetrack in Havana's Parque Oriental on 8 February 1947, however. Advised by the office of the legal attaché of the U.S. embassy, the chief of Cuba's secret police, Benito Herrera, went to the racetrack and informed Luciano that he would need to visit the secret police offices. Luciano did so two days later.[17] According to Luciano, Lansky had already spoken "with his friend" Alfredo Pequeño, Cuba's interior minister, regarding an extension of Luciano's six-month residency visa.[18]

U.S. officials began to pressure the Cuban government to expel Luciano from the island. Anslinger's request to that end received little or no reaction from Cuban authorities, and he responded by ordering an embargo on the export to Cuba of drugs for medical use, alleging that Luciano's organization could intercept and redirect them to illegal markets. Anslinger further decreed that the embargo would be lifted only when the government expelled Luciano.[19]

High officials of the Cuban government argued publicly and privately for the suspension of the embargo. Cuba's minister of health, for example, branded the measure "arbitrary and unjust."[20] Pedro Nogueira, director of the ministry's office of public health, took a more strident line, pointing out that Anslinger's statements "invite the supposition that this ministry would be capable of allowing the putative diversion [of legal drugs] and therefore [are] an accusation aimed directly at our health workers." Nogueira added that he would demand that Anslinger retract his statements.[21] Cuba's national health and welfare committee approved a motion of protest against the embargo, terming it "rash," "offensive," "arbitrary, abusive, and undeserved" and pointing out that Luciano was "a gangster molded [in the United States] and set free by the American authorities before completing his term of punishment."[22] In private, Nogueira and the health minister conveyed their intense displeasure to American diplomats in Havana. U.S. officials responded that their government was not lodging any accusations against the Cuban leaders personally but that the embargo would nonetheless be maintained until Luciano was expelled.[23]

The United States had previously placed embargoes on its export of legal drugs to Cuba. In 1943, U.S. officials took such action after an investigation found that legal drugs exported to Cuba had been illegally reexported back into the United States by a group of American drug traffickers belonging to Tampa's Antinori crime family. This group had been assisted by Juan Manuel Alfonso, a high-level Cuban government official.[24] And in 1940, Anslinger had embargoed the export of drugs to Mexico on the grounds that the country's health department failed adequately to regulate its department of drug addiction and that addicts who received drugs thus could reexport them illegally to the United States.[25]

On 26 February, Guillermo Belt, Cuba's ambassador to the United States, conveyed to Secretary of State George Marshall his country's displeasure with American actions and in particular with Anslinger's statements to the press; however, Belt also promised that Luciano would be deported within a matter of days and contended that such a quick response constituted proof of

Cuba's good faith, since the process normally took a month and a half.[26] The next day, Grau and Prío Socarrás signed a decree that outlined Luciano's past involvement in drug trafficking and prostitution and detailed findings that he was attempting to build up criminal operations in Cuba. As a result, the Cuban officials declared, Luciano was "undesirable" and should therefore be deported to Italy.[27] In fact, Luciano had been arrested on 22 February and was being held in the Camp Triscornia immigration center.[28]

Although the United States squeezed Cuba to expel Luciano, the island government proved more resistant when its neighbor to the north threatened Cuba's domestic economic interests, as a case involving air traffic between the two countries demonstrates. Aerovías Q, which was subsidized by the Cuban government and was the only airline company largely capitalized by the Cubans themselves, was also the only commercial line granted the right to use the military airport at Camp Columbia. All other carriers had to use the Rancho Boyeros airport, which was situated much farther from Havana. Displaying "a rapidly developing nationalistic attitude," in the words of one U.S. diplomatic official, the Grau administration in 1946 requested that a policy of reciprocity be adopted in the concession of air routes between the United States and Cuba.[29] Similarly, Grau and Belt held strongly to the position that Cuba's sugar quota should be preserved unconditionally, with the ambassador publicly voicing his objections to a U.S. initiative that would tie an increase in the quota to the resolution of other pending issues and threatening to boycott inter-American conferences planned for Río de Janeiro and Bogotá, retaliate against American economic interests in Cuba, and restrict Cuba's importation of manufactured goods. After a period of diplomatic sparring, however, the U.S. Congress and the White House worked out an agreement that Belt and Grau found satisfactory.[30] Given Cuba's proximity to the U.S. mainland and the close connections between the two countries, the U.S. Department of State ultimately saw the "maintenance of economic and political stability" on the island as the central consideration driving its Cuban policy and the U.S. market for sugar as the foundation on which such stability rested.[31]

Luciano continued to fight his deportation, telling reporters that he would leave Cuba voluntarily: "I'm trying to live decently and peacefully, but can't do even that. If they don't want me to be here, I'll go. I don't want to be in any place where I'm not wanted."[32] Nevertheless, Luciano continued to use his Cuban connections to fight the deportation order.[33] When his legal challenges failed, his Cuban cronies tried other maneuvers. José Suárez Rivas, a representative in the Cuban Congress and brother of Senator Eduardo Suárez Rivas, suggested that in response to the U.S. medicine embargo, President Grau should stop further shipments of sugar to the United States until the Americans deported a Spaniard — the alleged "head of the black market for sugar" — living in Miami.[34] Senators Manuel Capestany (a lawyer who had defended Chinese opium traffickers during the 1920s) and Francisco Prío Socarrás pressed for Luciano's freedom. The U.S. government, however, remained firm, insisting that the crime lord had to be deported to Italy and furthermore that he had to be sent on a ship. Luciano could not be allowed to leave Cuba by air because he held entry visas for Colombia and Venezuela and might therefore go to one of those countries; he could not be allowed to leave of his own volition to prevent him from returning to Cuba.[35]

On 26 February, the United States lifted the embargo.[36] The Colombian government canceled the visa it had granted to Luciano in keeping with "the dispositions currently in force which prevent entry on the part of undesirable elements."[37]

At the same time that the U.S. government was pressing for Luciano's deportation, American and Cuban officials were investigating eight U.S. citizens living in Cuba who maintained connections with the crime boss. Among the eight were two artists who performed in nightclubs.[38]

Luciano remained in detention until 19 March, when he was deported from Cuba on a Turkish cargo ship, the *Bakir*, on the night of 19 March 1947.[39] On his way out of Cuba, Luciano told Herrera that he would return to the United States "when its current government is no longer in power."[40] Herrera later claimed that Luciano had been expelled from Cuba not because of pressure from the United States but because he was considered a public enemy whose presence in the country could lead to a rise in drug trafficking. The secret police chief added that "from the moment [Luciano] stepped onto Cuban soil on 29 October 1946, my men have not let him out of their sight for even a single moment." When journalists asked if Cuba had a drug trafficking problem, Herrera responded in the affirmative, further contending that the traffickers had operated with the connivance of high officials in the previous government.[41] Whatever Herrera and other Cuban officials said publicly, however, Luciano clearly had been expelled from Cuba as a result of the U.S. campaign to force such an action.[42]

After the *Bakir* reached Genoa on 11 April, Italian authorities arrested Luciano and took him to a local prison.[43] At the beginning of May, he was transferred to a jail in Palermo.[44] Ten days later, he walked out of jail a free man.[45] He once again resumed his luxurious lifestyle, dividing his time between a penthouse in Naples and a villa on the island of Capri and frequenting the Naples racetrack and hobnobbing with important people.[46] Luciano also maintained his active involvement in American organized crime, albeit from a distance, receiving regular visits from U.S. syndicate associates and couriers.[47] The funding for this opulent lifestyle allegedly came, at least in part, from Luciano's participation in the organization headed by Frank Costello, who ran casinos in Newark, New Orleans, Chicago, and Florida.[48]

FBN officials still viewed Luciano as a major player in drug trafficking activities in both the United States and Italy.[49] According to U.S. authorities, Luciano and other Italian American mafiosi were associated with certain businessmen and pharmaceutical chemists in Milan in a racket to produce heroin, which was then shipped to the United States through Marseille.[50] Luciano was also suspected of having visited Germany to expand his range of illicit business activities.[51] U.S. authorities pressured the Italian government to cancel Luciano's passport and leaned on other European countries not to grant him entry visas.[52] FBN agents learned that a group of Italians was operating in Hamburg, dealing in black market transactions, foreign currency manipulation, and illegal import-export activities and consequently asked German officials to investigate illegal drug trafficking in their country.[53] With the help of the FBN, German police ultimately dismantled a gang that was processing cocaine, but Luciano was not linked to this case.[54] Luciano was definitely involved in other criminal activities, however, including smuggling goods through Mediterranean ports. In Naples, he controlled the counterfeiting racket and the black market for imports.[55]

For a number of years, Anslinger continued to insist that Luciano was distributing Cuban narcotics in the United States, a claim that prompted a U.S. congressman to make a fact-finding visit to Havana in 1958. A representative of the U.S. Treasury Department reported, however, that "to date, there has been no evidence whatsoever that Luciano is using Cuba" as an intermediate point for drug trafficking.[56] The FBN never built a drug-running case against Luciano. Anslinger blamed the failure to have Luciano tried and sentenced for his Italian activities on the impossibility of obtaining witnesses "who have the courage to declare publicly what they almost nonchalantly admit in private."[57] As Anslinger concluded, the mafia boss had the cunning of a fox and knew how to cover his tracks: "He leaves no trace because there is no trace. And still we know he is the man."[58] A U.S. senatorial commission, influenced directly by Anslinger and by the testimony of an FBN agent in Italy, noted in 1952 that Luciano was the "international kingpin" of the mafia, "a celebrated prostitution ringleader and drug trafficker."[59]

Luciano continued living in Naples, where he enjoyed celebrity status, especially in the eyes of tourists and U.S. sailors. He suffered a fatal heart attack on 26 January 1962 while waiting in the Naples airport to greet an American film producer who was going to make a movie about his life. Sometime later, his remains were interred in the Lucania family crypt on the burial grounds of New York's St. John's Cathedral, in the country he considered his true home.[60] The inscription on his tomb conjures up the image of a man who devoted himself to charity and public service:

HE FOUGHT IN DEFENSE OF ORDER AND JUSTICE
For democracy and on behalf of the oppressed
He gave succor to the poor and did only good
He rendered great service to the United States.[61]

Allegations of Luciano's involvement in large-scale heroin dealing were never proven.[62] He had only two brushes with U.S. law enforcement involving drugs, including a 1916 arrest for the possession and sale of heroin that led to a six-month stint in a reformatory.[63] The prosecution in his 1936 prostitution trial was unable to prove any involvement in drug trafficking on his part.[64]

Moreover, no evidence exists that Luciano engaged in drug trafficking while in Italy. Anslinger sought both to satisfy the public appetite for villains and to justify his position within the FBN by serving up a Sicilian gangster at a time when public hearings and extensive coverage had given both the U.S. Congress and the American media the image of a Sicilian Brotherhood that controlled and managed all illicit business dealings in the United States.[65] For years, Anslinger had exploited the tactical device of exaggeration to solidify his standing.[66] The FBN director propounded the idea that Luciano was the evil genius behind international drug trafficking and worked to create an image of him as a diabolical figure as a means of compensating for the bureau's failures. In practice, however, Anslinger managed only to irritate Luciano.[67]

Private statements by some Italian authorities indicate that they did not embrace either morally or as a matter of practical politics the crusades undertaken by U.S. officials. In response to the official U.S. point of view, one police chief asked,

What is the real crime that he committed? Look, I've got his FBI record here in the United States. As a boy he was arrested once for selling narcotics, and just a little bit. After that came the outrageous sentence that he got for forcing [some women] into prostitution. I ask you, what is compulsory prostitution? There is no such thing; a woman is a prostitute because she wants to be. This guy Lucania was simply providing a service to meet popular demand; I don't see anything wrong in that. As far as I'm concerned, the man is innocent and is being persecuted. If he commits a crime under Italian law, we'll arrest him. But, why should I harass myself with the problems of the Americans?[68]

Although Anslinger had never proved his accusations against Luciano, the FBN director had used American power to impose his moralizing outlook on the Cuban and Italian governments, much to their annoyance. As these developments were unfolding, the Cuban people went to the polls and elected Carlos Prío Socarrás as their next president. Not only was he Cuba's last civilian president, but he was later revealed as a habitual cocaine user.

Chapter 6

The Prío Socarrás Government and Drug Trafficking

Under the government of President Carlos Prío Socarrás (1948–52), Cuba's reports to the United Nations continued to maintain that the country's drug problem involved primarily marijuana and a very limited amount of morphine and that the problem primarily affected lower-class elements of society.[1] Thus, for example, one report asserted that "the drug that addicts use most heavily is marijuana . . . out of Mexico, which, because it costs the least is used the most." The report continued that such findings were hardly surprising, "given that the majority of those using it are from the country's lower class." The same report indicated that during 1948, the Ministry of Health and Social Welfare had destroyed 222 marijuana cigarettes, 15 pounds of loose marijuana, and just 10 grams of cocaine. The document acknowledged, however, that the retail price of heroin was high "due to its scarcity."[2] The figures for 1949 did not differ significantly: 125 marijuana cigarettes, 5 pounds of loose marijuana, 399 vials of morphine, and 27 grams of cocaine were destroyed, and 63 drug cases came before the courts.[3] A report submitted the same year by a U.S. antidrug agent noted that because of excess supplies in New York, cocaine prices in Cuba were three times higher than in the United States.[4]

In 1950, however, Cuba's report to the United Nations showed that although Cuban authorities destroyed only 96 marijuana cigarettes and 8 pounds of loose marijuana, 1,117 grams of cocaine had been confiscated and the courts had heard 125 drug cases.[5] For 1951, the last full year of the Prío presidency, the Cuban government reported to the United Nations that the courts had heard 75 drug cases and that a much greater amount of drugs had been confiscated: 146 marijuana cigarettes, 1,360 grams of loose marijuana, 87 vials of morphine, 595 grams of opium, 592 grams of morphine powder, 1.5 grams of cocaine, and 350 grams of coca paste. Both drug dealing and drug use were generally the province of young men; of the 43 court cases in which the offenders' gender was specified, 42 involved men and only 1 involved a woman. Those accused ranged between twenty-four and thirty-six years of age.[6]

Claiming that the volume of drug trafficking taking place on merchant ships had increased noticeably since the Second World War, the U.S. government introduced a December 1950 United Nations resolution calling on member states to compile "a list of those crew on merchant ships who have been convicted, inclusive of the years 1946 to 1950, of crimes connected to drug smuggling." The measure also asked that "sailors' papers and officers' licenses be revoked when held by such people."[7] The Cuban government expressed its support for such an initiative to the Office of the Secretary-General.[8]

AT THE BEGINNING of 1950, Prío offered to support Eduardo Chibás in the 1952 presidential campaign; according to Chibás, he rejected the offer because "we do not conclude agreements with bandits. . . . The Orthodox movement can't line up in any way with those who steal from the public treasury, be they members of the government or of the opposition. For that reason, the three soul mates, Prío Socarrás, Grau, [and] Batista, are all equally rejected."[9] On another occasion, Chibás accused the president and his brother, Antonio, "of having embezzled millions of pesos."[10] Chibás also claimed to have documents suggesting that President Prío and Genovevo Pérez Dámera, head of the army, were prepared to accept a section of land in the province of Pinar del Río in return for helping an estate owner expel some squatters.[11]

Yet Chibás, the mercurial public face of anticorruption in Cuba, was tormented by private demons. Days before he died from a self-inflicted gunshot wound to the stomach, an act committed at the end of one of his weekly radio broadcasts, Chibás repeated his accusations against "the government of Carlos Prío for being the most corrupt of all those which the Republic has had up to the present."[12] Chibás also accused the president of having tolerated drug trafficking and contended that highly placed Prío Socarrás administration officials had profited from the business.[13] In January 1952, Fidel Castro, then a young firebrand in the political party founded by Chibás, also leveled corruption charges against Prío.[14]

Foreign governments echoed Chibás's, Castro's, and other Cuban reformers' views regarding Prío. One U.S. State Department internal report, for example, called attention to "the prevalence of graft and corruption . . . as a traditional feature of Cuban administrations."[15] The British embassy in Cuba noted that "it is difficult to regard [Prío] as an honest man."[16] Eighteen months later, British officials accused Prío of having arranged for the disappearance of a file dealing with the embezzlement of funds during the Grau administration, a scheme in which he was personally implicated.[17] Prío not only amassed personal wealth but also tried to pacify and buy off gunmen operating under the cover of political groups by using state funds to give them jobs and sinecures.[18]

Prío's government also supported democratic movements in the Caribbean basin. After the 1948 coup in Venezuela against Rómulo Gallegos, both Gallegos and Rómulo Betancourt received political asylum in Havana.[19] Prío also supported the efforts of the Caribbean Legion, a multicountry alliance of democratic political leaders across Latin America, to overthrow Rafael Leonidas Trujillo's dictatorship in the Dominican Republic and offered protection to Dominicans exiled in Cuba.[20] The Prío government's "sympathy with democratic principles" led it to organize the Inter-American Conference for Democracy and Freedom, which took place in Havana in May 1950 and was attended by both Latin American and North American delegates.[21]

At the beginning of 1952, journalist Mario Kuchilán made public rumors of an impending coup d'état against Prío, referring to "a conversation in which a conspiracy on the part of military men dressed in civilian clothing was taken to be a sure thing."[22] State security forces had in fact been monitoring Fulgencio Batista's activities and his connections with military retirees and those on active service. Batista had concluded that he lacked sufficient strength in the country at large to win the presidential election and that he could obtain power only via a campaign to discredit the Prío government whose logical end point would be a coup d'état.[23] The military officers who supported Batista knew that a third consecutive victory for a politician from civilian ranks would indefinitely exclude them from power.[24]

The coup took place on 10 March 1952 and was a relatively peaceful affair. At dawn, tanks pulled out of the Camp Columbia military barracks, heading toward the presidential palace. The police and the few soldiers guarding the palace fired a few shots, but rather than resisting, Prío and most of the members of his government fled to Miami. Several provincial military garrisons remained loyal to Prío, but they capitulated after learning that Batista followers controlled the Matanza and Camagüey detachments.[25] Some elements of the population protested the coup, and the students and workers who would eventually become the seedbed of opposition to Batista called a general strike.[26]

Edward G. Miller, then serving as the U.S. assistant secretary of state for inter-American affairs, received the news as a "complete surprise" and deplored "the manner in which the coup occurred." Although Miller acknowledged that Batista's government would be "basically friendly" toward the United States, Washington extended de facto recognition to the new Cuban government only after it had promised to fulfill its international obligations and to adopt a favorable posture toward private capital. Furthermore, Batista agreed that both he and the provisional government would do whatever could be done "under the law to eliminate the freedom and privileges which the communists were now enjoying in Cuba," an important change from his alliance with the communists during his first administration.[27] Not until two and a half weeks after the coup, under pressure from American lobbyists partial to Batista, did the United States recognize his government, long after the military dictatorships in Venezuela, Nicaragua, and the Dominican Republic had done so.[28] According to one of the ministers in Prío's government, the U.S. embassy "had nothing to do with the coup d'état"; rather, Batista's takeover arose from "his authority among the officer class."[29]

During the first months of Batista's government, the U.S. ambassador, Willard Beaulac, maintained a clear distance from the Cuban president. Almost three months after the coup, Beaulac wrote that although he had met Batista informally on two or three occasions, "I have consciously refrained from rushing in to see him." Beaulac entertained doubts about the stability of the new regime, noting, "This is not a happy situation down here. In fact, I get sick at heart when I think of the unfortunate developments that may possibly occur."[30] Miller concurred: "The Cubans seem to be headed for a terrific mess both politically and economically. . . . Our ability to limit these developments is almost non-existent."[31]

After the coup, Prío and his brothers faced a wide variety of charges of drug trafficking and cocaine use. Batista claimed that cocaine had been found in the presidential palace.[32] Although the U.S. Federal Bureau of Narcotics (FBN) assigned an agent to watch one of the brothers, Francisco, in Miami, the agent found no evidence to implicate Prío in drug use.[33] However, another FBN agent, J. Ray Olivera, maintained that he had heard about the Prío brothers' efforts to obtain cocaine in Havana.[34] In addition, an FBN informant indicated that he had met Francisco Prío in Miami through a Bolivian drug trafficker, Blanca Ibáñez de Sánchez, from whom Prío wanted to buy cocaine.[35] Taking advantage of these accusations, Carlos Prío's foes hatched a plot to draw him into involvement with drugs in the United States.[36] Though the scheme proved unsuccessful, rumors linking the Prío Socarrás brothers to drug trafficking and drug use persisted.[37]

The corruption and the looting of the public treasury that characterized the Prío Socarrás presidency were damaging enough to Cuban interests, but as the final months of Prío's government ticked away, a committee of the U.S. Senate enacted certain measures that eventually had important repercussions for both Cuba's economy and its domestic politics.

Chapter 7
· ·

Gambling in Cuba

I
n January 1950, Tennessee senator Estes Kefauver introduced a congressional resolution calling for a formal investigation into the network of organized crime in the United States. Kefauver was responding in part to an appeal made by the mayors of New Orleans, Los Angeles, and Portland for federal intercession to expose and combat syndicated crime. The American Municipal Association had expressed the mayors' concerns to the U.S. Department of Justice in December 1949, claiming that "the problem is too massive to be dealt with solely by local authorities; organized crime elements operate across state borders, on a national scale." The U.S. attorney general seemed to confirm the gravity of the situation and the validity of the association's claim by sponsoring a conference on organized crime. On the basis of these developments, the Senate created a committee to investigate and formulate recommendations for dealing with organized crime. In 1950 and 1951, the committee held hearings in Washington, D.C.; Tampa; Miami; New York; Cleveland; St. Louis; Kansas City; New Orleans; Chicago; Detroit; Philadelphia; Las Vegas; Los Angeles; and San Francisco. More than eight hundred sworn witnesses contributed thousands of pages of testimony subsequently published in a dozen volumes. Public interest in the matter was heightened considerably when the committee's New York hearings were televised, reaching an estimated audience of 20 to 30 million viewers despite the fact that television was still a relatively new medium.[1]

To ensure that the committee's conclusions would not contradict his ideas and outlook, the head of the Federal Bureau of Narcotics (FBN), Harry J. Anslinger, saw to it that the committee staff included several FBN agents, who arranged for dozens of drug addicts to testify anonymously.[2] The Internal Revenue Service also provided the committee with information about the activities of alleged criminals.[3] Although the committee was charged with investigating the full spectrum of syndicated crime in the United States, it focused on gambling and bookmaking, and its final recommendations primarily concerned these two areas.[4]

With the repeal of Prohibition, gambling had become the principal source of revenue for the American mafia. As a result, by 1931 the city of Chicago had ten plants that manufactured slot machines, with all of these establishments controlled by local crime bosses. The gambling business grew steadily, and by the 1940s, the country had some 140,000 slot machines in operation, generating estimated annual revenues of $540 million. In addition, other varieties of casino gambling generated millions more. The mafia operated a numbers racket, or *bolita*, in Chicago's black neighborhoods and financed bookmakers who arranged bets on horse and dog racing via telegraph. The mafia also gained substantial revenue through loan sharks, charging exorbitant interest rates to people who had accumulated large gambling debts.[5]

The Kefauver Committee discovered that casino employees who worked in South Florida and in Cuba during the winter months returned to do the same work in the same type of business establishments in the North and Midwest during the spring and summer.[6] Betting on horse races had been legal in Florida since 1931, when despite strong opposition by several groups, the legislature had approved it as a means of boosting the state treasury.[7] The Senate committee's Florida hearings moved a number of influential citizens and the local press to denounce illegal casinos in the state and to organize an effort to suppress them by supporting the creation of the Crime Commission of Greater Miami.[8] As the result of the work done by Kefauver's committee, Meyer Lansky and other underworld figures came under investigation for running illegal casinos. Lansky's Florida casinos were promptly shut down, and he was fined. Furthermore, Lansky spent two months in jail in 1953 following exposure of his gambling operations in Saratoga Springs in upstate New York.[9]

Because the senatorial investigation focused on gambling, which for the most part took place in the country's urban centers, it also spotlighted the political machines that protected or at least tolerated the mafia bosses behind such activity. In the main, these machines belonged to the Democratic Party, which dominated political life in the cities. As a consequence of these politico-geographic alignments, Democratic Party leaders had not displayed a great deal of interest in the formation of the Senate's anticrime committee.[10] Kefauver paid a high political price for going against the wishes of the leaders of his party. In 1952, riding a wave of popularity, he sought the Democratic presidential nomination and received a majority of the primary delegates to the party's national convention in Chicago. The delegates gradually withdrew their support, however, and instead chose Adlai Stevenson as their candidate.[11]

In his book on Al Capone, Laurence Bergreen ties the tensions or dichotomies that play out along an urban-rural axis to the additional factors of class and ethnicity. As Bergreen explains, the sons of the first generation of Italian, Irish, and Jewish immigrants, who remained apart from older and established groups within the white Anglo-Saxon Protestant population, formed a prominent element of the American underworld because that world offered solidarity and an avenue of escape. In addition, the underground economy provided recently arrived ethnic groups that faced discrimination with a means of social mobility. Generally, then, the children of Protestant immigrants from northern Europe, many of whom had rural backgrounds, pursued criminals of Italian origin from urban areas.[12] Illegal economic activity thus became a way in which many immigrants could realize the American dream, avoiding the rigidities and discipline that characterized the Protestant corporate world.[13] However, many of those who enjoyed and benefited from illegal services provided by the underworld were urban-dwelling members of the Protestant community.

The Kefauver Committee uncovered the cozy relationships between Florida's casino owners and police chiefs and spotlighted the governor's complacent attitude.[14] Faced with unwanted public scrutiny and damaging revelations, some mafia bosses elected to move their businesses to Cuba, while others laundered their fortunes and invested in legitimate businesses.[15] Some, like Meyer and Jake Lansky, did both. In addition to expanding their operations in Havana, the Lanskys invested in Las Vegas's burgeoning casino business.[16] The fallout from the Kefauver Committee's investigations continued for some time. In March 1955, Santo Trafficante Jr., who controlled the lottery rackets in the Tampa and St. Petersburg areas, was convicted on charges of tax evasion stemming from profits on his *bolita* gambling operations. The Florida Supreme Court, however, overturned the conviction before he entered prison. Like other mafia bosses before him, Trafficante decided to look south and to cash in on the opportunity to invest in gambling operations in Havana.[17]

ALTHOUGH CUBA under Fulgencio Batista became a fertile ground for American gambling interests, gambling itself was not an activity that U.S. criminal elements introduced to Cuba. On the contrary, gambling was firmly rooted in a Spanish tradition that went back to colonial times and therefore constituted an integral part of Cuban life, though one that was nevertheless frequently criticized for its negative influences. An article that appeared in the December 1790 issue of the *Papel Periódico de la Habana* typified such criticism: "We were not put on this earth to play games but to live responsibly and occupy ourselves in purposeful and important matters. One need only peer closely into all of the communities and corners of this island to be appalled at the sight of so many villagers who, having abandoned the respectable work of agriculture, spend their days and nights in dim-witted activities like card playing and other such odious vices."[18] An early-nineteenth-century critic of Cuban gambling, José Antonio Saco, wrote, "There is no city, village, or corner of the island of Cuba into which this all-consuming cancer has not spread. . . . Gambling dens are a hideout for the idle, a school of corruption for youth, the tomb of family fortune, and the nefarious origin of most of the misdeeds that tarnish the society in which we live."[19] In addition to gambling, another reason for the vagrancy that existed among whites, according to Saco, was that the arts and crafts were monopolized by the black population.[20] Fernando Ortiz has noted that during the first third of the nineteenth century, "One gravitated in short measure from idleness and vagrancy to gambling. Everyone in Cuba gambled, and everything was fair game; nothing was sacred." Moreover, "to crown the demoralizing effects produced by gambling, in 1812 the government established the national lottery . . . which took hold so deeply that it became a 'fierce love of the public.'"[21] An 1838 novel by Ramón de Palma y Romay, *La Pascua en San Marcos*, criticized gambling among the country's upper classes.[22]

Nineteenth-century visitors to Cuba from both Europe and the United States noted that gambling was widespread and embedded, crossing all social and racial boundaries to include both whites and persons of color, the elite and the populace. Even parish priests were capable of "delaying the Mass to see the end of a cockfight."[23] In 1893, a Havana newspaper commented on the city's "dens of iniquity, where crimes are plotted, robberies are planned, and the habit of lazing about becomes an occupation in itself, where one is disposed to do anything other than work: those hundreds of daily raffles, of charades and gambling sites, worth pots of money but absent all dignity. . . . Havana today is a gigantic gambling den."[24]

Given gambling's popularity, attempts to crack down were bound to elicit spirited opposition. Two decades into the twentieth century, a newspaper published in Ciego de Avila, in the country's heartland, printed some lines of mordant verse after an illegal gambling establishment there was shuttered:

A great uproar broke out
among the people up above
some want it to be played,
to continue to be a gambling house,
this sick republic,
which, already sick, raves on . . .

He who doesn't play cards
plays Chinese charades
and he who isn't playing billiards
is off playing the lottery.

Oh! country of gamblers,
freeloaders, pickpockets,
ne'er-do-wells of an evil ilk,
poetasters, mountebanks.[25]

Cuban and Spanish immigrants brought the form of lottery gambling known as *bolita* to Tampa at the end of the nineteenth century. Although *bolita* was illegal in Florida, Anglo authorities tolerated it. Beginning in the 1930s, Sicilian immigrants became involved in the numbers game in the state, but in the mid–twentieth century, Cubans continued to handle much of the *bolita* business.[26] In Key West, both local residents and tourists bet on the results of the Cuban national lottery.[27]

Chinese immigrants also brought their gambling traditions to Cuba. According to Ortiz, "The Chinese have spread . . . that form of fraudulent criminality, very typical of their character, *paco pío* and *chiffá* games of chance and raffles, more popularly known as charade."[28] The Chinese charade, a scheme for playing the lottery involving the divination of numbers, "was popularized so effectively that it became a pastime taken up even within the highest echelons of Cuban society."[29]

In 1910, Orestes Ferrara, president of the Cuban House of Representatives, suggested that the Compañía de Fomento del Turismo receive a thirty-year concession on an area of land in Marianao, between Camp Columbia and the sea, on which it would develop a number of structures, including a casino. The project encountered strong opposition from American politicians and social reformers who believed that the proposed casino would attract gamblers from the United States. The U.S. government exerted so much pressure against the project that both the Cuban Senate and the country's president opposed Ferrara's initiative. The project's investors, both Cuban and American, were not easily defeated, and they attempted to revive it, but it again went down in the face of renewed opposition from the U.S. diplomatic legation in Havana.[30] The idea could not be killed off, and in 1919, the Compañía de Fomento won approval for the project, the development of which was assigned to another company, the Casino de la Playa. The opportunities for personal enrichment ultimately proved irresistible. In approving the project, Cuban president Mario García Menocal directly benefited his financial interests, since his family had the concession for jai alai matches (*pelota vasca*). Ricardo Dolz, president of the Cuban Senate, became the director of a new tourism commission and of a company that promoted horse racing. Furthermore, one of the three principal shareholders in the Casino de la Playa was Carlos Miguel de Céspedes, previously a lawyer in the department of public works and manager of the Cuban Ports Company in 1911 and eventually minister of public works, justice, and education in Gerardo Machado's administration.[31]

Memoirs, travel literature, and even academic reports described Cubans' passion for gambling. A 1928 guide for North American tourists, for example, observed that the Cuban "doesn't consider a game worth playing unless he can bet on it. . . . He always believes that his luck will change."[32] In 1933, Carleton Beals noted that "the Cuban worships none but the god of chance. An inveterate gambler, he will spend his last copper for lottery tickets. . . . The Cuban propensity for amusement and gambling reveals little regard for the day after tomorrow."[33] Invited by the Cuban government to visit the island in the mid-1930s, a commission of American academics emphasized that "the habit of gambling" was "widespread" among all social classes and that the purchase of lottery tickets discouraged Cubans from saving.[34]

Controlled by the government, the national lottery was a weekly event for Cubans, who ritualistically turned on their radios to hear the results of the drawings, conducted in Old Havana.[35] The revenue generated by the lottery was a self-renewing source of corruption. The monies bought off congressmen and newspaper editors, underwrote the costs of political campaigns, and paid the salaries of *botellas*, persons who appeared on the government payroll without ever reporting to work.[36] Cuba's presidents used the lottery to influence congressional decisions by handing out lottery tickets to congressmen, who would collect commissions by selling the tickets to distributors. This system of allocation was given the name *colecturías* (collectorships).[37]

Cubans in the capital pursued their passion for gambling in the Parque Oriental as well as in Havana's various casinos, including the Gran Casino

Nacional, a favored meeting place for the city's elite.[38] The gambling-addicted locals also enjoyed betting on jai alai games, while residents across the entire island attended baseball games and seized the opportunity to place every type of bet.[39]

Under Batista, the Cuban army took control of the national lottery beginning in 1937.[40] In 1938, according to a British diplomat, the military began to exploit its power to induce people to gamble as a way of extracting profits. In one case, a sugar mill owner prohibited his workers from gambling anywhere on the mill premises to prevent them from squandering their money. In response, an army sergeant tried to shake down the owner for a monthly payment, most of which would go to the sergeant's superiors. When this tactic failed, the sergeant opened a gambling den in the sugar mill, remitting part of the profits to his local barracks and keeping the remainder.[41] Military zone commanders collected the profits from gambling, kept part of the money, and sent the balance to Havana, where it went into a fund that financed different armed forces programs, including military schools.[42] The confluence of civil and military authority and gambling interests sometimes extended to extremes. For example, the vice president under Carlos Prío Socarrás, Guillermo Alonso-Pujol, and a group of friends set up a *timba* (gambling establishment) at army headquarters.[43]

Organized groups of Cuban women, generally drawn from the upper and middle classes, staunchly criticized not only gambling but also drug trafficking, alcohol consumption, and prostitution.[44] At the end of 1949, the Lyceum and Lawn Tennis Club, a venerable Cuban ladies' organization that promoted education and sports among women as well as community assistance programs, charitable works, and social activities, organized a series of twelve conferences on "The Theory and Explanation of Dissolute Habits," one of which was "Vice and Gambling."[45] This same club and more than twenty other social and religious organizations issued an October 1956 statement declaring, "This is a timely moment in which to stress the truly serious harm that gambling produces in the social fabric. It is a whirlpool that devours people's money and destroys the underpinning and well-being of the family, the principal building block of our society; it promotes thievery, crime, and prostitution, . . . causes a dislike for work, . . . leads to laziness and an attitude of indifference, [and] ends by undermining the strongest foundations of the nation." The statement concluded by asking for a crackdown on both legal and illegal gambling, both of which amounted to "organized games of chance, exploited for the sake of profits."[46]

Other voices also joined the Cuban antigambling chorus in the mid–twentieth century. Reformer Eduardo Chibás asserted that "Cuba had to stand up against an evil that corrupted the very essence of its nationhood and encased the country within the sphere of a colossal gaming establishment, where the degrading spectacle of gambling was witnessed on every corner."[47] Another author sharply critical of Cuba's infatuation with gambling wrote that "the pseudo-revolutionary governments set us down the path of crime. . . . [T]hey have implanted the all-consuming cancer of gambling within the hearts of Cubans."[48] Yet another critic likewise faulted the Cuban state for its central role in legitimizing gambling: "Gambling and principally its organized, official status [is] a powerful factor in the collapse of city life."[49]

Other Cubans complained about the negative international image of the island created by its casinos and cultivation of gambling.[50] A lengthy report prepared by a World Bank technical mission that had visited Cuba in 1950 also drew attention to gambling's deleterious effect on both the country's entrepreneurial spirit and its capacity to generate savings:

> The gambling spirit in the economy has a distorting effect on the spirit of enterprise. It is one of the reasons for the relative scarcity of capital and business initiative in the development of new industries. For the large owner of capital, what may be won in the fluctuating and unpredictable international sugar market — comparable almost to the lottery — can quickly overshadow all of the possible profits from a new venture which would necessarily take much time, toil, and trouble. . . .
>
> For the small man, in an economy where opportunities for business growth and job advancement seem to be few — a lottery ticket or any of the many betting games that flourish throughout Cuba may seem a more attractive use for money than saving. Besides providing excitement, it seems they offer a better hope of getting ahead than the prosaic process of steady saving, planning and hard work.[51]

In 1959, after the Cuban Revolution, an influential intellectual and Havana city historian, Emilio Roig de Leuchsenring, wrote, "From earliest colonial times to the present republican period, gambling has been the greatest and most persistent vice of Cubans. Bequeathed to us by our ancestors, the first Spaniards to settle on the island, gambling quickly took root among us. This perverse liking is so powerful and widespread as to merit being called the overriding passion of Cubans."[52] Soon after taking power, the country's revolutionary government abolished the national lottery, although it retained a remnant of the system, issuing numbered bonds whose purchasers were eligible for draw-ings with a top prize of one hundred thousand dollars. As American political activist and novelist Waldo Frank wrote, "The old gambling passion of the people hoping to get 'something for nothing' . . . is thus re-channeled into a legitimate means of gain with *the role of chance* still present."[53]

Whatever the dictates and reforms of the new governing order, the love of gambling and the thrills it offered did not disappear. In one popular song, *Espíritu Burlón*, a medium brings "a message from beyond":

O flee from me, mocking spirit,
mocking spirit, flee from me.

In a meeting one day,
they told me to play
bolita, and charades,
and the lottery, too.

I did as they ordered,
put down what they told me to,
now I'm without any money
and they've left me in the street.

My woman has given me the slip,
I've landed without any work,
but worst of all I came down sick,
and now I've disgusted myself.

I've got to give it up,
can't take any more bad luck,
I've got to rid myself
of this ever-mocking spirit.[54]

BOTH MEYER LANSKY'S connections to the world of Cuban gambling and casinos and his relationship with Fulgencio Batista went back to the 1930s.[55] As the country's president in the 1950s, Batista actively promoted tourism, in-cluding casinos, so that the country's economy would not depend exclusively on the unstable, fluctuating market for sugar, whose movements were deter-mined largely by external forces.[56] Tourism had long been seen as an effective though problematic tool for spurring Cuban economic development. In 1939, Chibás, for example, had supported the promotion of tourism in Cuba "as the most important of all initiatives that our country could undertake on behalf of its definitive political liberation — through its no less definitive economic redemption."[57] During the early 1950s, a surplus of sugar on the international market had triggered a drop in its price, creating a Cuban budget deficit.[58] In addition, as with other tropical commodities, the terms of trade had turned against sugar, and Cuba's imports were growing more quickly than its exports, reducing the surplus in the nation's balance of trade, although it remained positive as late as 1957.[59]

But even as Cuban authorities sought to promote tourism and gambling, visitors from the United States began to complain that they were being victimized by dishonest croupiers in various casinos.[60] Like tourism, the problem of Cubans taking advantage of visitors was not new to the island. In the same 1939 speech in which he had extolled the virtues of tourism, Chibás had criticized Cubans who "under the knowing eye of the authorities spend their time wheedling and exploiting the tourist . . . getting involved in one outrage after another . . . free as a bird and never penalized." After proposing that tourist brochures touting Cuba be distributed "in profusion" across the United States, Chibás warned, "It is less harmful to let tourists go to other seaside resorts, where they are welcomed and shown a more refined form of hospitality, than it is to have them turn into vocal critics of Cuba."[61]

The *Saturday Evening Post* spread the negative image with an article, "Suckers in Paradise," that infuriated Batista, who responded by ordering the deportation of American casino workers known to have cheated tourists.[62] Thirteen U.S. citizens who worked in casinos in the Hotel Varadero Internacional, Tropicana, Jockey Club, and Sans Souci were arrested and deported.[63] Batista then called on Lansky to clean up the business and restore gamblers' confidence and goodwill.[64]

In 1955, the Cuban government had granted tax benefits for the construction of new hotels and facilitated the placement of casinos in both hotels and nightclubs.[65] The law was framed within the context of the country's National Program for Economic Action, which sought to diminish Cuba's dependence on sugar exports.[66] Lansky had immediately taken advantage of the new law, beginning construction of the Hotel Riviera in 1956.[67] Both the Le Parisién nightclub and the Casino Internacional, in the Hotel Nacional, opened for business on 20 January 1956.[68] With officials from the government joining the festivities, Tampa-based crime boss Santo Trafficante Jr. inaugurated the Hotel Capri in 1957. Trafficante was also the owner of the Sans Souci nightclub and maintained a financial interest in other hotels as well. In 1958, he hired Hollywood actor George Raft, who had appeared in a number of movies about mobsters, to work as a host at the Sans Souci, greeting people who came into the casino. Raft was no stranger to such work, having performed the same duties some years earlier for the Sands Hotel, in Las Vegas.[69] Lansky also had an interest in the construction of the Hotel Jagua on the Bay of Cienfuegos, a particularly lovely seafront area.[70] By the end of the 1950s, Lansky and other U.S. mafia bosses had taken control of Cuba's principal hotels and casinos.[71] At the beginning of 1958, Havana's Hotel Nacional, Sans Souci, Tropicana, and Hotel Riviera employed one hundred Americans, many of them from gangster backgrounds.[72]

Havana increasingly seemed to have become the Las Vegas of Latin America, and the shows put on in its hotels and nightclubs featured a revolving cast of top international stars. Reflecting both the uneasy admixture of the legitimate and the illegitimate within the world of gambling and the related attempt by casino interests to buy respectability, the casino in the Hotel Nacional gave the profits realized from its grand opening to the League against Cancer.[73] (Similarly, Martín Fox, owner of the Tropicana, and Roberto Fernández Miranda, Batista's brother-in-law, donated part of the profits from slot machine rentals to support the program of soup kitchens [comedores populares] set up by Marta Fernández de Batista, Cuba's First Lady.)[74]

When asked why the presence of American gangsters was tolerated in Cuba, the U.S. ambassador, Earl Smith, replied candidly, "It's strange, but it seems to be the only way to get honest casinos."[75] In his Havana Hilton casino, Conrad Hilton hired an expert to spot the croupiers who were trying to cheat tourists, and *Life* magazine blandly pointed out that mafia kingpins such as Lansky "have recognized for some time that honesty [in the casinos] is the best policy."[76] According to Lansky's Cuban chauffeur and bodyguard, "Lansky really insisted on honesty. He used to say that a good dealer had no reason to be a crook," since operators of gambling establishments always come out ahead.[77]

IN THE WAKE OF the Second World War, Cuba's central banking system was reorganized. At the end of December 1948, the National Bank of Cuba, the country's central bank, was founded. The state controlled just over 50 percent of the bank's shares, while private banks controlled the remainder. Cuba's president received authority to appoint the president of the bank's board of directors, which also included the president of the country's Bank of Agricultural Credit, the director of the country's Currency Stabilization Fund, a representative of Cuba's private banks, and an individual from the foreign banking community in Cuba. Regulating credit numbered among the national bank's functions.[78]

Following the broader Latin American pattern in this period, Cuba also established a government-run bank to promote development, the Cuban Bank for Agricultural and Industrial Development (BANFAIC), which began operations in 1951.[79] In addition to promoting agriculture and industry, the BANFAIC encouraged the development of tourism, hydroelectric power, transportation, and mining projects.[80] The bank also tried to mitigate cyclical disruptions in the national economy by financing public works projects.[81] Batista's government maintained a high level of state spending by borrowing from the national bank and then issuing bonds to finance its budget deficits.[82]

Yet another state-run development bank, the Bank for Economic and Social Development (BANDES), was established in 1954 and began operating the following year. The purpose of this bank, whose sole shareholder was the Cuban government, was "to facilitate short-, medium-, and long-term credit transactions to carry out a policy of economic and social development."[83] BANDES financed up to 50 percent of the capital required by foreign as well as Cuban investors in the construction of new hotels. As part of this policy, investors also received five-year exemptions from Cuban taxes.[84] The bank made loans amounting to almost $450 million for infrastructure projects and for projects within the agricultural, industrial, and service sectors. Of this total, $55 million went to help build up the hotel industry.[85]

Meyer Lansky's Hotel Riviera was a prominent beneficiary of the BANDES program, with its investors receiving a $5.5 million loan, half of the hotel's estimated cost. The corporation that managed the hotel's construction was formed in February 1956. Eduardo Suárez Rivas, onetime president of the Cuban Senate and a friend of Lucky Luciano, sat on its board of directors and served as the corporation's secretary.[86] Another hotel built at the end of the 1950s, the Havana Hilton, had construction costs of $24 million. The building was owned by the Caja de Retiro del Sindicato Gastronómico (Food Workers Union Pension Fund), which had financed a major part of the investment portfolio. BANDES and BANFAIC also made significant loans for the Hilton's construction.[87]

Cuban writer Enrique Cirules contends that BANDES was "one of the institutions established by Batista to legalize the business dealings of the mafia" as well as to support other U.S. business ventures in the public service and mining sectors. Moreover, Cirules categorizes tourist companies as "fronts" to launder money from drug trafficking.[88] However, BANDES supported multiple Cuban and foreign investment projects, not just those involving Lansky and his ilk. In addition, although Cuba's drug business was significant, it was very small relative to the revenues generated by casinos, which, although distasteful to some observers, were entirely legal ventures. Furthermore, casinos were highly profitable. For example, between December 1957 and November 1958, and despite the difficult political situation and the fact that the establishment had just opened, the casino at the Hotel Riviera declared a net profit of four hundred thousand dollars.[89] During the 1950s, according to Louis A. Pérez, gambling revenue from Havana's casinos surpassed five hundred thousand dollars per month.[90]

The high-end tourist business was so profitable that even as the country was engulfed in civil war and Batista's fall neared, BANDES maintained a backlog of requests for loans to finance the construction of new luxury hotels. One corporation proposed construction of the 656-room Hotel Monte Carlo, in Barlovento, twenty minutes west of Havana. The corporation included both Cuban shareholders drawn from the sugar industry and Americans representing show business, Las Vegas and Miami hotels, the construction industry, and the political world.[91] Another entity that explored the possibility of securing a loan from BANDES was the Antillean Hotel Corporation, which represented "a group of North American investors with great experience in the hotel construction business in Miami [and in] the southwestern region of the United States." This group proposed a 600-room luxury hotel in the El Vedado district, the heart of Havana's hotel and casino complex.[92]

Despite the influence exerted by the United States, then, the culture of gambling in Cuba and the development of the physical infrastructure that supported it were a Cuban phenomenon, the fruit of a historical process internal to the country's society and economy. The Cuban government recruited men whom U.S. officials saw as crime barons to invest in and run businesses on the island. Even after Fidel Castro seized power, he initially found himself with no alternative but to allow these Americans to continue running Cuba's hotels and casinos to maintain the flow of tourist dollars that Cuba's economy required.

Chapter 8

The Andean Connection

T he 1940s and 1950s saw the furtherance of trade in illegal drugs within a triangle connecting the Andean countries, Cuba, and the United States. Both Cuban drug traffickers and their Andean counterparts, a large majority of them foreign-born immigrants, were very opportunistic, time and again demonstrating the ability to adapt to changing circumstances and to contest and deflect U.S. pressure against drug trafficking.

THE EMERGENCE of the Andean countries — in particular, Peru — on the hemispheric drug trafficking scene was related in a circuitous way to economic and political developments in the Far East. The first link in the chain appeared in 1878, when the Dutch introduced coca plants to their Javanese colony. From that point on, shored up by support from the Koloniale Bank of Amsterdam, coca leaf production on the island steadily expanded, and in 1920 Java exported seventeen hundred tons of coca.[1] When the Japanese occupation of British and Dutch colonies cut off the Asian coca supply during the Second World War, the demand for Peruvian coca increased significantly. With the end of the war and the reopening of the Asian supply lines to the West, the need for legal importation of Peruvian coca shrank to prewar levels, but the market dynamics had fundamentally changed, and Peru remained the principal source of cocaine in the Western Hemisphere.[2] One barometer marking this change involved the number of confiscations made in the United States of the illegal drug. In 1945, the U.S. Federal Bureau of Narcotics (FBN) seized 702 grams of cocaine originating in Peru and shipped from either Peruvian or Chilean ports; four years later, that number had jumped to more than 13.5 kilos.[3] The activities of sailors served as another indicator of the change. During the war, sailors traveling between the United States and South America focused on smuggling U.S.-produced items that had become scarce elsewhere; immediately after the war, however, they shifted their focus to transporting drugs.[4]

Some of the traffickers in Peruvian drugs were Cuban, while others were Peruvian and still others were of different nationalities.[5] When shipped by sea, Peruvian cocaine passed through Panama and was off-loaded in Cuba, where some was retained for local use and the rest packaged for reexport to the United States.[6]

Taking advantage of the pro-U.S. orientation of Peru's military government, FBN director Harry J. Anslinger worked through the Peruvian ambassador in Washington to persuade his country's leaders to close Peru's legal cocaine factories.[7] In addition, the volume of Peru's illegal drug traffic dropped as a consequence of the prosecution of several important traffickers, including Eduardo Balarezo, a Peruvian former sailor born in 1900 and living on New York's Long Island.[8] Balarezo headed a group of traffickers, composed primarily of Peruvians and Chileans, who carried the drug on commercial flights or while working as sailors on ships run by the Grace Line.[9] According to the supervisor of the FBN's New York district office, "It is a sure thing that any Grace Line ship which docked in El Callao, Peru, between the years 1947 and 1949, carried contraband cocaine to Charleston, South Carolina, New York, and other American ports."[10] During that time, Balarezo's gang smuggled an estimated one hundred kilos of cocaine into the United States.[11] In 1950, U.S. courts convicted Balarezo and six of his associates on drug trafficking charges, and he was sentenced to five years in federal prison.[12] The publicity generated by the case was such that both the secretary of the Peruvian embassy in Washington and a representative of the Peruvian police sat in on the trial of Balarezo and his comrades in New York.[13] Between 1950 and 1951, Peruvian authorities also arrested dozens of persons processing cocaine, including a number of chemists and others who had for years been legally manufacturing the drug.[14]

When Balarezo was arrested in New York in 1949, authorities also rounded up more than a dozen others, including several Cubans.[15] In this period, prior to the Cuban influx to South Florida in the wake of the 1959 revolution, 40 percent of Cubans living in the United States resided in the New York area.[16] *La vida real*, Miguel Barnet's novel about a Cuban immigrant to New York in the mid–twentieth century, alludes to the involvement of members of the city's Cuban community in drug trafficking.[17]

A September 1950 article in the Cuban magazine *Bohemia* referred to the

Cuba-Peru-U.S. drug triangle, describing locations in New York where drugs could be obtained and used and how both Cubans and Puerto Ricans distributed cocaine through a "complicated scheme that connected Lima, Havana, and New York."[18] This criminal operation was headed by Abelardo Martínez Rodríguez del Rey and Octavio Jordán, nicknamed El Teniente and El Cubano Loco, respectively, and imported drugs to Cuba from Peru. From there, they were smuggled into the United States through New York and Miami.[19] In 1952, El Teniente and another trafficker were arrested in Peru.[20]

Despite U.S. efforts to clamp down on the drug trade, the smuggling of cocaine from Peru to its distribution platforms in Cuba and Mexico persisted during the 1950s.[21] The traffickers' ingenuity and determination was evident when a secret laboratory set up for the production of cocaine was discovered inside a Lima jail in 1957.[22] According to a Cuban diplomatic envoy in Lima, "One reason the cocaine traffickers are tolerated [in Peru] lies in the huge profits they are making right now."[23] Nevertheless, the United Nations declared the same year "that the trafficking of illegal drugs from Peru has ceased to be an international problem."[24]

As government efforts in both North and South America gradually suppressed Peruvian drug trafficking, the volume of cocaine smuggled out of Bolivia picked up considerably.[25] In 1955, for example, U.S. officials confiscated 5.5 kilos of cocaine, with the bulk of the seizures taking place in New York and involving drugs from Bolivia.[26]

At the outset of the twentieth century, cocaine used in Bolivia for medical purposes had been imported from Germany, Belgium, and France.[27] Although Bolivian landowners legally grew coca leaf, the plant was not processed into cocaine there, a distinction the government stressed in resisting both League of Nations and United Nations campaigns to eradicate the cultivation of coca leaf.[28] With the suppression of trafficking of Peruvian cocaine, however, Bolivian suppliers took up at least part of the slack, and authorities discovered quantities of Bolivian cocaine ready for shipment not just to North America but also to Argentina.[29]

Because Bolivia lacked basic antinarcotics laws, drug enforcement agents faced particular challenges there. In October 1951, for example, a gang, several of whose members were of Syrian-Lebanese origin, was discovered operating a laboratory on the outskirts of La Paz.[30] Even though authorities soon discovered another laboratory in Cochabamba run by the same gang, all of those apprehended during the first raid were set free for the simple reason that Bolivian law imposed no penalty for processing cocaine.[31] At the end of February 1953, officials in Cochabamba found another cocaine-producing laboratory apparently run by the same gang.[32]

In April 1955, Rodríguez Martínez del Rey sent an associate, Manuel Méndez Marfa (known as Manolín), to La Paz to pay a trafficker, Rames Harb, ten thousand dollars for a shipment of drugs.[33] Harb maintained processing laboratories in La Paz and in Rurrenabaque, a settlement on the Beni River north of the Bolivian capital. Harb, who also trafficked in Chile, operated under the protection of a high-level Bolivian police official, Freddy Henrich, who in turn frequently traveled to the northern Chilean port city of Arica to deliver cocaine.[34] In May 1955, Méndez Marfa and another Cuban, Miguel Angel González, were arrested in New York while in possession of 3.5 kilos of cocaine.[35] The FBN followed the drugs' trail back to El Teniente by watching the movements of his lover, a Spanish dancer from Barcelona whom he used as his courier.[36]

Méndez Marfa and two other men were arrested in Havana in May 1954 while in possession of a large amount of cocaine.[37] Another Cuban, Jorge Juan Lemes García, was arrested in Bolivia in 1954 in possession of a batch of cocaine ready to be shipped to Havana. On previous occasions, Lemes García had sent cocaine to an associate in the Cuban capital, who apparently reshipped the drugs to the United States.[38] Another Bolivian trafficker, Mario Spechar, also sold drugs to Cuban traffickers, and in February 1956, officials raided another Bolivian processing laboratory whose chemist was Chilean.[39]

The third node on the triangle, the United States, continued to figure prominently. An American father and son, Charles Tourine Sr. and Charles Tourine Jr., and an Argentine, Carmen Di Marco, transported cocaine from Bolivia to New York via Havana, where they apparently had connections with El Teniente's brother, Jorge Martínez Rodríguez del Rey, known as El Bacardí.[40] Blanca Ibáñez Sánchez, another of the principal Bolivian suppliers of the cocaine that found its way through Havana to New York, maintained laboratories on the outskirts of La Paz as well as in Cochabamba and Santa Cruz.[41] In 1958, according to the Bolivian Department of the Interior, shipments of cocaine from Bolivia to Cuba reached the level of thirty kilos per month, much of it reexported to the United States.[42]

Chilean engagement in illegal drug operations predated the country's involvement in Bolivian-based cocaine trafficking. During the 1920s, the port of Valparaíso served as an important center for the sale of opium, whose principal buyers included American sailors.[43] In 1938, the Santiago newspaper *La*

Hora published a series of articles and editorials on the subject of drug trafficking, calling on the authorities to act swiftly to counter the problem. The newspaper also noted that Valparaíso was home to 150 traffickers, "known to one and all," who freely mixed the use of cocaine with prostitution and other allures of cabaret night life. In both Santiago and Valparaíso, *La Hora* reported, "hundreds of businesses . . . cafeterias, hotels renting rooms by the hour, restaurants and bars" supposedly were "used as places of distribution by the traffickers."[44] Drug use also penetrated further into the country: in 1942, officials discovered a brothel in Antofagasta where U.S. sailors were obtaining cocaine and marijuana. The proprietor of the establishment had previously been deported from Bolivia on drug trafficking charges.[45] In the northern Chilean port of Tocopilla, too, sailors regularly used marijuana while visiting the town's brothels.[46] American diplomatic personnel stationed in Chile also reported the case of a Chinese shopkeeper found to be selling opium in his Valparaíso store as well as the discovery of an opium den in Santiago and subsequent arrest of eleven Chinese men.[47] The multinational character of the drug problem again became apparent in January 1951, when Chilean officials broke up a gang of cocaine traffickers that included people from Chile, Argentina, and Bolivia.[48] Chile also served as a point of transshipment for drugs on their way to Argentina, Panama, Cuba, and the United States.[49] Chile's director-general of investigations, Luis Brun D'Avoglio, expressed to U.S. officials his concerns that his country was being used in this fashion, citing the cases of traffickers who funneled Bolivian cocaine through Chile before smuggling it into Cuba and the United States.[50] Some Italian diplomats agreed, expressing their belief that traffickers who had earlier operated out of Mexico had transferred their operations to Santiago.[51] Another route favored by traffickers in Chile involved transporting cocaine in boats from Arica and its environs to Valparaíso, from whence crewmen on Grace Line ships carried it to New York.[52]

The flow of drugs and the diplomatic response to it impinged on broader relations between Chile and the United States. In the early 1940s, the FBN took the same approach toward Chile as toward Cuba, refusing to approve the export of opiates intended for medical use to pressure the country to stop allowing the cultivation of poppies, even for medicinal uses, and to participate in additional international drug agreements. Furthermore, when Chile responded to the U.S. embargo by importing drugs from Great Britain, Anslinger pressured the British to put an end to the practice.[53] U.S. officials argued that Asia and Eastern Europe produced more than enough poppies for legal purposes and that "the United States, whenever the opportunity presents itself, has discouraged such production in this hemisphere."[54] The United States and Chile remained at a standoff for several months until the Chilean government, backed into a corner, used the liquidation of the Chilean pharmaceutical company that had grown and legally processed poppies as cover for a ban on the issuance of new licenses for such activity.[55] In the face of pressure from Chilean pharmacists, however, the government quickly revoked the new decree. The U.S. government, whose mouthpiece on the issue was Anslinger, retaliated harshly: "All requests for exports to Chile are to be rejected and all those still pending are cancelled."[56] The Chilean government yielded, and the embargo was lifted.[57]

In 1946, the same year as the U.S.-Chilean impasse, the United States also pressured Argentina to end both poppy cultivation and the production of opiates. American officials blocked the issuance of a permit Argentina needed to bring a shipment of five hundred kilos of opium paste from Afghanistan to Argentina, arguing that Argentine medical and scientific needs could be satisfied by opiates from the United States and Europe.[58] Although American diplomatic personnel in Buenos Aires expressed reservations about pressuring the Argentine government in light of the tense relations between the United States and President Juan Domingo Perón and questioned "whether the United States government possessed the authority to exercise police powers," the State Department remained adamant.[59] Perón, however, was equally determined; he ignored the pressures, allowing two factories licensed to produce opiates to continue doing so and authorizing the ministry of agriculture to distribute free poppy seeds to the country's farmers in hopes of making the country self-sufficient in this regard.[60]

Ecuador was also part of the network of opium trafficking that fed into Cuba and the United States. Two of its provinces, Riobamba and Imbabura, contained poppy-growing fields. One of the country's principal drug traffickers was Joffre Torbay, a chemist based in the coastal city of Guayaquil. Torbay was associated with Oscar Méndez, a Cuban who worked for El Teniente on the island. Quito also served as an important site of both drug processing and trafficking. Physician Enrique Alarcón was the city's principal drug trafficker; he also sold arms to politicians from Colombia's Liberal Party, who were embroiled in a bloody power struggle with their Conservative counterparts during the 1950s. Two other Colombians, Carlos Rodríguez Téllez, a former member of the country's military, and Guillermo Cadena, bought large quantities of opium paste in Ecuador for processing in Colombia.[61] Guillermo

Lozano, a Colombian who purported to be a lawyer and political exile, also smuggled drugs between Ecuador and Colombia, as did many others, allegedly including a retired captain in the Colombian army.[62] Still another person within this segment of the Andean connection was the Cuban Jesús Moms, alias Orejitas. Like so many others, Moms was associated with El Teniente and traveled between Ecuador and Cuba to deliver cocaine.[63] In 1953, FBN agent George H. White, who had been a lieutenant colonel in the CIA's predecessor agency, the Office of Strategic Services, collaborated with the Ecuadorian police by going undercover to pass as a drug buyer. The sting operation, carried out in Quito, resulted in the capture of seven individuals and the confiscation of drugs valued at half a million dollars.[64]

The attempt to puncture drug operations in the north-central Andean countries revealed the extent of their interconnections. According to the FBN, Luis Martínez Swett, a leader of the Guayaquil police force, had a background in narcotics dealing, and his former wife was married to a Peruvian trafficker. In 1955, two traffickers were captured in Peru; the two men sold drugs to three Ecuadorians. Another Guayaquileño who trafficked in cocaine, Juan Aníbal Pérez, had been deported from Peru as a convicted drug trafficker.[65]

In the mid-1950s, the FBN sent special agent Samuel Levine to the Andean countries to assess the drug situation. Levine summed up for his superiors what he encountered in Ecuador: "The authorities show little concern for applying the laws. . . . Insofar as drugs are concerned, the situation is very bad, and, as time passes, gets much worse. There seems to be no desire on the part of responsible authorities to enforce laws in order to get the job done. Whether this is the result of their being personally implicated, or of their own fear of stepping on the toes of those who are well connected, is not clear."[66] Levine's pessimism would have been greater still had he incorporated into his analysis the development of the French Connection, another drug trafficking triangle, this one involving heroin, that linked the United States and Cuba with drug traffickers in the Mediterranean basin.

Chapter 9
· ·

Contacts in France

ven before Cuba became a focal point on the international drug scene, the Mediterranean port of Marseille had been a center for narcotics processing and trafficking. Marseille was part of a chain of production that started in Asia: poppies cultivated and processed into opium paste in that part of the world made their way to French laboratories for conversion into heroin. Before reaching its eventual markets, the illegal heroin had first to be shipped through different transit points, and Cuba became a principal conduit through which the drug was smuggled to distributors in the United States.

IN JULY 1930, Reginald Lee, vice consul of the British legation in Marseille, vanished under mysterious circumstances. Lee, who cultivated sleuthing as a hobby, had been on the track of drug trafficking gangs during previous consular postings in both Havana and Savannah, Georgia. Shortly before his disappearance, Lee's detective work had led him to discover that a British ship docked in Marseille was concealing a shipment of morphine and heroin, so police surmised that he had been assassinated by members of the Marseille underworld.[1] Authorities in Marseille periodically confiscated great quantities of opium, cocaine, and heroin, giving the city a reputation as a perennial haunt of criminals and outcasts. One U.S. journalist described the port as "inhabited by the French, Italians, Greeks, Poles, and Algerians . . . and the riffraff of every nation on the globe." Moreover, drugs found "a ready market and eager buyers among the flotsam and jetsam who make up the population."[2]

The size and sophistication of the Marseille drug trade was cast in high relief in November 1933, when police investigators confiscated 2,000 kilograms of opium in a nearby town.[3] In March 1939, authorities found another laboratory operating in Marseille and seized 750 kilos of opium and 2 kilos of

TABLE 9.1. Persons Arrested for Possession of Drugs in France, 1936–1939

	Paris	Marseille	Other Cities	Total
1936	263	30	44	337
1937	327	40	23	390
1938	384	28	20	432
1939	528	56	47	631

Source: League of Nations, "The Drug Situation and the Control of Narcotic Drugs in France," O.C. Special 9, Geneva, 6 June 1944, Record Group 170, Records of the Drug Enforcement Administration, U.S. National Archives and Records Administration, College Park, Md., 74-12, Box 24.

TABLE 9.2. Drugs Confiscated in France, 1936–1939 (in Kilograms)

	Opium	Morphine	Heroine	Cocaine	Hashish
1936	195	3	15	10	6
1937	52	2	9	3	0.2
1938	103	0.4	101	3	3.6
1939	864	0.8	19.5	1.5	7

Source: League of Nations, "The Drug Situation and the Control of Narcotic Drugs in France," O.C. Special 9, Geneva, 6 June 1944, Record Group 170, Records of the Drug Enforcement Administration, U.S. National Archives and Records Administration, College Park, Md., 74-12, Box 24.

heroin. Drugs processed at the lab went primarily to the United States, either via Marseille or via the northern port of Le Havre, although some remained in France.[4] League of Nations statistics demonstrate France's central role in the illegal drug business during the 1930s (tables 9.1 and 9.2).

Although Cuba had not yet emerged as a major transshipment center, some markers of its future status already existed. At the beginning of the 1930s, for example, a Paris-based trafficker who manufactured heroin in his own laboratory with raw material from Marseille paid several visits to Cuba, the United States, and Canada. He traveled across the Atlantic with a Peruvian diplomat who took advantage of his privileged position to traffic in heroin.[5] After the Second World War, Cuba became a much more important gateway for heroin smuggling. The war almost completely cut off the Western Hemisphere's supply of heroin and opium from Europe and the Far East, and Cuban and Mexican traffickers moved in to fill the vacuum.[6] When the flow of heroin from Europe resumed after the end of hostilities, Italians and later Corsicans got into the business. Laboratories in Milan and Genoa produced the drug legally but then diverted it to illegal markets. When Italian authorities, assisted by agents of the U.S. Federal Bureau of Narcotics (FBN), intervened, the processors moved their operations to Marseille.[7]

Marseille served as a center for the processing and smuggling of various opium derivatives. In addition to being a major Mediterranean port, favored by its relative proximity to the Atlantic Ocean and by its strategic position in the geographic center of trade and communication lines connecting Europe, the Middle East, Africa, and the Americas, Marseille was a cosmopolitan city, visited regularly by ships and sailors from every continent. Not coincidentally, the city also served as a site for the smuggling of a wide range of products and goods. The city's criminal organizations were dominated by people of Corsican origin.[8] Marseille's vibrant cosmopolitanism was reflected in its rich mosaic of nationalities. Out of a total population of approximately 700,000 at the end of the 1930s, the city hosted 125,000 Italians, 20,000 Spaniards, 15,000 Armenians, 10,000 Middle Easterners, 5,000 Greeks, 5,000 Russians, and 60,000 Corsicans.[9] The city had an image, in part as a result of the efforts of the North American press, as the world capital of "dope, whores, and street violence."[10] Seeking a pithy label that would express the interplay between Marseille's rough-and-tumble political life and its gangsters, the Parisian press started referring to the city as "Marseille-Chicago."[11]

Since the 1920s, politicians had used local gangsters as electoral enforcers who used violence to compel cooperation. Marseille's politics thus combined violence with fraud and clientelism, a system of political organization and fulfillment that had deep roots in Corsica.[12] For example, Simon Sabiani, a key political figure in Marseille and a native of Corsica, employed Paul Venture (alias Paul Carbone) and François L. Spirito as electoral enforcers. Carbone had begun his criminal career trafficking in opium from the Middle East. Protected by Sabiani, Carbone also organized prostitution rings in Argentina, Spain, and Egypt.[13] For his part, after his conviction on drug trafficking charges in New York, Spirito returned to Marseille and worked in a gang headed by Joseph Orsini, another Corsican who had also served time in New York for drug trafficking.[14] For years, various groups called on Corsicans inside the criminal underworld to help advance specific political agendas. Corsicans lent support to the French fascists, for example, and were recruited by the Gestapo to counter communist intrigues. Immediately after the Second World War, the U.S. Central Intelligence Agency paid Corsicans to break up communist-organized strikes.[15]

Marseille also served as a hub for human trafficking, enjoying a dubious reputation as the center of the South American white slave trade.[16] Marseille attracted Jewish refugees seeking a bridge to Palestine and Italian immigrants entering France illegally. The long list of other sorts of smuggling that flourished in the city included arms, drugs, and foodstuffs.[17] The city's criminal gangs were also involved in smuggling American cigarettes between Marseille, Tangiers, and Naples and in the production of counterfeit dollars.[18] Chinese sailors and members of the Marseille's Vietnamese and Chinese communities participated in the opium trade, Middle Eastern businessmen sold hashish, while the French (either native or of Corsican origin) and Italians dominated heroin trafficking.[19] Near the end of the 1940s, the city's police noted that the French Riviera, including Marseille, had roughly two hundred thousand drug users.[20]

An indifferent if not negligent bureaucratic and judicial system threw up additional obstacles to suppressing the rampant local drug business. The Marseille police, for example, complained about not being given the resources they needed to combat the broad span of smuggling.[21] Charles Siragusa, the FBN's man in Marseille, pointed out that although French law recommended a maximum jail sentence of two years for large-scale traffickers, judges for the most part handed down "ridiculous" sentences of between one and six months and systematically ignored directives from Paris to increase their severity: "Marseille persistently ignores everyone. . . . The excellent efforts of the French Police in executing [the law] are cancelled out by the Marseille courts."[22] The penalties Marseille's judges imposed for drug trafficking were lighter than those imposed for smuggling cigarettes, leading a U.S. journalist to explain to his readers, "The cigarette running evades the high French tax and causes immediate harm to the French economy. Drug smuggling does little or no damage to France economically."[23] Nearly two decades later, U.S. officials continued to complain that French president Charles de Gaulle displayed an "evident insensitivity to narcotics problems and . . . distaste for cooperation with the United States."[24]

Marseille was part of a drug network that included a wide circle of countries in Europe, the Middle East, and along the Mediterranean. For example, a large portion of the opiates originating in Turkey entered Marseille via Beirut, another wealthy, cosmopolitan city and a commercial center since antiquity with the creature comforts and high life to cater to bons vivants.[25] By the mid–twentieth century, Lebanon had become a major financial and commercial center, with its ports serving as gateways through which imported goods reached not only the local market but also Syria and from which Middle Eastern petroleum was exported to other parts of the world.[26]

Lebanese drug traffickers bought the opium base, processed from Turkish poppies, in Aleppo, Syria, and sold it to Corsicans.[27] Turkey complicated the drug picture, because the country was burdened with local users addicted to hashish, opium, and/or heroin.[28] Turkey as well as Iran also exported opium in its crude form to France.[29] In addition, French traffickers had imported crude opium from Yugoslavia since the 1930s.[30]

According to both French diplomatic personnel and FBN agents, Lebanon's drug business involved not only opium but other narcotic drugs such as hashish and reached into the highest levels of the government.[31] Since Lebanon imposed only very low fines on people convicted of growing marijuana, a substantial segment of the population did so. Even the president of the national congress, the richest landowner in the Bekaa Valley, cultivated marijuana on some of his land. According to Farid Shehab, director of the country's criminal investigation department, other Lebanese politician-landowners were also involved in the production of marijuana. Moreover, some officials from the southern part of the country facilitated the export of hashish from the ports of Tyre and Sidon to the Egyptian city of Alexandria. Egypt, where the drug had been used for decades, served as the principal market for Lebanese-produced hashish.[32] Greece, too, produced hashish.[33]

Denizens of Beirut smoked hashish openly in public, and users apparently bore no social stigma. U.S. sailors on shore leave in Beirut used hashish, as did the American employees of Beirut-based oil companies, who also took cocaine when frequenting the city's brothels.[34] The cocaine sold in Beirut and in the vacation resorts nestled in Lebanon's mountains either was stolen from medical inventories in Europe or was purchased by Lebanese gangsters from their Bolivian, Peruvian, and Cuban associates.[35]

France's northern port city of Le Havre served not only as an embarkation site for narcotics but also as one of the principal centers for the smuggling of American cigarettes, a much sought-after commodity in Europe during the early postwar years.[36] Before the outbreak of war, Le Havre had been the port where American sailors collected drugs to transport to New York on ships sailing under the U.S. flag.[37] After the war, however, drugs moving from Europe to the United States, whether leaving from Le Havre or from Marseille, were carried by sailors working on French and British as well as North American ships.[38]

In the initial postwar years, authorities at U.S. and Canadian ports confiscated a number of large shipments of heroin that had originated in France. Two 1947 seizures in New York netted 14.5 kilos — more than all of France's legal stock of heroin, with a street value of nearly $1.3 million — from a French vessel, the *Saint Tropez*, and nearly 3 kilos from a North American ship.[39] In January 1949, 18 kilos of Iranian opium were found hidden on a French ship, *Bastia*, that had docked in New York; later that month, 3.5 kilos of opium were discovered on a North American ship, *Excalibur*, when it arrived in the port of Jersey City after departing from Marseille.[40]

The significant confiscations continued during the next decade. In October 1953, authorities found 5 kilos of heroin on the French ship *Flandre*; during the Atlantic crossing, the drugs had been stored in two of the vessel's fire extinguishers. This seizure resulted from a six-month investigation, coordinated jointly by the FBN and France's criminal investigation bureau, and was accompanied by the arrest of two members of a Marseille gang that had organized the operation and used couriers from Le Havre and New York to transport the drugs from Europe to the United States.[41] Two years later, several confiscations of heroin transported on French ships occurred. New York authorities found 13.5 kilos, while Montreal officials netted 14 kilos and Brooklyn officials discovered nearly 10.[42] In July 1957, in Port Everglades, a distribution hub located next to Fort Lauderdale, Florida, north of Miami, antinarcotics agents arrested two crew members from a French ship that had come from Marseille who were in possession of more than 4 kilos of heroin.[43] U.S. authorities suspected that these drugs coming from France originated not only in illegal, clandestine laboratories but also in the country's legal medical laboratories, which in 1959, for example, produced seventeen times more morphine than international standards indicated that the country required.[44]

During the 1950s, the quantity of heroin brought into the United States by Corsicans also shot up significantly.[45] As U.S. officials instituted tight controls on the country's East Coast and increased the number of confiscations, traffickers began to look for new routes to bring drugs to North America. Latin America as a whole and Cuba in particular seemed promising.[46]

IN THE MID-1950S, the FBN took steps to alert Cuban authorities to the presence of Corsican drug traffickers in their country.[47] One of these traffickers was Paul Damien Mondolini. In August 1949, Mondolini and others had robbed the Aga Khan's wife at gunpoint on the French Riviera, taking her jewelry, a high-profile crime for which he was sentenced in absentia in 1953 in Marseille. Mondolini pursued his renegade adventures on at least three continents, and by the mid-1950s, he headed a France-based group of traffickers that imported drugs into the United States through Canada, Mexico, and Cuba.[48] In December 1956, authorities in Havana arrested Mondolini, and he was extradited to Paris in February 1957.[49] The Corsican fought his deportation through every means he could muster, reportedly including having the minister of the interior intercede on his behalf, bribing officials, and marrying a Cuban. The French ambassador, however, pressed strongly for Mondolini's extradition, and Colonel Orlando Piedra, chief of the Bureau of Investigations and director of the Cuban secret police, personally conveyed the deportation decree to President Fulgencio Batista. Back on French soil, Mondolini received a two-year prison sentence for armed robbery but spent only five months behind bars.[50]

Another trafficker who worked the Cuba-U.S. drug pipeline during this period, Ansan Albert Bistoni, had previously worked as a sailor for the Messageries Maritimes shipping company in the Far East. In March 1953, he was arrested in France while in possession of 4 kilos of heroin hidden in a double-bottomed suitcase. Bistoni confessed under interrogation that he had already sent 6 kilos to the United States in a similar suitcase. A short while later, he turned up in Havana, where he had interests in several nightclubs and from whence he sent heroin to North America. Bistoni was arrested in Havana in October 1956 and shortly thereafter was deported to France.[51]

The roster of French and Corsican drug traffickers operating in Cuba also included Jean Baptiste Croce, a native of Bastia, Corsica. Like Bistoni, Croce had been employed as a sailor by the Messageries Maritimes company. The owner of two Havana nightclubs, Croce had connections to both Bistoni and Mondolini.[52] Antinarcotics agents followed Croce's and Bistoni's movements beginning in June 1956, when the two men traveled from Montreal to Havana.[53] Interpol's efforts led to Croce's and Bistoni's capture in Havana, and their confessions enabled the Cuban authorities to seize Mondolini as well. Like Bistoni, Croce was expelled from Cuba, in large measure because of pressure brought by French officials, who in turn were responding to pressure from the U.S. government.[54]

Canada also figured in the geography of drug trafficking between Europe, the United States, and Cuba. The kingpin of illicit trafficking in Canada was Lucien Rivard, a French Canadian who lived in Montreal. Rivard, who supplied drugs to addicts in Montreal and Vancouver and dealt illegally in Canadian gold that he transferred to the black market in France, allied himself with Mondolini, Bistoni, and Croce to smuggle drugs into the United States through Mexico and Cuba. Together with Mondolini and a third gangster, Norman Rothman, Rivard owned El Morocco, a nightclub in the prosperous Cuban interior city of Camagüey. William "Butch" Munroe acted as a courier for Rivard, frequently traveling between Montreal and both Camagüey and Havana.[55] Rivard also had a financial interest in the casino at Havana's Hotel Plaza, which opened in November 1958.[56]

Various other criminals took part in drug-running operations that used Cuba as a point of transshipment. Dominique Albertini, a Corsican who lived in Marseille and whom the FBN considered France's principal operator of heroin laboratories, had for a quarter of a century supplied heroin to various gangs of traffickers.[57] Others who played key roles included the brothers Giuseppe and Vincent Cotrone, who lived in Montreal and trafficked drugs in Cuba; Joseph Patrizi, a native of Ogliastro, Corsica, and resident of Marseille who organized heroin shipments for Bistoni and Croce; Lucien Gabriel Graziani, a Marseille native who worked as a courier for Croce, traveling frequently among France, North America, Cuba, and South America; and Antranik (André) Paroutian, a Frenchman of Armenian ancestry and Marseille resident whose contributions included obtaining morphine base in the Middle East and accompanying Graziani on several trips to Cuba.[58]

According to the FBN, Croce and Mondolini first oversaw the production of heroin in the Marseille laboratories, a process that typically lasted several months. After accumulating between 50 and 150 kilos of the drug, they then traveled to Havana, where they sold the heroin to traffickers from the United States, Canada, and Mexico.[59] Rivard and Mondolini used Camagüey as their Cuban base because it was close to the ports of Nuevitas and Tarafa, where heroin could be landed. The drug was then reexported from Camagüey to the United States by air. Unrefined opium from India also made its way to Cuba's Chinese community through Nuevitas, where the drug passed for jute, a fibrous material used to manufacture sugar sacks.[60] Both Nuevitas, the world's leading sugar-exporting port, and Tarafa, which played a prominent role in Cuba's international trade, were pivotal to the well-being of the island's economy.[61] Like other places in Cuba, Camagüey had been the site of active drug trafficking decades before Rivard and Mondolini made their presence felt there.[62]

The FBN aggressively monitored the movements and activities of the drug traffickers operating in Cuba. In this connection, one of the bureau's agents, John Cusack, proposed visiting Camagüey with a fellow agent, Salvatore Vizzini.[63] In August 1958, the two men arrived in Havana on a mission to investigate Mondolini and his associates. Passing himself off as a drug trafficker, Vizzini made his way to Camagüey, accompanied by a Cuban informant, but was unable to locate either Mondolini or Rivard. Their nightclub, El Morocco, had closed, and Rivard, having lost $180,000 in the venture, had gone back to Havana. Vizzini spotted Rothman at the airport with an American who specialized in repairing slot machines. Some days later, Vizzini again tried and failed to find Rivard at Havana's Hotel Plaza.[64]

By the eighteenth century, the province of Camagüey, situated between the middle of the island and its eastern end, had become an important center for smuggling.[65] During the nineteenth-century wars of independence, the port of Nuevitas, in the northern part of the province, served as an entry point for the delivery of large quantities of arms for the insurgent forces.[66] Twentieth-century improvements and innovations in transportation further spurred the province's development as a haven for smugglers. Pan American Airways had maintained a landing strip along the highway to Nuevitas since 1928, and the adjacent airport was modernized for strategic reasons during the Second World War. With assistance provided by the United States, the physical facilities were upgraded, and two full-length runways as well as a military barracks were constructed.[67] By the end of the 1940s, Pan American used the Camagüey airport for connecting passengers on Cubana de Aviación flights to Havana and as a stopover on its Miami–Buenos Aires and Miami-Balboa routes, while Cubana de Aviación used the airport to streamline connections to the Antilles and South America.[68] Even though the population of the municipal district of Camagüey scarcely exceeded 110,000, the city claimed one of the most important airports in the Caribbean region, served by several foreign carriers, including KLM.[69]

With such a major air facility, then, Camagüey provided a natural passageway for drug trafficking. In 1958, officials arrested a Cubana de Aviación crew member who resided in Camagüey after discovering that he was using his position to transport cocaine to New York.[70] The same year, authorities followed a Puerto Rican who had bought small amounts of narcotics in Havana to Camagüey, where he supposedly intended to acquire larger amounts.[71] In a third 1958 case, a Cuban trafficker was arrested in Camagüey while holding a quarter of a kilo of cocaine.[72] Finally, also in 1958, several people, one of whom had a criminal past that included prostitution and running a numbers racket in Tampa, Florida, were investigated on suspicion of sending heroin from Camagüey to Tampa.[73] In short, the city's geographic position, economic wealth, proximity to two highly important ports, and sophisticated air transport and communications infrastructure (developed with U.S. government assistance) helped to make the city an important Cuban drug distribution center. On a more general level, too, Cuba's relative prosperity and its success in attracting international flows of both people and goods also helped to create the conditions that persuaded criminal elements to use the island during the final years of the Batista dictatorship.

Chapter 10

The Batista Dictatorship and Drug Trafficking

ccording to Harry J. Anslinger, the director of the U.S. Federal Bureau of Narcotics (FBN), while serving as Cuba's dictator between 1952 and 1958, Fulgencio Batista failed to cooperate with U.S. antidrug efforts: "Our agents made more than fifty cases against Cuban pushers and dealers in the Batista era. The Batista government did nothing about putting these men in jail in spite of our co-operation in working with their own people to get the evidence."[1] This lack of cooperation stemmed from the corruption that existed more generally in Cuba during this period. As Louis A. Pérez has trenchantly written, "Millions of dollars were distributed among Cuban officials high and low in the form of graft and rake-offs. Criminal activities expanded on all fronts, most notably drugs and prostitution, without the slightest interference from Cuban authorities and wholly free of any fear of local prosecution."[2]

That graft and corruption pervaded Cuba during this period is incontestable. With respect to drug trafficking, however, the reality was more shaded, since evidence indicates both that in certain key cases, Batista's government collaborated in apprehending foreign criminals and in approving requests for their deportation and that in other cases, the laxness of the Cuban judiciary allowed drug traffickers to escape punishment.

Although Batista's detractors accused him of corruption and of governing dictatorially, they never charged that he was linked to drug trafficking. Fidel Castro did not include such an allegation in the manifesto he issued prior to his July 1953 assault on the Moncada Barracks in Santiago.[3] Orthodox Party leader Eduardo Chibás lodged a slew of other charges against Batista, however: "What I accuse General Batista of is having stolen, during his period of government, many millions of pesos from funds for hospital medicines, local road projects, school breakfast programs, military pensions, etc., etc."[4]

El Acusador, a news sheet published in 1952 by Castro and other younger Orthodox Party members, alleged that "all of [Batista's] fortune has been made underhandedly."[5] Castro's charges of corruption against various Cuban leaders went back to his years as a political militant while a university student, and he assailed Ramón Grau San Martín's and Carlos Prío Socarrás's administrations in the same terms he later used against Batista. Thus, Castro logically chose to follow Chibás when he established his own political party.[6]

As various studies have shown, Batista clearly used his power shamelessly to enrich himself. By 1958, his press secretary estimated his personal fortune at $300 million, the bulk of it invested in Switzerland, Mexico, Florida, and New York.[7] He also had numerous investments on the island, including ownership of businesses, land, media outlets, and tourist properties.[8] Cuba's revolutionary government estimated that Batista's regime had appropriated the equivalent of $424 million in gold and U.S. currency from the country's treasury reserves, and only months after Castro took power, a new ministerial-level department, established to recover assets stolen or misappropriated from the government, had repossessed properties registered to Batista and his relatives valued at $3.5 million.[9]

IN PREPARATION for the sixteenth meeting of the United Nations Economic and Social Council (ECOSOC), to be held in Geneva beginning on 30 June 1953, Miguel A. Campa, Batista's minister of state, provided instructions to Cuba's United Nations ambassador:

> Cuba should give its support to the resolution . . . of ECOSOC, under which the United Nations will convoke a General Conference, charged with formulating and establishing a protocol related to limiting the production of opium. . . . Cuba should support as many measures as are adopted to impede or limit to the utmost the exportation of coca, whose open trade would bring great harm to humanity and to the people of Cuba in particular.[10]

Cuba was already complying with earlier United Nations conventions, submitting required reports on the country's narcotic usage in a timely manner.[11]

In the mid-1950s, Cuba's military intelligence service set up an antinarcotics squadron that carried out several important confiscations of marijuana. In December 1955, furthermore, a smaller group was formed to pursue individuals who were selling cocaine. The group included a major and two officers of lesser rank who received direct training from an FBN agent in Havana and was charged with carrying out surveillance and sweeps of the city's nightclubs and casinos.[12]

Three years earlier, Cuba had joined the International Criminal Police Organization (Interpol). At that time, Jorge A. de Castroverde, a dental surgeon in the national secret police, was named director of the newly established Cuban National Central Bureau, the country's liaison with Interpol.[13] De Castroverde served as Cuba's delegate to several of Interpol's yearly international assemblies.[14] At the 1958 meeting, held in London, de Castroverde insisted on "the need to deny the benefit of bail to high-profile traffickers or traffickers caught in flagrante delicto and to ratchet up the penalties."[15] The sentences imposed for drug trafficking in Cuba, while not as severe as those handed down in the United States, were at least in theory much stronger than those elsewhere around the world. In Australia and the United Kingdom, for example, the sentences imposed for drug trafficking were generally measured just in weeks, with a maximum of several months, and in many cases were limited to the imposition of a fine.[16]

In the United States, however, the 1956 Narcotic Control Act further strengthened the already severe penalties for drug trafficking, lengthening sentences over what the 1951 Boggs Act had required and forbidding defendants from receiving credit for time spent either on bail or on trial.[17] The first-time sale of illegal drugs brought convicted offenders between five and twenty years in prison; a second offense carried a penalty of between ten and forty years imprisonment. Juries had the option of recommending the death penalty for anyone convicted of selling heroin to someone under age eighteen.[18]

Under these circumstances, U.S. mafia leaders convened a meeting in Apalachin, New York, at which the majority decided to disassociate themselves entirely from the drug trade; those who elected to remain involved would henceforth operate at a relatively high level, importing heroin through the Sicilians and the Corsican-born French while leaving the distribution of the drug in New York, the country's largest drug-consuming market, to other groups — in particular, to blacks and Puerto Ricans.[19] Nonetheless, the FBN declared in 1964 that in the eight years since the Apalachin meeting, no fewer than 206 members of the mafia had been tried and convicted on drug trafficking charges.[20] Among the notorious crime bosses who suffered this fate was Vito Genovese, who was arrested with twenty-four of his associates in 1958. Tried and convicted on the charge of importing heroin from Europe and

Cuba, Genovese received a sentence of fifteen years in prison, where he died of natural causes. Fourteen of those arrested with him received prison sentences of between five and twenty years.[21]

Although Cuban courts heard 79 drug cases in 1952 and 128 the following year, the only prohibited substance that was confiscated, according to the trial summaries, was marijuana, "which is brought into the country by crews coming from Mexico who pass through our ports, since at no time in Cuba are there marijuana crops."[22] FBN officials believed, however, that Cuba's drug trafficking problem was far more serious. In 1953, William Johnston, the U.S. Treasury Department's representative in Havana, reported that substantial amounts of cocaine and opiates were available in the city—more than had been available in previous years.[23] A rather dramatic police action had occurred in October 1952 when 75 pounds of marijuana were confiscated after being thrown in a suitcase from a Spanish ship, the *Marqués de Comillas*, into Havana Bay in front of the Hotel Nacional. Three Cubans caught trying to recover the suitcase were arrested, as was the gang's leader, Roberto Arce Valdés, alias Papagayo. Arce had previously been charged with trafficking drugs between Mexico and Cuba.[24] Two months later, authorities confiscated 40 pounds of marijuana found on the eastern end of the island packed in boxes and ready for shipment to Havana.[25] In 1953, in addition to small, routine confiscations, several major operations yielded 218 pounds of marijuana. In one case, the marijuana had come into Cuba from Mexico; in another, the packages were again tossed from a Spanish ship; and in a third, a shipment that had come by train from Guantánamo was seized at the Havana railway station.[26] The amount of marijuana seized in large-scale confiscations declined to 90 pounds the following year but subsequently rebounded: between August and October 1955, agents confiscated hundreds of pounds of marijuana from the provinces of Oriente and Pinar del Río.[27] Most attention focused on Oriente, however, because authorities discovered a field in which marijuana was being grown, the harvest from which came to approximately 5,000 pounds.[28] Drug seizures remained high in 1956: in March, agents belonging to Cuban military intelligence confiscated hundreds of pounds of marijuana, and another four seizures between June and August yielded 117 pounds of the drug.[29] In addition, a good many small-scale sellers were also identified and arrested. Indeed, some months during the 1950s averaged one such arrest per day.[30] Sellers and users arrested in this period had their names published in police reports in the daily press.[31] One newspaper article reported that a man arrested for selling marijuana and released on bail had fled to New York but was recaptured and returned to Havana.[32] The press also included accounts of U.S. sailors arrested for using marijuana in Cuba.[33]

Although other drugs had become much more of a problem than in earlier years, authorities continued to deal with the sale and use of opium in the Chinese community during the 1950s.[34] Most significantly, in January 1956, officials arrested four Indians and a Chinese man, all of them members of the crew on an English ship, and a Chinese resident of Havana who were caught in possession of forty pounds of opium, the largest amount of the drug confiscated in Cuba in many years.[35]

Because Cuba was an island, a high percentage of the drugs smuggled into the country arrived on ships. As in years past, ships flying under the Spanish flag figured prominently in this traffic during the 1950s, especially with regard to cocaine and opiates. At times, sailors acted on their own in bringing in these drugs; at other times, Cuban smugglers arranged the transport. According to William Johnston, the amounts smuggled in ranged from a few grams to several kilos.[36] Spanish ships took a higher profile in carrying drugs to Cuba from Europe in part because of Italian and French authorities' efforts to suppress the export of drugs.[37]

Drugs also came into Cuba from the Middle East, smuggled in by Cubans of Middle Eastern ancestry. José Flaifel Moubarak, known as Pepe el Cubano, was arrested in April 1954 in Beirut while holding thirteen kilos of opium. Following the familiar pattern, he paid a fine and soon was released from jail. Flaifel Moubarak then left Lebanon but not the drug trade, shifting his efforts to trafficking cocaine from Bolivia and Peru. Flaifel Moubarak apparently followed his father into the family business. At the time, Nicolás Flaifel Yapur, a Lebanese immigrant who had settled in Cuba, was serving a U.S. prison sentence for drug trafficking. After his release and return to Cuba, authorities again sought out Flaifel Yapur, who fled to Beirut, where he was arrested in April 1957. Flaifel Yapur escaped serious punishment and made his way to Syria, where police caught him in January 1958 with 500 grams of morphine base. He was grabbed as he left a processing laboratory run by one of Syria's principal drug traffickers, from whom police confiscated 28 kilos of Turkish opium.[38]

In April 1956, Khossee Kholian Martínez Minanoz, another Cuban drug trafficker of Middle Eastern origin, was arrested in the Beirut airport, about to board a flight to Havana with 2 kilos of Turkish morphine base. Lebanon freed him a few months later, but in February 1957, he was again arrested, this time in the company of Flaifel Moubarak and a third Cuban, José Gabriel Pérez Fernández, for attempting to sell 1,300 grams of cocaine to an undercover FBN agent in Havana.[39] Both Flaifel Moubarak and Pérez Fernández posted bail and regained their freedom.[40]

Under Batista, Cuban officials continued to break up drug gangs and make arrests. In May 1954, the secret police confiscated 6 kilos of pure cocaine and several pounds of coca paste from a year-old laboratory that sent drugs to the U.S. market. This raid netted officials gang leader Manuel Méndez Marfa as well as Oscar Méndez Pérez, Pedro Perdomo Oviedo, and chemist Carlos Aulet Curbelo. Agents subsequently seized 200 grams of cocaine and arrested four traffickers, Francisco Femeniar Lores, Pastor Rodríguez Yzuaga, Apolonio Regalado Falcón, and Abel Mera. Both Regalado and Mera were pilots, while Mera was associated with the infamous El Teniente. In another case, the authorities confiscated 300 grams and arrested Manuel Arias Izuozu; his daughter, Virginia Arias Cruz; Germán Pérez Carballo; Jorge González López; and José Salas Fonseca. An informant had told police that Méndez Pérez had traveled to South America to bring back coca paste. He returned on 19 May with the drugs, valued at two hundred thousand dollars, hidden in a double-bottomed suitcase and immediately made his way to a house in Wajay, a rural area near Havana, where Méndez Marfa was waiting. Police arrested both men and searched the building, discovering a laboratory. Méndez Marfa, who was also connected to El Teniente, admitted under questioning that he sold drugs to distributors in the United States and that he had lived for a year in Ecuador, Bolivia, and Mexico, establishing contacts and learning how to produce cocaine, morphine, and heroin. On 22 May, the gang members were indicted and freed on bail. Méndez Marfa skipped bail and was recaptured in New York in May 1955 with Miguel Angel González Hernández and more than 5.5 pounds of Bolivian cocaine, which they had transported from Mexico City via Brownsville, Texas, in yet another double-bottomed suitcase. A third person, Miguel Angel González Lastra, a Mexican, was also involved in this case.[41]

William Johnston believed that the Cuban success in fighting drug trafficking merited recognition. Given "the magnitude and international ramifications of the confiscations," he wrote in 1954, American officials should send letters of congratulations to Colonel Orlando Piedra and his immediate subordinates.[42] Piedra, who had collaborated with U.S. agents, had received direct orders from Batista to combat drug trafficking.[43] Johnston was not alone in praising Cuban efforts, which another American agent described as "more effective than in many of the countries where we have operated." He concluded, "If we had the same carte blanche in France, for example, I believe that heroin trafficking would be substantially reduced."[44] In response to Johnston's recommendation, Anslinger wrote to Piedra that "your efforts are a boon to anti-narcotic agents everywhere and a blow to the international traffic in illicit drugs."[45] Cuba also participated in a 1957 multinational collaboration that helped identify and break up a large network of drug traffickers operating in the United States.[46]

U.S. agents' description of Piedra as "an important and merciless police power in Havana" clearly fit the ruthless head of the Bureau of Investigations.[47] When his longtime friend Batista asked how to fight the guerrillas in the Sierra Maestra, Piedra answered, "Total war. Everything that lived had to be killed." Piedra recalled that "the trigger happy were made to pay for it. If one of them cut down one of my officers . . . he had no hope of not catching a bullet himself."[48] Piedra was unconcerned with observing the niceties of diplomatic or political protocol. In 1956, for example, he rushed into the Haitian embassy, shooting indiscriminately, in pursuit of a group of government opponents who had taken refuge in the building.[49] Not surprisingly, in light of his methods, Piedra made many enemies, and an attempt on his life occurred in January 1957.[50] He fled the country when Batista's government fell, and soon thereafter *Bohemia* published an article about the dictator's principal deputies, replete with photographs, under the title "Gallery of Assassins." The piece acknowledged that Piedra "was not one of the bloodiest" but also pointed out that the headquarters of Piedra's Bureau of Investigations "had been turned into a true fortress with electrified fencing, like in the Nazi camps, and dungeons in which the regime's goons had their torture chambers."[51]

In October 1955, Cuba's police arrested Abelardo Martínez Rodríguez del Rey, El Teniente. Piedra and Johnston personally questioned the Cuban drug lord, and Martínez Rodríguez del Rey admitted having taken five kilos of cocaine on two trips to Houston and New Orleans.[52] He also revealed that an official of the Cuban police attached to the country's embassy in Mexico was a party to his dealings.[53] In June 1958, the Cuban police struck again, arresting El Teniente's brother, Jorge Martínez del Rey, known as El Bacardí, after catching him and another trafficker in possession of several bottles containing cocaine. The police had been operating based on information provided by two women captured in New York while holding a kilo of cocaine that they had received from El Bacardí.[54] By this time, however, El Teniente had regained his freedom, and in October 1958 he was recaptured in the company of three associates when the police, under Piedra's command, raided a cocaine processing laboratory in El Vedado, one of Havana's hotel and residential districts.[55]

During the final years of Batista's dictatorship, the connection between Cuban traffickers and their counterparts in the Andean region continued to challenge law enforcement. In early 1958, for example, the authorities discovered that an Ecuadorian trafficker had sold 900 grams of cocaine to Darío Güell, the owner of a Havana furniture store and the brother of a high Cuban government official.[56] In February of that year, a Bolivian drug trafficker was captured in Cuba with 26 kilos of coca paste but according to Johnston went free after bribing a highly placed police official.[57]

Antidrug efforts benefited from the cooperation of inside sources. At the beginning of July 1958, Piedra and Johnston gained access to Frank Martin, a courier for the criminal organization run by Juan Suárez and formerly a courier for a Camagüey drug trafficker, Jorge Fernández Trujillo. Martin traveled to Bolivia to obtain drugs, which he then transported to the United States. His source for cocaine in La Paz was Blanca Ibáñez de Sánchez, who also used a Bolivian woman known as Melvis to smuggle cocaine into Cuba and the United States. After entering the United States, the drugs were given to Fernández Trujillo's brother, José, who lived in New York.[58]

In August 1958, Cuban officials unraveled more of the Andean connection, when they apprehended another Bolivian trafficker, Luis González Aguilera, in Havana. González was arrested with only a half a pound of cocaine, but after several days of intensive questioning by police officials, including Piedra, he confessed that he possessed another six kilos and that he had a laboratory in his apartment in El Vedado. González then offered to collaborate with the authorities. Piedra requested special assistance from the FBN, which sent an agent, Sal Vizzini, to Havana. González gave Vizzini, Johnston, and Piedra the names of his Bolivian contacts.[59]

In 1957, Giuseppe Catalanotti, born in Sicily and a resident of the Detroit area, was deported from the United States to Italy. Five years earlier, he had been convicted of illegal possession of heroin. By May 1958, however, Catalanotti was living in the Havana house of an Italian friend, Onofrio Minaudo. Prodded by the FBN, the Cuban police rounded up and detained the two Italians, who were suspected of drug trafficking, on 20 November 1958. Continuing his collaboration with U.S. authorities, Piedra asked the Cuban minister of state to prepare the way for the deportation of the two foreign residents, and the process started in December.[60]

Miami and southern Florida also served as key U.S. transit points for drug trafficking from Cuba. Situated less than 250 miles from Havana, Miami was a natural gateway through which heroin and cocaine could be smuggled to their biggest market, New York City. In one typical large-scale drug-running case, for example, a Cuban trafficker traveled to Miami to negotiate a large drug deal with two Italian Americans, who planned to travel to Havana to inspect the drugs firsthand.[61]

Drug traffickers used all types of couriers to transport drugs. In one case, an American woman married to a Cuban official carried drugs to her contacts — three American men — in Florida. In another instance, a Cuban woman who ran a bar in Miami was suspected of bringing in cocaine from the island to her clients, one of whom was supposedly Prío Socarrás, the former Cuban president.[62] Other couriers operating between Cuba and Miami included a North American who owned a Havana bar and a Cuban woman intercepted carrying cocaine to Cuban exiles in Miami who was freed by the Havana courts.[63] Couriers between Key West and Cuba included people who drove automobiles onto the ferry between Cuba and the keys, crew members on the ferry, and shrimpers working the local waters.[64] Although Miami's Cuban population remained relatively small at the beginning of the 1950s, the city had become a favored destination for Cuban tourists, with between forty and fifty thousand visiting per year.[65] The number of people traveling between Cuba and the United States was very high; by 1948, for example, when foreign travel had yet to become commonplace, Cuba exchanged more visitors with the United States than did any other country.[66]

Between 1954 and 1957, Johnston's reports from Havana repeatedly stressed that for all the Cuban police's success in the fight against drug trafficking, defeating the political and armed opposition to Batista's government remained a higher priority.[67] Violence had again become ubiquitous in Cuban life, with bombs exploding throughout the country on a nightly basis.[68] Furthermore, the 26 July Movement, led by Fidel Castro, had embarked on a campaign to sabotage the sugar harvest. In March 1958, under the cry "either Batista without the *zafra* [sugarcane harvest], or the *zafra* without Batista," the guerrillas announced that they had set fires in all of the country's cane-producing provinces, destroying two million tons of sugar.[69] Several months earlier, in October 1957, George H. Gaffney, an FBN district supervisor, had warned Anslinger that Havana's drug traffic was increasing by "alarming proportions" and that the island was becoming a "refuge for important people on the run."[70] Drug traffickers took advantage of the worsening security situation, slipping easily into Havana as authorities focused on quelling the civil war and suppressing political opposition.[71]

DESPITE THE INROADS made by Cuban and U.S. antinarcotics agents and the corresponding arrest of a string of traffickers, the level of cocaine and heroin traffic reached a new peak in the United States. At the end of the 1950s, American agents viewed Cuba as "the most important transit point in this traffic of death, . . . administered in a disciplined way by organized criminal gangs of various nationalities."[72] Despite the "shoulder-to-shoulder" cooperation of Cuban authorities in numerous confiscations and arrests, U.S. officials complained, Cuban courts let many of the accused go free in a matter of weeks or even days.[73] Concluded FBN agent John Cusack, "At present, the Cuban court system is the real obstacle to applying that country's anti-drug laws."[74] For better or for worse, Cuba's judiciary acted autonomously, free of executive branch interference.[75]

Those tried, convicted, and imprisoned for drug trafficking in Cuba during the 1950s came from society's bottom rungs and generally were convicted of marijuana offenses. People of means who used cocaine avoided prosecution. Indeed, a study of thirty individuals convicted on drug charges and sent to jail during the 1950s reveals that all of those imprisoned were males and were sent to the men's national prison on the Isle of Pines. Twenty-five were aged between twenty and thirty-five, while only five were older than forty; most were unmarried. Nineteen of the thirty lived in the greater Havana area, while five lived in Oriente province, three in Camagüey, two in Matanzas, and one in Las Villas. As a group, these men were poor, earning their living as day laborers or craftsmen and working only seasonally or sporadically. Almost half of the men were of mixed race (primarily mulatto, although classified as mestizo), while 25 percent were white, including one Spaniard; one was a Cantonese immigrant, and the remainder were black. Few foreigners were involved as a consequence of the end of large-scale immigration to Cuba at the time of the Great Depression. Reflecting Cuba's high levels of literacy even before the revolution, only the few campesinos were illiterate; men from the cities generally had received at least some formal education. Only in isolated cases had any of the accused been convicted of nondrug crimes such as rape or battery. The bulk of those who were repeat offenders had been convicted of transgressions involving prohibited substances, the only one of which specifically cited was marijuana.[76]

Chapter 11

Revolution

A s the guerrilla fighters of the 26 July Movement steadily gained the upper hand and achieved a series of military victories in different parts of the country, Fulgencio Batista, facing inevitable defeat, fled Havana shortly after midnight on 31 December 1958. In the aftermath of his departure and the collapse of his government, mobs roamed the city's streets, destroying and looting parking meters, and invaded the casinos, where they plundered the slot machines.[1] The casinos of both the Sevilla Biltmore and Plaza hotels, situated in the heart of the capital, were laid to waste.[2] The magazine *Bohemia* got to the heart of the matter: "In the first hours after victory, people vented their anger at one of the hallmarks of the old regime, gambling, especially in its most ostentatious guise, the hotels and casinos."[3] The parking meters and slot machines symbolized entrenched graft and corruption and were linked to Batista and his family, inasmuch as the dictator and his brother-in-law, General Roberto Fernández Miranda, had a personal stake in those businesses.[4]

Yet whatever their political sympathies, hotel and casino employees stood their ground and confronted the crowds, attempting to prevent the destruction of the buildings — and their jobs.[5] The militia of the 26 July Movement and the members of the revolutionary directorate intervened to help restore order; when less aggressive tactics proved insufficient, the militia opened fire on looters.[6]

In April 1958, Ernesto Betancourt, then serving as Fidel Castro's spokesman and representative in the United States, had declared to a New York City newspaper that when Batista fell and Castro assumed power, the new government would purge the island of its mafia presence.[7] Thus, immediately after the revolution, Castro announced that legitimate U.S. businesses in Cuba would be protected but not the businesses belonging to "those gangsters," the casino owners.[8] The first voices to protest this policy, however, were not those of the casino owners but those of the hotel and cabaret workers whose livelihoods depended on the casinos.[9] A second break in revolutionary unity quickly occurred when the anarchist leaders of the food workers' union quarreled with the new government about the country's political course.[10] Objections regarding the economic consequences of a crackdown on casino gambling continued to be heard. Waiters, bartenders, croupiers, musicians, and even prostitutes soon joined the chorus of protest, demanding that the revolution not deprive them of their livelihoods.[11]

In this unsettled atmosphere, an American columnist for the *Havana Post* observed presciently, "Even though Fidel Castro is an idealist, a couple of his most influential supporters are materialistic. They want to keep that tourist money churning into Havana."[12] Charles Baron, executive vice president of the Hotel Riviera, warned that if the casinos were shut down, the luxury hotels would cease to earn profits.[13] The Riviera's owner, Meyer Lansky, remained in Havana until 9 January, when he boarded a Pan American flight to Miami. Lansky returned to Havana to oversee his business interests at the end of February and then departed Cuba again in April, never to return.[14]

Contrary to some expectations, Castro's pragmatic side initially won out over any impulse on his part to move in a more radical direction. Just ten days into the new era, the Cuban leader used the front page of the *Havana Post* to send a message to American tourists and businessmen:

> I wish to invite the American tourists and the American businessmen to come back to Cuba with the assurance that they will be welcomed by all citizens of our country. We are back to normal in Cuba, a Cuba where there is liberty, peace, and order; a beautiful land of happy people. Our hotels, shops, and offices are open and we want our friends from the United States to come and see this beautiful land of Cuba, which can now be counted among the countries where freedom and democracy are a reality.[15]

At the same time, Cuba's president, Manuel Urrutia, told journalists that all types of gambling, including that in the large casinos, should henceforth be forbidden. This position was reinforced on 16 January, when Prime Minister José Miró Cardona declared that "the government stands absolutely opposed to the reestablishment of gambling in any of its forms, and this stance will not be altered." Such assurances were premature, however, and Castro promptly disavowed them. The casinos reopened for business subject to one condition — they were asked to pay a new tax as a way of contributing to the recently created Instituto Nacional de Ahorro y Vivienda (National Savings and Housing

Institute).[16] The only type of gambling prohibited was cockfighting, as the government sought to wean the campesino population from the long-held custom of betting on these contests.[17] Urrutia and Castro's differences over the issue of casino gambling persisted until Urrutia resigned from office on 1 July 1959.[18] Castro announced that although in principle he opposed the casinos, they would remain open to avoid depriving their employees of work.[19] Gambling was now restricted to four hotels and two nightclubs, however, and slot machines were banned.[20] Much as government officials disliked the idea, they had no choice but to continue working with American mafiosos, who ran the casinos and hotels.[21] Only in September 1961, after tourism had disappeared from Cuba, were all the casinos finally closed.[22]

Castro had already displayed his political realism during the guerrilla war in the Sierra Maestra, when he tolerated campesinos' practice of growing and selling marijuana to avoid losing their support.[23] However, his tolerance on this matter had its limits: in October 1958, he invoked a total prohibition on the cultivation, trafficking, and use of marijuana.[24]

The revolutionaries saw Cuba as a fallen land in which, under Batista's rule, "all was misery, violence, corruption, gambling, prostitution, pleasures for the taking; in a word: the U.S.' brothel."[25] This reductionist slant gave birth to a purifying vision of the future in which "the revolution triumphant is directed, in part, against the other Havana, the Havana of before. It's about the reaction — moralistic, puritanical, prudish — of the real nation against the 'decadent' spectacle represented by the capital. . . . [T]he places of 'vice' are closed one after another. . . . The 'new man' needs a good education (or good indoctrination) and to be of sound mind and body, more than fleeting pleasures."[26] In addition, homosexuality would be "violently repressed, because it constituted the most provocative demonstration of impermissible individual freedom."[27] In still another expression of this moralizing impulse, authorities prohibited the screening of the 1961 documentary film *P.M.* (*Pasado Meridiano*), which tracked Havana's night life, on the grounds that it expressed "counterrevolutionary tendencies and was pornographic."[28]

According to American journalist Herbert L. Matthews, the puritanical character of the Cuban Revolution was nowhere better revealed than in Castro's decision that mass marriage ceremonies be carried out to legalize unmarried unions.[29] The minister of justice and his wife acted as witnesses at these Operación Matrimonio ceremonies, which took place across the length and breadth of the country.[30] Even battle-hardened fighters from the Sierra Maestra, including Raúl Castro and Ernesto "Ché" Guevara, fell into line and married their companions in formal ceremonies during the first months after the revolution.[31]

The revolution's quickening tempo soon dampened tourism. Fernando Benítez, a Mexican journalist who sympathized with the new regime, saw this development in positive terms, writing, "The tourists have disappeared from Havana. . . . The engine propelling this clean industry has been weakened beyond repair. The sea that caresses, the beaches with their heavy sand like slivers of marble, the frozen daiquiris, the games of roulette, the show in the Tropicana — the world's most fabulous cabaret — the girls of Virtudes Street, are still here, more alluring than ever, and the [North] Americans stay away."[32] Others, too, saw Cuba under Batista as "a fount of iniquity."[33]

Observers have often exaggerated the number of prostitutes operating in Cuba prior to the revolution, citing figures between 100,000 and 150,000 despite a lack of empirical evidence to justify such numbers. Furthermore, the notion that prerevolutionary Cuban prostitution developed primarily in response to American tourists' demands is similarly inaccurate. In reality, Cuban prostitutes, many of whom were of campesino origin, principally served a Cuban clientele in both the cities and the countryside, although they preferred U.S. clients, who paid more. During the sugar harvest, thousands of prostitutes moved into the country to offer their services to the cane cutters.[34] In Havana, young Cuban men comprised a high percentage of the prostitutes' clientele.[35]

Many Cubans saw Fidel Castro as a messianic figure who had come down from the mountains to cleanse the cities of corruption.[36] In Carlos Franqui's view, Fidel and Raúl Castro and Ché Guevara were united in seeing fiestas and merrymaking as a popular form of vice and in believing that leaders needed to create and nourish a new kind of spartan morality in the Cuban people.[37] Such a morality would draw its strength and inspiration from the soldiers who had formed the heart and soul of the revolution. As Luis E. Aguilar wrote in the March 1959 issue of the magazine *Revolución*, "The revolution has emanated from the countryside, its victory made possible by simple young men from small villages, admirable fighters who put on none of the airs of liberators."[38] Furthermore, these bearded revolutionaries did not get drunk, had scrupulously avoided looting, and behaved "like saints."[39] The fact that Castro was thirty-three years old when he formed his government and that the guerrilla fighters had long hair and beards and carried rosary beads inspired the facile notion that he and his band of revolutionaries resembled Christ and his apostles.[40] Indeed, some Cubans portrayed Castro as the reincarnation of Christ, the redeemer who had produced the miracle of the revolution and rekindled the spiritual faith of the Cuban people.[41] The lyrics of a song composed by Carlos Puebla, the Troubadour of the Revolution, evoked and championed the reformist and moralistic spirit of the new Cuba as well as the apotheosis of Castro as the emancipator, leading his people out of a submissive wilderness of decadence and crime into an unspoiled future:

> They were planning to go on here,
> devouring more and more of the land,
> without ever suspecting that in the Sierra
> the future was being lit up.

> And continuing in a cruel way
> the custom of crime
> turning Cuba into a gambling den
> and that's when Fidel arrived.

> And that was the end of the party,
> the commander arrived and ordered it to stop.[42]

Several days after Castro entered Havana, *Lyceum*, the magazine of the Lyceum and Lawn Tennis Club, printed an editorial conveying the same message of moral renewal and extolling the virtues of the rank-and-file revolutionary from the heartland: "Faced with the decadence and corruption of the regime that ruled until now, it was essential," the editorial asserted, "to put front and center the cultivation of the goodly virtues of honor, loyalty, sincerity, and fidelity to ethical principles." In addition, the piece described the revolutionary army as "noble and honorable," drawing "its strength mainly from the ranks of the peasantry — that is, from the purest, most uncorrupted element of the Cuban population."[43] To help develop and implement this type of thinking on a policy level, the government named Elena Mederos de González, a diplomat, social reformer, and cofounder of both the Lyceum and the University of Havana's program in social work, as the country's minister of social welfare.[44]

The task of building a new country and new institutions under the aegis of the revolution likewise left no room for drug addicts, a point a former addict firmly addressed in *Bohemia*:

> We must put vice behind us. A country of dissolute people may be a country, but it will not be a great country. If a people are degenerate, they are made that way more by their indulgence in vice than by anything else. And

Cuba, a wondrous land, a country now restored to beauty, steered toward the future by the revolution, must in the days to come play a great role. . . . I wish to contribute with these spontaneous and sincere declarations to the work of renewal that the revolution has in every sense commanded and imposed.[45]

Jorge A. de Castroverde, the director of Interpol in Cuba, joined in celebrating Batista's fall and the dawn of a new era, describing himself as "brimming over with joy and satisfaction . . . in the liberation of our country which was forced to groan under seven long years of brutal dictatorship. Now Cuba is free and sovereign through the will of its people, strong in the hope that never more must we experience anything like what happened in the past."[46] He compared the Cuban and French Revolutions, denouncing the Batistianos who oppressed their fellow Cubans as "base criminals" and expressing his dismay at foreign press condemnations of the execution of those he saw as "war criminals."[47] After having fulfilled the duties of his office since 1952 "without a salary or any kind of stipend," he claimed to have achieved "the partial eradication of international crime in Cuba," despite the fact that "some of these individuals were sheltered by ministers of the regime now in flight."[48]

Castro's support from elements of the elite stemmed from his war against Batista. Indeed, members of the anti-Batista bourgeoisie eventually contributed several million dollars to the guerrilla movement in the Sierra Maestra. The contributors included sugar barons, cattle ranchers, bankers, industrialists, and politicians, including Carlos Prío Socarrás. The guerrilla struggle also received the enthusiastic backing of the Bosch-Bacardí clan, owners of the Bacardi Rum and Hatuey beer labels: José M. Bosch even offered to pay his 1959 taxes in advance.[49] As always, politics and the shifting scales of power could make strange bedfellows. In 1958, for example, Martín Fox, the owner of the Tropicana nightclub and a close ally of the Batista government, "donated" five thousand dollars to an envoy from the revolutionary movement.[50] The guerrilla fighters also extracted a "war tax" from the sugar mills, setting fire to any facilities whose owners refused to contribute.[51]

In April 1959, still leaning in a pragmatic direction, Castro declared at a New York press conference that his government wanted to make tourism Cuba's principal industry, attracting between two and three million visitors annually.[52] With this goal in mind, the Cuban tourism commission was reorganized and a campaign was launched to lure people to the island.[53] Castro also announced that over the next four years, the government would spend

$200 million to promote tourism.[54] The new Cuban government asked the American Society of Travel Agents (ASTA) not to drop Havana as the site of its next annual conference, scheduled for October 1959.[55] The conference remained in Havana, and Castro presided over its opening at the massive Blanquita Theater, after which "brigades of voluntary workers, coming from all social classes, lent themselves to the task of tidying up the city [and] of helping in the construction of a new airport." That night, President Osvaldo Dorticós hosted a dinner at the capitol building for two thousand ASTA delegates. Fidel Castro attended, spending an hour and a half bantering with the visitors and signing autographs. Raúl Castro shared a table with U.S. ambassador Philip Bonsal.[56]

Based on such goodwill, the island's tourist industry might have appeared to have a bright future. Yet events quickly buried the effects of Castro's charm offensive. Cuban anti-aircraft batteries fired tracers at airplanes dropping antigovernment flyers, and counterrevolutionaries carried out assassination attempts by throwing grenades from moving automobiles. The flyers were dropped by Pedro Luis Díaz Lanz, former commander of the Revolutionary Air Force, who had supplied Castro with arms from Costa Rica and the United States but went into exile in the United States after Batista's fall to protest the "indoctrination classes" to which members of the military were being subjected. The mood was also darkened by the resignation and subsequent capture of Huber Matos. Matos, who had fought with Castro in the Sierra Maestra and attained the rank of major (*comandante*) in the revolutionary army, was arrested on Castro's orders for committing "treasonous" acts and "for conspiring against the revolution." Castro personally traveled to Camagüey to present the charges against Matos. When combined with the broadsides that Castro was beginning to deliver against the United States, these developments effectively scuttled the possibilities for reviving tourism. In Bonsal's words, "As the travel agents took their departure, they were hardly in an optimistic mood as to future bookings. They were convinced that it would be a waste of time to promote tourism by Americans to Cuba."[57] Unwilling to concede total defeat on this front, however, the Cuban government provided a group of U.S. black leaders with an all-expense-paid trip to the island during the 1959 Christmas holidays. In addition to spreading its political message, the government hoped to encourage black American tourists to visit Cuba.[58]

For the typical tourist, the vicissitudes of the revolution clearly constituted a source of uncertainty and discomfort, and by 1960, U.S. tourism had virtually disappeared from the island.[59] Despite the special promotions that attempted to bolster the 1959–60 winter tourist season, numerous cruises into Havana were canceled.[60] The U.S. embassy in Havana, monitoring the situation, informed the State Department on 30 October that the city's hotels had received "significant cancellations."[61]

With U.S. tourism rapidly drying up, the Cuban government refocused, looking for ways to attract Latin American tourists. First, Cuban officials sponsored the third Congress of Latin American Tourist Organizations, which took place in Havana in April 1960. President Dorticós greeted the six hundred representatives from eighteen countries who attended the congress in the same theater in which he had welcomed the ASTA delegates. In addition to participating in the congress' Havana activities, the delegates traveled into Cuba's interior "to get to know the centers of tourist attraction opened up by the revolution."[62] The government also tried to entice Soviet citizens to visit, and the first contingent arrived in Havana at the end of December 1960.[63] Nevertheless, despite this spurt of attention, the tourism industry entered a period of steep decline that lasted for years. Between 1960 and the end of the 1970s, sixteen hotels closed, overall hotel capacity fell by 50 percent, and the quality of service steadily eroded.[64]

The political arrests, summary trials, and executions that gripped Cuba played a powerful role in stopping American tourism on the island. The public trials without due process and the executions that followed (originally of Batista's followers, then of opponents of the new regime or those accused of opposing it) enjoyed wide popular support throughout the country, even in small towns and villages. In some instances, trenches were bulldozed so that prisoners could be lined up, machine-gunned, and then immediately dumped into the mass graves. In one case, seventy-one prisoners were shot and thrown into a common grave on the grounds of a Santiago military barracks.[65] Ché Guevara personally signed more than fifty death sentences, and Raúl Castro allegedly directly oversaw the execution by firing squad of soldiers who had belonged to Batista's army.[66]

The firing squads provoked a strong international reaction.[67] Nonetheless, the executions went on, with crowds chanting, "Up against the wall! . . . [T]o the wall, the wall, the wall!" One survey found that 93 percent of the Cuban population supported the executions.[68] Furthermore, to exploit the popular thirst for justice and revenge, the government broadcast some of the executions on television.[69] Moreover, *Bohemia*, which enjoyed the highest circulation of any publication in Cuba, printed graphic photo spreads showing the bloody corpses.[70]

Castro justified the firing squads on the grounds that those being executed were assassins, not mere opponents of the new order.[71] Moreover, he contended that "there is not the slightest doubt, either among the public at large or on the part of any individual," about the guilt of the victims and the correctness of the verdicts.[72] In response to foreign critics of the trials and executions such as the Argentine government and an Oregon senator who had previously criticized Batista and supported the rebels, Castro thundered that the United States could send in the Marines and there would be "200,000 dead gringos."[73]

Yet the tensions between Cuba and the United States were not caused solely by internal developments on the island. U.S. foreign policy certainly helped drive a wedge between the two countries, although the United States did not take a monolithic approach toward Cuba immediately after the revolution. U.S. Department of State officials recommended that ambassador to Cuba Earl E. T. Smith be removed as a consequence of concerns that the new government would declare him persona non grata because he had worked to have someone other than Castro succeed Batista.[74] Such concerns were justified: Cuban officials dismissed the meddling Smith as a "servant of the despot."[75] His successor, Bonsal, was a career diplomat currently serving as the U.S. ambassador to Bolivia and previously ambassador to Colombia. Bonsal had lived in Cuba as an employee of ITT and subsequently as the American consul in Havana.[76]

In the interests of preserving relations and protecting investments, a committee of American businessmen in Havana and the secretary of state recommended that the United States recognize the revolutionary government as soon as feasible. The British government agreed, and both countries granted diplomatic recognition to the new government on 7 January 1959.[77] Behind the formalities of diplomatic protocol, however, President Dwight D. Eisenhower made no attempt to hide his hostility toward Castro, even weighing the possibility of denying an entry visa to the new Cuban leader, whom the American Society of Newspaper Editors had invited to Washington, D.C. CIA director Allen Dulles, however, believed that such an action would be counterproductive in light of what he believed to be a growing anti-Castro movement in Cuba: "We must be careful not to do anything which would tend to discourage the growth of this movement."[78]

Ambassador Bonsal construed the matter differently than Eisenhower. For some months, Bonsal recommended that the United States demonstrate patience and indeed take a positive attitude toward Castro and the revolution in hopes of influencing Castro and isolating him and drawing him away from the communist elements his group.[79] At an April 1959 meeting of U.S. ambassadors to Caribbean and Central American countries held in El Salvador, Bonsal defended his position against Robert C. Hill, U.S. ambassador to Mexico, who argued for a hard line toward Castro.[80]

Another link in the chain of worsening relations between the two countries snapped into place on 17 May, when the Cuban government promulgated its new law of agrarian reform. This development prompted the representatives of American-financed sugar mills to meet with Bonsal to express their sense of unease.[81] Bonsal pressed the matter with the Cuban government, requesting that it listen to the concerns of the sugar companies, especially with regard to the issue of compensation.[82] Although various members of the U.S. Congress were extremely displeased with Castro, the State Department continued to advocate a more temperate line to avoid alienating moderate Cuban groups and to change the design and impact of the planned agrarian reform.[83] Nor did Bonsal sway from his recommendation that the United States should "continue [a] policy of friendship toward Castro and the government of Cuba, using our influence in every way to guide it onto solid economic ground."[84]

As relations between the two countries became increasingly strained, the State Department altered course and stiffened its policy toward Cuba. In September 1959, the department instructed its diplomatic missions in Latin America to undertake what was in effect a disinformation campaign against Fidel Castro: "It is to the interest of the United States that the tendencies of Latin American opinion to become skeptical of Castro on the issues of dictatorship, intervention, and Communism be intensified and accelerated. . . . It remains important, however, particularly at this stage, that any awakening public skepticism about Castro retain the appearance of being an indigenous Latin American reaction."[85] This policy change caused Bonsal to give up hope that Cuban-U.S. relations could be normalized.[86]

On 4 March 1960, the French ship *La Coubre* arrived in Havana harbor with a cargo of Belgian arms and munitions ordered by the government. While being unloaded, the ship exploded at dockside, resulting in the death of more than one hundred crew members, dock workers, and armed forces personnel on the vessel and the pier. Fidel Castro immediately and publicly blamed the U.S. government for the explosion, and he and Raúl met with

Soviet envoy and KGB agent Alexandr Alekseev to request Soviet military and economic assistance.[87]

According to Bonsal, Castro's very public accusation tipped the balance and convinced the U.S. government to intervene in Cuba by authorizing the Central Intelligence Agency (CIA) to train Cuban exiles who would spearhead the effort to overthrow Castro.[88] Not only in Florida but also in Mexico and the Dominican Republic, groups of Cuban exiles had been waiting for this moment.[89] The CIA's "Program of Covert Action against the Castro Regime" formed part of the agency's larger program of covert operations against "international communism," which the National Security Council had authorized during the 1950s.[90]

In June 1960, as part of the campaign to bring down Castro and in line with advice from the U.S. government, U.S. oil companies announced that they would refuse to refine oil from the Soviet Union. Cuba responded by expropriating the American-owned refineries. Escalating the confrontation, the United States in July suspended the purchase of Cuban sugar; in response, the Soviet Union and China committed to buying it.[91] The following month, the Cuban government expropriated the holdings of the principal American companies operating on the island, including the sugar mills. The U.S. government retaliated with an embargo on all American exports to Cuba except for food and medicine.[92] The two countries had passed the point of no return. By the time the embargo went into effect, the CIA had already begun conspiring with the U.S. mafia to have Castro assassinated.[93] Vice President Richard M. Nixon hoped not simply to overturn Cuba's government but also somehow to eliminate Castro and to orchestrate both events before the November 1960 presidential election, in which Nixon was the Republican candidate.[94]

The ill will between the two countries, which resulted in the official severing of relations in the first week of January 1961, affected their handling of the issue of drug trafficking. The earlier collaboration that had led to the arrest and prosecution of numerous traffickers turned into yet another source of disagreement and distrust and at its lowest ebb even served to inflame and reinforce Cold War stereotypes.

Chapter 12

The Diplomacy of Drug Trafficking at the Beginning of the Revolution

I n early 1959, as the Cuban Revolution unfolded, Harry J. Anslinger, director of the U.S. Federal Bureau of Narcotics (FBN), demanded that the new government deport the mafia bosses who administered the island's casinos, asserting that they were directly responsible for importing drugs from Cuba to the United States. Fidel Castro shrewdly parried Anslinger's demand by asking for a list of the traffickers and stating that he was disposed not to deport them but to have them brought before a firing squad.[1] He also pointed out that he believed that the Cubans who had sought refuge in the United States after the revolution were "gangsters" and "war criminals" and that the United States should therefore deport them back to Cuba.[2]

Just days after the revolutionaries had seized power, FBN officials stressed to the Cuban government that it needed to take strong measures against the drug traffickers. FBN agents suggested that anyone convicted of trafficking receive a prison term of between ten and twenty years and complained about the laxness of the judiciary, noting that courts had too often in the past freed drug traffickers. The agency also compiled a dossier of the names of various drug traffickers so that the individuals could be brought to justice.[3] The officials also requested the deportation to the United States of "hardened and dangerous" American traffickers such as Carmine Galante and John Ormento so that they could be tried.[4] The New York–born Galante was considered "an extremely important figure in the international drug trade."[5] Ormento, likewise a native of New York, had been convicted several times on drug trafficking charges in the United States.[6] In all, the FBN prepared case reports on forty-one mafiosos it wanted deported from Cuba, with Meyer Lansky's name atop "the list of gangsters who [should] never [be] allowed to return to Cuba."[7]

At the beginning of April 1959, Efigenio Almejeiras, chief of Cuba's national revolutionary police, offered Joseph H. Dillon of the U.S. Department of the Treasury complete cooperation in arresting drug traffickers. From his post at Camp Libertad, the name given by the government to the old Camp Columbia, Captain Raúl Cros, chief of the intelligence division of the revolutionary air force, made a similar commitment.[8] Dillon then met with Comandante Aldo Vera Serafín, who promised to pursue persons arrested for drug trafficking under the previous government and to work with the courts to see that justice was applied.[9] Discussions on these matters continued, and on 17 April 1959, Steve Minas, a U.S. customs agent in Havana, met with Lieutenant Adolfo Díaz Lorenzo, chief of the narcotics unit in Cuba's Bureau of Investigation. Minas had given the chief a list of cases involving drug traffickers; Díaz reported that he was working with the list and that people whose names appeared on it were by and large the same as the people on a list that Charles Siragusa had given Antonio de la Carrera, private secretary to President Manuel Urrutia, the previous January. Minas also met with Mario Fernández y Fernández, Cuba's attorney general and prosecutor for the Supreme Tribunal, and with Jorge de Castroverde. Both Fernández and de Castroverde agreed that a new narcotics law needed to be implemented, and according to Minas, Fernández believed that repeat traffickers should be denied the right to remain free on bail and favored applying the death penalty in certain drug cases.[10] American embassy personnel believed that the new revolutionary police force, "disorganized and inexperienced" as it may have been, was nonetheless eager to assist in apprehending criminals sought by the U.S. authorities.[11]

Two months earlier, in fact, agents of the Cuban Bureau of Investigation had arrested Abelardo Martínez Rodríguez del Rey, the irrepressible El Teniente, and one of his associates, Ricardo Borroto Díaz, as they were preparing to board a plane at the Rancho Boyeros airport. The two, who between them had $18,891 in currency and $1,300 in traveler's checks, were planning to fly first to Panama and then to Argentina and Peru to buy cocaine for resale on the Cuban market. They were equipped with two suitcases with false bottoms.[12] In addition, Cuban antinarcotics agents arrested El Teniente's brother, Jorge Martínez Rodríguez del Rey (El Bacardí), and their father, Abelardo Martínez Arenas, in Havana on 10 April 1959 in possession of a kilo of cocaine sent to them from La Paz, Bolivia, by Martín Binder.[13] Under questioning, El Bacardí disclosed that his network encompassed two countries, Mexico and Venezuela, and that the cocaine had been brought into Cuba in 1958. In addition, he offered to reveal the names of other drug traffickers if he were promised a civil rather than military trial, since he feared that the latter would mean facing a firing squad. The three Martínezes were held in the La Cabaña fort.[14] On 15 April, authorities confiscated an additional 800 grams of cocaine from the closet of El Bacardí's beach residence in Marianao.[15] The state attorney requested a six-year prison term for Jorge Martínez Rodríguez del Rey for a separate 1958 case, and he was required to post twenty-five thousand pesos bail on this charge.[16]

In addition to the high-profile Martínez brothers, Cuban authorities captured other cocaine traffickers on the island during 1959 as well as pursued leads outside the country.[17] In May 1959, for example, the government requested that Brazilian authorities collaborate in helping capture Enrique and Celina Saucedo, two Bolivian citizens known to have brought cocaine into both Cuba and the United States.[18]

In April 1959, Anslinger privately acknowledged that the Cuban government "is apparently taking strenuous measures" against drug trafficking, and he congratulated Cuban authorities for their success in arresting the Martínezes.[19] Publicly, Anslinger was even more positive, declaring to the magazine *Bohemia*, "We are pleased to have seen that the new government has taken an interest in fighting drug trafficking in Cuba. . . . Cuba is a member of Interpol and that organization's representative in Havana, Jorge [de] Castroverde, has also demonstrated great interest. . . . [De] Castroverde's activity is further proof of the interest shown by the new Cuban government, a fact which pleases us enormously."[20]

During 1959 and 1960, Cuban police arrested a great number of people caught selling marijuana, ranging from large-scale traffickers apprehended with shipments valued in the thousands of dollars to persons possessing only handfuls of marijuana cigarettes. Yet while the size of seizures may have varied, the point of origin of the marijuana did not — either Cuba's Sierra Maestra or Mexico.[21] The number of drug-related arrests shot up in 1959 before beginning to decline in 1960, although hundreds of cases, involving marijuana in particular, continued to be reported over the rest of the decade.[22] In 1960, Cuban courts dealt with 586 cases relating to either the sale or the possession of marijuana and imposed jail sentences ranging between one and six years.[23] In April 1959, a military court invoked the death penalty against someone convicted of selling marijuana. Although this sentence was ultimately commuted to imprisonment, Rubén Acosta Carrasco, the country's director general of immigration, told FBN agent Charles Siragusa that the

Cuban government had already executed a convicted marijuana trafficker.[24] Those arrested in Cuba on charges of marijuana possession included New Yorker Joseph John Hogan, who was sentenced to prison on the Isle of Pines, and Denver resident Walter Graham.[25]

In 1961, the United Nations adopted a new convention on narcotic drugs, which Cuba ratified the following year.[26] The 1962 report of the United Nations Commission on Narcotic Drugs drew attention to the fact that Cuba's revolutionary government had made important strides in curtailing the use of marijuana by means of educational programs or when necessary by instituting more severe penalties.[27] Anslinger, however, chose to plant seeds of doubt by invoking Cold War stereotypes and using scare tactics: "No one knows yet," wrote the director, "to what extent Cuba is participating in the efforts to undermine the United States with drugs. But certainly, geared as it is for all kinds of warfare, actual and psychological, the Communists may be expected to employ narcotics against America."[28]

On the night of 6 May 1959, Cuban police arrested Jake Lansky and Dino Cellini, the manager and personnel director, respectively, of the casino at Havana's Hotel Riviera.[29] Also arrested around the same time were three other gangsters, Charles Tourine Jr., Giuseppe Di Giorgio (alias Pierre Cavanese), and Lucien Rivard.[30] All of these police actions evidently conformed to a broad antidrug initiative, as on 11 May, less than a week after the Lansky and Cellini arrests, Cuba's attorney general, Mario Fernández y Fernández, announced that the government had embarked on a campaign to stamp out drug trafficking on the island and would as part of this effort deport foreign traffickers.[31] Cellini's arrest was especially important, since an FBN memorandum had identified him as "a threat to the application of the anti-narcotics laws."[32] Cellini's criminal associates included Joseph Lo Piccolo, who was involved in heroin dealing and had recently been arrested in New York, and Di Giorgio, who ran the casino at the Club Tropicana and was suspected of involvement in drug dealing.[33]

The opportunity presented to law enforcement by the arrests of Lansky, Cellini, and Tourine was temporarily lost when the U.S. consul general in Havana reported that none of the three were currently wanted on any drug charges in the United States.[34] Cuban authorities thus released the men, and Lansky decamped for Florida.[35] Upset over Cellini's release, the antidrug agents speculated that an "idiot . . . or at least a good friend [of Cellini] in the U.S. embassy" had facilitated the release of the three men.[36] In June 1959, however, Di Giorgio, Tourine, and Rivard received notice that they were being deported from Cuba.[37] Tourine was sent to Miami, while Rivard was returned to Toronto via Jamaica.[38] Tourine later spent a few years in prison in the United States and then, supported by the earnings from his casino interests, lived in considerable luxury in an apartment facing New York's Central Park.[39] In July 1960, another American, Sicilian-born mobster Frank Cammarata, was captured in Havana with a supply of cocaine estimated to be worth sixteen thousand dollars.[40]

In June 1959, Santo Trafficante Jr., owner of Havana's Capri and Comodoro hotels as well as the Sans Souci casino, had been arrested and placed in the Triscornia detention center. Some officials suspected that he was a drug trafficker simply because of his surname.[41] Even the U.S. authorities resorted to joking about his name, calling it "most suitable . . . for this thug."[42] U.S. agents' suspicions about Trafficante rested on more solid ground, however: his uncle had been sentenced in Tampa for drug trafficking, and the FBN noted clear indications that Trafficante was involved in running drugs between Havana and New York.[43] Nevertheless, *La Gaceta*, a Spanish-language newspaper published in Tampa, came to Trafficante's defense, portraying him in essence as an ordinary member of the local community whom the FBN seemed intent on slandering:

> Santo Trafficante, a Tampa man who has lived for five years in Cuba, is locked up in Triscornia (near Havana), with deportation proceedings having been initiated against him as an "undesirable." . . . Trafficante has committed no crime in Cuba and apart from a civil claim over taxes is not charged with any felony in this country. . . . Mr. Anslinger, the Commissioner of Narcotics, believes him to be connected to the traffic in hard drugs but does not directly accuse him because he lacks the proof. If he has such proof and doesn't request his extradition, then he is prevaricating! . . . Why keep him locked up now, in Cuba? Because his lovely and cultivated daughter is going to be married this coming Sunday in a Havana hotel to a fine young Tampa man?[44]

The Cuban government granted Trafficante permission to attend his daughter's wedding at the Havana Hilton, but immigration officials and the chief of Cuba's secret police kept a watchful eye on Trafficante during the ceremony.[45] In light of the fact that no charges were pending against him "in matters concerning the illicit traffic in narcotic drugs," Cuba's Interior Department ultimately ordered his release, and Trafficante left Cuba for Tampa in November 1959.[46] In the United States, however, Trafficante faced another potential legal threat. He was suspected of having ordered the assassination of mafia boss Albert Anastasia, who was gunned down in a New York City barber shop in October 1957. Officials theorized that Trafficante, Joseph Silesi, and Meyer Lansky had wanted to prevent Anastasia from competing with them in the casino business in Havana. In addition, several Cubans had warned Anastasia not to meddle in gambling operations on the island.[47]

One of Trafficante's hotels, the Capri, was not, strictly speaking, arbitrarily taken over by Cuba's revolutionary government. Rather, in April 1959, the establishment had received a line of credit with a loan from state funds, and the line was bolstered again six months later. Given the drop in tourism, however, Trafficante's company could not make payments on the loan, so the hotel and the shops and stores that formed its commercial complex passed into the state's hands.[48]

In August 1959, the government took over Lansky's hotel, the Riviera.[49] Like all hotels, the Riviera had suffered considerable losses during 1959, with the November shortfall alone amounting to nearly $800,000.[50] The hotel was nationalized in October 1960 as part of the broad wave of nationalization of U.S. business enterprises on the island.[51] By the time the books were finally closed, Lansky and his partners had lost at least $8 million of their investment in the Riviera.[52]

Despite the deportation of some mobsters from Cuba and the departure of others, as soon as U.S.-Cuban relations began to sour, the FBN's top brass condemned the country for supposedly failing to pursue drug traffickers. Siragusa, for example, asserted that Cuba offered "international gangsters" "a secure refuge to continue their criminal activities, including drug trafficking."[53]

A segment of the North American press began to reflect this line of attack against the Cuban government. A syndicated column by Ruth Montgomery, for example, described Castro as an "egocentric bearded man" and declared that the smuggling of cocaine from Cuba to the United States had tripled since Batista's fall. Montgomery reported that this surge had resulted in part from the complicity of the Cuban government and constituted part of the strategy of "international communism [that] for years has used drugs as a favorite means of subverting the poor and of obtaining money to finance its undercover activities in foreign lands." She further suggested that Castro was "probably" a cocaine "addict," which facilitated his "ability to rant and rave for five or six hours when making speeches."[54] The accusations that Castro was addicted to cocaine continued for several years. In one version, Castro's fondness for the drug not only enabled him to deliver his long addresses but was also "the source of his unceasing energy" and made "his appetite for women insatiable."[55]

At the end of 1961, at an inter-American meeting on drug control held in Rio de Janeiro, Siragusa reported that Miguel Uriguen Bravo, the Cuban delegate, had handed out an "anti-U.S. pamphlet [with] communist propaganda." The pamphlet, titled *Desarrollo Económico y Salud* (Economic Development and Health) had been produced by Cuba's Ministry of Public Health and bore Uriguen's personal inscription, "Patria o muerte, ¡venceremos!" (The fatherland or death, we shall be victorious!) An offended Siragusa added that delegates from several Latin American countries, including the Brazilian who presided over the meeting, sympathized openly with Uriguen Bravo and demonstrated open hostility toward the United States.[56] A year later, while participating in another inter-American meeting dealing with coca leaf, Siragusa complained that the delegate from Colombia made no attempt to disguise his friendship with the representative from Cuba despite the fact that the two countries had broken off diplomatic relations and that, "whether drunk or sober," the Colombian freely expressed his sympathy for Castro and his disapproval of U.S. foreign policy.[57]

The opportunity to demonize Fidel Castro and Cuba's embrace of revolutionary radicalism by linking the two to drugs, organized crime, and the evils of international communism proved too tempting to ignore. Siragusa, for example, in the best tradition of Cold War rhetoric, wrote that "Fidel Castro had found relations with the Mafia not only profitable, but also in line with his communist objectives." Moreover, according to Siragusa, "Pumping cocaine into the United States in order to weaken and even destroy the minds of Americans would certainly be applauded by the dictator's bosses in Moscow."[58] The canard that the Cuban government was using drug smuggling as a tool to demoralize and destabilize the U.S. government retained currency for years.[59]

Anslinger was the first to plow this ground. He subsequently accused Castro's government of sending opium acquired in China to the United States to "break the will" of Americans and obtain dollars. These two objectives supposedly formed part of a global plan devised by "Soviet Russia and its communist allies."[60] Anslinger's accusations, seconded by Siragusa, reflected not only their virulent anticommunism but also the fact that in mid-March 1962, four Cuban refugees had been arrested in Miami and charged with the possession and sale of opium after one of them sold half a pound of the drug to an undercover FBN agent.[61] The controversy did not recede, and when the

Czechoslovak embassy in Washington, D.C., announced that it would transmit a protest from Cuba over these accusations, Siragusa advised Anslinger to speak with the State Department to find a way to "use the press to exploit this issue."[62] Predictably, when the Cuban government's letter of complaint reached the State Department, it refused to accept the missive, charging that it employed "insulting and abusive language."[63]

Several days later, another group of Cubans holding six pounds of cocaine was captured in a Miami raid. Siragusa claimed that the drug had come from Cuba and was "definitely" part "of a communist project" intended, among other things, to discredit the exile community.[64] Although one of the traffickers had arrived from Cuba just a few days earlier and declared that a diplomat from mainland China had given him the opium in Havana, he could not identify the individual.[65]

The Cubans charged in the two cases were convicted and sentenced to prison terms of between five and ten years. Yet no one looking into the affair found any connection between them and the Castro government. On the contrary, their political sympathies pointed in the other direction. One of the traffickers had been a member of the Cuban intelligence service during Batista's dictatorship, and another had commanded a landing craft during the April 1961 Bay of Pigs invasion.[66] The arrest of these Cubans in Miami dealt an emotional blow to the area's growing refugee community, which was characterized by its resolve to earn an honest living through hard work. Indeed, the Dade County grand jury that heard the cases noted that the Cuban community "has behaved for the most part in exemplary fashion. They have shown dignity, patience, and initiative."[67] In addition, many of the first Cuban refugees were physicians, educators, and other professionals, and most were quickly recognized for their entrepreneurial spirit and capacity for work.[68]

Authorities in New York also arrested Cubans for drug trafficking. In January 1962, police booked Juvenito Pablo Guerra for possessing two pounds of cocaine. The antinarcotics agents who captured him noted that his apartment contained "a supply of communist literature and pictures of Fidel Castro." Guerra and two other Cubans were tried amid the glare of press accusations that they had smuggled cocaine into the United States "to obtain arms or cash for Fidel Castro." Nevertheless, the judge who found Guerra and a female accomplice guilty of drug trafficking stressed, "I do not want another word said about [their] political faith of communism. There was no charge that these defendants violated any laws having to do with political beliefs or even subversion."[69] In American authorities' interpretations, however, Cuba's defense against charges of cynically conspiring with drug traffickers to wage political warfare amounted to an offhanded admission of guilt. Said one U.S. government spokesman, "The unnecessary denial by the Cuban government regarding its participation [in drug trafficking] must reveal its own guilty conscience."[70]

These accusations against Cuba were being made at the same time that the U.S. government, following the failed Bay of Pigs invasion, was planning Operation Mongoose, designed to bring down Castro. U.S. officials also feared that Cuba would export revolution to the rest of the continent both by example and through military training offered to aspiring Latin American guerrilla forces.[71] Operation Mongoose, authorized by U.S. president John F. Kennedy, sought to use the "elements at our disposal . . . to help Cuba bring down the communist regime."[72] Specifically, the operation attempted to remove Castro from power by fomenting a counterrevolutionary movement that would garner popular support, would be backed by psychological and economic warfare, and would have the support of paramilitary groups in charge of carrying out sabotage and armed resistance against the government.[73] To gain intelligence for the effort, U.S. government agents subjected Cuban exiles in Miami to rigorous questioning.[74] As part of the operation, flyers inciting sabotage were distributed in Cuba, and millions of comic books containing stories designed to cast aspersions on Castro and the revolution were handed out across Latin America.[75] In addition, the Central Intelligence Agency launched a second round of attempts to assassinate Castro, this time obtaining aid from some of the mobsters who had owned and lost casinos in Cuba and were eager to revive their old businesses. The mafiosos were asked to contact their former associates on the island, whom the agency could then recruit to provide intelligence.[76] One plan, coordinated by both President Kennedy and his brother, Attorney General Robert F. Kennedy, without any involvement by mafia bosses, contemplated a 1 December 1963 assassination of Castro coupled with a coup against the government. This plan entailed the participation of U.S. military forces, which would back up a provisional governing junta.[77] Kennedy asked Florida senator George Smathers if "people would be gratified" in the event Castro were assassinated. John and Robert Kennedy had in fact discussed the subject many months earlier, in the fall of 1961.[78] The Kennedy brothers had made the toppling of Castro a personal matter; engineering his demise would help avenge the Bay of Pigs fiasco. The attorney general described the Cuban leaders as "black-bearded communists," and he traveled with Central Intelligence Agency operatives to the camps where Cuban exiles were being trained to monitor and coordinate activities.[79]

Anslinger's statements about the flow of drugs from Cuba to the United States quickly provoked public reaction. The Brooklyn Division of the Protestant Council, which represented 573 churches and 500,000 parishioners in New York City, as well as the Kings County branch of the city's American Legion organization asked for official investigations by both the Congress and the White House. The *New York Journal-American* editorialized that Cuba, "a country inclined to such depravity, has no place among civilized nations."[80] A *Baltimore News-Post* editorial informed readers that "Havana was already the center of opium smuggling from Red China" and urged the United Nations "to boot" Cuba's "representatives onto the street."[81] The media attacks on Fidel Castro and its allegations about his supposed drug addiction also continued, with one syndicated journalist calling him "the king of cocaine."[82] The rising public clamor affected official Washington. The Subcommittee on Internal Security of the U.S. Senate's Judiciary Committee met in New York and declared "that the cases under investigation in New York reveal a relationship between Red China and Cuba's drug operations." The subcommittee warned that New York City "enjoys the invidious distinction of having the largest concentration of drug addicts in the United States" and pointed out that "New Yorkers, therefore, have a special interest in checking this drug smuggling and in denouncing this communist treason." The senators concluded by asking whether "the Communist Party of the United States was connected in some way with the illicit trafficking of drugs from Cuba."[83] Siragusa, who had been invited to testify before the subcommittee, claimed that "the evidence we possess . . . indicates that this cocaine traffic is connected to Castro's regime." To reinforce his argument, he quoted selectively from his presentation made as head of the U.S. delegation to the First Inter-American Conference on the Illicit Traffic in Cocaine and Coca Leaves, held in Rio de Janeiro in March 1960.[84] Siragusa's original presentation had indeed made the point that "almost all of the contraband hydrochloride cocaine in the United States and Canada comes from Cuba," but he had also grouped Cuba with the United States, Canada, and nine other Latin American countries as "actual or potential victims" of such traffic.[85]

Seeking information that might shed light on the supposed China-to-Cuba opium connection, a U.S. Secret Service agent attached to the Treasury Department's Miami office contacted Cuban refugees in the last months of

1962. The agent concluded that while the presence of mainland Chinese in Cuba was a source of concern, no information elucidated the nature of their activities on the island. U.S. officials also could not prove that the Cuban government was using the diplomatic pouch to send narcotic drugs to New York via Mexico City. In the absence of any hard evidence, the Miami office closed the investigation.[86] Authorities in Washington disagreed, however, and insisted on keeping the opium issue alive. They next decided to study aerial photographs to pinpoint the location of the fields in Cuba where poppies were being cultivated.[87] Henry L. Giordano, who had replaced Anslinger as director of the FBN in 1962, picked right up where his predecessor left off, declaring in 1963 that Cuba and China were the principal sources of the cocaine and heroin entering the United States and Canada.[88]

Nevertheless, an official report issued in August 1965 contradicted the director, concluding that "we have no concrete evidence to date about the cultivation of poppies in Cuba."[89] Giordano eventually embraced that view, acknowledging in a note to the Department of State that although Cuban exiles maintained important drug trafficking networks between Latin America and the United States, "Cuba as such does not appear to be bound up in these activities." He likewise endorsed the finding that Mexico City had replaced Havana as the main center of activities by criminal organizations.[90]

During his tenure, Anslinger had also accused Communist China of being "the dope-vending dragon of the East."[91] According to Anslinger, the Chinese government vigorously opposed the use of drugs domestically but encouraged their processing for export as a weapon in the soft war against Japan and the United States.[92] More concretely, Anslinger accused China of growing opium and of processing it into heroin to be sent to Japan.[93] Taiwan's representative to the United Nations contributed to the disinformation campaign against China.[94] During the Korean War, furthermore, Anslinger had accused North Korea of serving as the pipeline through which Chinese heroin made its way to South Korea.[95] In every year from 1953 through 1962 with the exception of 1960, the FBN's annual reports repeated the charge that China was one of the main sources of heroin entering the United States.[96]

Anslinger never wavered in his position on China, but contrary to his repeated accusations, the Chinese communists had long since clamped down on the processing and trafficking of opium. According to historian Charles O. Walker, the coup de grâce against opium trafficking had been delivered during the Chinese Revolution.[97] Indeed, the Chinese communists, who had maintained a strong antidrug line since the 1920s, launched massive campaigns between 1949 and 1952 to obliterate opium trafficking and use as part of the construction of "new China."[98] China's communists had departed from their antidrug policy only between 1941 and 1946, when they relied on money coming from opium to help finance their military campaigns.[99] Similarly, revolutionary Cuban campaigns directed toward forming a "new man" ceded no ground at all to drug use or trafficking.

Epilogue

he foreign traffickers who smuggled drugs from either Europe or Latin America to the United States using Cuba as a transit point abandoned the island after the revolution and relocated in other countries. Corsican Paul Mondolini left Cuba for Madrid in January 1960, returned to Havana at the beginning of the next month, and then quickly left again, this time for Mexico City. Mondolini later met up with his Canadian associate, Lucien Rivard, in Acapulco. The two drug lords continued making trips to Mexico for some years to come.[1] Mondolini also maintained his heroin operations in France, as did Jean-Baptiste Croce and Ansan Bistoni, and his client networks in Mexico, Canada, and South America. He also joined a criminal organization run by Edouard Toudayan. Bistoni operated a processing laboratory near Cros-de-Cagnes, in France, and established a second facility, in partnership with Croce, in Corsica.[2] By 1966, French drug traffickers had begun to base some of their operations in Madrid and Barcelona, and both Mondolini and Croce frequently traveled to Spain.[3] On the other side of the Atlantic, the Corsican mafia now transported heroin from France to the United States via Argentina and Mexico.[4] The Corsican traffickers also operated in reverse, sending cocaine from Buenos Aires to Europe.[5] In 1967, more than seven years after he had last stood on Cuban soil, Mondolini was captured in France, indicted, and put on trial.[6]

Lucien Rivard, who owned a summer resort near Montreal, was captured and jailed in Canada in June 1964. He attempted to avoid extradition to the United States, where he faced charges of having imported heroin from Europe via Mexico and Canada. The Rivard case erupted into a political scandal when one of the assistants to the Canadian minister of justice was accused of attempted bribery on behalf of Rivard. The scandal broadened when the justice minister and a member of Parliament stepped down after admitting that they had failed to investigate the assistant's actions. Further embarrassing the government, Rivard escaped from jail in March 1965 and remained on the lam until he was captured in his hideout in provincial Quebec four months later. He was extradited to Laredo, Texas, and tried for having arranged four deliveries of between seventy and seventy-five pounds of heroin. Rivard was convicted and sentenced to twenty years in prison, while three of his Canadian associates received prison terms ranging between twelve and fifteen years.[7]

The monitoring and pursuit of other traffickers who had operated or found sanctuary in Cuba during the time of Batista's dictatorship continued to yield results. Antranik Paroutian, another of the French drug runners who had brought heroin into Cuba during the 1950s, was captured in Beirut in March 1960. Paroutian was extradited to the United States, tried, and sentenced to twenty years in prison for bringing heroin into the country. Testimony revealed that Paroutian had transferred more than half a million dollars from several New York banks to secret numbered Swiss accounts. He appealed his case to the U.S. Supreme Court, which declined to consider it.[8]

Mexico also became home to several gangs of Cuban drug traffickers who needed a new location in which to continue their illicit activities.[9] On 30 June 1960, authorities discovered a cocaine-processing laboratory in Mexico City as the result of an investigation in which U.S. Federal Bureau of Narcotics (FBN) agents stationed in both Cuba and Mexico shared information with their Mexican and Cuban counterparts. The raid turned up 3 kilos of cocaine and 11 kilos of heroin.[10] Some months later, six more Cubans were captured, along with a Mexican associate, after a cocaine laboratory exploded in Cuernavaca.[11] Despite these successes, however, other Cuban drug traffickers who had relocated to Mexico continued to ship cocaine, obtained from South America, to the Miami and New York markets.[12]

After the revolution, the Cubans who headed the island's drug trafficking gangs generally stayed away from the United States, since their names appeared on the list of criminals sought by American agents. At the same time, however, New York's long-established Cuban drug distribution networks gained strength.[13] Cubans were involved in drug trafficking in Miami, California, and Texas. At least eighty-six Cubans were convicted and sentenced for violating U.S. antidrug laws between July 1959 and early 1966, providing some indication of the measure of their involvement. Forty-nine of these individuals operated in the New York–New Jersey area, while thirty-five operated in Florida. Furthermore, nearly three-quarters of the group came from Havana and its environs. Their sentences ranged from as little as one year in prison to twenty-five years behind bars, but most terms ran between five and ten years.[14]

Between 1959 and 1966, virtually all of the Cubans convicted in Florida on drug trafficking charges had arrived in Miami after the revolutionary government took power. With some exceptions, these people trafficked for the most part in cocaine.[15] The pattern in New York City differed somewhat, however: Cubans formed the largest group among those convicted of cocaine trafficking during the period, while a smaller but still significant number were convicted of selling heroin to New York's huge market for that drug, in which traffickers of various nationalities participated. These Cubans generally were arrested for making retail sales of the drug on the street.[16]

In addition to their involvement on the U.S. mainland, Cubans also participated in drug trafficking in Puerto Rico. As the director of the Puerto Rican Division of Drugs and Narcotics declared at the end of the 1970s, "Many [Cubans] increased the traffic and use of drugs, especially cocaine."[17]

Central America also figured in the new scheme, as Cuban exiles set up a laboratory in Managua, doing so, according to U.S. authorities, with the likely complicity of the head of Nicaragua's immigration service. This gang included Cubans who lived in Miami as well as in Nicaragua, and its members used young Americans as their mules. The gang had extensive networks that reached as far as Detroit.[18]

Before the revolution, Cuba's cocaine trafficking had been handled by people of other nationalities, and they, too, continued sending the drug to the United States after Castro took power. In August 1965, for example, chemist Luis González Aguilera shipped eighteen pounds of cocaine to the United States using Blanca Ibáñez as his courier. Ibáñez, however, was intercepted by agents in the Miami airport and subsequently convicted and imprisoned.[19]

Extant records offer no further information regarding the drug-related activities of Colombian brothers Rafael and Tomás Herrán Olózaga, although in 1958 one FBN agent reported to his dismay that they were free on bail and that "reliable information existed that they had gone back into trafficking."[20] Colombia, however, had figured in the international drug trade well before the time of the Herrán Olózaga brothers. During the 1930s and 1940s, illegal drugs were smuggled into Colombia from Europe through the coastal ports of Cartagena and Barranquilla. Some of the contraband drugs were consumed locally, though their high cost restricted them only to the well-to-do, while the remainder was reexported to the United States.[21]

After 1965, a new dimension of the Andean connection was opened when Colombian drug traffickers, in tandem with traffickers of other nationalities, including Americans, began to establish distribution networks in the United States. Its main centers were New York and Miami. Los Angeles served as a secondary hub. Cubans who had settled in the United States helped to set up these networks, through which cocaine and to a lesser extent marijuana were distributed. In addition to the department of Antioquia, Colombian drug traffickers came in considerable numbers from the cities of Bogotá, Barranquilla, and Cali. Some managed to exist in two worlds, running both legal businesses and clandestine laboratories in which they processed coca paste from Peru. Still others combined drug trafficking with emerald smuggling. Typically, mules (citizens of countries increasingly tied to the U.S. economy) would bring cocaine and marijuana on commercial flights to Miami and New York, hoping to blend unremarkably into the larger pool of Colombians traveling between the two countries. Not all, however, got past the customs and drug enforcement agents, and several of the intercepted mules were found to be carrying false passports, suggesting that the traffickers had developed relatively sophisticated criminal networks.[22]

Inevitably, the higher volume of drug trafficking was reflected in law enforcement statistics. According to one official report, Florida's crime rate increased 60 percent during the 1960s. Moreover, the report concluded, Florida suffered under "conditions of organized crime that were among the most aggravated in the United States."[23] Yet the scope of the drug problem in Florida was a matter of degree, since in the mid-1950s, Florida's Office of Narcotic Drugs had already reported that the state was witnessing a rise in the number of arrests and convictions stemming from violations of the drug laws.[24] Despite warning against the inference that a "disproportionate amount of illegal activity" could be attributed to the large colony of Cuban refugees, subsequent reports issued by the same Florida agency noted that the cocaine "found in insignificant amounts before the arrival of the Cubans, is now being confiscated on a frequent basis and in great quantities."[25] However, the pattern of involvement by citizens of different countries in drug trafficking in Florida was simply too diverse to permit any single and unvarying cause-and-effect relationship.

Nevertheless, Cubans and South Americans from other countries had significant influence, and a considerable number of Americans were also involved in the Florida drug trafficking business during the 1960s.[26] For the most part, the illegal substances involved were heroin, cocaine, and marijuana. In a significant number of cases, those selling the drugs were addicts themselves.[27] Thus, drug trafficking in Florida could not be ascribed purely to foreign interests or portrayed merely as something that had been "imported." Rather, much as in Cuba in earlier years, drug trafficking both in Florida and in the rest of the United States became a multinational business whose participants (who accorded the law little if any respect) included both Americans and foreigners as well as fortune-seeking, business-minded immigrants.

On the basis of this mixture of ingredients and players, drug trafficking networks took shape and filled the exploding demand for illegal drugs in the United States. Beginning in the mid-1960s, drug use in the United States ceased being peculiar to fringe groups and became, on a massive scale, an activity pursued by middle-class youth for whom drugs provided an outlet for anti–Vietnam War protests and their rejection of the values transmitted by their parents and older Americans as a whole.[28] The enormous growth in U.S. drug use and the development of domestic and international trafficking networks to service it are part of a different history.

Notes

Abbreviations

BDFA	*British Documents on Foreign Affairs: Reports and Papers from the Foreign Office Confidential Print*
FBN	U.S. Treasury Department, Federal Bureau of Narcotics
FBNC	Fondo Banco Nacional de Cuba, Archivo Nacional de Cuba, Havana
FC	Fondo Chibás, Archivo Nacional de Cuba, Havana
FME	Fondo Ministerio de Estado, Archivo Nacional de Cuba, Havana
FRUS	U.S. Department of State, *Foreign Relations of the United Status*
FSE	Fondo Secretaría de Estado, Archivo Nacional de Cuba, Havana
FSP	Fondo Secretaría de la Presidencia, Archivo Nacional de Cuba, Havana
PAWA	Collection 341, Pan American World Airways, Archives and Special Collections Department, Richter Library, University of Miami, Miami, Fla.
RG21NE	Record Group 21, Records of the District Courts of the United States, U.S. National Archives and Records Administration, Northeast Region, New York
RG21SE	Record Group 21, Records of the District Courts of the United States, U.S. National Archives and Records Administration, Southeast Region, East Point–Ellenwood–Morrow, Georgia
RG59	Record Group 59, General Records of the Department of State, U.S. National Archives and Records Administration, College Park, Md.
RG170	Record Group 170, Records of the Drug Enforcement Administration, U.S. National Archives and Records Administration, College Park, Md.
USDCM	Criminal Dockets, U.S. District Court of Miami

Introduction

1. Arango Mejía, *Genealogías*, 1:274, 467–68, 2:137–38; Carrizosa Argáez, *Linajes*, 232.

2. "Ocupó la Policía un cargamento de heroína valorado en $16,000," *Diario de la Marina*, 27 December 1956, 16B; "16,000 in Heroin Seized in Vedado," *Havana Post*, 27 December 1956, 1; "Ocupan drogas," *El Mundo*, 26 December 1956, 8A; "20 mil pesos de fianza a unos traficantes," *Diario de la Marina*, 29 December 1956, 20B; William W. Johnston, Treasury Representative in Charge, to the Commissioner of Customs, Division of Investigations, Bureau of Customs, Havana, 31 December 1956, RG170-74-12, Box 22; William W. Johnston, Treasury Representative in Charge, Monthly Activity Report, Havana, 31 December 1956, RG170-74-12, Box 22; Henry L. Giordano, "District

Supervisor Gaffney's Trip to Medellín, Colombia," Washington, D.C., 18 February 1957, RG170-74-12, Box 21; FBN, *Traffic in Opium, 1957*, 22; Steve Minas, Customs Agent, to Commissioner of Customs, Division of Investigations, Bureau of Customs, Havana, 27 April 1959, RG170-74-12, Box 22; Stewart H. Adams, Senior Customs Representative, to Commissioner of Customs, Division of Investigations, Bureau of Customs, Monthly Activities Report, Havana, 4 August 1959, RG170-74-12, Box 22; Charles Siragusa to A. de la Carrera, Alexandria, Va., 20 January 1959, RG170-71A-3555, Box 8; Arturo Robledo, Secretario, Ministerio de Trabajo, Higiene y Previsión Social, to Ministro de Relaciones Exteriores, Bogotá, 22 May 1939, Fondo Ministerio de Relaciones Exteriores, transferencia 10, caja 120, carpeta 940, folios 115–16, Archivo General de la Nación, Bogotá; Departamento de Organismos Internacionales to Ministro de Relaciones Exteriores, Bogotá, 25 May 1939, Fondo Ministerio de Relaciones Exteriores, transferencia 10, caja 120, carpeta 940, folio 117. See also Sáenz Rovner, "Prehistoria: Serie documental," 90; Sáenz Rovner, "Prehistoria: Temores norteamericanos."

3. For a critique of the argument that purports to show a direct correlation between drug trafficking and poverty, see Thoumi, *Illegal Drugs*, 48–50.

4. Moya, "Spanish Emigration," 17.

5. Dye, *Cuban Sugar*, 2–8.

6. Moya, "Spanish Emigration," 24.

7. Luis, *Culture and Customs*, 68–69.

8. Pérez-Stable, *Cuban Revolution*, 27–31. See also Marrero, *Geografía*, xxi–lii; Falcoff, *Cuba*, 29–30; Farber, *Origins*, 19–22.

9. Ely, *Cuando reinaba*, 83–86. See also Álvarez Estévez, *Huellas francesas*.

10. Freire, *Historia*, 305.

11. Moya, "Spanish Emigration," 16.

12. Moreno Fraginals, *Cuba/España*, 265, 296; Levine, *Tropical Diaspora*, 2, 16–17, 34, 50; Naranjo Orovio, "Población española," 122. On the immigration of Middle Easterners, Koreans, Japanese, and Germans, see Menéndez Paredes, *Componentes*; Ruiz and Kim, *Coreanos*; Álvarez Estévez and Guzmán Pascual, *Japoneses*; Álvarez Estévez and Guzmán Pascual, *Alemanes*.

13. See Louis A. Pérez Jr., *Cuba and the United States*, 123–24; Louis A. Pérez Jr., *On Becoming Cuban*, 107–10; Le Riverend, *República*, 68–70; Aguilar, *Cuba 1933*, 24; Cirules, *Conversación*; Jesús Guanche, *Componentes*, 107–8; Verrill, "Treasure Island," 137; Jenks, *Our Cuban Colony*, 144–50.

14. Deere, "Here Come the Yankees!"

15. Masterson and Funada-Classen, *Japanese*, 110.

16. Naranjo Orovio, "Immigration," 160.

17. Maluquer de Motes, *Nación e inmigración*, 132–33.

18. Soler Martínez, *Españoles*, 5.

19. Moya, "Spanish Emigration," 22–23.

20. Maluquer de Motes, *Nacion e inmigración*, 123, 125–28; Maluquer de Motes, "Inmigración," 138–40.

21. Moya, *Cousins and Strangers*, 502 n. 94; de la Fuente, *Nation for All*, 101.

22. Naranjo Orovio, *Del campo*, 83–84. The complex remains in use today as a gathering and educational center for political officials and cadres of Cuba's governing Communist Party. One author has described Triscornia as "a den of crime and corruption" through which its administrators made fortunes by turning the granting of entry permits into a profit-making venture. See Barnet, *Gallego*, 268 n. 8.

23. Naranjo Orovio, *Del campo*, 159; Maluquer de Motes, *Nación e inmigración*, 138–39; Louis A. Pérez Jr., *Cuba under the Platt Amendment*, 60–61; McAvoy, *Sugar Baron*, 7.

24. Aguilar, *Cuba 1933*, 8, 21; Louis A. Pérez Jr., *Cuba under the Platt Amendment*, chapter 1; Louis A. Pérez Jr., *On Becoming Cuban*, 143–47.

25. Louis A. Pérez Jr., *On Becoming Cuban*, 166–67.

26. Robert F. Smith, *United States and Cuba*, 17.

27. O'Brien, *Revolutionary Mission*, 210.

28. Christian M. Allen, *Industrial Geography*, 1, 16, 26, 61.

29. "Memorandum to Division of Foreign Control, Deportation, Persons Charged Smuggling Liquor, Aliens or Narcotics from Cuba to the United States," Havana, 5 September 1927, RG170-74-12, Box 22; F. T. F. Dumont, Report, Havana, 25 January 1933, RG59, 837.114Narcotics/42; F. T. F. Dumont, Report, Havana, 16 February 1933, RG59, 837.114Narcotics/43; F. T. F. Dumont, American Consul General, to Secretary of State, "Smuggling Activities in Cuba," 29 June 1933, RG59, 837.114Narcotics/64; C. R. Cameron, American Consul General, to Secretary of State, "Deportation from Cuba of Atanasio Kaineros, Greek Citizen, Alleged Narcotic, Alien, and Liquor Smuggler," Havana, 28 March 1935, RG59, 837.114Narcotics/82.

30. Thoumi, "Ventajas competitivas ilegales," 7. Thoumi has also argued this point in *Economía política y narcotráfico*, 54, and *Illegal Drugs*, 54.

31. For the view of Cuba as neocolonial victim of drugs, see Arias Fernández, *Cuba*.

32. Topik, Marichal, and Frank, introduction to *From Silver to Cocaine*, 3. For more on this approach with specific reference to cocaine, see Gootenberg, "Cocaine in Chains."

33. On corruption in Cuba, see Díaz-Briquets and Pérez-López, *Corruption in Cuba*, esp. chapter 3, which deals with the period prior to the revolution.

34. Montaner, *Cuba*, 29–30. Nevertheless, various sectors of Cuban society took up the outcry against corruption in the struggle against Batista during the 1950s; see, e.g., De Palma, *Man*, 70, 93, 103, 200–201.

35. Thoumi, "Ventajas competitivas ilegales," 6. See also Thoumi, *Illegal Drugs*, 76.

36. Meyer and Parssinen, *Webs of Smoke*, 5.

37. Courtwright, Joseph, and Des Jarlais, *Addicts*, 1.

38. Damián J. Fernández, introduction, xv.

39. The discussion over following the transnational versus "nation-state" approach in the analysis of U.S. history has heated up in recent years. See, e.g., Tyrrell, "American Exceptionalism"; McGerr, "Price"; Daniel T. Rodgers, "Exceptionalism"; Fredrickson, *Comparative Imagination*, 46–65; Bender, *Rethinking*; Louis A. Pérez Jr., "We Are the World."

40. See Cirules, *Imperio*; Cirules, *Mafia in Havana*; Cirules, *Vida*; Cirules *Mafia en Cuba*. See also Cirules, "Mafia norteamericana," parts 1–4.

41. Buajasán Marrawi and Méndez Méndez, *República*, 34.

42. On the quantitative and qualitative magnitude of illicit activities in general since the 1990s, see Naím, *Illicit*.

43. Cited by Meyer and Parssinen, *Webs of Smoke*, 243. Anslinger's position is in line with what Thoumi calls the "moralistic" North American model, in which "crime reflects a conception of life as a continuous struggle between good and evil" (*Illegal Drugs*, 19–20).

44. For example, in 1939, when Alfred R. Lindesmith, a professor of sociology at Indiana University, criticized Anslinger's punitive outlook, Anslinger sent one of his agents to the university to denounce Lindesmith as "connected with a criminal organization." In 1962, when Lindesmith published a work critical of Anslinger, the FBN investigated both Lindesmith and Indiana University Press. See Kinder, "Bureaucratic Cold Warrior," 175–76, 191.

45. Acker, *Creating*, 2–4.

46. Ibid., 19.

47. Courtwright, *Forces*, 178.

48. Acker, *Creating*, 8.

49. Musto, *American Disease*, 294.

50. Cited by Thoumi, *Illegal Drugs*, 15.

51. Juan Vega y Vega, *Los Delitos* (Havana: Instituto del Libro, 1968), cited by Salas, *Social Control*, 50.

52. For this reason, I cannot agree with William O. Walker III's assertion that "Cuba in the 1950s . . . offered to traffickers in good standing with the Batista regime a reliable locale from which to ship drugs to the United States" (*Drugs*, 170–71).

53. Valle, *Jineteras*, 113–14, 155, 192. See also Elizalde, *Flores*, 24.

54. Valle, *Jineteras*, 152, 155.

55. Louis A. Pérez Jr., *Essays*, 147.

56. Mormino, *Land*, 92–93, 95, 100, 283.

57. Yongming, *Anti-Drug Crusades*, 2–5, 95.

58. Brook and Wakabayashi, "Introduction," 2.

59. Dikötter, Laamann, and Xun, *Narcotic Culture*, 3, 8.

60. William O. Walker III, *Drug Control*, xii.

61. Ibid.

62. Ibid., 1–2.

63. Ibid., 12.

64. William O. Walker III, "Drug Control," 381.

65. William O. Walker III, *Drugs*, xiv.

66. Nelli, *Business*, 11.

67. Griffith, "Geography," 98–99, 109. Griffith also develops these arguments in *Drugs*, 2.

68. As Christian M. Allen has pointed out in his analysis of the economic geography of drug trafficking, "The development of economic systems in time and space does not result simply from 'geographic' processes like the friction of distance, but also from wider economic, political and cultural contexts" (*Industrial Geography*, 7).

69. Orlando J. Pérez, "Drugs," 143–44; U.S. Congress, Senate, *Drugs*, 69–70. See also U.S. Congress, Senate, *Haitian Narcotics Activities*; Richard C. Steiner to John Conyers Jr. and Alfred A. McCandless, Washington, D.C., 28 December 1994, U.S. General Accounting Office, 15391 GAO Documents.

70. Henríquez, *Farmacodependencia*, 85–87; Velásquez Mainardi, *Narcotráfico*, 13–15, 19, 41–42; U.S. Congress, House of Representatives, *Dominican Drug Trafficking*, 19.

71. Chevannes, "Background," 28–30.

72. Gootenberg, *Cocaine*, 67, 70, 185–86, 188.

73. Meyer and Parssinen, *Webs of Smoke*, 261–62.

74. Schwartz, *Pleasure Island*.

75. Valentine, *Strength*.

Chapter 1

1. Escohotado, *Historia*, 252.

2. Russo, *Outfit*, 4.

3. Courtwright, *Forces*, 175–76.

4. Mason, *Rum Running*, 13–14.

5. Russo, *Outfit*, 6.

6. Kolko, *Main Currents*, 31–32.

7. Frederick Lewis Allen, *Only Yesterday*, 206.

8. Gordon, *New Deals*, 80.

9. Mason, *Rum Running*, 16–19.

10. Ibid., 35–46, 69, 79–80, 107–9; Eisenberg, Dan, and Landau, *Meyer Lansky*, 79–83, 90–91, 107.

11. Recio, "Drugs and Alcohol," 31–33.

12. Meyer and Parssinen, *Webs of Smoke*, 242.

13. Mason, *Rum Running*, 144–45.

14. Kavieff, *Purple Gang*, 71, 76–77.

15. See, e.g., Dubro and Rowland, *King*.

16. Quoted by Sann, *Lawless Decade*, 90.

17. Louis A. Pérez Jr., *On Becoming Cuban*, 169.

18. Schwartz, *Pleasure Island*, 44.

19. Louis A. Pérez Jr., *On Becoming Cuban*, 166.

20. Ibid., 183, 187.

21. Levi and Heller, *Cuba Style*, 9.

22. González Echevarría, *Pride*, 159.

23. Kohn, *Dope Girls*, 20.

24. Quoted in Moya, *Cousins and Strangers*, 156.

25. Guy, *Sex and Danger*, 124, 149–50; Benedetti, *Mejores letras*, 348–497.

26. Ortiz, *Negros curros*, 14.

27. See Calvo Ospina, *Ron Bacardí*, 24; Frederick H. Smith, *Caribbean Rum*, 229; the advertisements in *Who's Who among Visitors to Havana*, 6 March 1932, pp. 8, 24, PAWA, Box 64.

28. "Dry Raiders Search 400 on Ship from Miami; Hundreds of Bottles of Fine Liquors Seized," *New York Times*, 9 March 1929, 21.

29. McCarthy, *Aviation*, 20, 131.

30. "Big Mail Plane Hits Hard Rain near Havana; First Trip of Regular Schedule Got under Way Here at 8:25 This Morning," *Key West Citizen*, 28 October 1927, PAWA, Box 248; McCarthy, *Aviation*, 14.

31. Pan American Airways, Public Relations — Miami, Florida, "Pan American Airways — World's Largest — Started with Key West Hop 16 Years Ago," 17 October 1943, PAWA, Box 248; Pan American World Airways, Public Relations — Latin American Division, "PAA Completing 25th Year of Miami-Havana Service," 4 September 1953, PAWA, Box 357. See also McCarthy, *Aviation*, 14.

32. Schwartz, *Pleasure Island*, 3–4, 67–68.

33. Ibid., 4, 19, 34–35, 37.

34. Knight, *Caribbean*, 236.

35. Solicitor, Department of State, 13 January 1925, RG59, 711.379/orig; Enoch M. Crowder, American Ambassador, 2 February 1935, RG59, 711.379/orig. For the treaty with Canada, see Calvin Coolidge, Executive Order no. 4306, 13 September 1925, RG59. For the agreement with Mexico, see *Convention between the United States and Mexico*.

36. Frank B. Kellogg to Enoch H. Crowder, 11 March 1925, RG59, 711.379/1.

37. Mabel Walker Willebrandt, Assistant Attorney General, to Secretary of State, Washington, D.C., 26 August 1925, RG59, 71.379/19. On the smuggling of illegal immigrants, see also Levine, *Tropical Diaspora*, 69.

38. Mellon, Secretary of the Treasury, to Frank B. Kellogg, Secretary of State, Washington, D.C., 10 June 1925, RG59, 711.37/3.

39. Crowder to Secretary of State, Havana, 4 September 1925, RG59, 711.379/15.

40. Hemingway, *To Have and Have Not*; Serpa, *Contrabando*.

41. Foster, the Solicitor, Department of State, to Vallance, 6 February 1925, RG59.

42. Greene, Office of the Solicitor, Department of State, to Barnes, 20 January 1926, RG59, 711.379/47.

43. Enoch H. Crowder to Secretary of State, Havana, 15 September 1925, RG59, 711.379/18.

44. Beals, *Crime*, 376; López Leiva, *Bandolerismo*, 18–19.

45. Le Riverend, *Historia*, 101.

46. Beals, *Crime*, 60.

47. Moreno Fraginals, *Cuba/España*, 72–73.

48. Guerra y Sánchez, *Manual*, 87, 140.

49. Serpa, *Contrabando*, 104.

50. Enoch H. Crowder to Gerardo Machado, Havana, 6 August 1925, FSP, Legajo 89, no. 16.

51. Kellogg to American Embassy in Havana, Washington, D.C., 5 January 1926, RG59, 711.379/39.

52. Consultor, Secretaría de Estado, to Miguel Angel de la Campa, Subsecretario de Estado, Havana, 15 July 1925, FSE, Legajo 204, no. 2451. See also Portell-Vilá, *Nueva historia*, 336.

53. See *Convention between the United States and Great Britain*; *Convention between the United States and Norway*; *Convention between the United States and Denmark*; *Convention between the United States and Germany*; *Convention between the United States and Sweden*; *Convention between the United States and Italy*; *Convention between the United States and Panama*; *Convention between the United States and the Netherlands.*

54. See "Notas confidenciales, correspondencia relativa al Convenio entre Cuba y Estados Unidos para la supresión de contrabando, 8 octubre–12 noviembre, 1925," FSE, Legajo 204, no. 2453.

55. See *Gaceta Oficial de la República de Cuba*, Edición Extraordinaria no. 12, 13 July 1926, 1; *Convention between the United States and Cuba: Prevention of Smuggling*; *Convention between the United States and Cuba: To Suppress Smuggling.*

56. "Cuban Distillers Will Lose Millions of Dollars If Rum Treaty Is Approved," *Havana Post*, 2 March 1926.

57. "The National Alcohol Industry Will Loose [*sic*] More Than One Million Dollars If the Rum Treaty with the U.S. Is Approved," *Heraldo de Cuba*, 1 March 1926, RG59, 711.379/77 (English translation).

58. Editorial, *El Mundo*, 7 June 1926, RG59, 711.379/102 (English translation).

59. "Visit to President by Commission of Cuban Distillers to Solicit Repeal of Certain Decrees and to Censure the U.S.-Cuba Liquor Treaty," Clipping, 1 September 1927, RG59, 711.379/123; C. B. Curtis, Chargé d'Affaires ad interim, to Secretary of State, Havana, 25 April 1928, RG59, 711.379/124; "Campaign on Here for the Abrogation of the Liquor Treaty," 3 September 1928, RG59, 711.379/131; Noble Brandon Judah to Secretary of State, Havana, 4 September 1928, RG59, 711.379/125; "Se Dispone Cuba Para Denunciar el Tratado Del Ron con los E.U. En la Secretaría de Estado se está redactando un interesante memorandum acerca de esa material; El Estado Cubano no recibe beneficio con ese Convenio," *Heraldo de Cuba*, 29 August 1928, clipping, RG59, 711.379/125.

60. Robert F. Smith, *United States and Cuba*, chapter 3; Aguilar, *Cuba 1933*, 95–96.

61. Copley Armory Jr., Memorandum, 15 February 1929, RG59, 711.379/1327w.

62. Hickerson to Gilbert, Vallance, and Baker, 27 March 1930, RG59, F.W.711.379/135.

63. Regarding such complaints and pressures, see C. B. Curtis, Chargé d'Affaires ad interim, to Secretary of State, Havana, 25 April 1928, RG59, 711.379/124; "Se Dispone Cuba Para Denunciar el Tratado del Ron con los E.U.," *Heraldo de Cuba*, 29 August 1928; "Campaign on Here for the Abrogation of the Liquor Treaty," 3 September 1928, RG59, 711.379/131.

64. The operational patterns described in this paragraph are based on the analysis of dozens of cases contained in the record. See FSE, Legajo 257.

65. Sann, *Lawless Decade*, 94.

66. See Subsecretario de Hacienda to Subsecretario de Estado, Havana, 27 March 1928, FSE, Legajo 257, no. 4249; Miguel Angel Carbonell, Encargado del Despacho, Secretaría de Estado, to Subsecretario de Estado, Havana, 17 December 1928, FSE, Legajo 257, no. 4251.

67. For a sampling of cases, see Harold L. Williamson, Chargé d'Affaires ad interim, Embassy of the United States of America, to Rafael Sánchez Aballí, Acting Secretary of

State, Havana, 11 October 1927, FSE, Legajo 257, no. 4248; C. B. Curtis, Chargé d'Affaires ad interim, to Rafael Martínez Ortiz, Secretary of State, Havana, 4 November 1927, FSE, Legajo 257, no. 4248; Noble Brandon Judah to Rafael Martínez Ortiz, Secretary of State, Havana, 29 February 1928, FSE, Legajo 257, no. 4249; C. B. Curtis to Rafael Martínez Ortiz, Secretary of State, Havana, 28 November 1928, FSE, Legajo 257, no. 4251.

68. See, e.g., Enoch H. Crowder to Rafael Martínez Ortiz, Secretary of State, Havana, 18 April 1927, FSE, Legajo 257, no. 4256; Harold L. Williamson, Chargé d'Affaires ad interim, Embassy of the United States of America, to Rafael Sánchez Aballí, Acting Secretary of State, Havana, 1l October 1927, FSE, Legajo 257, no. 4248; C. B. Curtis to Francisco María Fernández, Acting Secretary of State, Havana, 6 December 1928, FSE, Legajo 257, no. 4251.

69. See, e.g., Subsecretario de Hacienda to Subsecretario de Estado, Havana, 1 May 1928, FSE, Legajo 257, no. 4249; Subsecretario de Hacienda to Secretario de Estado, Havana, 15 November 1928, FSE, Legajo 257, no. 4250; Subsecretario de Hacienda to Subsecretario de Estado, Havana, 29 November 1928, FSE, Legajo 257, no. 4251; Subsecretario de Hacienda to Subsecretario de Estado, Havana, 10 December 1928, FSE, Legajo 257, no. 4251; Subsecretario de Hacienda to Secretario de Estado, Havana, 5 January 1929, FSE, Legajo 257, no. 4251; José Lamillar, Jefe de la Sección de Aduanas, to Subsecretario de Estado, Havana, 7 August 1929, FSE, Legajo 257, no. 4267.

70. Frederick Lewis Allen, *Only Yesterday*, 208–9.

71. Leuchtenburg, *Franklin D. Roosevelt*, 9.

72. Russo, *Outfit*, 89.

73. Leuchtenburg, *Franklin D. Roosevelt*, 10.

74. Gordon, *New Deals*, 70–285; Wall, *Alfred I. du Pont*, 519; Burnham, *Bad Habits*, 32, 35.

75. See the correspondence found in FSE, Legajo 254, no. 4104.

76. See "Confidencial: Contrabando de Licores a los Estados Unidos desde El Mariel," Cuba, 22 May 1934, FSE, Legajo 254, no. 4104; José Argamasilla Grimany, Inspector, Secretaría de Hacienda, to Sr. Jefe de la Sección de Impuesto del Empréstito de 35 millones, Havana, 22 June 1935, FSE, Legajo 254, no. 4104.

77. "Memorandum para el señor presidente de la República: O. Ferrara, Secretaría de Estado," Havana, 10 May 1933, FSE, Legajo 254, no. 4103; F. T. F. Dumont, Cónsul General Americano, to Honorable Señor Subsecretario de Estado, Havana, 10 June 1934, FSE, Legajo 254, no. 4104; J. Martínez Sáenz, Secretario de Hacienda, to Sr. Jefe de Aduanas, Havana, 26 May 1934, FSE, Legajo 254, no. 4104.

78. See Sáenz Rovner, "Elites, estado, y política," 87. See also *FRUS, 1934*, 108–81.

79. Portell-Vilá, *Nueva historia*, 340.

80. "El Dr. Roberto A. Netto replica a los destiladores explicando su actuación como investigador," *Diario de la Marina*, 21 October 1934, clipping, FSE, Legajo 254, no. 4104.

81. J. Martínez Sáenz, Secretario de Hacienda, to Guillermo de Blanck, Subsecretario de Estado, Havana, 26 May 1934, FSE, Legajo 254, no. 4104.

82. See "Confidencial: Contrabando de Licores a los Estados Unidos desde el Mariel, Cuba," 22 May 1934, FSE, Legajo 254, no. 4104; J. Martínez Sáenz, Secretario de Ha-

cienda, to Guillermo de Blanck, Subsecretario de Estado, Havana, 26 May 1934, FSE, Legajo 254, no. 4104; "Posee Hacienda los Hilos de una Vasta Organización con Varios Barcos y Hombres," *El Mundo*, 4 August 1934, clipping, FSE, Legajo 254, no. 4104; "Ocho millones de pesos Dejó de Recaudar el Fisco Americano por Alcoholes Procedentes de Cuba," *El País*, 28 August 1934, clipping, FSE, Legajo 254, no. 4104.

83. "Protestan los destiladores de alcoholes de la campaña que realize el Dr. Roberto Netto," 20 October 1934, clipping, FSE, Legajo 254, no. 4104.

84. See, e.g., Charles E. Hughes, Secretary of State, to Carlos Manuel de Céspedes, Minister of Cuba, Washington, D.C., 24 October 1921, FSE, Legajo 537, no. 12552; Subsecretario, Asuntos Consulares, to Carlos M. de Céspedes, Ministro de Cuba en Washington, Havana, 27 March 1922, FSE, Legajo 537, no. 12552; Isaac L. Smith, Inspector in Charge, U.S. Department of Labor, Immigration Service, to Florencio Guerra, Consulado de la República de Cuba, Miami, 18 November 1931, FSE, Legajo 418A, no. 8734; Pedro J. Cartaza, Comisionado de Inmigración, to Secretario de Estado, Havana, 11 February 1932, FSE, Legajo 418ª, no. 8374.

85. "Bribery in Bringing Chinese into U.S. Laid to Vice Consul," *Washington Post*, 30 May 1924, 2.

86. See, e.g., Noble Brandon Judah to Rafael Martínez Ortiz, Secretary of State, Havana, 1 April 1928, 18 April 1928, 28 April 1928, FSE, Legajo 257, no. 4249; C. B. Curtis to Rafael Martínez Ortiz, Secretary of State, Havana, 9 March 1929, FSE, Legajo 257, no. 4265; C. B. Curtis to Francisco María Hernández, Acting Secretary of State, Havana, 22 June 1929, FSE, Legajo 257, no. 4266; Alfonso L. Fors, Jefe de la Policía Nacional, to Secretario de Estado, Havana, 31 August 1929, FSE, Legajo 257, no. 4266; "Very Urgent: Embassy of the United States of America," Havana, 8 April 1930, FSE, Legajo 257, no. 4266.

87. F. T. F. Dumont, American Consul General, to Secretary of State, "Smuggling Activities in Cuba," 29 June 1933, RG59, 837.114Narcotics/64. See also Levine, *Tropical Diaspora*, 60.

88. S. R. Sarabasa, Encargado de Negocios, Legación de Cuba, to Dr. Juan J. Remos, Secretario de Estado, Port-au-Prince, 7 October 1938, FSE, Legajo 212, no. 2704; F. S. León Blanco, S.D., Supervisor de la Policía Nacional, Secretaría de Justicia, to Dr. Miguel Angel Campa, Subsecretario de Estado, Havana, 29 November 1938, FSE, Legajo 212, no. 2704.

89. Guerra y Sánchez, *Sugar and Society*, 27, 76, 144–45; Jesús Guanche, *Componentes*, 91–92; O'Brien, *Revolutionary Mission*, 212.

90. De la Fuente, *Nation for All*, 46–47, 100–102.

Chapter 2

1. Grant Watson to John Simon, Havana, 26 March 1934, 15 June 1934, *BDFA*, part 2, series D, 11:196, 301–2.

2. Suchlicki, *University Students*, 30–31.

3. Aguilar, *Cuba 1933*, 108–18, 125–26; Lazo, *Dagger*, 56.

4. Argote-Freyre, "Fulgencio Batista," 75.

5. See Marconi Braga, "To Relieve the Misery."

6. Pérez-Stable, *Cuban Revolution*, 40–41.

7. Ibid., 41; Portell-Vilá, *Nueva historia*, 408.

8. Caffery to Acting Secretary of State, Havana, 10 January 1934, 837.00/4591: Telegram, *FRUS, 1934*, 95.

9. Whitney, *State and Revolution*, 6.

10. Louis A. Pérez Jr., *Cuba and the United States*, 196–97. See also Argote-Freyre, "Fulgencio Batista," 146.

11. Phillips, *Cuba*, 100–101.

12. Fernández Miranda, *Mis Relaciones*, 44.

13. Caffery to Acting Secretary of State," Havana, 15 January 1934, 837.00/4619: Telegram, *FRUS, 1934*, 101; Caffery to Acting Secretary of State, Havana, 16 January 1934, 837.00/4622: Telegram, *FRUS, 1934*, 102; Caffery to Acting Secretary of State, Havana, 17 January 1934, 837.00/4626: Telegram, *FRUS, 1934*, 103; Matthews to Acting Secretary of State, Havana, 19 January 1934, 837.00/4662, *FRUS, 1934*, 105; Secretary of State to Caffery, Washington, D.C., 23 January 1934, 837.01/70: Telegram, *FRUS, 1934*, 107; Caffery to Secretary of State, Havana, 23 January 1934, 837.01/71: Telegram, *FRUS, 1934*, 107.

14. "Treaty of Relations between the United States of America and the Republic of Cuba, Signed at Washington, May 29th, 1934," *FRUS, 1934*, 183–84; Phillips, *Cuba*, 161.

15. Suchlicki, *University Students*, 42; Suárez Suárez, *Insurreccional*, 19–22, 25–29.

16. Argote-Freyre, "Fulgencio Batista," 301–4.

17. Phillips, *Cuba*, 161–63; Grant Watson to John Simon, Havana, 13 October 1934, *BDFA*, part 2, series D, 12:121.

18. Rees to John Simon, Havana, 6 July 1934, *BDFA*, part 2, series D, 12:32.

19. Ibid., 22 August 1934, 63.

20. Ibid., 64.

21. Ibid., 5 September 1934, 73.

22. Ibid.

23. Ibid., 74; Grant Watson to John Simon," Havana, 2 October 1934, *BDFA*, part 2, series D, 12:108–9.

24. Grant Watson to John Simon," Havana, 13 October 1934, *BDFA*, part 2, series D, 12:121.

25. Phillips, *Cuba*, 108.

26. Grant Watson to John Simon, Havana, 10 January 1935, *BDFA*, part 2, series D, 13:71.

27. Ibid., 21 February 1935, 133; Phillips, *Cuba*, 164.

28. Grant Watson to John Simon, Havana, 7 March 1935, 16 March 1935, 29 March 1935, *BDFA*, part 2, series D, 13:140, 155, 169–70; Phillips, *Cuba*, 165; Lazo, *Dagger*, 64; Portell-Vilá, *Nueva historia*, 442–44; Suchlicki, *University Students*, 44.

29. Grant Watson to John Simon, Havana, 8 May 1935, *BDFA*, part 2, series D, 13:220; Snow to Samuel Hoare, Havana, 5 July 1935, *BDFA*, part 2, series D, 13:274; Portell-Vilá, *Nueva historia*, 445; Suárez Suárez, *Insurreccional*, 36–37, 41–44; Suchlicki, *University Students*, 44; Argote-Freyre, "Fulgencio Batista," 329–33.

30. Grant Watson to John Simon, Havana, 8 November 1934, 23 September 1934, 24

October 1934, 13 December 1934, 10 April 1934, 25 April 1934, *BDFA*, part 2, series D, 12:150, 93–94, 126, 161, 11:225, 244.

31. "Inquieta saber cuál habrá sido el consumo de drogas en 1932, cuando el sobrante ha sido tan fabuloso," *El País*, 10 March 1933, clipping, RG59, JA837.14Narcotics/52.

32. "Treinta y Una Jefaturas de Sanidad, Dejaron de Informar Sobre el Consumo de Drogas," *El País*, 14 March 1933, clipping, RG59, JA837.14Narcotics/52.

33. Blohm, Report, Havana, 25 April 1933, RG59, 837.14Narcotics/60.

34. See "Alleged Smuggler Chief Held," *Washington Post*, 5 March 1930, 3.

35. F. T. F. Dumont, American Consul General, to Secretary of State, Havana, 8 April 1933, RG59, 837.14Narcotics/51.

36. García Álvarez, *Gran burguesía*, 86–87; Naranjo Orovio, *Cuba*, 100; Naranjo Orovio, *Del campo*, 73.

37. F. T. F. Dumont, American Consul General, to Secretary of State, "Smuggling Activities in Cuba," 29 June 1933, RG59, 837.114Narcotics/64.

38. Meyer and Parssinen, *Webs of Smoke*, 25–26, 121–22.

39. Gil Carballo, *Expendedores*, 19.

40. F. T. F. Dumont, American Consul General, to Secretary of State, "Smuggling Activities in Cuba," 29 June 1933, RG59, 837.14Narcotics/64.

41. See C. R. Cameron, American Consul General, to Secretary of State, "Movements of the Vessel OL-PAL, Suspected of Smuggling Narcotic Drugs into Cuba," Havana, 4 September 1934, RG59, 837.114Narcotics/73; C. R. Cameron, American Consul General, to Secretary of State, "Suspicious Operations of the American Vessel Adventuress," Havana, 4 December 1934, RG59, 837.114Narcotics/75; C. R. Cameron, American Consul General, to Secretary of State, "Movements of the American Vessel Adventuress," Havana, 10 December 1934, RG59, 837.114Narcotics/76; C. R. Cameron, American Consul General, to Secretary of State, "Movements of the American Vessel Adventuress," Havana, 20 December 1934, RG59, 837.14Narcotics/79.

42. Meyer and Parssinen, *Webs of Smoke*, 31–32, 130; Friman, *NarcoDiplomacy*, 26–31.

43. Meyer and Parssinen, *Webs of Smoke*, 131.

44. Claude A. Follmer, "Special Cuban Assignment SE-202," 21 July 1943, RG59, 837.14Narcotics/230, p. 69.

45. Guillermo de Blanck, Delegado Permanente, to R. Martínez Ortinez, Secretario de Estado, Geneva, 26 October 1928, FSE, Legajo 447, no. 9857.

46. Other Latin American countries likewise demonstrated no great concern over the matter of drug trafficking, which they did not view as a local problem, and they did not even bother to prepare in timely fashion the annual reports that existing agreements required (William O. Walker III, *Drug Control*, 46–47, 83).

47. Société des Nations, "Trafic de l'opium et autres drogues nuisibles: Rapports annuels des gouvernements pour 1935, Cuba," Geneva, 16 November 1936, RG59, 837.114Narcotics/121.

48. Société des Nations, "Trafic de l'opium et autres drogues nuisibles: Rapports annuels des gouvernements pour 1936, Cuba," Geneva, 7 October 1937, RG59, 837.114Narcotics/134; Société des Nations, "Trafic de l'opium et autres drogues nuisibles: Rap-

ports annuels des gouvernements pour 1937, Cuba," Geneva, 15 November 1938, RG59, 837.14Narcotics/157.

49. Quoted by Zenón Zamora, secretary of health and welfare, Havana, 5 May 1937, FSE, Legajo 545, no. 12781A.

50. See "Records of Leading Personalities in Cuba," *BDFA*, part 2, series D, 20:156.

51. Gerardo Fernández Abreu to Junta Nacional de Sanidad and Beneficencia, Havana, 8 December 1936, FSE, Legajo 545, no. 12781A.

52. Secretaría de Sanidad y Beneficencia, Memorandum, Havana, 8 November 1937, FME, Legajo 470, no. 7338; Miguel Angel Campa, Subsecretario de Estado, to Manuel Contales Latutú, Secretario de Sanidad y Beneficencia, Havana, 15 August 1938, FME, Legajo 470, no. 7338.

53. See related correspondence in FME, Legajo 470, no. 7339.

54. Enrique Giral Moreno, Jefe de la Oficina de Conexión con las Instituciones Internacionales, Ministerio de Estado, to Dr. Emilio Iglesias Cartaza, Médico Inspector Auxiliar de Estupefacientes, Ministerio de Salubridad, Havana, 9 August 1947, FME, Legajo 384, no. 6110.

55. Secretary-General, United Nations, to Rafael P. González Muñoz, Minister of State, New York, 8 July 1947, FME, Legajo 470, no. 7338.

56. Antonio E. de la Puente and Fernando I. Zayas to Junta Nacional de Sanidad y Beneficencia, Havana, 26 February 1937, FSE, Legajo 545, no. 12781A.

57. Barroso, "Toxicomanía," 16–17; Cardelle y Penichet, "Contribución," 16–17.

58. Sobrado López, *Vicio*, 50.

59. Cardelle y Penichet, "Contribución," 14–16.

60. Sobrado López, *Vicio*, 81–82; Fernández Robaina, *Historias*, 50, 100, 107, 36.

61. Cardelle y Penichet, "Contribución," 16.

62. Sobrado López, *Vicio*, 62–63. See also Arias Fernández, *Cuba*, 22–23.

63. Commission on Cuban Affairs, *Problems*, 30.

64. See, e.g., Sáenz Rovner, "Prehistoria: Serie documental," 84–85; Piccato, *City*, 199.

65. See FBN, *Traffic in Opium, 1929*, 15. See also Musto, *American Disease*, 219–23.

66. Himmelstein, *Strange Career*, 4, 58–71; Morgan, *Drugs*, 138–42; William O. Walker III, *Drug Control*, 99–107.

67. Barroso, "Toxicomanía," 14.

68. Quoted by Jonnes, *Hep-Cats*, 160.

69. Caballero, "Droga," 184.

70. Sobrado López, *Vicio*, 56, 60–61, 69.

71. Fernández Miranda, *Mis relaciones*, 85–86.

72. Lino Gato, "Origen," 204.

73. Immigrants from the Middle East often changed their first and last names from Arabic to Spanish. See Menéndez Paredes, *Componentes*, 31.

74. F. T. F. Dumont, American Consul General, to Secretary of State, "Smuggling of Aliens into the United States," Havana, 15 December 1933, RG59, 837.114Narcotics/65; "Muerto misteriosamente anoche, un individuo en la barriada del Vedado," *Diario de la Marina*, 9 December 1933, 12.

75. William C. Beers, Treasury Representative, to Commissioner of Customs, Havana, 4 January 1945, 1 May 1945, RG170-74-12, Box 22.

76. Alfonso L. Fors, Jefe de la Policía Judicial, to Sr. Fiscal de la Audiencia de La Habana, Havana, 15 May 1931, FME, Legajo 472, no. 7369; "$15,000 in Narcotics Seized aboard Ship," *Washington Post*, 8 October 1930, 10.

77. Fernández's criminal history has been reconstructed from Gil Carballo, *Expendedores*, 145–53; Claude A. Follmer, "Special Cuban Assignment SE-202," 21 July 1943, RG59, 837.14Narcotics/230, pp. 85–90; James Bennett, Memorandum, Havana, 16 April 1946, RG170-74-12, Box 22; Jose Sobrado to Jefe de la Policía Secreta, Havana, 5 May 1940, RG170-74-12, Box 22; "Traffic in Drugs between Cuba and North America" [translation], n.d., RG170-74-12, Box 22; "File Sensational Suit of Illegal Drug Traffic" [translation], *Prensa Libre*, 6 November 1943, RG170-74-12, Box 22; Wilson C. Beers, Treasury Representative, to Commissioner of Customs, Havana, 1 May 1945, RG170-74-12, Box 22; Joseph A. Fortier, Treasury Representative in Charge, to Commissioner of Customs, Division of Investigations and Patrol, Bureau of Customs, Havana, 17 February 1947, RG170-74-12, Box 22; Ernest M. Gentry, Narcotic Agent, to H. J. Anslinger, Miami, 15 June 1950, RG170-74-12, Box 22; Vicente Cubillas Jr., "Nueva York: Capital del vicio; cocaína y marihuana: Un relato de Salvador Cancio Peña ('Saviur')," *Bohemia*, 10 September 1950, 102.

Chapter 3

1. Courtwright, *Forces*, 33–36; Escohotado, *Historia*, 22, 147–52, 162; Jonnes, *Hep-Cats*, 27; Hanes and Sanello, *Opium Wars*; Meyer and Parssinen, *Webs of Smoke*, 10; William O. Walker III, *Opium*, 3–7.

2. Dikötter, Laamann, and Xun, *Narcotic Culture*, 4–7, 56–57.

3. Ibid., 65–66.

4. Berridge, *Opium*, 196–201.

5. Jay, *Emperors*, 83.

6. Acker, "From All Purpose Anodyne," 124–25.

7. Corbitt, *Study*, 23. Corbitt arrived at this total by consulting the Havana newspaper *Diario de la Marina*, which published daily figures for the number of individuals granted entry into the country. Chang, "Chinese," 15, similarly estimates that 125,00 Chinese arrived in Cuba during the period.

8. Moreno Fraginals, *Ingenio*, 261.

9. Moreno Fraginals, *Historia*, 120.

10. Zanetti and García, *Sugar and Railroads*, 121–23.

11. Chang, "Chinese," 12, 14, 16–17; Corbitt, *Study*, chapters 4, 5; Franklin W. Knight, *Slave Society*, 116, 119; Pérez de la Riva, "Viaje," 191–94; Moreno Fraginals, *Historia*, 132.

12. Franklin W. Knight, *Slave Society*, 15; Scott, *Slave Emancipation*, 29.

13. Corbitt, *Study*, 61, 69, 79, 81; Franklin W. Knight, *Slave Society*, 71, 117, 119; Scott, *Slave Emancipation*, 29, 32–33.

14. Louis A. Pérez Jr., *To Die in Cuba*, chapter 1.

15. Helg, *Lo que nos corresponde*, 48.

16. Quoted by Cabrera Déniz, *Canarios*, 32.

17. Crespo Villate, *Legación*, 9.

18. Hu-DeHart, "Coolies," 10–11, 20.

19. Corbitt, *Study*, 21–24. See also Jiménez Pastrana, *Chinos*, chapter 5.

20. Corbitt, *Study*, 87–90, 92–94.

21. Moreno Fraginals, *Ingenio*, 261; Corbitt, *Study*, 91.

22. Moreno Fraginals, *Historia*, 132.

23. Jesús Guanche, *Componentes*, 79.

24. Ibid., 77. Cristina García, *Monkey Hunting*, winds together all of these different strands of the Chinese immigrant experience in Cuba.

25. Musto, *American Disease*, 3–6, 294; Courtwright, *Violent Land*, 152–68; Courtwright, *Dark Paradise*, 62–66; Escohotado, *Historia*, 169; Jay, *Emperors*, 81; Jonnes, *Hep-Cats*, 27–30; Meyer and Parssinen, *Webs of Smoke*, 240; Sloan, *Our Violent Past*, chapter 7; Kwong and Miščević, *Chinese America*, chapter 7.

26. Quoted by Hill, "Anti-Oriental Agitation," 52.

27. See Kohn, *Dope Girls*, 18–19, 57–63.

28. Chang, "Chinese," 25; Corbitt, *Study*, chapter 8.

29. Chang, "Chinese," 70.

30. Ibid., 63, 65.

31. Ibid., 98, 132.

32. Fermor, "Havana Carnival," 153–54.

33. "Good-Sized Chinatown," *Who's Who among Visitors to Havana*, 6 March 1932, p. 9, PAWA, Box 64.

34. Phillips, *Cuba*, 23; de la Torriente Brau, *Testimonios y reportajes*, 184, 188; Román, *Así era Cuba*, 15; Coyula, *Habana*, 18, 28, 43, 91.

35. Moreno Fraginals, *Cuba/España*, 141–42.

36. Louis A. Pérez Jr., *Cuba under the Platt Amendment*, 62.

37. *Directorio Telefónico de la Habana, 1958*, 625.

38. Phillips, *Cuban Dilemma*, 97–98.

39. F. T. F. Dumont, American Consul General, to Secretary of State, "Smuggling Activities in Cuba," 29 June 1933, RG59, 837.114Narcotics/64.

40. "Report of Dr. Domingo F. Ramos, 1 June 1935, to the Secretary of Sanitary and Public Charity in Cuba, Submitting Data for Reply to a Questionnaire of the League of Nations," in William B. Murray, American Vice Consul, "Notes on Traffic in Narcotics," RG59, 837.114Narcotics/89.

41. Gil Carballo, *Expendedores*, 75, 46.

42. Sobrado López, *Vicio*, 37.

43. Schwartz, *Pleasure Island*, 89.

44. See "Actas, declaraciones etc. del sumario #598 de 1934 contra el asiático Armando Chirig SOA y otros por poseer en su casa un fumadero de opio en Camagüey," Índice del Fondo Juzgado de Instrucción del Partido Judicial de Camagüey, 1899–1954, Legajo 334, no. 4159, Archivo Histórico Provincial de Camagüey, Camagüey; "Incidente

de prisión del sumario #598 contra el Asiático Armando Chirig SOA y otro por poseer en su casa un fumadéro de Opio en Camagüey," Índice del Fondo Juzgado de Instrucción del Partido Judicial de Camagüey, 1899–1954, Legajo 334, no. 4160.

45. Sobrado López, *Vicio*, 39.

46. Vélez, *Geografía*, 56; Vélez, *Páginas*, 163.

47. "Pide Cuarentenas trasladen del Mariel a los narcómanos," *Diario de la Marina*, 4 October 1952, 23.

48. Rodríguez, Oficial Spdrio. Aux. Delegado Gob., to Secretario Gobernación, Guanajay, 8 September 1926, FSP, Legajo 69, no. 17.

49. Gil Carballo, *Expendedores*, 129–37, 141–43.

50. Ibid., 142.

51. Roberts, *Havana*, 229.

52. Moreno Fraginals, *Historia*, 144.

53. See "Expediente mecanografiado y manuscrito que contiene cartas, acuses de recibo, informes policíacos, decreto, recortes de periódicos, actas, etc.; en relación con la causa 1091 de 1926 seguido por el Juzgado Especial por el asesinato del asiático Andrés Chiu Lion y la complicidad de la Sociedad China Chi-Kong-Tong en el mismo. Fechada: Havana, Camagüey, Matanzas, Santiago de Cuba, 9 de abril hasta 13 de diciembre de 1926," FSP, Legajo 25, no. 52; Guillermo Villarronda, "Memorias de un Viejo Reportero Policíaco: El Asesinato de Andrés Chiu Lion," *Bohemia*, 1 May 1960, 46–47.

54. See, e.g., Secretario, Secretaría de Gobernación, to Sr. Teniente José Prado Sánchez, Delegado de la Secretaría de Gobernación de Santa Clara, Havana, 2 September 1926, FSP, Legajo 25, no. 20.

55. A. González Lanuaza, Capitán del Ejército Supervisor, to Secretario de Gobernación, Morón, 8 September 1926, FSP, Legajo 25, no. 25; Rogelio Zayas Bazán, Secretario de Gobernación, to Sr. Gobernador Provincial de Oriente, Havana, 16 September 1926, FSP, Legajo 25, no. 26; Luis Pérez Arocha, Delegado de Gobernación, to Subsecretario de Gobernación, Cienfuegos, 9 September 1926, FSP, Legajo 25, no. 27; Alcalde Municipal to Subsecretario de Gobernación, Cienfuegos, 14 September 1926, FSP, Legajo 25, no. 28; Alcalde Municipal to Secretario de Gobernación, Matanzas, 28 September 1926, FSP, Legajo 25, no. 29; Angel Mas, Capitán de la Guardia Rural, to Sr. Secretario de la Gobernación, Santiago de Cuba, 9 September 1926, FSP, Legajo 25, no. 31; "Antecedentes penales de la directiva de la Sociedad Chin Con Yun en Salud 14," Havana, n.d., FSP, Legajo 25, no. 33; Alcalde Municipal to Secretario de Gobernación, Ciego de Avila, 3 October 1926, FSP, Legajo 25, no. 46.

56. Antonio Madruga, Delegado de Gobernación, to Secretario de Gobernación, Cárdenas, 8 September 1926, FSP, Legajo 25, no. 34; Antonio Madruga, Delegado de Gobernación, to Secretario de Gobernación, Cárdenas, 25 August 1926, FSP, Legajo 25, no. 48.

57. See, e.g., "Expediente mecanografiado que contiene las investigaciones realizadas por la Policía Nacional, Judicial y Secreta, a fin de comprobar las actividades y antecedentes penales del asiático Loo Puec Ken. Fechada: La Habana, del 10 de febrero al 8 de marzo de 1927," FSP, Legajo 78, no. 58; Asunción Martínez to Presidente de la República, Havana, 30 June 1927, FSP, Legajo 25, no. 21.

58. Gustavo Chang Suy to Secretario de Gobernación, Havana, 1 September 1926, FSP, Legajo 25, no. 30.

59. Aguilar, *Cuba 1933*, 51.

60. Rogelio Zayas Bayán, Secretario de Gobernación, to Gustavo Chang Suy, Presidente de la Asociación de la Colonia China, Havana, 26 September 1926, FSP, Legajo 25, no. 30.

61. Subsecretario de Estado to Secretario de Estado, Havana, 30 December 1926, FSP, Legajo 108, no. 69.

62. Subsecretario to Secretario de la Presidencia, Havana, 12 January 1927, FSP, Legajo 108, no. 68.

63. Wu to Adee, Washington, D.C., 20 August 1902, no. 253, U.S. Department of State, *Papers, 1902*, 263–65; Minister Gonzales to Secretary of State, Havana, 12 April 1915, 837.55/27, U.S. Department of State, *Papers, 1915*, 271; Crespo Villate, *Legación*, 22.

64. Commission on Cuban Affairs, *Problems*, 35.

65. Barroso, "Toxicomanía," 15–16.

66. *El Comercio*, 30 July 1917, 2, quoted in Galván Tudela, *Canarios*, appendix 1, 151.

67. López Leiva, *Bandolerismo*, 33–34.

68. Gil Carballo, *Expendedores*, 164.

69. Ortiz, *Negros esclavos*, 12.

70. Astorga, *Drogas*, 23.

71. Ham Chande, "Migración," 170.

72. Recio, "Drugs and Alcohol," 34–35; Astorga, *Drogas*, 17; Cardiel Marín, "Migración," 216–17.

73. Recio, "Drugs and Alcohol," 38.

74. Ibid., 39.

75. H. S. Creighton, Supervising Customs Agent, to Commissioner of Customs, Houston, 11 December 1940, RG170-71A-3554, Box 22; W. J. Harmon, Supervising Customs Agent, to District Supervisor, Bureau of Narcotics, Houston, 23 February 1944, RG170-71A-3554, Box 22; Frederick H. Gardner, Supervising Customs Agent, to Commissioner of Customs, San Francisco, 15 February 1945, RG170-71A-3554, Box 22; Astorga, *Drogas*, 36.

76. George A. Morlock, Department of State, Memorandum of Conversation, "The Narcotics Situation in Mexico," Washington, D.C., 9 April 1943, RG170-71A-3554, Box 22; S. C. Peña, Special Employee, to Commissioner of Customs, Mexico, D.F., 21 December 1943, 27 September 1945, RG170-71A-3554, Box 22; S. C. Peña, Special Employee, Memorandum for the Treasury Representative in Charge, Mexico, D.F., 16 March 1945, RG170-71A-3554, Box 22.

77. "Estados Unidos Mexicanos, Gobierno del Territorio Norte de la Baja California, Inspección General de Policía, Estadística de la labor desarrollada por esta inspección contra el tráfico de enervantes y juegos prohibidos de acuerdo con el plan delineado por el C. Gral. De Div. Juan Felipe Rico Islas gobernador y comandante de la 2ª Zona militar del territorio," Tijuana, 31 March 1945, RG170-71A-3554, Box 22.

78. A. A. Berle Jr. to George S. Messersmith, Washington, D.C., 11 May 1943, RG170-71A-3554, Box 22; Manuel Tello to C. Jefe del Departamento de Salubridad Pública,

Mexico, D.F., 9 September 1943, RG170-71A-3554, Box 22; T. S. Simpson, Customs Agent, to Commissioner of Customs, El Paso, Texas, 3 June 1944, RG170-71A-3554, Box 22.

79. G. A. Morlock, Excerpts from the Annual Reports of the U.S. Government on the Traffic in Opium and Other Dangerous Drugs Regarding Mexico, n.d., RG170-71A-3554, Box 22.

80. Astorga, *Drogas*, 267; Young W. Chinn, Narcotic Agent, to Terry A. Talent, District Supervisor, El Paso, Texas, 16 September 1946, RG170-71A-3554, Box 22; Young W. Chinn, Narcotic Agent, to Terry A. Talent, District Supervisor, "Opium Situation in the Interior of Mexico," El Paso, Texas, 15 March 1947, RG170-71A-3554, Box 22; Young W. Chinn, Narcotic Agent, to Terry A. Talent, District Supervisor, "Opium Situation in Mexico," El Paso, Texas, 14 April 1947, RG170-71A-3554, Box 22.

81. D. J. DeLagrave, Treasury Representative in Charge, to Commissioner of Customs, Mexico, D.F., 27 December 1947, RG170-71A-3554, Box 22.

82. Recio, "Drugs and Alcohol," 38, 39.

83. Cardiel Marín, "Migración," 243.

84. Astorga, *Drogas*, 22–23.

85. Ibid., 164.

86. Ham Chande, "Migración," 185; Cardiel Marín, "Migración," 241.

87. Ham Chande, "Migración," 169, 173, 179; Cardiel Marín, "Migración," 230, 243–46, 249.

88. Sánchez-Albornoz, *Population*, 151.

89. Transcription, *El Comercio*, 22 January 1932, in Fred Morris Dearing to Secretary of State," Lima, 3 May 1933, RG170-71A-3554, Box 23.

90. "Ley no. 4428 of 26 November 1921," RG170-71A-3554, Box 23; Edwin McKee, American Vice Consul, "Constitution and Operation of Peruvian Government Opium Monopoly," Lima, 21 June 1933, RG170-71A-3554, Box 23.

91. Transcription, *El Comercio*, 22 January 1932, in Fred Morris Dearing to Secretary of State, Lima, 3 May 1933, RG170-71A-3554, Box 23; transcription, *La Noche*, 11 December 1936, in Fred Morris Dearing to the Secretary of State, Lima, 16 December 1936, RG170-71A-3554, Box 23.

92. Gootenberg, "Reluctance or Resistance," 53–54.

93. Laurence A. Steinhardt to Secretary of State," Lima, 18 March 1938, RG170-71A-3554, Box 23.

Chapter 4

1. Memorandum, 15 December 1942, RG170-0480-172 #4B; George A. Morlock, Department of State, Division of Far Eastern Affairs, to Scherer, 30 March 1943, RG59, 837.114Narcotics/223.

2. George A. Morlock, Department of State, Division of Far Eastern Affairs, to Scherer, 30 March 1943, RG59, 837.114Narcotics/223.

3. Braden to Secretary of State, Havana, 8 May 1950, RG59, 837.114Narcotics/222; Herbert E. Gaston, Assistant Secretary of the Treasury, to Secretary of State, Washington, D.C., 31 May 1943, RG59, 837.114Narcotics/225; Department of State, Memorandum of

Conversation, "Request of the American Embassy at Havana for the Sending of a Narcotics Agent to Cuba," 2 June 1943, RG59, 837.114Narcotics/226.

4. Charles H. Ducoté, Commercial Attaché, to Secretary of State, Havana, 12 June 1943, RG59, 837.114Narcotics/229; Ministerio de Estado, Registro de Confidenciales, Memorandum, Havana, 5 June 1943, RG59, 837.114Narcotics/229.

5. Russo, *Live*, 214.

6. Claude A. Follmer, "Special Cuban Assignment SE-202," 21 July 1943, RG59, 837.14Narcotics/230, p. 65 (translated from Spanish).

7. Ibid., 70 (translated from Spanish).

8. G. Ogilvie-Forbes to Eden, "Records of Leading Personalities in Cuba," Havana, 23 July 1941, *BDFA*, part 3, series D, 3:55; G. Ogilvie-Forbes to Eden, Havana, 5 February 1941, part 3, series D, 3:29.

9. Lazo, *Dagger*, 76.

10. Washington Chancery to the North American Department—Foreign Office, Washington, D.C., 30 December 1942, *BDFA*, part 3, series D, 6:133.

11. Foreign Office, Summary of Anglo-Cuban Relations, London, 29 April 1943, *BDFA*, part 3, series D, 6:372.

12. Spruille Braden to Secretary of State, Havana, 13 January 1944, RG59, 837.14Narcotics/237 (translated from Spanish).

13. Gellman, *Roosevelt and Batista*, 210.

14. Wilson C. Beers, Treasury Representative, to Commissioner of Customs, Division of Investigation and Patrol, Treasury Department, Havana, 18 January 1945, RG170-74-12, Box 22 (translated from Spanish).

15. Memorandum, [1944?], FC, Legajo 41, no. 1292; Wilson C. Beers, Treasury Representative, to Commissioner of Customs, Division of Investigation and Patrol, Treasury Department, Havana, 18 January 1945, RG170-74-12, Box 22. See also Lowinger and Fox, *Tropicana Nights*, 95.

16. Louis A. Pérez Jr., "Cuba, c. 1930–1959," 442.

17. Lino Lemes García, "El gobierno de Batista tiene que ponerle una fuerte barrera a los vicios, al contrabando y al clandestinaje commercial," Guantánamo, 8 November 1940, FSP, Legajo 44, no. 75; Lino Lemes García to Presidente de la República, Guantánamo, 23 November 1940, 11 June 1942, FSP, Legajo 44, no. 75.

18. Spruille Braden to José Agustín Martínez, Minister of State, Havana, 8 March 1943, FME, Legajo 262, no. 3453.

19. Angelo A. Zurlo, Narcotic Agent, "Suspected Smuggling of Narcotics from Cuba by Winthrop Gardiner," New York, 8 April 1948, RG170-74-12, Box 22.

20. Franklin W. Knight, *Slave Society*, 238. According to Leff, "Economic Development," 308, foreigners living in underdeveloped countries are often "persistent critics of corruption," perhaps because they become frustrated at obstacles in conducting business and other affairs or because of a sense of moral superiority that causes them to see corruption as both the cause and consequence of a backward state of development.

21. See, e.g., Whitney, *State and Revolution*, 17.

22. Benjamin, *United States and the Origins*, 104.

23. Louis A. Pérez Jr., *Cuba and the United States*, 205–6.

24. Montaner, *Cuba*, 27.

25. Lazo, *Dagger*, 81–82; Padula, "Fall," 14, 19, 25, 66–69; Thomas, *Cuba*, 737–40; Costa, *Imagen*, 303; Damián J. Fernández, *Cuba*, 52–53.

26. See, e.g., Galvis and Donadío, *Colombia Nazi*, chapter 7; Donadío, *Uñilargo*; Sáenz Rovner, *Ofensiva empresarial*, chapters 4, 7; Niblo, *Mexico*, chapter 5; Whitehead, "High-Level Political Corruption," 111–12; Bunge, *Perón*, chapter 7; Krauze, *Presidencia*, 124–26, 142–43; Levine, *Brazilian Legacies*, 89–90; Smallman, *Fear and Memory*, 71, 123–25.

27. Eduardo Palacios Planas to H. J. Anslinger, Havana, 4 August 1943, RG170-74-12, Box 22.

28. Ibid., 13 October 1943.

29. Société des Nations, "Trafic de l'opium et autres drogues nuisibles: Rapports annuels des gouvernements pour 1940, Cuba," Geneva, 24 November 1941, RG59, 837.114Narcotics/213; League of Nations, "Traffic in Opium and Other Dangerous Drugs: Annual Reports of Governments for 1941, Cuba," RG59, 837.114Narcotics/11-243.

30. *Records of the Conference*, 1:379.

31. Eduardo Palacios Planas, Comisionado de Drogas, to H. J. Anslinger, Havana, 1 September 1943, RG59, 837.14Narcotics/230.

32. Breckinridge Long, Department of State, to Spruille Braden, Washington, D.C., 13 December 1943, RG170-74-12, Box 22; Spruille Braden to Emeterio S. Santovenia, Ministro de Estado, Havana, 24 December 1943, RG59, 837.14Narcotics/237.

33. Spruille Braden to Secretary of State, Havana, 25 January 1944, RG59, 837.114Narcotics/238.

34. Charles H. Ducoté, Memorandum, Havana, 17 March 1944, RG59, 837.114Narcotics/244; Spruille Braden to Jorge Mañach, Minister of State, Havana, 17 March 1944, RG59, 837.114Narcotics/244; Charles H. Ducoté to Secretary of State, Havana, 22 March 1944, RG59, 837.114Narcotics/244; Spruille Braden to Secretary of State, Havana, 31 April 1944, RG59, 837.114Narcotics/245.

35. Charles H. Ducoté, "Discussion of Narcotics Situation with Dr. Alberto Recio, Minister of Health," Havana, 30 March 1944, RG59, 837.114Narcotics/247.

36. Ibid.; Charles H. Ducoté to Secretary of State, Havana, 3 April 1944, RG59, 837.114Narcotics/247; James Bennett, "Control of Narcotic Drugs," Havana, 21 November 1944, RG59, 837.114Narcotics/12-2044.

37. Eduardo Palacios Planas to H. J. Anslinger, Havana, 31 March 1944, RG59, 837.114Narcotics/248.

38. Charles H. Ducoté, "Proposed Decree Establishing the Office of Narcotics Control," Havana, 2 June 1944, RG59, 837.114Narcotics/262; Charles H. Ducoté to Secretary of State, Havana, 6 June 1944, RG59, 837.114Narcotics/262; James Bennett to Charles H. Ducoté, Havana, 20 July 1944, RG59, 837.114Narcotics/7-2644; Charles H. Ducoté to Secretary of State, Havana, 26 July 1944, RG59, 837.114Narcotics/7-2644; James Bennett to Charles H. Ducoté, Havana, 22 August 1944, RG170-74-12, Box 22; James Bennett to H. J. Anslinger, Havana, 15 December 1944, RG59, 837.114Narcotics/12-2044.

39. Reynaldo Geerken Saladrigas, Jefe de Despacho del Ministerio de Salubridad y Asistencia Social, to Sr. Subsecretario de Estado, Havana, 6 October 1947, FME, Legajo 384, no. 6110; James Bennett to H. J. Anslinger, Havana, 14 June 1945, RG59, 837.114Nar-

cotics/8-845; Department of State, Memorandum of Conversation, "Control of Narcotic Drugs in Cuba," Washington, D.C., 21 August 1945, RG59, 837.114Narcotics/8-2145.

40. James Bennett to H. J. Anslinger, Havana, 29 January 1946, RG59, 837.114Narcotics/1-3146; E. H. Foley Jr., Assistant Secretary of the Treasury, to Secretary of State, Washington, D.C., 2 May 1946, RG59, 837.114Narcotics/5-246; United Nations, "Annual Reports of Governments: Government of Cuba, Annual Report for 1946," p. 5, RG59, 837.114Narcotics/12-147.

41. Antonio Gil Carballo, "El tráfico de las drogas heroicas en Cuba," *Bohemia*, 8 October 1944.

42. Wilson C. Beers, Treasury Representative, to Commissioner of Customs, Division of Investigation and Patrol, Treasury Department, Havana, 4 January 1945, RG170-74-12, Box 22.

43. James Bennett to H. J. Anslinger, Havana, 3 January 1946, RG170-74-12, Box 22; James Bennett, Memorandum, Havana, 16 April 1946, RG170-74-12, Box 22.

44. James Bennett, Memorandum, Havana, 16 April 1946, RG170-74-12, Box 22.

45. José Sobrado López and Antonio García Betancourt, "Report on Services Rendered by Group Number Eight, Bureau of Narcotics, National Secret Police, during the Year 1946" [translation], RG170-74-12, Box 22.

46. United Nations, Economic and Social Council, "Annual Reports by Governments for 1945: Cuba," RG59, 837.114Narcotics/9-1047; United Nations, "Government of Cuba: Annual Report for 1946," RG59, 837.114Narcotics/12-247. See also FME, Legajo 383, no. 6102.

Chapter 5

1. M. Jay Racusin, "Luciano Legend of Service Laid to 2 Affidavits," *New York Herald Tribune*, 25 February 1947, clipping, RG170-71A-3555; George H. White, District Supervisor, to H. J. Anslinger, "Charles Luciano 'Lucky,'" 5 February 1951, NARG170-71A-3555; Eisenberg, Dan, and Landau, *Meyer Lansky*, chapters 24–27; Lacey, *Little Man*, chapter 7; Feder and Joesten, *Luciano Story*, chapters 7–9; Repetto, *American Mafia*, 175–76.

2. H. J. Anslinger to Garland H. Williams, Washington, D.C., 3 May 1946, RG170-71A-3555; H. J. Anslinger to J. W. Bulkley, 4 September 1946, RG170-71A-3555; George R. Davis to R. W. Artis, Los Angeles, 9 September 1946, RG170-71A-3555; Garland H. Williams to John C. Cross, 17 September 1946, RG170-71A-3555; Henry L. Manfredi to Irwin Greenfeld, 12 January 1947, RG170-71A-3555.

3. Joseph A. Fortier to Commissioner of Customs, Havana, 1 November 1946, RG170-71A-3555.

4. "Solicitud de venta de giros Que por conducto de First National Bank of Boston Ha presentado el Señor Salvatore Lucania Por valor de $4,000.00 = Cheques Viajeros, República de Cuba, Ministerio de Hacienda, Sección Especial de Investigaciones de la Oficina de Control de Cambios y Movimiento de Monedas Extranjeras," 18 January 1947, RG170-71A-3555; Feder and Joesten, *Luciano Story*, 230–31.

5. Repetto, *American Mafia*, 143.

6. Robert C. Ruark, "Shame Sinatra!," 20 February 1947, clipping, RG170-71A-3555;

"The Luciano Myth," *New York World Telegram*, 25 February 1947, clipping, RG170-71A-3555; Francis L. McCarthy, "Luciano Back at His Old Trade — in Havana," *Daily News*, 21 February 1947, clipping, RG170-71A-3555; Henry Hillman, "Café Society Beauty Seen with Luciano; Italy to Arrest Him," *Daily Mirror*, 26 February 1947, clipping, RG170-71A-3555.

7. J. Ray Olivera, Narcotic Agent, to Garland H. Williams, District Supervisor, Bureau of Narcotics, New York, 21 March 1947, RG170-71A-3555; Joseph H. Dillon, Treasury Representative, to Treasury Representative in Charge, 18 March 1947, RG170-71A-3555; Garland Williams, District Supervisor, Memorandum for File, New York, 31 March 1947, RG170-71A-3555; "AEROVIAS Q, S.A., 72 Cienfuegos St., Habana, Cuba," RG170-71A-3555; Scarpaci, Segre, and Coyula, *Havana*, 98; Jiménez, *Empresas*, 29; Valentine, *Strength*, 67.

8. District Supervisor, Bureau of Narcotics, District no. 2, to Yutronich et al., 2 May 1947, RG170-71A-3555.

9. Eisenberg, Dan, and Landau, *Meyer Lansky*, 234.

10. Levine, *Tropical Diaspora*, 172; Thomas, *Cuba*, 739.

11. Grau Alsina and Ridderhoff, *Mongo Grau*, 97. Regarding her activities in her role as First Lady, see, e.g., "Cocktail en honor de la Primera Dama de la República Sra. Paulina Alsina Vda. De Grau, que tendrá lugar en los salones del Lyceum Lawn Tennis, Calzada y 8 Vedado, el día 4 de enero de 1945, a las 6 P.M.," Fondo Grau, Legajo 25, no. 907, Archivo Nacional de Cuba, Havana; "Folleto y carta enviados a Paulina Alsina relacionados con su actividad social, Febrero 7 y mayo 15 de 1947," Fondo Grau, Legajo 25, no. 959.

12. See Dodds to Bevin, "Cuba Annual Report for 1947," Havana, 31 January 1948, *BDFA*, part 4, series D, 5:52.

13. Portell-Vilá, *Nueva historia*, 552.

14. Ameringer, *Cuban Democratic Experience*, 23.

15. Davis, *Mafia Dynasty*, 72, 122; Denton and Morris, *Money*, 55–56; Gosch and Hammer, *Last Testament*, 311–18; Turkus and Feder, *Murder*, 291; Eisenberg, Dan, and Landau, *Meyer Lansky*, 232–33. Sinatra had grown up in New Jersey in a socioeconomic milieu quite similar to that of many Italian American mafiosi, and Sinatra's father and maternal uncles had been involved in smuggling alcohol during Prohibition. The singer's relationship with Luciano and other members of the underworld in both New York and Miami went back a good many years (Summers and Swan, *Sinatra*, chapters 3, 5, 13).

16. Sondern, *Brotherhood*, 115.

17. Joseph A. Fortier to Commissioner of Customs, Havana, 11 February 1947, RG170-71A-3555.

18. Gosch and Hammer, *Last Testament*, 308.

19. T. J. Walker to Garland H. Williams, New York, 21 February 1947, RG170-71A-3555; "No mandará narcóticos E.U. a Cuba," *Diario de la Marina*, 22 February 1946; "Cancelará E.U. la suspensión de embarques de drogas para Cuba si se expulsa a Lucky," *Diario de la Marina*, 23 February 1946; H. W. Sharpe, "Habrá que expulsarlo," *El Mundo*, 23 February 1947; Anslinger, *Murderers*, 106.

20. "No hay fuerza legal alguna que prohiba a Cuba recibir su cuota normal de drogas," *Diario de la Marina*, 22 February 1947.

21. "Protesta enérgicamente el Dr. Nogueira por la suspensión del envío de drogras a Cuba," *Diario de la Marina*, 26 February 1947, 14.

22. "Enérgica protesta contra comisionado de drogas de EE.UU. en relación con 'Lucky,'" *Diario de la Marina*, 1 March 1947, 16.

23. J. Ray Olivera, Narcotic Agent, to Garland H. Williams, District Supervisor, Bureau of Narcotics, New York, 25 February 1947, 21 March 1947, RG170-71A-3555; Joseph H. Dillon, Treasury Representative, to Treasury Representative in Charge, 18 March 1947, RG170-71A-3555.

24. Claude A. Follmer, "Special Cuban Assignment SE-202," 21 July 1943, RG59, 837.14Narcotics/230, pp. 50–51. See also Nelli, *Business*, 236.

25. Astorga, *Drogas*, 218–27.

26. Memorandum of Conversation, "Luciano Narcotics Case, Department of State," Washington, D.C., 26 February 1947, RG59, 837.14 NARCOTICS/2-2647; "Aclaraciones del Dr. Belt," *Diario de la Marina*, 27 February 1947, 1.

27. "Firmado ya el decreto contra Lucky Luciano," *Diario de la Marina*, 28 February 1947, 2; Decreto no. 416, *Gaceta Oficial*, 28 February 1947, clipping, RG170-71A-3555.

28. "Hállase sujeto a expediente de expulsión Lucky Luciano, conocido gangster de los E.U.," *Diario de la Marina*, 23 February 1947, 4.

29. Howard, Commercial Attaché in Cuba, Memorandum, Havana, 21 October 1946, 837.796/10-2346, *FRUS, 1946*, 750–53; "Aerovías Q. under Way as Third Cuban Scheduled Airline," *International Aviation*, 27 December 1946, PAWA, Box 59; "Airlines in Cuba Form Trade Association," *International Aviation* 6, 25 July 1947, PAWA, Box 59. Regarding Cubana and Pan American, see Clark, *All the Best*, 8, 166.

30. Walker, Assistant Chief of the Division of Caribbean Affairs, Memorandum of Conversation, Washington, D.C., 5 March 1947, 800.8836/3-547, *FRUS, 1947*, 606–8; Walker, Assistant Chief of the Division of Caribbean Affairs, Memorandum of Conversation, Washington, D.C., 29 May 1947, 837.61351/5-2947, *FRUS, 1947*, 613–14; Secretary of State to Harry S. Truman, Washington, D.C., 26 June 1947, 837.61351/6-2647, *FRUS, 1947*, 616–17; Duncan A. Mackay, Division of Caribbean Affairs, Memorandum of Conversation, Washington, D.C., 1 July 1947, 837.61351/7-1147, *FRUS, 1947*, 617–19; Secretary of State to Embassy in Cuba, Washington, D.C., 8 August 1947, 837.61351/8-847, *FRUS, 1947*, 622; Armour, Assistant Secretary of State, Memorandum of Conversation, Washington, D.C., 8 August 1947, 837.61351/7-847, *FRUS, 1947*, 622–24.

31. Department of State, Memorandum, Washington, D.C., 29 July 1948, 71.37/8-548, *FRUS, 1948*, 562–63.

32. "Foils Plot in Role of Capone," *New York Journal-American*, 24 February 1947, clipping, RG170-71A-3555; "Promete Lucky dejar a Cuba e irse a Italia," *Diario de la Marina*, 25 February 1947, 1; Francis L. McCarthy, "Vivo decentemente y estoy muy viejo para andar con juegos, declara Ch. Lucky," *Diario de la Marina*, 25 February 1947, 14.

33. J. Ray Olivera, Narcotic Agent, to Garland H. Williams, District Supervisor, Bureau of Narcotics, New York, 25 February 1947, RG170-71A-3555.

34. Francis L. McCarthy, "Italy Waiting to Grab Luciano as He Docks," *Daily News*, 26 February 1947, clipping, RG170-71A-3555.

35. J. Ray Olivera, Narcotic Agent, to Garland H. Williams, District Supervisor, Bu-

reau of Narcotics, New York, 21 March 1947, RG170-71A-3555; Oscar Loinaz, Capitán Inspector, to Mayor General Pablo Mendieta, Havana, 15 April 1926, FSP, Legajo 25, no. 23; Pablo Mendieta, Jefe de Policía, Policía Nacional, to Sr. Secretario de Gobernación, Havana, 27 April 1926, FSP, Legajo 25, no. 23. On the opposite flank, Senator Eduardo "Eddy" Chibás, who was known for his campaigns against corruption and had distanced himself from President Grau, maintained that the government was reluctant to deport Luciano for fear that he would reveal the names of his "Cuban associates," including Francisco Prío Socarrás. This accusation led Chibás and Prío Socarrás to come to blows in the Congress. The Cuban Senate urged that "in the interests of this body," the two men "settle their grievances in a duel." The two men faced off with swords in the capitol building's Hall of Arms, with both sustaining superficial sword wounds (Conte Agüero, *Eduardo Chibás*, 490–94; Ameringer, *Cuban Democratic Experience*, 40; Thomas, *Cuba*, 751; Alavez Martín, *Ortodoxia*, 80).

36. T. J. Walker, Narcotic Inspector, to Garland H. Williams, District Supervisor, New York, 27 February 1947, RG170-71A-3555.

37. "Colombia no lo admitirá," *El Mundo*, 23 February 1947.

38. "8 Americans Eyed by Cuba in Lucky Probe," *Daily News*, 27 February 1947, clipping, RG170-71A-3555.

39. "Esperan hoy al Bakir, donde será reembarcado para Génova, Italia, Charles Lucky Luciano," *Diario de la Marina*, 13 March 1947, 19; "Embarcan hoy hacia Italia a Lucky Luciano," *Diario de la Marina*, 19 March 1947, 1; "Fue embarcado por la noche Lucky Luciano," *Diario de la Marina*, 20 March 1947, 1. Ironically, the *Bakir* had docked in Jersey City a few weeks earlier and was found to have carried six kilos of opium from Istanbul (FBN, *Traffic in Opium, 1947*, 17).

40. "Lucky piensa volver a los Estados Unidos," *Diario de la Marina*, 21 March 1947, 1.

41. *Avance*, 19 March 1947, clipping, RG170-71A-3555 (translation); "Declaraciones de Herrera en torno a Lucky," *Diario de la Marina*, 21 March 1947, 16.

42. Cirules, *Imperio*, 96, has written that Luciano's departure from Cuba resulted not from "pressures and demands from Washington" but from "the internal differences that existed between mafia families brought on by jealousies and struggles for power." However, this conclusion flies in the face of the evidence.

43. Lester L. Schnare, American Consul General, to Secretary of State, Genoa, 15 April 1947, RG170-71A-3555; Gosch and Hammer, *Last Testament*, 327.

44. "Luciano in Sicilian Jail," *New York Times*, 3 May 1947, clipping, RG170-71A-3555.

45. "Luciano Released from Palermo Jail," *New York Times*, 15 May 1947, clipping, RG170-71A-3555.

46. A. Pagani, Il Questore, to Consulate General of the United States, Naples, 24 August 1947, RG170-71A-3555; Feder and Joesten, *Luciano Story*, 249.

47. Feder and Joesten, *Luciano Story*, 252; Davis, *Mafia Dynasty*, 124; Lacey, *Little Man*, 174.

48. George H. White, District Supervisor, to H. J. Anslinger, "Charles Luciano 'Lucky,'" 5 February 1951, RG170-71A-3555; Vizzini, Fraley, and Smith, *Vizzini*, 48, 156, 218–19.

49. U.S. Congress, Senate, *Investigation*, part 14, 345–56.

50. Terry S. Rizza, Special Investigator, Alcohol Tax Unit, to Garland H. Williams, Bureau of Narcotics, 14 May 1948, RG170-71A-3555; Charles Siragusa, Narcotic Agent, to H. J. Anslinger, Trieste, 10 February 1951, RG170-71A-3555; Charles Siragusa, U.S. Narcotic Agent, to H. J. Anslinger, Milan, 19 April 1951, RG170-71A-3555; Joseph Amato to Charles Siragusa, Naples, 7 May 1951, RG170-71A-3555. See also Siragusa, *Trail*, 83; Anslinger, *Murderers*, 106–7; Feder and Joesten, *Luciano Story*, chapter 12; Jonnes, *Hep-Cats*, 151–52; Streatfeild, *Cocaine*, 181, 195.

51. Joseph Amato to Charles Siragusa, Frankfurt, 15 February 1951, RG170-94-004, Box 24; Hudson to Secretary of State, Milan, 12 April 1950, RG170-94-004, Box 24.

52. Charles Siragusa, Narcotic Agent, to H. J. Anslinger, Progress Report no. 13, Hamburg, 9 March 1951, RG170-94-004, Box 24.

53. Charles Siragusa, Narcotic Agent, to H. J. Anslinger, Progress Report no. 17, Hamburg, 17 March 1951, RG170-94-004, Box 24.

54. Charles Siragusa, Narcotic Agent, to H. J. Anslinger, Progress Report no. 21, Hamburg, 28 March 1951, RG170, 94-004, Box 24; Hudson to Secretary of State, Milan, 12 April 1951, RG170-94-004, Box 24; "History of the Hamburg, Germany, Cocaine Case involving Dr. Walter Buchler, et al., made by Nar. Agt. Joseph Amato, March–April 1951," RG170-94-004, Box 24.

55. Feder and Joesten, *Luciano Story*, 259; Davis, *Mafia Dynasty*, 121; Joseph Amato, Narcotic Agent, Memorandum for File, Munich, 1 April 1951, RG170-71A-3555.

56. William W. Johnston, Treasury Representative in Charge, to Commissioner of Customs, Havana, 8 February 1958, RG170-74-12, Box 22.

57. Anslinger, *Murderers*, 107.

58. Ibid., 108.

59. U.S. Congress, Senate, *Investigation*, part 14, 345–46; Kefauver, *Crime*, 29.

60. "Luciano Dies at 65; Was Facing Arrest," *New York Times*, 27 January 1962, 1, 45; "Racket Boss Luciano Falls Dead in Italy," *Washington Post*, 27 January 1962, A1, A3; Gosch and Hammer, *Last Testament*, 380, 445–50; Marino, *Padrinos*, 256–57.

61. Quoted by Escohotado, *Historia*, 372 n. 16 (translated from Spanish).

62. Messick, *Of Grass*, 13.

63. Nelli, *Business*, 106; Jonnes, *Hep-Cats*, 142, 144.

64. Frattini, *Mafia*, 102.

65. Meyer and Parssinen, *Webs of Smoke*, 285–86.

66. Davenport-Hines, *Búsqueda*, 333–35.

67. Jonnes, *Hep-Cats*, 160–61. My research bears out these findings. Numerous documents contained in U.S. federal archives — including the final, sober-minded reports made by FBN agents stationed in Italy, hundreds of photographs documenting the private and public life of Luciano in Naples, and a series of personal letters written to him that the agents intercepted — provide no evidence that proves any of the connections claimed by Anslinger. By September 1951, Anslinger had gained approval from both the U.S. Department of State and the Italian government to open a permanent FBN office in Rome. For more on this point, see Nadelmann, *Internationalization*, 131.

68. Quoted by Sondern, *Brotherhood*, 114.

Chapter 6

1. United Nations, "Annual Report for 1948, Communicated by the Government of Cuba," RG59, 837.114Narcotics/10-1549; United Nations, "Annual Report for 1949, Communicated by the Government of Cuba," RG59, 837.53/10–50.

2. Manuel Riaño Jauma, Jefe de Despacho del Ministerio, Ministerio de Salubridad y Asistencia Social, to Subsecretario de Estado, Havana, 16 June 1949, FME, Legajo 383, no. 6102.

3. Bernardo Gómez Toro, Jefe Superior Médico, Sección Estupefacientes, Ministerio de Salubridad y Asistencia Social, to Señor Director de Salubridad, Havana, 5 May 1950, FME, Legajo 383, no. 6102.

4. James C. Ryan, Report, Havana, August 1949, RG170-74-12, Box 22.

5. United Nations, "Annual Report for 1950, Communicated by the Government of Cuba," RG59, 837.53/7-1651. See also FME, Legajo 383, no. 6102.

6. See "Bernardo Gómez Toro, Jefe Superior Médico, Secc. Estupefacientes, Ministerio de Salubridad y Asistencia Social, "Informe al Comité Central Permanente del Opio con relación a datos adicionales sobre tráfico ilícito de narcóticos conforme al cuestionario remitido conteniendo las siguientes preguntas que aparecen en forma de informes anuales," Havana, 5 March 1952, FME, Legajo 383, no. 6103; Bernardo Gómez Toro, Jefe Superior Médico, Secc. Estupefacientes, Ministerio de Salubridad y Asistencia Social, to Sr. Director de Salubridad, Havana, 8 March 1952, FME, Legajo 383, no. 6103; United Nations, "Cuba, Annual Report for 1951," E/NR 1951/76, 25 September 1952, FME, Legajo 377, no. 6023.

7. "Proyecto de resolución propuesto por el representante de los Estados Unidos de América en la Comisión de Narcóticos. Tráfico ilícito de narcóticos por las tripulaciones de los barcos mercantes," n.d., FME, Legajo 384, no. 6112.

8. Raúl Ruiz Hernández, Subsecretario de Estado, to Byron Price, Secretario General de las Naciones Unidas, Havana, 4 October 1951, FME, Legajo 384, no. 6112.

9. Eduardo Chibás, Report, 4 February 1950, reproduced as "Enjuicia Chibás Discurso de Prío," *El Mundo*, 5 February 1950, FC, Legajo 8, no. 220.

10. Quoted by Conte Agüero, *Eduardo Chibás*, 682–83.

11. See Alicia Toscano vda. De Wilmot, "Documento Privado," Las Pozas, 26 April 1949, FC, Legajo 9, no. 270; Alicia Consuelo Toscano Sauvalle vda. De Wilmot to Carlos Prío Socarrás, Presidente de la República, Las Pozas, 8 June 1950, FC, Legajo 9, no. 270; Néstor G. Mendoza, Bufete de Mendoza, to Alicia Toscano vda. De Wilmot, Havana, 28 May 1951, FC, Legajo 9, no. 270.

12. Chibás, "Último aldabonazo," 18.

13. On these points, see Vignier and Alonso, *Corrupción*, 189.

14. Szulc, *Fidel*, 204–5. After Prío was exiled to Miami, he contributed healthy amounts of money to help Castro in his anti-Batista guerrilla war, even providing funds for the purchase of the *Granma*, the yacht on which Castro and his band of revolutionaries sailed from Mexico to Cuba in December 1956 (Szulc, *Fidel*, 366–67; Casuso, *Cuba*, 12).

15. Department of State Policy Statement, Washington, D.C., 1 January 1951, 61.37/1-1151, *FRUS, 1950*, 845.

16. Dodds to Bevin, "Presidential Elections in Cuba, Nomination of Candidates," Havana, 16 March 1948, *BDFA*, part 4, series D, 5:59.

17. Holman to Bevin, "Leading Personalities in Cuba," Havana, 14 September 1949, *BDFA*, part 4, series D, 7:109. Martínez-Fernández, "Prío Socarrás," 182, contends that "it was estimated that Prío illegally appropriated $90 million."

18. Skierka, *Fidel Castro*, 21.

19. Ameringer, *Cuban Democratic Experience*, 90.

20. Ameringer, *Caribbean Legion*, 83, 128; Ameringer, *Cuban Democratic Experience*, 92–93.

21. Phillips, *Cuba*, 248, 253.

22. Mario Kuchilán, "Babel," *Prensa Libre*, 30 January 1952, clipping, Fondo Donativos y Remisiones, Archivo Nacional de Cuba, Havana, Legajo 615, no. 75.

23. Salvador Díaz-Versón Rodríguez, Capitán S.M.E., D. en S., en el S.I.M., Confidencial, Ciudad Militar, 8 February 1952, Fondo Donativos y Remisiones, Archivo Nacional de Cuba, Havana, Legajo 615, no. 75.

24. Thomas, *Cuba*, 778.

25. Aguilar-León, "'Década trágica,'" 73; Portell-Vilá, *Nueva historia*, 624–25; Fernández Miranda, *Mis relaciones*, 121; Coltman, *Real Fidel*, 60.

26. García-Pérez, *Insurrection and Revolution*, 2, 6, 8–9.

27. "Editorial Note," *FRUS, 1952–54*, 868; Beaulac, Ambassador in Cuba, Memorandum of Conversation, Havana, 22 March 1952, 737.02/3-2452, *FRUS, 1952–54*, 868–70; Secretary of State to President, Washington, D.C., 24 March 1952, 611.37/3-2452, *FRUS, 1952–54*, 871–72. The U.S. ambassador to Cuba was rarely on the island, perhaps contributing to American officials' surprise at the coup (López-Fresquet, *My Fourteen Months*, 31; Portell-Vilá, *Nueva historia*, 670).

28. Portell-Vilá, *Nueva historia*, 631; Coltman, *Real Fidel*, 64.

29. Curti, "Habana," 131. Despite a lack of evidence to support such claims, various authors have argued that the 1952 coup was carried out "with the connivance of the Yankee embassy" (Vignier and Alonso, *Corrupción*, 28), "had the well-deserved and obligatory blessing" of the U.S. government (Calvo Ospina, *Ron Bacardí*, 30), and "was one of so many imperialist crimes" (Rousseau González, *Sociedad*, 125). According to Ibarra Guitart, *Sociedad*, 16, "Batista carried out the coup, positive that there would be little delay in obtaining recognition by the United States." Similarly, Le Riverend has written that "with American knowledge and consent, Batista . . . decided to stage a military coup on 10 March 1952" (*Habana*, 233), while Clerc has declared that the U.S. government was "delighted" by the coup ("Democracia," 89). The list of scholars who argue the thesis of American patronage and involvement is not easily exhausted. Arboleya has stressed that "whatever might have been [the U.S. government's] participation in the Batista-led coup, it turned out to be a development that was well received by the American power structure, since it was in line with the assertion of a hegemonic will that was needed to maintain stability on the continent, a stability that was understood

to begin with the maintenance of strict control over Latin American governmental institutions" (*Contrarevolución*, 32). Cantón Navarro has stated that Batista "had American approval" and "played his role like Washington's compliant agent" (*Historia*, 148). Rodríguez Mesa, an economist, has further argued that through the coup, "the U.S. government wiped out what democracy and freedom had been able to yield in Cuba under the capitalist system. . . . The Batista regime was imperialism's political response to the crisis of the Cuban economy" (*Proceso*, 125). Cirules has contended that not only did Washington support the coup but also that "those who organized and directed the operation . . . were the same elements who shaped the thinking behind American domination: financiers — the mafia-special services," concluding that "the installation of a military dictatorship [was] promoted from Washington" (*Imperio*, 138; see also Cirules, *Vida*, 8, 14–15). Finally, Pino Santos has argued that the coup resulted from an alliance among American financial interests, the Central Intelligence Agency, and the State Department "to impose on Cuba the government that was needed for the defense of their interests." Although Pino Santos describes his explanation as only "a working hypothesis," he also points out "the remarkable and logical convergence of events, which other facts help confirm" (*Asalto*, 122–23).

30. Beaulac, Ambassador in Cuba, to Miller, Assistant Secretary of State for Inter-American Affairs, Havana, 2 June 1952, Miller Files, lot 53 D 26, "Cuba-1952," *FRUS, 1952–54*, 873–74.

31. Miller, Assistant Secretary of State for Inter-American Affairs, to Beaulac, Ambassador in Cuba, Washington, D.C., 10 June 1952, Miller Files, lot 53 D 26, "Cuba-1952," *FRUS, 1952–54*, 875.

32. W. F. Kelly, Assistant Commissioner, Enforcement Division, Immigration and Naturalization Service, to Commissioner of Narcotics, Washington, D.C., 2 April 1952, RG170-74-12, Box 22; Joseph H. Dillon, Acting Treasury Representative in Charge, to Commissioner of Customs, Bureau of Customs, Havana, 30 June 1952, RG170-74-12, Box 22.

33. K. C. Rudd, Narcotic Agent, to T. W. McGreever, District Supervisor, Miami, 30 July 1952, RG170-74-12, Box 22.

34. J. Ray Olivera, Narcotic Agent, Report, New York, 27 February 1953, RG170-74-12, Box 22.

35. "The Blanca Ibáñez de Sánchez Gang of International Illicit Cocaine Traffickers," Washington, D.C., 26 November 1962, RG170-74-12, Box 10.

36. J. Edgar Hoover to John W. Ford, Washington, D.C., 30 January 1953, RG170-74-12, Box 22.

37. John T. Cusack, District Supervisor, to H. J. Anslinger, 12 January 1959, RG170-71A-3555, Box 8. U.S. historian Alfred L. Padula interviewed nearly one hundred Cuban exiles at the beginning of the 1970s and heard many accusations that Carlos Prío was a cocaine addict ("Fall," 51 n. 48).

Chapter 7

1. Kefauver, *Crime*, 15, 22; Anderson and Blumenthal, *Kefauver Story*, chapters 16–17; Gorman, *Kefauver*, 74–78, 86, 92; Halberstam, *Fifties*, 191–92; Repetto, *American Mafia*, 254–55.

2. Denton and Morris, *Money*, 82; Jonnes, *Hep-Cats*, 162. See also "Witnesses (anonymous)," in U.S. Congress, Senate, *Investigation*, part 14.

3. Kefauver, *Crime*, 22.

4. Lacey, *Little Man*, 243; Kefauver, *Crime*, 247–52.

5. Russo, *Outfit*, 112–15, 117, 187–89, 249.

6. Lacey, *Little Man*, 200.

7. Rogers, "Fortune and Misfortune," 290; Rogers, "Great Depression," 305.

8. Kefauver, *Crime*, 82–87.

9. Lacey, *Little Man*, 208–12.

10. Gorman, *Kefauver*, 79; Halberstam, *Fifties*, 190; Repetto, *American Mafia*, 255–56.

11. Denton and Morris, *Money*, 121–26.

12. Bergreen, *Capone*.

13. Bell, *End*, chapter 7.

14. Russo, *Outfit*, 254, 267.

15. Levine, *Tropical Diaspora*, 203; Louis A. Pérez Jr., *On Becoming Cuban*, 196; Russo, *Outfit*, 275–76.

16. "Memorandum, Jack Lansky," 2 May 1959, RG170-71A-3555, Box 8.

17. K. C. Rudd, Narcotic Agent, "Report of Criminal Activities of Santo Trafficante Jr. at Tampa and St. Petersburg, Fla.," 29 May 1959, RG170-71A-3555, Box 8.

18. Quoted by Roig de Leuchsenring, *Males*, 205–6.

19. Saco, *Vagancia*, 30.

20. See Moreno Fraginals, *Cuba/España*, 180.

21. Ortiz, *Negros curros*, 210, 211.

22. Luis, *Culture and Customs*, 102.

23. Louis A. Pérez Jr., *Slaves, Sugar, and Colonial Society*, 16, 38, 53, 135, 139, 147, 152, 222, 225–26. See also Ely, *Cuando reinaba*, 767–73.

24. *El Comercio*, 25 March 1893, quoted by Díaz Martínez, "Sociedad, violencia, y criminalidad," 64.

25. *El Pueblo*, 26 May 1921, quoted by Reynaldo González, *Fiesta*, 204–5.

26. Mormino and Pozzeta, *Immigrant World*, 281–86; Ragano and Raab, *Mob Lawyer*, 1, 16; Deitche, *Cigar City Mafia*, 19; Kefauver, *Crime*, 95.

27. Ogle, *Key West*, 217.

28. Ortiz, *Negros esclavos*, 12. See also Fernández Robaina, *Historias*, 20.

29. Shelton, *Cuba*, 82. Relations between China and Cuba were temporarily tainted during the first decade of the twentieth century when an illegal gambling establishment owned by Cubans was uncovered in Shanghai (Crespo Villate, *Legación*, 71–74).

30. Schwartz, *Pleasure Island*, 25–27.

31. Beals, *Crime*, 224; Schwartz, *Pleasure Island*, 16–17, 30–34; Suchlicki, *Historical Dictionary*, 125.

32. Quoted by Lowinger and Fox, *Tropicana Nights*, 33–34.

33. Beals, *Crime*, 84, 90.

34. Commission on Cuban Affairs, *Problems*, 73, 364.

35. Hermer and May, *Havana Mañana*, 60; Clark, *All The Best*, 145–46.

36. O'Brien, *Revolutionary Mission*, 209.

37. Meyer Berger, "Gambling Control Is Varied Greatly," *New York Times*, 5 December 1951, 42; Phillips, *Cuba*, 137; Phillips, *Cuban Dilemma*, 53–54; Thomas, *Cuba*, 738.

38. Hermer and May, *Havana Mañana*, 65–66, 143–45.

39. Ibid., 76; de Castroverde, *Que la patria*, 65–66; González Echevarría, *Pride*, 62, 99, 156, 187, 195, 275.

40. Phillips, *Cuba*, 183.

41. Grant Watson to Viscount Halifax, Havana, 19 July 1938, *BDFA*, part 2, series D, 19:189.

42. Ibid., 20 July 1939, 20:142.

43. Portell-Vilá, *Nueva historia*, 602.

44. Stoner, *From the House*, 130.

45. Lyceum y Lawn Tennis Club, *Memoria 1949–1951*, Collection 0124, Lyceum and Lawn Tennis Club, La Havana, Cuban Heritage Collection, University of Miami, Miami, Fla., Box 5; Rodríguez-Luis, *Memoria*, 118.

46. "Exhortan Instituciones a Combatir el Juego en La Habana," *El Mundo*, 12 October 1956, 1A, 8A.

47. Quoted by Alavez Martín, *Ortodoxia*, 72.

48. De Arce, *Vagancia*, 41.

49. Juan de Dios Pérez, *Juego*, 28.

50. Emma Pérez, "Arrecia en los Estados Unidos la campaña de descrédito contra Cuba," *Bohemia*, 13 January 1957, 70–72.

51. International Bank for Reconstruction and Development, *Report*, 58.

52. Roig de Leuchsenring, *Males*, 203–5.

53. Frank, *Cuba*, appendix 3.

54. Jorrín, "Espíritu Burlón," 78.

55. Eisenberg, Dan, and Landau, *Meyer Lansky*, 152, 173; Lacey, *Little Man*, 108–9.

56. Batista, *Piedras*, 267–68; Mesa-Lago, *Economy*, 8; Paterson, *Contesting Castro*, 52.

57. Eduardo Chibás, "La piedra angular de nuestro turismo: Proyecto leído por su autor en la sesión rotaria del día 6 de noviembre de 1939," FC, Legajo 41, no. 1315.

58. Beaulac, Ambassador in Cuba, to Department of State, Havana, 14 July 1953, 737.5MSP/7-1453, *FRUS, 1952–54*, 893. See also Zanetti, *Cautivos*, 154–55.

59. Pérez-Stable, *Cuban Revolution*, 16; Comisión Económica, *Economía cubana*, 65–66.

60. Charles Schwartzman to State Department, Cincinnati, 8 January 1953, RG59, 837.45/1-853; Hyman Goldberg, Counselor at Law, to U.S. Embassy, New York, 9 March 1953, RG59, 837.45/3-1753; M. B. Hirsch to Willard L. Beaulac, U.S. Ambassador to Cuba, Cincinnati, 22 April 1953, RG59, 837.45/5-653; Charles W. Tobey, Committee on Interstate and Foreign Commerce, to John Foster Dulles, Secretary of State, 27 May 1953, RG59, 837.45/5-2753; "A Game of Casino," *Time*, 20 January 1958, 32.

61. Eduardo Chibás, "La piedra angular de nuestro turismo: Proyecto leído por su autor en la sesión rotaria del día 6 de noviembre de 1939," FC, Legajo 41, no. 1315.

62. Paul J. Reveley, American Consul General, to Department of State, "Illegal Gambling Enterprises in Cuba," Havana, 21 April 1953, RG59, 837.45/4-2153; "Suckers in Paradise," *Saturday Evening Post*, 28 March 1953, 32–33, 181–83.

63. Paul J. Reveley, Memorandum for Files, Havana, 14 April 1953, RG59, 837.45/4-2153; Scott McLeod, Administrator, Bureau of Security and Consular Affairs, to Senator Charles W. Tobey, Chairman, Committee on Interstate and Foreign Commerce, 9 June 1953, RG59, 837.45/5-2753.

64. Lacey, *Little Man*, 227–28; Paterson, *Contesting Castro*, 55.

65. "A Game of Casino," *Time*, 20 January 1958, 32; "Mobsters Move in on Troubled Havana and Split Rich Gambling Profits with Batista," *Life*, 10 March 1958, 35; Lacey, *Little Man*, 231.

66. Pérez-Stable, *Cuban Revolution*, 22.

67. Lacey, *Little Man*, 231, 235.

68. *Havana Post*, 19 January 1956, 3; "Casinos Gambling on Big Tourist Payoff," *Havana Post*, 19 January 1956, 1.

69. Paterson, *Contesting Castro*, 54–56; Ragano and Raab, *Mob Lawyer*, 41; Munn, *Hollywood Connection*, 231, 240–41; Cirules, *Vida*, 124–25.

70. Cirules, *Vida*, 164.

71. Louis A. Pérez Jr., *On Becoming Cuban*, 196.

72. Albert G. Vaughan to Regional Commissioner — Richmond," Havana, 5 February 1958, 19 March 1958, RG170.

73. *Havana Post*, 19 January 1956, 3; "Casinos Gambling on Big Tourist Payoff," *Havana Post*, 19 January 1956, 1.

74. Lowinger and Fox, *Tropicana Nights*, 254.

75. Lacey, *Little Man*, 236.

76. Dubois, *Fidel Castro*, 9; "Mobsters Move in on Troubled Havana and Split Rich Gambling Profits with Batista," *Life*, 10 March 1958, 34.

77. Quoted by Cirules, *Vida*, 148.

78. Le Riverend, *Historia*, 646–47.

79. Banco de Fomento Agrícola e Industrial de Cuba, *Memoria, 1951–1952*, 9, 11; Le Riverend, *Historia*, 648.

80. Banco de Fomento Agrícola e Industrial de Cuba, *Memoria, 1952–1953*, 14–15, 17, 76, 78, 86–87, 93.

81. Banco de Fomento Agrícola e Industrial de Cuba, *Memoria, 1953–1954*, 12.

82. García-Pérez, *Insurrection and Revolution*, 40.

83. See "Copia de escritura de préstamo, constitución de hipoteca y emisión de bonos otorgada en 23 de mayo de 1957 por la Compañía de Hoteles La Riviera de Cuba S.A. al Banco de Desarrollo Económico y Social y el Banco Financiero S.A. relativa a la construcción del Hotel Havana Riviera," FBNC, Legajo 517, no. 17. See also Rodríguez Mesa, *Proceso*, 127.

84. Teobaldo Valle, Depto. De Crédito y Valores, BANDES, to Dr. Julio A. Díaz

Rodríguez, Havana, 18 October 1956, FBNC, Legajo 479, no. 24; Ectore Reynaldo, Assistant Manager, BANDES, to Frederic E. Michel, International Corporation Company, Havana, 20 April 1957, FBNC, Legajo 479, no. 24; Segundo T. Valle to Comité de Crédito, Havana, 14 November 1957, FBNC, Legajo 380, no. 19; Jorge F. Diago to Sr. Jefe de Crédito y Valores, Havana, 10 December 1957, FBNC, Legajo 380, no. 19.

85. Batista, *Piedras*, 202–3; Mascarós, *Historia*, 103–4.

86. See "Copia de escritura de cancelación de hipteca ororgada el 31 de octubre de 1958 a la sociedad anónima denominada Inversiones Bonti S.A. y la Compañía de Hoteles La Riviera S.A.," FBNC, Legajo 517, no. 11; "Copia de escritura de cancelación otorgada el 31 de octubre de 1958 por el Banco de Desarrollo Económico y Social, El Banco Financiero S.A. y la Compañía de Hoteles La Riviera de Cuba, S.A.," FBNC, Legajo 517, no. 12; "Copia de escritura de préstamo, constitución de hipoteca y emisión de bonos otorgada el 23 de mayo de 1957 por la Compañía de Hoteles La Riviera de Cuba S.A., el Banco de Desarrollo Económico y Social y el Banco Financiero S.A. relativa a la construcción del Hotel Havana Riviera," FBNC, Legajo 517, no. 17.

87. Banco de Fomento Agrícola e Industrial de Cuba, *Memoria, 1953–1954*, 15, 28; Phillips, *Cuba*, 283; de Paz Sánchez, *Zona Rebelde*, 63.

88. Cirules, *Imperio*, 189–91, 195.

89. The same audit, performed in July 1959 by Castro's revolutionary government, that revealed this figure also indicated, without any firm proof, that over the four months of the winter quarter of 1957–58, the casino's profits "exceeded TRES MILLONES DE PESOS." See "Oscar Méndez Carbonell, Compañía de Hoteles la Riviera de Cuba S.A., Informe de intervención," Havana, 31 July 1959, FBNC, Legajo 517, no. 18. In this period, the Cuban peso was on a par with the dollar.

90. Louis A. Pérez Jr., *Cuba and the United States*, 223–24. Years later, when Lansky was arrested and put on trial after being deported to the United States from Israel, the government charged him with tax evasion and contempt of court. No charge of drug trafficking was ever brought against him. See *United States v. Meyer Lansky*, Criminal Docket 71-136-Cr-JLK, U.S. District Court, Miami; *United States v. 1) Meyer Lansky 2); Dino Cellini*, Criminal Docket 72-415-Cr-JE, USDCM; *United States v. Meyer Lansky*, Criminal Docket 73-140Cr-JE, USDCM.

91. See "Expediente relative al financiamiento del proyecto de construcción del Hotel Monte Carlo de la Habana solicitado por la Compañía Hotelera del Oeste S.A. al Banco de Desarrollo Económico y Social," FBNC, Legajo 526, no. 7.

92. See Eugenio Desvernine, Vice-Secretario, Antillean Hotel Corporation, to Dr. Joaquín Martínez Sáenz, Gerente, Banco de Desarrollo Económico y Social, Havana, 14 January 1958, FBNC, Legajo 479, no. 23; Eugenio Desvernine, Secretario, Antillean Hotel Corporation, to Sr. Gerente General Banco de Desarrollo Económico y Social, BANDES, Calle 23 no. 171 Vedado, Havana, 18 December 1958, FBNC, Legajo 479, no. 24.

Chapter 8

1. Zaitch, *Trafficking Cocaine*, 74–75.

2. Gagliano, *Coca Prohibition*, 147–48.

3. FBN, *Traffic in Opium, 1946*, 15; FBN, *Traffic in Opium, 1947*, 13–14; FBN, *Traffic in Opium, 1948*, 14; FBN, *Traffic in Opium, 1949*, 13.

4. "Cocaine Renaissance," in M. L. Harney, Bureau of Narcotics, Office of the Assistant to the Commissioner, to Garland H. Williams, Washington, D.C., 28 February 1950, RG170-74-4, Box 19.

5. Garland H. Williams to H. J. Anslinger, Report, in "Peruvian Cocaine Traffic," New York, 5 August 1949, RG170-74-12, Box 29.

6. James C. Ryan, Narcotic Agent, to H. J. Anslinger, Lima, 16 August 1949, RG170-74-12, Box 29; James C. Ryan, Narcotic Agent, to Garland H. Williams, Lima, 3 September 1949, RG170-74-12, Box 29; M.L.H., "Peruvian Cocaine Traffic," 23 September 1949, RG170-74-12, Box 29.

7. Anslinger and Tompkins, *Traffic*, 281; Gootenberg, "Between Coca and Cocaine," 140.

8. FBN, *Traffic in Opium, 1950*, 18.

9. Charles Siragusa, "Investigation of Eduardo Balarezo and Members of His Cocaine Smuggling Ring," New York, 21 April 1949, RG170-74-12, Box 29; Garland Williams to H. J. Anslinger, New York, 27 May 1949, RG170-74-12, Box 29.

10. James C. Ryan, District Supervisor, to M. L. Harney, "Illicit Cocaine Traffic," New York, 3 December 1949, RG170-74-4, Box 19 (translated from Spanish).

11. "Cocaine Renaissance," in M. L. Harney, Bureau of Narcotics, Office of the Assistant to the Commissioner, to Garland H. Williams, Washington, D.C., 28 February 1950, RG170-74-4, Box 19.

12. Garland H. Williams, District Supervisor, to H. J. Anslinger, New York, 7 March 1950, RG170-74-12, Box 29; FBN, *Traffic in Opium, 1949*, 14; "Leader of Ring Jailed," *New York Times*, 22 October 1949, 2.

13. "3 Go on Trial Here in Narcotics Case," *New York Times*, 11 October 1949, 37; "Ship's Aide Guilty in Narcotics Case," *New York Times*, 18 October 1949, 54.

14. Gootenberg, *Cocaine*, 71.

15. "Peruvian Cocaine Traffic; Opium from Ecuador; Interest in Producing Heroin," 23 September 1949, RG170-74-12, Box 23; "Memorandum: Santos Trafficante Jr.," RG170-71A-3555, Box 8.

16. Antón and Hernández, *Cubans*, 117.

17. Barnet, *Vida real*.

18. Vicente Cubillas Jr., "Nueva York: Capital del vicio: Cocaína y marihuana: Un relato de Salvador Cancio Peña ('Saviur')," *Bohemia*, 10 September 1950, 48–52, 101–2.

19. Garland H. Williams, District Supervisor, to H. J. Anslinger, "Abelardo Martínez alias El Teniente," New York, 16 March 1950, RG170-74-12, Box 29; Garland H. Williams, District Supervisor, to H. J. Anslinger, "Octavio Jordán alias El Cubano Loco," New York, 18 April 1950, RG170-74-12, Box 22.

20. Edward V. Lindberg, American Vice Consul, to Department of State, Lima, 16 January 1952, RG170-74-12, Box 29.

21. Subsecretaría Técnica, Embajada de Cuba, to Gonzalo Güell y Morales del Castillo, Ministro de Estado, Lima, 8 April 1957, FME, Legajo 431, no. 6781.

22. Orlando Daumy Amat to Gonzalo Güell y Morales del Castillo, Ministro de Estado, Lima, 16 January 1957, FME, Legajo 431, no. 6781.

23. Orlando Daumy Amat to Gonzalo Güell, Ministro de Estado, Lima, 5 June 1957, FME, Legajo 431, no. 6781.

24. Cotler, *Drogas*, 84.

25. Gootenberg, "Between Coca and Cocaine," 142.

26. FBN, *Traffic in Opium, 1955*, 19.

27. Lema, "Coca Debate," 102.

28. Ibid., 103–12.

29. David A. de Lima, Commercial Attaché, to Department of State, La Paz, 23 July 1951, RG170-74-12, Box 19.

30. Ibid., 16 October 1951.

31. Ibid., 28 November 1951.

32. Charles Bridgett, Commercial Attaché, to Department of State, La Paz, 5 March 1953, RG170-74-12, Box 19.

33. Samuel Levine, Narcotic Agent, to James Noland, Lima, 1 June 1955, RG170-74-12, Box 33.

34. Samuel Levine, Narcotic Agent, "Bolivia: Memorandum for the Commissioner of Narcotics," New York, 15 August 1955, RG170-74-12, Box 33.

35. Samuel Levine, Narcotic Agent, to William W. Johnston, Lima, 1 June 1955, RG170-74-12, Box 33.

36. Samuel Levine, Narcotic Agent, to Ellis O. Briggs, Lima, 5 June 1955, RG170-74-12, Box 33.

37. Samuel Levine, Narcotic Agent, to James C. Ryan, 23 June 1955, RG170-74-12, Box 33.

38. "Copy of Foreign Service Dispatch #339 (A. Embassy, La Paz), dated 2/3/55," RG170-74-12, Box 19; Samuel Levine, Narcotic Agent, to James Noland, Quito, 22 June 1955, RG170-74-12, Box 33.

39. Samuel Levine, Narcotic Agent, "Bolivia: Memorandum for the Commissioner of Narcotics," New York, 15 August 1955, RG170-74-12, Box 33; Charles Bridgett, Commercial Attaché, to Department of State, La Paz, 29 February 1956, RG170-74-12, Box 19.

40. "Memorandum: (A) Charles Tourine, Jr. . . . (B) Charles Tourine, Sr.," RG170-71A-3555, Box 8.

41. "U.S. Treasury Department, Bureau of Narcotics: The Blanca Ibáñez de Sánchez Gang of International Illicit Cocaine Traffickers," Washington, D.C., 26 November 1962, RG170-74-4, Box 10.

42. U.S. Embassy to Department of State, La Paz, 24 March 1958, RG170-74-12, Box 19.

43. Davenport-Hines, *Búsqueda*, 266.

44. See *La Hora*, 10, 12, 14, 18 February, 1 March 1938, transcription of clippings in Renwick S. McNiece, American Consul, to Secretary of State, Valparaíso, 13 April 1938, RG170-74-12, Box 21.

45. L. E. Gilbert, Naval Attaché, "Intelligence Report: Activities in Narcotic Traffic in Antofagasta," Santiago de Chile, 12 October 1942, RG170-74-12, Box 21.

46. Bingham to Secretary of State, Antofagasta, 30 April 1947, RG170-74-12, Box 21.

47. Gilson G. Blake, American Consul General, to Secretary of State, Valparaíso, 15 July 1949, RG170-74-12, Box 21; "Memorandum Report: Narcotic Traffic in the Republic of Chile," New York, 18 July 1950, RG170-74-12, Box 21.

48. Luis Brun D'Avoglio, Director General de Investigaciones, to J. Edgar Hoover, Santiago de Chile, 31 January 1951, RG170-74-12, Box 21.

49. Telex, 16 July 1951, RG170, 179-74-12, Box 21.

50. "Memorandum for File: Luis Brun D'Avoglio," 18 July 1951, RG170-74-12, Box 21.

51. Joe M. Uberuaga, Treasury Representative, to Commissioner of Customs, Mexico City, 28 September 1951, RG170-74-12, Box 21.

52. F. Clayton, Local Clerk, American Consulate, Report, Valparaíso, 18 December 1953, RG170-74-12, Box 21; "Reported Smuggling of Cocaine," Valparaíso, 21 December 1953, RG170-74-12, Box 21.

53. H. J. Anslinger, U.S. Commissioner of Narcotics, to F. Thornton, Deputy Chief Inspector, Dangerous Drugs, 25 April 1944, RG170-74-12, Box 21.

54. Claude G. Bowers, Ambassador, to Joaquín Fernández Fernández, Ministro de Relaciones Exteriores de Chile, Santiago de Chile, 13 October 1944, RG170-74-12, Box 21.

55. Claude G. Bowers to Secretary of State, Santiago de Chile, 22 January 1945, RG170-74-12, Box 21; A. Quintana Burgos, Departmento de Política Comercial, Ministerio de Relaciones Exteriores, to Claude G. Bowers, Santiago de Chile, 14 May 1945, RG170-74-12, Box 21; Claude G. Bowers to Secretary of State, 25 May 1945, RG170-74-12, Box 21; W. E. D. to Secretary of State, 25 May 1945, RG170-74-12, Box 21.

56. Claude G. Bowers to Secretary of State, Santiago de Chile, 2 July 1946, 5 July 1946, RG170-74-12, Box 21; H. J. Anslinger to Wood and Breidenback, 11 July 1946, RG170-74-12, Box 21.

57. Claude G. Bowers to Secretary of State, Santiago de Chile, 25 November 1946, 6 February 1947, RG170-74-12, Box 21; Marshall to American Embassy, Washington, D.C., 11 February 1947, RG170-74-12, Box 21.

58. William L. Clayton, Assistant Secretary for Economic Affairs, to John M. Cabot, American Chargé d'Affaires ad Interim, Washington, D.C., 20 February 1946, RG170-74-12, Box 19.

59. Howard H. Tewsbury, Counselor of Embassy for Economic Affairs, to Secretary of State, Buenos Aires, 26 April 1946, RG170-74-12, Box 19.

60. John Ordway, Second Secretary of Embassy, and Clarence T. Breaux, Third Secretary of Embassy, "Argentine Government Fosters Poppy Production," Buenos Aires, 7 July 1948, RG170-74-12, Box 19.

61. George H. White, "Report on Illicit Drug Traffic in Ecuador," Quito, 5 March 1953, RG170-71A-3555, Box 8.

62. Ibid., 12 March 1953.

63. Samuel Levine, Narcotic Agent, to James C. Ryan, Quito, 2 May 1955, RG170, 71-A-3555, Box 8.

64. "Assignment in Quito," *Time*, 6 April 1953, 46; Agnew, *Undercover Agent*, 119–24.

65. Samuel Levine, Narcotic Agent, "Ecuador: Memorandum for the Commissioner of Narcotics," New York, 22 August 1955, RG170-74-12, Box 33.

66. Ibid. (translated from Spanish).

Chapter 9

1. "Consul's Slaying Laid to Drug Ring," *Washington Post*, 13 July 1930, M4.

2. Robert M. Collyer, "Illicit Drugs Flooding France," *New York Sun*, 27 December 1930, clipping, RG170-74-12, Box 24 (translated from Spanish).

3. League of Nations, Advisory Committee on Traffic in Opium and Other Dangerous Drugs, O.C.S. 165, Geneva, 2 February 1945, RG170-74-12, Box 24.

4. League of Nations, "The Drug Situation and the Control of Narcotic Drugs in France," O.C. Special 9, Geneva, 6 June 1944, RG170-74-12, Box 24.

5. Meyer and Parssinen, *Webs of Smoke*, 256–57, 260–61.

6. Courtwright, *Dark Paradise*, 147.

7. "France and the Narcotic Traffic," n.d., RG170-94-004, Box 11; Forst, *Heroin Trail*, 75, 82, 137; McCoy, *Politics*, 48; Courtwright, *Dark Paradise*, 148.

8. Moscow, *Merchants*, 95–96.

9. Jankowski, *Communism*, 3, 5.

10. Fisher, *Considerable Town*, 3.

11. Jankowski, *Communism*, 36.

12. Ibid., 10–12, 16–19.

13. Ibid., 29; Attard-Maraninchi, *Panier*, 111 n. 233.

14. "François Spirito" and "Joseph Orsini," in "France and the Narcotic Traffic," n.d., RG170-94-004, Box 11.

15. McCoy, *Politics*, 46–47, 60–61.

16. Fisher, *Considerable Town*, 42.

17. C. W. Gray, American Consul General, to Secretary of State, Marseille, 18 June 1948, RG170-74-12, Box 24.

18. Attard-Maraninchi, *Panier*, 16 n. 251; McCoy, *Politics*, 48; Charles Siragusa, U.S. Narcotic Agent, to Barrett McGurn, Rome, 3 March 1953, RG170-74-12, Box 24; Tully, *Treasury Agent*, 262–64.

19. Gray to Secretary of State, Marseille, 22 June 1948, RG170-74-12, Box 24; George H. White, District Supervisor, to H. J. Anslinger, Marseille, 26 June 1948, RG170-74-12, Box 24; Charles Siragusa, Narcotic Agent, to H. J. Anslinger, Progress Report no. 41, Marseille, 3 May 1951, RG170-74-12, Box 24; Charles Siragusa, Narcotic Agent, to H. J. Anslinger, Progress Report no. 45, Marseille, 8 May 1951, RG170-74-12, Box 24; Valentine, *Strength*, 103–4.

20. George H. White, District Supervisor, to H. J. Anslinger, Marseille, 26 June 1948, RG170-74-12, Box 24.

21. C. W. Gray, American Consul General, to Secretary of State, Marseille, 18 June 1948, RG170-74-12, Box 24.

22. Charles Siragusa, Narcotic Agent, to H. J. Anslinger, Progress Report no. 45, Marseille, 8 May 1951, RG170-74-12, Box 24; Charles Siragusa, U.S. Narcotic Agent, to Barrett McGurn, Rome, 3 March 1953, RG170-74-12, Box 24.

23. Barrett McGurn, "Courts 'Easy' in Drug Cases at Marseilles," *Washington Post*, 5 May 1953, 31.

24. "Narcotics Cooperation with France," *Washington Post*, 1 January 1970, 34.

25. Moscow, *Merchants*, 65–68; Vizzini, Fraley, and Smith, *Vizzini*, 176.

26. "Líbano," 977; Rodríguez Zahar, *Líbano*, 184–85.

27. Henry L. Giordano, Acting Commissioner of Narcotics, to A. Gilmore Flues, Assistant Secretary of the Treasury, 3 October 1960, RG170-74-12, Box 28; Charles Siragusa, Narcotic Agent, to H. J. Anslinger, Progress Report no. 29, Beirut, 9 September 1950, RG170-74-12, Box 28; "U.S. Smashes Middle East Narcotic Ring," *Washington Post*, 3 December 1954, 3.

28. Paul E. Knight, "Turkey — Survey Report," Rome, 10 March 1959, RG170-74-12, Box 32.

29. "Illicit Traffic: Need for Closer International Co-Operation," *United Nations Bulletin*, 15 May 1952, 407.

30. League of Nations, "Opium Production and the Control of Narcotic Drugs in Yugoslavia," O.C. Special 2, Geneva, 3 February 1944, RG170-74-12, Box 32; FBN, *Traffic in Opium, 1951*, 22–23.

31. Kuniholm to Secretary of State, Beirut, 21 July 1948, RG170-74-12, Box 28; Paul E. Knight, Narcotic Agent, to H. J. Anslinger, "Lebanon," Rome, 12 April 1954, RG170-74-12, Box 28.

32. Charles Siragusa, Narcotic Agent, to H. J. Anslinger, Progress Report no. 29, Beirut, 9 September 1950, RG170-74-12, Box 28; Charles Siragusa, District Supervisor, to H. J. Anslinger, "Lebanon," Rome, 1 November 1954, RG170-74-12, Box 28; Garland H. Williams, District Supervisor, to H. J. Anslinger, "Hashish Traffic in Lebanon," Istanbul, 14 February 1949, RG170-74-12, Box 28; Valentine, *Strength*, 121.

33. Davenport-Hines, *Búsqueda*, 239–40.

34. Charles Siragusa, Narcotic Agent, to H. J. Anslinger, Progress Report no. 29, Beirut, 9 September 1950, RG170-74-12, Box 28; Charles Siragusa, Narcotic Agent, to H. J. Anslinger, Progress Report no. 31, Beirut, 14 September 1950, RG170-74-12, Box 28.

35. Henry L. Giordano, Acting Commissioner of Narcotics, to A. Gilmore Flues, Assistant Secretary of the Treasury, 3 October 1960, RG170-74-12, Box 28.

36. See clipping in H. J. Anslinger to Leon Steinig, Director, Division of Narcotic Drugs, United Nations, 25 May 1948, RG170-74-12, Box 24.

37. Garland H. Williams, District Supervisor, to M. L. Harney, Assistant to the Commissioner of Narcotics, New York, 12 April 1950, RG170-74-12, Box 24.

38. Charles Siragusa, U.S. Narcotic Agent, to Barrett McGurn, Rome, 3 March 1953, RG170-74-12, Box 24.

39. FBN, *Traffic in Opium, 1947*, 13; "Old and New Narcotic Perils: World Drug Control in Operation," *United Nations Weekly Bulletin*, 16 September 1947, 361–62.

40. FBN, *Traffic in Opium, 1949,* 9, 15.

41. FBN, *Traffic in Opium, 1953,* 16–17; "6 Arrested in Dope Haul," *Washington Post,* 13 October 1953, 8; "Pair Given Five Years as Dope Smugglers," *Washington Post,* 9 February 1957, A3.

42. James C. Ryan, District Supervisor, to H. J. Anslinger, New York, 17 November 1955, RG170-74-12, Box 24; FBN, *Traffic in Opium, 1955,* 18; Charbonneau, *Canadian Connection,* 93.

43. FBN, *Traffic in Opium, 1957,* 17.

44. James C. Munch to Harry J. Anslinger, Landsdowne, Pa., 8 November 1959, RG170-71A-3555, Box 8.

45. Davenport-Hines, *Búsqueda,* 337.

46. McCoy, *Politics,* 48.

47. William W. Johnston, Treasury Representative in Charge, Monthly Activity Report, Havana, 13 August 1956, RG170-74-12, Box 22.

48. "5 Seized in Theft of Aga Khan Gems," *New York Times,* 21 January 1950, 6; "Police Seize 6 in Gem Holdup of Aga Khan," *Washington Post,* 21 January 1950, 5; "France and the Narcotic Traffic," RG170-94-004, Box 11; Secrétariat Général, Commission Internationale de Police Criminelle, Interpol, "Drug Traffic between North America and Western Europe," Paris, 20 March 1957, p. 26, RG170-94-005, Box 24; John T. Cusack, District Supervisor, to William W. Johnston, 4 September 1958, RG170-74-12, Box 22; Charbonneau, *Canadian Connection,* 75–77, 88 n. 2, 97.

49. International Criminal Police Organization, Report Submitted by the General Secretariat, "International illicit Drug Traffic — 1957," p. 31, RG170-94-005, Box 22.

50. William W. Johnston, Treasury Representative in Charge, Monthly Activity Report, Havana, 31 December 1956, RG170-74-12, Box 22; Jorge A. de Castroverde to Marcel Sicot, Secretario Gral. OIPC, Havana, 7 January 1959, FME, Legajo 377, no. 6029; "Reclamado por la Embajada de Francia Paul Damián Mandolina [*sic*]," *El Mundo,* 27 December 1956, 8A; Charbonneau, *Canadian Connection,* 104.

51. "France and the Narcotic Traffic," RG170-94-004, Box 11; Secrétariat Général, Commission Internationale de Police Criminelle, Interpol, "Drug Traffic between North America and Western Europe," Paris, 20 March 1957, p. 19, RG170-94-005, Box 24; Charbonneau, *Canadian Connection,* 95.

52. "France and the Narcotic Traffic," RG170-94-004, Box 11.

53. "NY Bur of Narcs, Agent Amato on line, Message for Mr. Cunningham," 27 June 1956, RG170-74-12, Box 22; Charbonneau, *Canadian Connection,* 76.

54. Secrétariat Général, Commission Internationale de Police Criminelle, Interpol, "Drug Traffic between North America and Western Europe," Paris, 20 March 1957, p. 26, RG170-94-005, Box 24; K. C. Rudd, Narcotic Agent, to Wayland L. Speer, Assistant to the Commissioner of Narcotics, Miami, 9 January 1959, RG170-71A-3555, Box 8; Charles Siragusa to A. de la Carrera, "Case no. 40," Alexandria, Va., 2 February 1959, RG170-71A-3555, Box 8; Charbonneau, *Canadian Connection,* 103.

55. "Canada and the Narcotic Traffic," RG170-94-004, Box 1; Charles Siragusa to A. de la Carrera, "Case No. 38," Alexandria, Va., 2 February 1959, RG170-71A-3555, Box 8; Valentine, *Strength,* 187; Charbonneau, *Canadian Connection,* 67, 104.

56. John T. Cusack, District Supervisor, to H. J. Anslinger, 4 November 1958, RG170-74-12, Box 22.

57. "France and the Narcotic Traffic," RG170-94-004, Box 11.

58. Charles Siragusa to A. de la Carrera, "Case no. 39," Alexandria, Va., 2 February 1959, RG170-71A-3555, Box 8; "France and the Narcotic Traffic," RG170-94-004, Box 11; Charles Siragusa to A. de la Carrera, "Case no. 23," Alexandria, Va., 2 February 1959, RG170-71A-3555, Box 8; Charles Siragusa to A. de la Carrera, "Case No. 26," Alexandria, Va., 2 February 1959, RG170-71A-3555, Box 8; Charbonneau, *Canadian Connection*, 115.

59. John T. Cusack, District Supervisor, to H. J. Anslinger, "Paul Daniel [*sic*] Mondolini, Jean Baptiste Croce, and Lucienne [*sic*] Rivard," 24 November 1958, RG170-71A-3555, Box 8. See also Valentine, *Strength*, 187.

60. John T. Cusack, District Supervisor, to H. J. Anslinger, 4 November 1958, RG170-74-12, Box 22.

61. Marrero, *Geografía*, 570.

62. See, e.g., "Actas, declaraciones, etc. del sumario #1055 de 1926 contra Pedro Varela Coo y Segundo Corripio Fernández por infracción de la Ley #25 de Julio de 1919 por drogas en Camagüey," Índice del Fondo Juzgado de Instrucción del Partido Judicial de Camagüey (1899–1954), Archivo Histórico Provincial de Camagüey, Camagüey, Legajo 334, nos. 4155, 4156; "Autos de Sentencia, etc. del sumario #1055 de 1926 contra Pedro Varela Coo y Segundo Corripio Fernández por infracción de la Ley #25 de Julio de 1919 por drogas en Camagüey," Índice del Fondo Juzgado de Instrucción del Partido Judicial de Camagüey, Legajo 334, no. 4157; "Incidente del sumario #1055 de 1926 contra Pedro Varela Coo y Segundo Corripio Fernández por infracción de la Ley #25 de Julio de 1919 por drogas en Camagüey," Índice del Fondo Juzgado de Instrucción del Partido Judicial de Camagüey, Legajo 334, no. 4158; "Comunicaciones, certificaciones, etc., del sumario #1322 de 1939 contra Alberto Muñiz Rodríguez por traficar drogas en Camagüey," Índice del Fondo Juzgado de Instrucción del Partido Judicial de Camagüey, Legajo 334, no. 4161; "Sentencia, autos, etc. del sumario #426 de 1941 contra Julia Barreto Arrieta y otros por tráfico de drogas estupefacientes en Camagüey," Índice del Fondo Juzgado de Instrucción del Partido Judicial de Camagüey, Legajo 334, no. 4162; "Actas, comunicaciones, etc. del sumario #426 de 1941 contra Julia Barreto Arrieta y otros por tráfico de drogas estupefacientes en Camagüey," Índice del Fondo Juzgado de Instrucción del Partido Judicial de Camagüey, Legajo 334, no. 4163.

63. John T. Cusack, District Supervisor, to H. J. Anslinger, Atlanta, 14 July 1958, RG170-74-12, Box 22.

64. John T. Cusack to H. J. Anslinger, 27 August 1958, RG170-74-12, Box 22.

65. Moreno Fraginals, *Cuba/España*, 212–13.

66. Freire, *Historia*, 472.

67. Pan American Airways, Airport Development Program, "Chronological Record, Camagüey—Cuba, Agremonte [*sic*] Field," n.d., PAWA, Box 505; Carbajo, *Recuerdo*.

68. U.S. Civil Aeronautics Board, "Pan American Airways, Inc., et al., Latin American Route Amendment Case," 31 March 1949, PAWA, Box 64; *Alas Cubanas sobre el Mundo: Reporte Anual Compañía Cubana de Aviación S.A., 1947*, p. 4, PAWA, Box 59.

69. Clark, *All the Best*, 8, 183; Fergusson, *Cuba*, 64. Vallina Mendoza, *Disparos*, 1.

70. John T. Cusack, District Supervisor, to George H. Gaffney, 11 July 1958, RG170-74-12, Box 22; John T. Cusack, District Supervisor, to H. J. Anslinger, Atlanta, 14 July 1958, RG170-74-12, Box 22.

71. William W. Johnston, Treasury Representative in Charge, Monthly Activity Report, Havana, 31 August 1958, RG170-74-12, Box 22.

72. Steve Minas, Customs Agent, Monthly Activity Report, Havana, 30 November 1958, RG170-74-12, Box 22; Steve Minas, Acting Treasury Representative in Charge, Monthly Activity Report, Havana, 19 December 1958, RG170-74-12, Box 22.

73. K. C. Rudd, "Alleged Heroin Smuggling at Tampa, Florida, from Havana, Cuba," Miami, 11 August 1958, RG170-74-12, Box 22; K. C. Rudd, "Search of Minerva Pedrero @ Minerva Pérez at Tampa, Florida, 15 August 1958," Miami, 3 September 1958, RG170-74-12, Box 22; K. C. Rudd, "Additional Information of Minerva Pedrero of Tampa and José Valdés of Cuba," Miami, 9 September 1958, RG170-74-12, Box 22.

Chapter 10

1. Anslinger, *Murderers*, 205.

2. Louis A. Pérez Jr., *Cuba and the United States*, 224.

3. Szulc, *Fidel*, 252.

4. Eduardo Chibás, untitled document, 10 January 1951, FC, Legajo 8, no. 220. See also Conte Agüero, *Eduardo Chibás*, 719–20.

5. *El Acusador*, 16 August 1952, FC, Legajo 86, no. 3631.

6. Coltman, *Real Fidel*, 23, 25–26, 55–57.

7. Thomas, *Cuba*, 1027.

8. For details on Batista's numerous investments and holdings, see Jiménez, *Empresas*, 28, 30, 40, 49, 158, 160, 207, 246, 266, 270–72, 275, 362–63, 372, 376, 385–86, 454–55, 458–59, 492–93, 502, 510–11, 513, 535, 554, 593, 595.

9. Skierka, *Fidel Castro*, 65; Buch Rodríguez and Suárez Suárez, *Otros pasos*, 72.

10. Miguel A. Campa, Ministro de Estado, to Emilio Núñez Portuondo, Embajador Delegado Permanente de Cuba ante las Naciones Unidas, Havana, 19 June 1953, FME, Legajo 480, no. 7505.

11. Gonzalo Güel, Subsecretario de Estado, to Presidente del Comité Central Permanente del Opio, Havana, 14, 19 August 1952, FME, Legajo 480, no. 7508.

12. William W. Johnston, Treasury Representative in Charge, Monthly Activity Report, Havana, 29 February 1956, RG170-74-12, Box 22.

13. Luis Rodolfo Miranda, Subsecretario de Estado, to Víctor Vega Ceballos, Ministro de Gobernación, Havana, 14 October 1941, FSP, Legajo 68, no. 26.

14. Ministro-Consejero, Encargado de la Alta Dirección de Asuntos de las Naciones Unidas, to Secretario Técnico Político, "Memorándum Antecedentes sobre la Organización Internacional de Policía Criminal (OIPC)," Havana, 17 February 1959, FME, Legajo 377, no. 6029.

15. Jorge A. de Castroverde Cabrera and Andrés Díaz Rojas to Dr. Gonzalo Güel, Ministro de Estado, Havana, 6 October 1958, FME, Legajo 377, no. 6029.

16. United Nations Economic and Social Council, E/NM.1956/2, "List of Merchant

Seafarers and Members of Civil Air Crews Convicted of Narcotic Offenses," 26 July 1956, FME, Legajo 377, no. 6024.

17. Moscow, *Merchants*, 132–33; Courtwright, *Dark Paradise*, 156.

18. John T. Cusack, "Lecture #3: Combating the Illicit Drug Traffic: The Illicit Drug Traffic in the United States," in John T. Cusack, District Supervisor, to H. J. Anslinger, Commissioner of Narcotics, "Interpol International Seminar on the Illicit Narcotic Traffic," Rome, 25 March 1958, RG170-94-005, Box 22; Musto, *Drugs*, 276–81.

19. Moscow, *Merchants*, 133, 198.

20. Messick, *Of Grass*, 17.

21. "Genovese Guilty in Narcotics Plot," *New York Times*, 4 April 1959, 1; FBN, *Traffic in Opium, 1959*, 24; Davis, *Mafia Dynasty*, 92–94.

22. Sección de Control de Drogas Estupefacientes, Ministerio de Salubridad y Asistencia Social, to Sr. Director General de Salubridad, Havana, 9 March 1953, FME, Legajo 383, no. 6103; Carlos Salas Humara, Subsecretario Administrativo, Ministerio de Salubridad y Asistencia Social, to Sr. Ministro de Estado, Havana, 22 March 1954, FME, Legajo 377, no. 6024.

23. William W. Johnston, Treasury Representative in Charge, Monthly Activity Report, Havana, 1 September 1953, 4 January 1954, RG170-74-12, Box 22.

24. Ibid., 6 November 1952; "Preso al jefe de una banda de contrabandistas de marihuana," *Diario de la Marina*, 24 October 1952, 21.

25. William W. Johnston, Treasury Representative in Charge, Monthly Activity Report, Havana, 2 January 1953, RG170-74-12, Box 22.

26. Ibid., 3 February 1953, 31 March 1953, 2 October 1953.

27. Ibid., 2 April 1954, 5 October 1954, 12 September 1955, 30 September 1955, 31 October 1955.

28. Ibid., 30 September 1955.

29. Ibid., 30 March 1956, 29 June 1956, 31 August 1956.

30. Ibid., 2 March 1953, 1 September 1953, 3 November 1953, 2 February 1954, 3 May 1954, 2 June 1954, 2 August 1954, 29 February 1956, 28 September 1956, 30 June 1957.

31. See, e.g., *Diario de la Marina*, 22 May 1954, 10; 11 August 1955, 16A; 26 January 1956, 18B; 27 December 1956, 16B; 29 December 1956, 20B; 30 December 1956, 2A; 8 January 1957, 8A; 9 January 1957, 18B; 10 January 1957, 8A; 12 January 1957, 8A; 15 January 1957, 20B; 19 January 1957, 20B; 20 January 1957, 8A; 22 January 1957, 18B; 27 January 1957, 8B; 2 February 1957, 16B.

32. "Detenido al llegar a los E.U., un reclamado por tráfico de drogas," *Diario de la Marina*, 9 December 1952, 32.

33. William W. Johnston, Treasury Representative in Charge, Monthly Activity Report, Havana, 2 May 1955, RG170-74-12, Box 22.

34. Ibid., 2 January 1953, 3 November 1953, 2 August 1954.

35. Ibid., 29 February 1956.

36. Ibid., 30 June 1953, 2 October 1953, 3 November 1953, 4 January 1954, 29 June 1956; William W. Johnston, Treasury Representative in Charge, to Commissioner of Customs, Havana, 28 December 1953, RG170-74-12, Box 22.

37. C. A. Emerick, Deputy Commissioner, to U.S. Treasury Representative in Charge —Havana, Cuba, 21 December 1953, RG170-74-12, Box 22.

38. José Manuel Cortina Corrales, Subsecretario de Estado, to Dr. Carlos Salas Humara, Ministro de Salubridad y Asistencia Social, Havana, 12 March 1957, FME, Legajo 429, no. 6733; Felix Fernández Teriza to Subsecretario de Estado, Havana, 25 October 1957, FME, Legajo 383, no. 6103; "Examples of Significant Cases in the Illicit Traffic," n.d., RG170-74-12, Box 28; K. C. Rudd, Narcotic Agent, to Wayland L. Speer, Assistant to the Commissioner of Narcotics, Miami, 9 January 1959, RG170-71A-3555, Box 8; "Turkey," Washington, D.C., 24 March 1959, RG170-74-12, Box 32; Menéndez Paredes, *Componentes*, 128.

39. "Turkey," Washington, D.C., 24 March 1959, RG170-74-12, Box 32; K. C. Rudd, Narcotic Agent, to George H. Gaffney, Havana, 14 February 1957, RG170-74-12, Box 22; William W. Johnston, Treasury Representative in Charge, Monthly Activity Report, Havana, 28 February 1957, RG170-74-12, Box 22.

40. William W. Johnston, Treasury Representative in Charge, to K. C. Rudd, Havana, 24 December 1957, RG170-71A-3555, Box 8.

41. William W. Johnston, Treasury Representative in Charge, Monthly Activity Report, Havana, 2 June 1954, RG170-74-12, Box 22; "Agentes de la Policía Secreta ocuparon cocaine por $200,000," *Diario de la Marina*, 22 May 1954, 38; Jorge A. de Castroverde to Commissioner of Narcotics, Havana, 8 June 1955, RG170-74-12, Box 22; Jorge A. de Castroverde to U. E. Baughman, Chief of the U.S. Secret Service, Havana, 1 June 1955, RG170-74-12, Box 22; C. W. Cunningham, Acting U.S. Commissioner of Narcotics, to Jorge A. de Castroverde, Washington, D.C., 6 July 1955, RG170, 170-74-12, Box 22; Astorga, *Drogas*, 296.

42. William W. Johnston, Treasury Representative in Charge, to Commissioner of Customs, Havana, 27 May 1954, RG170-74-12, Box 22.

43. Ibid., 23 April 1954; John T. Cusack, District Supervisor, to H. J. Anslinger, Atlanta, 14 July 1958, RG170-74-12, Box 22.

44. John T. Cusack, District Supervisor, to H. J. Anslinger, 3 November 1958, 10 November 1958, RG170-71A-3555, Box 8.

45. H. J. Anslinger to Colonel Orlando Piedra Negueruela, Washington, D.C., 11 June 1954, RG170-74-12, Box 22.

46. "Global Dope Ring Broken, U.S. Says: 2 Men From D.C. among 46 Indicted," *Washington Post*, 5 September 1957, A3.

47. K. C. Rudd, Narcotic Agent, to George H. Gaffney, Miami, 22 June 1956, RG170-74-12, Box 22.

48. Raimundo, *Habla el Coronel*, 189–90; Fernández Miranda, *Mis relaciones*, 98.

49. "How Police Chief Was Shot in Haitian Embassy Here; Now It Can Be Told," *Havana Post*, 14 January 1959, 10.

50. "Anti-Terrorist Rule Applied to All Cuba," *New York Times*, 15 January 1957, 12.

51. "Galería de Asesinos," *Bohemia*, 1 January 1959, 157. At the end of 1959, U.S. authorities arrested Orlando Piedra's brother, Osvaldo, south of Miami while he and four other anti-Castro Cubans were loading a plane with three bombs that they planned to

drop somewhere over the island. (E. W. Kentworthy, "U.S. Seizes Bombs Headed for Cuba," *New York Times*, 2 December 1959, 1).

52. William W. Johnston, Treasury Representative in Charge, Monthly Activity Report, Havana, 31 May 1956, 31 October 1955, RG170-74-12, Box 22.

53. Ibid., 30 March 1956.

54. John T. Cusack, District Supervisor, to George H. Gaffney, 11 July 1958, RG170-74-12, Box 22.

55. John T. Cusack, District Supervisor, to H. J. Anslinger, 10 November 1958, RG170-71A-3555, Box 8.

56. William W. Johnston, Treasury Representative in Charge, to Commissioner of Customs, Havana, 6 March 1958, RG170-74-12, Box 22; William W. Johnston, Treasury Representative in Charge, Monthly Activity Report, Havana, 30 March 1958, RG170-74-12, Box 22.

57. William W. Johnston, Treasury Representative in Charge, Monthly Activity Report, Havana, 31 March 1958, RG170-74-12, Box 22.

58. John T. Cusack, District Supervisor, to H. J. Anslinger, 3 November 1958, RG170-74-12, Box 22.

59. John H. Windham, Acting District Supervisor, to H. J. Anslinger, Atlanta, 12 August 1958, RG170-74-12, Box 22; William W. Johnston, Treasury Representative in Charge, Monthly Activity Report, Havana, 31 August 1958, RG170-74-12, Box 22; S. Vizzini, Narcotic Agent, "Interview with Cuban Defendant Loius [sic] Gonzalaz [sic] Aguilera @ Armand Pérez Aguilera," Miami, 18 August 1958, RG170-74-12, Box 22; Raimundo, *Habla el Coronel*, 9–10.

60. John T. Cusack, District Supervisor, to Colonel Orlando Piedra Negueruela, 14 November 1958, RG170-71A-3555, Box 8; Steve Minas, Customs Agent, Monthly Activity Report, Havana, 30 November 1958, RG170-74-12, Box 22; Steve Minas, Acting Treasury Representative in Charge, Monthly Activity Report, Havana, 19 December 1958, RG170-74-12, Box 22; "The Illicit Interstate Narcotic Traffic from New York City throughout the Eastern Seaboard of the United States, Background Sheet 22," RG170-94-004, Box 11.

61. William W. Johnston, Treasury Representative in Charge, Monthly Activity Report, Havana, 4 January 1954, RG170-74-12, Box 22; H. J. Anslinger, Memorandum, Washington, D.C., 14 May 1956, RG170-74-12, Box 22.

62. William W. Johnston, Treasury Representative in Charge, Monthly Activity Report, Havana, 2 October 1953, RG170-74-12, Box 22; Steve Minas, Customs Agent, Monthly Activity Report, Havana, 30 November 1958, RG170-74-12, Box 22.

63. John T. Cusack, District Supervisor, to Steven Minas, 10 November 1958, RG170-74-12, Box 22; William W. Johnston, Treasury Representative in Charge, Monthly Activity Report, Havana, 3 May 1954, RG170-74-12, Box 22.

64. Ibid., 31 August 1956, 30 June 1957, 28 February 1958.

65. Antón and Hernández, *Cubans*, 126.

66. Lisandro Pérez, "Cuban Miami," 84–85.

67. William W. Johnston, Treasury Representative in Charge, Monthly Activity Report, Havana, 2 November 1954, 4 April 1955, 30 March 1956, 30 April 1956, 31 May 1956,

31 January 1957, 31 May 1957, 31 August 1957, 30 November 1957, RG170-74-12, Box 22.

68. Ibid., 30 April 1957, 31 May 1957; "Cuba Still Censors Incoming Journals," *New York Times*, February 1957, 3.

69. Louis A. Pérez Jr., *Cuba and the United States*, 234.

70. George H. Gaffney, District Supervisor, to H. J. Anslinger, Atlanta, 3 October 1957, RG170-74-12, Box 22.

71. William W. Johnston, Treasury Representative in Charge, Monthly Activity Report, Havana, 30 September 1957, 28 February 1958, RG170-74-12, Box 22.

72. "The Illicit Narcotic Traffic in Cuba," 16 January 1959, RG170-71A-3555, Box 8.

73. Ibid.

74. John T. Cusack, District Supervisor, to H. J. Anslinger, 10 November 1958, RG170-71A-3555, Box 8.

75. De Castroverde, *Que la patria*, 97.

76. See Fondo Presidios y Cárceles, Archivo Nacional de Cuba, Havana, Legajos 103, 105, 108, 347, 352, 413.

Chapter 11

1. Wayne S. Smith, *Closest of Enemies*, 40; Dubois, *Fidel Castro*, 349.

2. Phillips, *Cuban Dilemma*, 3; Geyer, *Guerrilla Prince*, 203; Glinn, *Havana*, 26.

3. "Contra el Juego," *Bohemia*, 11 January 1959, 126.

4. Paterson, *Contesting Castro*, 52; "Mobsters Move in on Troubled Havana and Split Rich Gambling Profits with Batista," *Life*, 10 March 1958, 36.

5. Paterson, *Contesting Castro*, 227.

6. Dubois, *Fidel Castro*, 353; Phillips, *Cuba*, 397; Phillips, *Cuban Dilemma*, 3; Paterson, *Contesting Castro*, 227; Earl E. T. Smith, *Fourth Floor*, 189; Quirk, *Fidel Castro*, 213; Franqui, *Camilo Cienfuegos*, 36.

7. Paterson, *Contesting Castro*, 56.

8. Schwartz, *Pleasure Island*, 196.

9. Phillips, *Cuban Dilemma*, 48–49; Schwartz, *Pleasure Island*, 196–97; Ragano and Raab, *Mob Lawyer*, 52.

10. Frank Fernández, *Cuban Anarchism*, 76.

11. Quirk, *Fidel Castro*, 227; Farr, *Rites*, 26; Lowinger and Fox, *Tropicana Nights*, 327–28.

12. Earl Wilson, "It Happened Last Night," *Havana Post*, 8 January 1959, 7.

13. "Cuban Tourism Hopeful; Gambling Still Question," *Havana Post*, 13 January 1959, 7.

14. Cirules, *Vida*, 195, 200–209.

15. "Castro Sends Message to U.S. Tourists and Businessmen," *Havana Post*, 13 January 1959, 1.

16. Phillips, *Cuban Dilemma*, 49–51; Portell-Vilá, *Nueva historia*, 706–7; Coltman, *Real Fidel*, 154; Orejuela Martínez, *Son*, 46; Lowinger and Fox, *Tropicana Nights*, 328.

17. Phillips, *Cuban Dilemma*, 275.

18. Buch Rodríguez and Suárez Suárez, *Otros pasos*, 21, 35. More than four decades

later, Castro declared that Urrutia's proposal had been "stupid" (Ramonet, *Fidel Castro*, 222).

19. E. A. Gilmore, Counselor of Embassy for Economic Affairs, to Department of State, Havana, 12 February 1959, RG59, 837.45/2-1259; Schwartz, *Pleasure Island*, 197.

20. Dubois, *Fidel Castro*, 374, 376.

21. Schwartz, *Pleasure Island*, 198; Pavia, *Cuba Project*, 47–48.

22. Dumur, *Cuba*, 59.

23. Matos, *Cómo llegó*, 122–23.

24. See Arias Fernández, *Cuba*, 70–73; Phyllis Greene Walker, "National Security," 348.

25. Machover, "Memoria," 17.

26. Ibid., 22.

27. Alejandro, "Primicias," 50. See also Lumsden, *Machos*, 59.

28. Lemogodeuc, "*Orígenes*, 155. See also Cabrera Infante, *Mea Cuba*, 100–101; Luis, *Culture and Customs*, 86–87.

29. Matthews, *Cuba*, 39.

30. Luis Rolando Cabrera, "La Operación Matrimonio: La Revolución ha legalizado ya miles de uniones," *Bohemia*, 24 January 1960, 36, 38, 96–97.

31. Gott, *Cuba*, 169.

32. Benítez, *Batalla*, 9.

33. Skierka, *Fidel Castro*, 2.

34. Lois M. Smith and Padula, *Sex and Revolution*, 21, 40; de la Torre Mulhare, "Sexual Ideology," 258–59, 261.

35. De Castroverde, *Que la patria*, 53, 57.

36. Geyer, *Guerrilla Prince*, 200, 204; Coltman, *Real Fidel*, 140.

37. Franqui, *Camilo Cienfuegos*, 23.

38. Aguilar, *Cuba 1933*, 102.

39. Thomas, *Cuba*, 1033.

40. Conde, *Operation Pedro Pan*, 4.

41. Quirk, *Fidel Castro*, 255.

42. Puebla, "Y en eso."

43. *Lyceum*, February 1959, 2–3, Collection 0124, Lyceum and Lawn Tennis Club, La Havana, Cuban Heritage Collection, University of Miami, Miami, Fla., Box 3, Folder 11.

44. Stoner, *From the House*, 46, 76, 143, 187; Portell-Vilá, *Nueva historia*, 702; Lois M. Smith and Padula, *Sex and Revolution*, 17, 35.

45. Carlos José Enríquez and Guillermo Villaronda, "Confesiones de un vicioso: ¡Yo fui mariguanero!," *Bohemia*, 17 May 1959, 4–6, 156–57.

46. Dr. Jorge A. de Castroverde to Marcel Sicot, Secretario Gral. OIPC, Havana, 7 January 1959, FME, Legajo 377, no. 6029.

47. Ibid., 9 February 1959.

48. Jorge A. de Castroverde to Roberto Agramonte, Havana, 5 January 1959, FME, Legajo 377, no. 6029.

49. Padula, "Fall," 74–109; Sweig, *Inside*, 20, 168, 170, 184; Thomas, *Cuba*, 1065.

50. Lowinger and Fox, *Tropicana Nights*, 5, 300.

51. Núñez, "Nací," 194–97; Sweig, *Inside*, 78.

52. Bonsal, *Cuba*, 293 n. 1; "Fidel y el turismo," *Bohemia*, 31 May 1959, 89.

53. "Cuban Tourist Commission Is Going Full-Speed-Ahead: Campaigning to Promote Good Will," *Havana Post*, 17 January 1959, 2.

54. U.S. Embassy in Cuba to Department of State, Telegram, Havana, 13 July 1959, 737.00/7-1359, *FRUS, 1958–60*, 556.

55. Schwartz, *Pleasure Island*, 198–99.

56. Mario G. del Cueto, "El despertar turístico de Cuba: La Jornada del ASTA," *Bohemia*, 25 October 1959, 72–74, 98; Bonsal, *Cuba*, 100–101; U.S. Embassy in Cuba to Department of State, Dispatch, Havana, 20 October 1959, 737.13/10-2059, *FRUS, 1958–60*, 628–29.

57. Phillips, *Cuban Dilemma*, 112–13; Bonsal, *Cuba*, 106; Hinckle and Turner, *Deadly Secrets*, 52; Coltman, *Real Fidel*, 163–64; Matos, *Como llegó*, 337–49; Sweig, *Inside*, 116, 163; Gott, *Cuba*, 171; U.S. Embassy in Cuba to Department of State, Telegram, Havana, 21 October 1959, 737.00/10-2159, *FRUS, 1958–60*, 631; U.S. Embassy in Cuba to Department of State, Telegram, Havana, 22 October 1959, 737.00/1-1259, *FRUS, 1958–60*, 632; "Editorial Note," *FRUS, 1958–60*, 642–43.

58. De la Fuente, *Nation for All*, 296–97.

59. Schwartz, *Pleasure Island*, 202–3.

60. Phillips, *Cuban Dilemma*, 125, 144.

61. U.S. Embassy in Cuba to Department of State, Telegram, Havana, 30 October 1959, 61.37/10-3059, *FRUS, 1958–60*, 649.

62. Mario G. del Cueto, "Unir la América Latina a través del turismo, es la consigna de la COTAL," *Bohemia*, 24 April 1960, 60–61.

63. Phillips, *Cuban Dilemma*, 281.

64. Falcoff, *Cuba*, 132.

65. See, e.g., "10 Armed Forces Officers Executed; Revolutionary Courts Set," *Havana Post*, 8 January 1959, 1; "Over 2,000 Persons under Rebel Arrest," *Havana Post*, 9 January 1959, 1; "Ex-Cárdenas Police Chief Executed," *Havana Post*, 11 January 1959, 1; "71 Batista Adherents Executed by Mass Grave; Some Smoke while Awaiting End," *Havana Post*, 13 January 1959, 1, 7; "Executions to Continue until Guilty Punished; Ernesto 'Che' Guevara Gives Views," *Havana Post*, 14 January 1959, 1; "Castro Prosecutor in War Crime Trials Here; Havana Trials Expected to Start Thursday," *Havana Post*, 20 January 1959, 1, 7; "Cubans Back Castro Policy; Hit Foreign Concessions; Trials Start Here Today," *Havana Post*, 22 January 1959, 1. See also Fuentes, *Narcotráfico*, 50; Macaulay, *Rebel*, 170–76; Fernández Barrios, *Blessed*, 19.

66. Gott, *Cuba*, 168.

67. "World Opinion Mounts against Executions Here," *Havana Post*, 15 January 1959, 1; Quirk, *Fidel Castro*, 224.

68. Quirk, *Fidel Castro*, 229; Skierka, *Fidel Castro*, 78.

69. Luis E. Aguilar, "¡Paredón, paredón!," *Prensa Libre*, Havana, 1 November 1959, in Aguilar, *Cuba*, 122–23; Montaner, *Viaje*, 111; Eire, *Waiting*, 214, 218–19; Matos, *Como llegó*, 358; Lowinger and Fox, *Tropicana Nights*, 326; "Embajada de Colombia, La Habana: Informe diplomático, Mes de octubre de 1959," Despacho Señor Presidente, 1959,

Archivo de la Presidencia de la República, Bogotá, Caja 108, folios 188–91. I thank Susana Romero, graduate student in history at the National University of Colombia, for sharing this document with me.

70. See, e.g., "Ajusticiado García Olayón," *Bohemia*, 11 January 1959, 52–53; "Criminal bombardeo en Santa Clara," *Bohemia*, 11 January 1959, 60–61; "La Caza del Implacable Jacinto Menocal: El Pueblo y los milicianos lo cercaron y herido de muerte se suicidó," *Bohemia*, 11 January 1959, 84–85; "Ya tienen la revolución: no la pierdan . . . ," *Bohemia*, 18–25 January 1959, 22–23; "El ajusticiamiento de Juan Centellas," *Bohemia*, 18–25 January 1959, 25; "El pueblo juzgó a los bárbaros tigres de Masferrer y los llevó ante el paredón," *Bohemia*, 1 February 1959, 66–68. *Bohemia* had great power to shape Cuban public opinion. Even at the outset of Batista's dictatorship, when authorities could have found ways to muffle its persistent criticism of the regime, more than two hundred thousand copies of each issue were printed and distributed (Mallory and Barber, *Political Handbook*, 48).

71. Coltman, *Real Fidel*, 149.

72. Quoted by Núñez Jiménez, *En marcha*, 64.

73. Phillips, *Cuban Dilemma*, 28; Quirk, *Fidel Castro*, 224; Conde, *Operation Pedro Pan*, 8–10.

74. Earl E. T. Smith, *Fourth Floor*, chapter 18.

75. "Bochorno para Norteamérica: El Embajador Smith; Servidor del Déspota," *Bohemia*, 11 January 1959, 76.

76. Christian A. Herter and Wilton B. Persons, Eisenhower Library: Herter Papers, Telephone Conversations, 6 January 1959, *FRUS, 1958–60*, 343; Gott, *Cuba*, 179.

77. U.S. Embassy in Cuba to Department of State, Telegram, Havana, 5 January 1959, Department of State: 737.00/1-659, *FRUS, 1958–60*, 345; Secretary of State to President, Washington, D.C., 7 January 1959, Eisenhower Library: Project "Clean Up" Records, Cuba, *FRUS, 1958–60*, 6:347; "U.S. Recognizes Cuban Govt; Castro Arrives Here Today; Ambassador Smith Delivers Note in Havana" and "Britain Recognizes Urrutia," *Havana Post*, 8 January 1959, 1.

78. "Memorandum of Discussion at the 400th Meeting of the National Security Council," Washington, D.C., 26 March 1959, Eisenhower Library: Whitman File, NSC, *FRUS, 1958–60*, 440–42; General Goodpaster, Memorandum, 3 April 1959, Eisenhower Library: Whitman File, DDE Diaries, *FRUS, 1959–60*, 446.

79. U.S. Embassy in Cuba to Department of State, Dispatch, Havana, 14 April 1959, Department of State: 737.001/4-1459, *FRUS, 1958–60*, 464.

80. Lazo, *Dagger*, 195–96.

81. U.S. Embassy in Cuba to Department of State, Telegram, Havana, 23 May 1959, Department of State: 837.16/5-2359, *FRUS, 1958–60*, 511.

82. "Memorandum of Conversation, Department of State," Washington, D.C., 27 May 1959, Department of State: 837.16/5-2759, *FRUS, 1958–60*, 514.

83. "Memorandum of Conversation," Washington, D.C., June 1959, Department of State: 7373.00/6-159, *FRUS, 1958–60*, 518. After the Second World War, the United States imposed a program of agrarian reform on Japan that was even more radical and far-reaching than the reforms envisioned by Cuba (Gott, *Cuba*, 180).

84. U.S. Embassy in Cuba to Department of State, Telegram, Havana, 7 July 1959, Department of State: 737.00/7-759, *FRUS, 1958–60*, 6:554.

85. "Instructions from the Department of State to All Diplomatic and Consular Posts in the American Republics," Washington, D.C., 15 September 1959, 61.37/9-1559, *FRUS, 1958–60*, 602.

86. Bonsal, *Cuba*, 108. See also Ambrose, *Eisenhower*, 499–500; Bundy, *Tangled Web*, 13.

87. Bissell, *Reflections*, 153.

88. Fursenko and Naftali, *"One Hell of a Gamble,"* 40–42; Bonsal, *Cuba*, 133–35; Coltman, *Real Fidel*, 172–73.

89. Pavia, *Cuba Project*, 66–67.

90. Bohning, *Castro Obsession*, 3. See also Pavia, *Cuba Project*.

91. Bonsal, *Cuba*, chapter 16; Ambrose, *Eisenhower*, 516; Gott, *Cuba*, 183–84.

92. Gott, *Cuba*, 184–85.

93. Summers and Swan, *Arrogance*, 184–93; Bissell, *Reflections*, 157.

94. Russo, *Live*, 8–10.

Chapter 12

1. Daniel M. Braddock, Minister-Counselor, to Department of State, Havana, 19 March 1959, RG59, 837.53/s-1959. See also William O. Walker III, *Drugs*, 170–72.

2. "'Gangster Exchange,' Suggested by Castro; He'll Send Back Dope Peddlers," *Washington Daily News*, 19 March 1959, clipping, RG170-71A-3555, Box 8; "Manden la lista de los gangsters," *Prensa Libre*, 19 March 1959, clipping, RG170-71A-3555, Box 8.

3. Charles Siragusa to A. de la Carrera, Alexandria, Va., 16 January 1959, RG170-71A-3555, Box 8; "Dope-Seller List Sent to Havana, Lost," *Washington Post*, 18 April 1959, A10.

4. Charles Siragusa to A. de la Carrera, Alexandria, Va., 20 January 1959, RG170-71A-3555, Box 8.

5. "The Illicit Interstate Narcotic Traffic from New York City throughout the Eastern Seaboard of the United States," RG170-94-004, Box 1, Background Sheet 47.

6. Ibid., Background Sheet 98.

7. Charles Siragusa to A. de la Carrera, "Case no. 22," Alexandria, Va., 2 February 1959, RG170-71A-3555, Box 8.

8. Joseph H. Dillon, Acting Senior Customs Representative, to Commissioner of Customs, Havana, 3 April 1959, RG170-74-12, Box 22.

9. Steve Minas, Customs Agent, to Commissioner of Customs, Havana, 24 April 1959, RG170-74-12, Box 22. Vera Serafín had led the underground resistance against Batista in the capital (Fuentes, *Narcotráfico*, 48).

10. Steve Minas, Customs Agent, to Commissioner of Customs, Havana, 24 April 1959, RG170-74-12, Box 22.

11. U.S. Embassy in Cuba to Department of State, Dispatch, Havana, 18 February 1959, 611.47/2-1859, *FRUS, 1958–60*, 403.

12. Joseph H. Dillon, Acting Senior Customs Representative, to Commissioner of Customs, Havana, 3 April 1959, RG170-74-12, Box 22.

13. Telex, 10 April 1959, 9:49 A.M., RG170-71A-3555, Box 8; H. J. Anslinger, Commissioner of Narcotics, to Gilbert E. Yates, Director, Division of Narcotic Drugs, United Nations, 13 April 1959, RG170-71A-3555, Box 8.

14. Treasury Department, U.S. Customs Service, Havana, Cuba, to Supervising Customs Agent, New York, 13 April 1959, RG170-71A-3555, Box 8.

15. Steve Minas, Customs Agent, to Commissioner of Customs, Havana, 24 April 1959, RG170-74-12, Box 22.

16. Jorge A. de Castroverde, Director del Buró Central Nacional — Interpol, to J. H. Ashlinger [sic], Havana, 28 April 1959, RG170-71A-3555, Box 8.

17. Stewart H. Adams, Senior Customs Representative, Monthly Activities Report, Havana, 30 April 1960, RG170-74-12, Box 22.

18. "Confidential Report of the Brazilian Delegation to the Inter-American Meeting on the Illicit Traffic in Coca Leaves and Cocaine," RG170-74-4, Box 10.

19. H. J. Anslinger, Commissioner of Narcotics, to Gilbert E. Yates, Director, Division of Narcotic Drugs, United Nations, 10 April 1959, RG170-71A-3555, Box 8; H. J. Anslinger, Commissioner of Narcotics, to Jorge A. de Castroverde, 23 April 1959, RG170-71A-3555, Box 8.

20. José Antonio Cabrera, "Cuba se convirtió durante los último años en el centro mundial del tráfico de drogas — dice Harry J. Anslinger, Jefe del Buró de Narcóticos de Estados Unidos," *Bohemia*, 31 May 1959, 46–47, 121.

21. Joseph H. Dillon, Acting Senior Customs Representative, to Commissioner of Customs, Havana, 3 April 1959, RG170-74-12, Box 22; Stewart H. Adams, Senior Customs Representative, Monthly Activities Report, Havana, 30 April 1960, 20 September 1960, RG170-74-12, Box 22.

22. Salas, *Social Control*, 52–53; Arias Fernández, *Cuba*, 56, 64.

23. United Nations Economic and Social Council, Commission on Narcotic Drugs, "Illicit Traffic: Cuba," E/CN.7/R.11/add.39, 7 April 1961, RG170-74-12, Box 22.

24. "Marijuana Seller Gets Death in Cuba," *New York Times*, 9 April 1959, 2; Phillips *Cuban Dilemma*, 68; Charles Siragusa to H. J. Anslinger, 17 April 1959, RG170-71A-3555, Box 8.

25. Stewart H. Adams, Senior Customs Representative, Monthly Activities Report, Havana, 31 January 1960, RG170-74-12, Box 22; Phillips, *Cuban Dilemma*, 203–4.

26. "Eleven Countries Ratify Convention on Narcotic Drugs," *United Nations Review*, November 1962, 59; Salas, *Social Control*, 55.

27. Cited by Anslinger, *Protectors*, 230.

28. Ibid., 223.

29. K. C. Rudd, Narcotic Agent, "Jack Lansky and Dino Vicente Cellini DiMarco," Miami, 11 May 1959, RG170-71A-3555, Box 8; "Americans Still Held," *New York Times*, 10 May 1959, 12.

30. Steve Minas, Customs Agent, to Commissioner of Customs, Havana, 13 May 1959, RG170-71A-3555, Box 8; K. C. Rudd, Narcotic Agent, "William Willie Lamy, Montreal Canada," Miami, 14 May 1959, RG170-71A-3555, Box 8; Charbonneau, *Canadian Connection*, 153.

31. Steve Minas, Customs Agent, to Commissioner of Customs, Havana, 13 May 1959, RG170-71A-3555, Box 8.

32. "Memorandum: Dino Vicente Cellini," 22 May 1959, RG170-71A-3555, Box 8.

33. Martín F. Pera, Narcotic Agent, "Investigation of Background and Associates of Dino Vincenzo Cellini," New York, 22 May 1959, RG170-71A-3555, Box 8.

34. James E. Brown Jr., Consul General, to Sr. César Blanco, Director General de Orden Público, Ministerio de Gobernación, Havana, 27 May 1959, RG170-71A-3555, Box 8.

35. Dr. Jorge A. de Castroverde, Director de la Oficina General Nacional, Interpol, to Wayland L. Speer, Asst. to Commissioner of Narcotics, Havana, 4 June 1959, RG170-71A-3555, Box 8.

36. See K. C. Rudd, Narcotic Agent, to H. J. Anslinger, Commissioner of Narcotics, Miami, 29 May 1959, RG170-71A-3555, Box 8; Charles Siragusa to H. J. Anslinger, 2 June 1959, RG170-71A-3555, Box 8; César Blanco, Director General de Orden Público y Asuntos Generales del Ministerio de Gobernación, to Wayland Speer, Havana, 5 June 1959, RG170-71A-3555, Box 8; Bonsal to Secretary of State, Havana, 5 June 1959, RG170-71A-3555, Box 8; Charles Siragusa to Files, 8 June 1959, RG170-71A-3555, Box 8; Wayland L. Speer, Assistant to the Commissioner, to District Supervisors, Districts 2, 6, 17, 9 June 1959, RG170-71A-3555, Box 8.

37. Dr. Jorge A. de Castroverde, Director de la Oficina Central Nacional, Interpol, to Wayland L. Speers, Asst. Commissioner, Bureau of Narcotics, Havana, 20 June 1959, RG170-71A-3555, Box 8; "Cuba Orders Two Deported," New York Times, 21 June 1959, 4.

38. Interpol Havana to Wayland Speer, Bureau of Narcotics, Havana, 1 July 1959, RG170-71A-3555, Box 8; K. C. Rudd, Narcotic Agent in Charge, to Ross B. Ellis, Atlanta District Supervisor, Miami, 17 August 1959, RG170-71A-3555, Box 8; Henry L. Giordano, Acting Commissioner of Narcotics, to District Supervisor Gaffney, 3 September 1959; Interpol Havana to Wayland Speer, Bureau of Narcotics, Havana, 1 July 1959, RG170-71A-3555, Box 8; Charbonneau, Canadian Connection, 154.

39. Lorenz and Schwarz, Marita, 173–76.

40. "5 Held in Cuba Narcotics Raid," New York Times, 30 July 1960, 3.

41. Ragano and Raab, Mob Lawyer, 53–62.

42. "Memorandum: Santos Trafficante Jr.," RG170-71A-3555, Box 8.

43. Ibid.

44. "El caso de S. Trafficante," La Gaceta, 19 June 1959, clipping, RG170-71A-3555, Box 8.

45. "Cuban Police Take Trafficante to Daughter's Wedding," Miami Herald, 22 June 1959; Pavia, Cuba Project, 64.

46. Dr. Jorge A. de Castroverde, Director de la Oficina Central Nacional, Interpol, to H. J. Anslinger, Havana, 15 November 1959; Interpol Havana to Wayland Speer, Bureau of Narcotics, Havana, 1 July 1959, RG170-71A-3555, Box 8.

47. Lawrence Lafer and Harry Schlegel, "Pair Hunted for Grilling on Anastasia," New York Daily News, 8 January 1958, clipping, RG170-71A-3555, Box 8; Joseph Martin and James Desmond, "Link Cuba Mob with Murder of Anastasia," New York Daily News, 9 January 1958, clipping, RG170-71A-3555, Box 8; Joseph Martin and James Desmond,

"Four Cubans Helped Warn Anastasia Off," *New York Daily News*, 10 January 1958, clipping, RG170-71A-3555, Box 8; Anthony John Falanga, Narcotic Agent, "Report: Santo Trafficante Jr.," New York, 1 September 1961, RG170-71A-3555, Box 8.

48. See "Convenio sobre apertura de crédito bancario entre Banco Financiero y la Compañía Hotelera Shepard, S.A.," Havana, 14 October 1959, FBNC, Legajo 483, no. 16; "Contrato de anticipo y otros compromisos," Havana, 30 November 1960, FBNC, Legajo 483, no. 16; A. García Álvarez to Tomás Regalado, Havana, 6 January 1961, FBNC.

49. "Oscar Méndez Carbonell, Compañía de Hoteles La Riviera S.A. Informe de Intervención," 31 August 1959, FBNC, Legajo 517, no. 18; Lorenz and Schwarz, *Marita*, 24.

50. "Informe financiero del Habana Riviera Hotel correspondiente a Nov. 30, 1959," FBNC, Legajo 517, no. 16.

51. Lacey, *Little Man*, 258.

52. Ibid., 257.

53. Charles Siragusa to H. J. Anslinger, 2 February 1960, RG170-71A-3555, Box 8.

54. See Ruth Montgomery, "Castro-Ruled Cuba Tops World in Use of Cocaine," *New Orleans Times-Picayune*, 27 June 1960, "Cuba Now 'Staging Area' for Drug Running to U.S.," *Baltimore News- Post*, 27 June 1960, "Reds Use Drug as Weapon," *New York Journal-American*, 28 June 1960, clippings, RG170-74-12, Box 22 (translated from Spanish).

55. Harvey Wilson, "Secret Report Reveals . . . Castro Is a Dope Addict," *National Police Gazette*, March 1966, clipping, RG170-74-12, Box 22.

56. "Classified Report of the United States Delegation to the Second Meeting of the Inter-American Consultative Group on Narcotics Control, Rio de Janeiro, Brazil, 27 November to 7 December, 1961, Submitted to the Secretary of State, Charles Siragusa, Chairman of the Delegation," 4 January 1962, RG170-74-4, Box 10.

57. Charles Siragusa, Deputy Commissioner, to H. L. Giordano, Commissioner of Narcotics, Lima, 30 November 1962, RG170-74-12, Box 10.

58. Siragusa, *Trail*, 196.

59. Emilio T. González, *Cuban Connection*, 2–4. Some scholars have found that Siragusa acted as a contact between the FBN and the CIA (Hinckle and Turner, *Deadly Secrets*, 28; Russo, *Live*, 50).

60. "Cuba Pushing Dope; China Opium Reaches Miami," *New York Mirror*, 15 March 1962, clipping, RG170-74-12, Box 22. See also "Narcotics Rise Laid to China and Cuba," *New York Times*, 1 June 1962, 2.

61. "Cuba Said to Push Opium Sales in the U.S.," *New York Times*, 16 March 1962, clipping, RG170-74-12, Box 22. See also Kinder, "Bureaucratic Cold Warrior," 190.

62. Charles Siragusa to H. J. Anslinger, 22 March 1962, RG170-74-12, Box 22.

63. "Abusive Cuban Note Handed Back by U.S.," *Washington Post*, 24 March 1962, A4.

64. "Big Cocaine Seizure Held Cuban in Origin," *New York Times*, 30 March 1962, 68; "Narcotics Worth $500,000 Seized," *Washington Post*, A1; "Cuba Plot Is Cited in Narcotics Raids," *New York Times*, 31 March 1962, 2; Valentine, *Strength*, 230.

65. Charles Siragusa, Acting Commissioner of Narcotics, to J. Edgar Hoover, Director, Federal Bureau of Investigation, 26 June 1962, RG170-74-12, Box 22.

66. *United States v. Ramon Bustillos and Eugenio Hernandez Villa*, Criminal Docket 131-62-M-Cr, USDCM; *United States v. José González Pérez and Ramon Bustillos*, Criminal Docket 134-62-M-Cr, USDCM; *United States v. Arturo Ojeda Rodriguez*, Criminal Docket 135-62-M-Cr, USDCM; *United States v. Luis Benitez Delgado, Jose Leon, Jose Adrian Barral, Rudolf Martinez, and Gabriela Giralt*, Criminal Docket 179-62-M-Cr, USDCM; *United States v. Arturo Ojeda Rodriguez*, Criminal Docket 224-62-M-Cr-EC, USDCM; "Cuban Aliens Convicted of Federal Narcotic Violations since July 1959," RG170, Cuba 1966–1967; *United States of America v. Ramon Bustillos and Eugenio Hernandez Villa*, no. 131-62-M-Cr-DD, RG21SE, Criminal Case Files, 1916–, Box 430; *United States of America v. José Gonzalez Perez and Ramon Bustillos*, no. 134-62-M-Cr-DD, RG21SE, Criminal Case Files, 1916–, Box 430; *United States of America v. Arturo Ojeda Rodriguez*, no. 135-62-M-Cr, RG21SE, Criminal Case Files, 1916–, Box 430; *United States of America, Plaintiff, v. Adolph Martin (with aliases), Defendant*, no. 189-62-Cr, RG21SE, Criminal Case Files, 1916–, Box 435; *United States of America v. Arturo Ojeda Rodriguez*, no. 224-62-M-Cr-EC, RG21SE, Criminal Case Files, 1916–, Box 436.

67. Dom Bonafede, "Islander Who Stayed to Dinner Worries Miami," *Washington Post*, 29 April 1962, E3.

68. See Masud-Piloto, *From Welcomed Exiles*, 33–34, 51; Grenier and Pérez, *Legacy of Exile*, 46–48.

69. "Big Cocaine Seizure Held Cuban in Origin," *New York Times*, 30 March 1962, 68; "3 Cubans Convicted of Cocaine Traffic," *New York Times*, 11 May 1962, 63; "U.S. Jails 2 in Narcotics Case; One Reported Close to Castro," *New York Times*, 2 June 1962, 47.

70. "Statement for the Press, March 23, 1962, U.S. Rejection of Insulting Cuban Note on Narcotics," RG170-74-12, Box 22.

71. Gleijeses, *Conflicting Missions*, 16, 22–23; Fursenko and Naftali, *"One Hell of a Gamble,"* 146–48.

72. John F. Kennedy, Memorandum, Washington, D.C., 30 November 1961, Kennedy Library, President's Office Files, Countries Series, Cuba, *FRUS, 1961–63*, 688. See also Russo, *Live*, 43; Rabe, *Most Dangerous Area*, 137; Valdés-Dapena, *Operación Mangosta*.

73. Lansdale, Chief of Operations, Operation Mongoose, Memorandum, Central Intelligence Agency, DCI (McCone) Files: Job 80-B01285A, Box 5, *FRUS, 1961–63*, 692; Lansdale, Chief of Operations, Operation Mongoose, Program Review, Washington, D.C., 18 January 1962, 737.00/1-2062, *FRUS, 1961–63*, 710; Fursenko and Naftali, *"One Hell of a Gamble,"* 158; Bissell, *Reflections*, 200.

74. Helms, Chief of Operations in the Deputy Directorate for Plans, to McCone, Director of Central Intelligence, Washington, D.C., 19 January 1962, Central Intelligence Agency, DCI (McCone) Files: Job 80-B01285A, Box 5, *FRUS, 1961–63*, 719; Bohning, *Castro Obsession*, 144. The FBI had been interrogating Cuban exiles in Miami since 1959. See Pavia, *Cuba Project*, 54.

75. Elliston, *Psywar*, 207–8.

76. "Memorandum for the Record," Washington, D.C., 14 May 1962, Central Intelligence Agency, DCI (McCone) Files: Job 80-B01285A, Box 11, *FRUS, 1961–63*, 807–9. See also *CIA Targets Fidel*; Kornbluh, *Bay of Pigs*, 9–10, 265, 294; Russo, *Live*, 51–52, 57, 60; Escalante Font, *Guerra secreta*.

77. See Waldron and Hartmann, *Ultimate Sacrifice*.

78. Dallek, *Unfinished Life*, 439.

79. Russo, *Live*, 22, 37, 47–48.

80. "Crush This Evil," *New York Journal-American*, 19 March 1962, clipping, RG170-74-12, Box 22.

81. "Boot Them Out," *Baltimore News-Post*, 3 April 1962, clipping, RG170-74-12, Box 22.

82. Victor Riesel, "'Cocaine Castro' Has No Thought for Food," *New York Mirror*, 6 June 1962, clipping, RG170-74-12, Box 22; Victor Riesel, "Cuban Agents Flood U.S. with Cocaine," *Dallas Morning News*, 11 June 1962, clipping, RG170-74-12, Box 22.

83. "Statement of Senator Kenneth B. Keating at Opening of Hearings on the Flow of Narcotics from the Communist Bloc, Internal Security Subcommittee of the U.S. Senate Committee on the Judiciary Meeting in New York, N.Y., Friday, April 13, 1962," RG170-74-12, Box 22 (translated from Spanish).

84. "Statement of Charles Siragusa, Assistant to the Commissioner of Narcotics, before the Sub-Committee on Internal Security, Senate Judiciary Committee, on 13 April 1962 at New York City," RG170-74-12, Box 22.

85. "Report of the U.S. Delegation to the First Inter-American Meeting on the Illicit Traffic in Cocaine and Coca Leaves, Rio de Janeiro, Brazil, March 21–25, 1960, Submitted to the Secretary of State, Charles Siragusa, Chairman of the Delegation," 14 April 1960, RG170-74-4, Box 10.

86. "U.S. Secret Service, Treasury Department, Investigation Made by SA Ernest I. Aragon," Miami, 31 January 1963, RG170-74-12, Box 22.

87. Patrick P. O'Carroll, Director, Narcotics Training School, to Charles Siragusa, Deputy Commissioner of Narcotics, 10 April 1962, RG170-74-12, Box 22.

88. "Cuba and Red China Called Dope Sources," *Washington Post*, 23 August 1963, A3.

89. Daniel P. Casey, District Supervisor, to Henry L. Giordano, Commissioner of Narcotics, "House Un-American Activities Committee Investigation, Cuban Narcotic Traffic," 31 August 1965, RG170-74-12, Box 22.

90. Henry L. Giordano, Commissioner of Narcotics, to David C. Acheson, Special Assistant to the Secretary, 7 March 1966, RG170-74-12, Box 22.

91. Anslinger, *Murderers*, 207; Kinder, "Bureaucratic Cold Warrior."

92. Anslinger, *Murderers*, 209–10.

93. "Illicit Traffic: Need for Closer International Co-Operation," *United Nations Bulletin*, 15 May 1952, 408. During the 1930 and 1940s, when Japan was a U.S. enemy, Anslinger had accused that country's government of promoting drug trafficking as a way of earning revenue, corrupting westerners, and enslaving people under the heel of the Japanese empire (Courtwright, *Forces*, 171).

94. Valentine, *Strength*, 102.

95. "War on Illicit Drug Traffic; Commission Assays Reports on Narcotics Control," *United Nations Bulletin*, 1 May 1953, 332.

96. Yongming, *Anti-Drug Crusades*, 176 n. 19.

97. William O. Walker III, *Opium*, 89–90, 187–88.

98. Yongming, *Anti-Drug Crusades*; Meyer and Parssinen, *Webs of Smoke*, 268–69, 272–74.

99. Meyer and Parssinen, *Webs of Smoke*, 271–72.

Epilogue

1. Joseph A. Fortier, Supervising Customs Agent, to the Commissioner of Customs, Miami, 3 January 1960, RG170-71A-3555, Box 8; Stewart H. Adams, Senior Customs Representative, Monthly Activities Report, Havana, 29 February 1960, RG170-71A-3555, Box 8; Benjamin S. White Jr., Senior Customs Representative, to Commissioner of Customs, Mexico City, 2 December 1960, RG170-71A-3555, Box 8; Charles Siragusa, Acting Commissioner of Narcotics, to James Green, Immigration and Naturalization Service, 11 June 1963, RG170-71A-3555, Box 8; Joseph Dino Jr., Staff Assistant, to John R. Enright, Assistant Commissioner, 1 November 1967, RG170-74-12, Box 40.

2. John T. Cusack, District Supervisor, to Anthony S. Pohl, Narcotic Agent, Rome, 18 July 1961, RG170-74-12, Box 24; Paul E. Knight, Narcotic Agent, "Albert Bistoni et al.," RG170-74-12, Box 24; Albert Garofalo, Narcotic Agent, "Clandestine Laboratories and Narcotic Organizations Operating in France," Marseille, 13 July 1965, RG170-74-12, Box 24.

3. Albert Garofalo, Memorandum Report: Activities of French Narcotic Traffickers at Barcelona and Madrid, Spain, Marseille, 20 January 1966, RG170-74-12, Box 30; Michael C. Picini, District Supervisor, to Director General de Seguridad Bureau Interpol, Madrid-España, Rome, 15 February 1966, RG170-74-12, Box 30.

4. Albert Garofalo, Narcotic Agent, "Buenos Aires, Argentina," New York, 15 May 1967, RG170-74-12, Box 24.

5. Valentine, *Strength*, 325.

6. Jacques I. Kierte, Narcotic Agent, "Execution of Rogatory Commissions, Comments by the Judge of Instruction," Paris, 13 January 1967, RG170-74-12, Box 40; Charbonneau, *Canadian Connection*, 247.

7. On the Rivard case and the ensuing political scandal, see the following *New York Times* articles: "Judge Is Appointed in Ottawa Inquiry into Bribe Charge," 26 November 1964, 52; Jay Walz, "Jailbreak Stirs Furor in Ottawa," 4 March 1965, 2; "Canadians Press Hunt for Fugitive," 5 March 1965, 10; "Minister Leaves Canadian Post after Criticism in Bribery Case," 30 June 1965, 13; "Ex-Pearson Aide Quits Commons in Bribe Case," 7 July 1965, 9; "Rivard, Fugitive, Caught in Canada," 17 July 1965, 5; "Canada Will Return Rivard to Face Charges in Texas," 22 July 1965, 17; "Smuggler Traces Heroin Operation," 15 September 1965, 28; "4 Heroin Smugglers Imprisoned; Leader Gets 20-Year Sentence," 13 November 1965, 60; "Bribery Case Ends in Ottawa Mistrial," 31 March 1966, 19. See also "Escapee Sends Apology from Another Prison," *Washington Post*, 25 December 1965, A9; Charbonneau, *Canadian Connection*, chapter 9.

8. "Heroin Smuggler Gets Top Penalty," *New York Times*, 5 November 1960, 48; "Actions in United States Supreme Court," *New York Times*, 7 June 1967, 63; "Proceedings in the U.S. Supreme Court," *New York Times*, 21 January 1969, 58; Charbonneau, *Canadian Connection*, 116–17.

9. Stewart H. Adams, Senior Customs Representative, Monthly Activities Report, Havana, 31 May 1960, 30 September 1960, RG170-74-12, Box 22.

10. Astorga, *Drogas*, 185–86; Stewart H. Adams, Senior Customs Representative, Monthly Activities Report, Havana, 31 July 1960, 30 September 1960, RG170-74-12, Box 22.

11. Astorga, *Drogas*, 186.

12. Edwin A. Lahey, "Cubans in Mexico Run Cocaine Ring," *Detroit Free Press*, 24 March 1965, clipping, RG170; George H. Gaffney, Acting Commissioner of Narcotics, to Paul G. Rogers, House of Representatives, 29 September 1965, RG170-74-12, Box 22.

13. David W. Costa, Narcotic Agent, "Cocaine Traffic between South America, Central America, and the United States," New York, 15 November 1961, RG170-74-12, Box 19.

14. "Cuban Aliens Convicted of Federal Narcotic Violations since July 1959," RG170, Cuba, 1966–1967.

15. See *United States of America v. Mario Escandar*, no. 11.433-M-Cr, RG21SE, Criminal Case Files, 1916–, Box 363; *United States of America v. Armando Villonga and Mary Suarez*, no. 11.439-M-Cr, RG21SE, Criminal Case Files, 1916–, Box 354; *United States of America v. Mario Escandar*, no. 11.525-M-Cr, RG21SE, Criminal Case Files, 1916–, Box 363; *United States of America v. Ramon Bustillos and Eugenio Hernandez Villa*, no. 131-62-M-Cr-DD, RG21SE, Criminal Case Files, 1916–, Box 430; *United States of America v. Jose Gonzalez Perez and Ramon Bustillos*, no. 134-62-M-Cr-DD, RG21SE, Criminal Case Files, 1916–, Box 430; *United States of America v. Arturo Ojeda Rodriguez*, no. 135–62-M-Cr, RG21SE, Criminal Case Files, 1916–, Box 430; *United States of America v. Arturo Ojeda Rodriguez*, no. 224-62-M-Cr-EC, RG21SE, Criminal Case Files, 1916–, Box 436; *United States of America, Plaintiff, v. Adolph Martin (with aliases), Defendant*, no. 189-62-Cr, RG21SE, Criminal Case Files, 1916–, Box 435; *United States of America, Plaintiff, v. Domingo del Cristo, also known as Juan Rodriguez, Defendant*, no. 521–62-Cr-DD, RG21SE, Criminal Case Files, 1916–, Box 458; *United States of America v. Antonio Padilla Samodevilla*, no. 63-256-Cr-DD, RG21SE, Criminal Case Files, 1916–, Box 476; *United States of America, Plaintiff, v. Jose Thomas Polledo, a/k/a Pancho*, no. 63-276-Cr-DD, RG21SE, Criminal Case Files, 1916–, Box 476; *United States of America v. Reinaldo Lopez Lima*, no. 63-418-Cr-EC, RG21SE, Criminal Case Files, 1916–, Box 482; *United States of America v. Antonio Padilla Samodevilla*, no. 63-511-Cr-DD, RG21SE, Criminal Case Files, 1916–, Box 492; *United States of America v. Santiago Garcia More and Jorgelina Canamero Rojas alias Garcia*, no. 63-553-Cr-CF, RG21SE, Criminal Case Files, 1916–, Box 494; *United States of America v. Ramon Cruz Diaz, Orestes Diaz Gestell, alias Pouchi Diaz, Carlos Lorenzo Gomez, and Maria Teresa Gestell Diaz*, no. 63-554-CR-CF, RG21SE, Criminal Case Files, 1916–, Box 494; *United States of America v. Ramon Cruz Diaz, Orestes Diaz Gestell, alias Pouchi Diaz, Carlos Lorenzo Gomez, and Maria Teresa Gestell Diaz*, no. 63-628-Cr-CF, RG21SE, Criminal Case Files, 1916, Box 501; *United States of America v. Gilbert Velez Rodriguez and Jose Luis Correa*, no. 63-675-Cr-CF, RG21SE, Criminal Case Files, 1916–, Box 523; *United States of America v. Rene Martinez Valdenades*, no. 64-50-Cr-CGY, RG21SE, Criminal Case Files, 1916, Box 509; *United States of America, Plaintiff, v. George Edwards and Fernando Rodriguez-*

Acon, no. 64-189-Cr-EC, RG21SE, Criminal Case Files, 1916–; *United States of America v. Oscar Figer Martinez, alias Red*, no. 64-248-Cr-DD, RG21SE, Criminal Case Files, 1916–, Box 522; *United States of America v. Jose Manuel Franchi-Alfaro Negrin, alias Frank*, no. 62-264-Cr-DD, RG21SE, Criminal Case Files, 1916–, Box 523; *United States of America v. Jose Manuel Franchi-Alfaro Negrin, alias Frank*, no. 64-305-Cr-DD, RG21SE, Criminal Case Files, 1916–, Box 525; *United States of America, Plaintiff, v. Manuel Calixto Rojas de Díaz, a/k/a, Carlos Rojas, and Eddy Sabugo, Defendants*, no. 64-320-Cr-DD, RG21SE, Criminal Case Files, 1916–, Box 482; *United States of America v. Ruben Giro-Herrera, alias Ruben Giro*, no. 64-358-Cr-DD, RG21SE, Criminal Case Files, 1916, Box 527; *United States of America v. Raul Estevez, Manuel Luis Rodriguez, and Pedro Aloma*, no. 65-263-CR-DD, RG21SE, 73A188, Box 582; *United States of America v. Jose de la Paz, and Alfredo Francisco Gonzalez,"* no. 66-6-Cr-WM, RG21SE, 73A188, Box 599; *United States of America v. Jose Diaz*, no. 66-425-Cr-CA, RG21SE, 73A188, Box 617.

16. See *United States of America v. Rolando Bardina, Rafael Panadeiros, Jose Estol Ramirez, Julian Frank Rojas, and Roberto Arce Valdes, Defendants*, RG21NE, Southern District, CR158-200; *United States of America v. Esteban Lastra, Osvaldo Machado, Francisco Rey, and Isaac Garcia, Defendants*, RG21NE, Southern District, CR160-17; *United States of America v. Albert Nunez*, RG21NE, Southern District, 60CR478; *United States of America v. Ramon Menendez, Defendant*, RG21NE, Southern District, 60CR616; *United States of America v. Pablo Guerra, Estella Prat, and Manuel Rivera, a/k/a Indio, Defendants*, RG21NE, Southern District, 62CR117; *United States of America v. Rafael Ochoa Carrillo, Defendant*, RG21NE, Southern District, 62CR951; *United States of America v. Rolando Rivera y Castenada, Defendant*, RG21NE, Southern District; *United States of America v. Julian Florencio Betancourt, Defendant*, RG21NE, Southern District, 63CR853; *United States of America v. Guillermo Harris and Antonio Hernandez, Defendants*, RG21NE, Southern District, 64CR106; *United States of America v. Maximo del Llano, Defendant*, RG21NE, Southern District, 64CR566; *United States of America v. Hiram Jesus Alonso, Defendant*, RG21NE, Southern District, 64CRIM799; *United States of America v. Jose Ramon Paz-Sierra and Luis Paz-Sierra, Defendants*, RG21NE, Southern District, 64CRIM848; *United States of America v. Jose Diaz Verdia, Defendant*, RG21NE, Southern District, 61CR364; *United States of America v. Sabino Concepcion, Defendant*, RG21NE, Southern District, 61CR669; *United States of America v. Pedro Pablo Padrone and Norman Ramis, Defendants*, RG21NE, Southern District, 62CR333; *United States of America v. Alberto Marin, Defendant*, RG21NE, Southern District, 63CR360; *United States of America v. Emilio Irizar, Defendant*, RG21NE, Southern District, 64CRIM923.

17. U.S. Congress, House, *Scope*, 44.

18. *United States of America v. Denise C. Betancourt*, no. 69-402-CR-WM, RG21SE, 77A0075, Box 14; *United States of America v. Denise C. Betancourt*, no. 68-461-CR-WM, RG21SE, 73A188, Box 666; *United States of America v. Pedro Luis Rodriguez y Paz, Raul Fernandez, Fernando Acosta, Anna Echevarry, Norberto Fernandez, Carlos Inchaustegui, Dulce Maria Espinoza, Lucrecia Lum, Clarence Hosea Jackson*, no. 69-443-Cr-JE, RG21SE, 77-0075, Box 18; "G. L. Latimer, Staff Assistant, to Commissioner of Customs," Miami, 10 January 1969, RG170-74-4, Box 9.

19. *United States of America v. Lucy Blanca Ybanez de Franco*, no. 65-370-Cr-DD, RG21SE, 73A188, Box 588.

20. John T. Cusack, District Supervisor, to H. J. Anslinger, Atlanta, 14 July 1958, RG170-74-12, Box 22.

21. On cases of drug trafficking in Colombia that predate the Herrán Olózaga era, see Sáenz Rovner, "Prehistoria: Serie documental," 69–70, 86–88.

22. For a series of such cases, see *United States of America against Jorge Ernesto Parra-Valdivieso, Defendant*," 66CR268, RG21NE, Eastern District; American Embassy in Bogotá to Ruesmo, American Embassy in Mexico, Bogotá, 20 June 1966, RG59, SOC 11-5 COL, Bogotá 1617; Carl F. Esposito, Acting Customs Agent in Charge, to Commissioner of Customs, New York, 6 July 1966, RG170-71A-3555, Box 8; American Embassy in Bogotá to Rueslm, American Embassy in Lima," Bogotá, 21 October 1966, RG59, SOC 11-5 COL, Bogotá 1862; Carlson, "Smuggling: Subject, A. Joseph Eliezer Antia, B. Ernesto Ardila Paez," Bogotá, 10 March 1967, RG170-71A-3555, Box 8; Richard J. Dunagan, Narcotic Agent, "Investigation of Julian Martinez et al., Bogotá, Colombia," Mexico City, 12 June 1967, RG170-74-12, Box 21; American Consul, Cali, to Department of State, Cali, 14 September 1967, RG170-71A-3555, Box 8; Carlson to Secretary of State, Bogotá, 22 December 1967, RG170-71A-3555, Box 8; *United States v. Homero Sanchez Pineda, Heriberto Lozano Castro, and Maria Hermelinda Montoya*, no. 67-267-CR-EC, RG21SE, Criminal Case Files, 1916–; *United States of America v. Gloria Amparo Velez-Tamayo*, no. 68-267-CR-TC, RG21SE, 73A188, Box 656; *United States of America v. Jairo de Jesus Ospina-Gomez*, no. 68-268-CR-TC, RG21SE, 73A188, Box 656; *United States of America v. Arnulfo Baquero Barreto*, no. 68-323-CR-JE, RG21SE, 73A188, Box 657; *United States of America v. Lilian Gomez de Torres*, 68CR274, RG21NE, Eastern District; *United States of America v. Ofelia Mejia Ramirez, also known as Josefa Emilia Montoya Zapata, and Maria Gonzales, also known as Maria Hermania Montoya Zapata, Defendants*, 68CR383, RG21NE, Eastern District; *United States of America v. Jose Pena-Pena, a/k/a Alirio R. Castillo; Gilberto Amaya Contreras; Domingo Diaz Granados, a/k/a William A. Carranza*, no. 69-359-CR-TC, RG21SE, 77A0075; *United States of America v. Aura G. de Peralta, Eduvigis P. de Conrado, Alcira R. de Torres, Jose A. Malagon Sanchez, and Wilfredo Ocasio, Defendants*, 69CR29, RG21NE, Eastern District; *United States of America v. Rocio Ramirez Tamayo, Maria Socorro Ortiz Munoz, and John Doe, also known as "Palitraqui," Defendants*, 69CR64, RG21NE, Eastern District; *United States of America v. Juan Carlos Velez*, 69CR64, RG21NE, Eastern District; *United States of America against Norelia Rodriguez Zapata, Defendant*, 69CR157, RG21NE, Eastern District; *United States of America against Juan Ramirez, also known as Santiago Eduardo Gomez-Restrepo, Defendant*, 69CR282, RG21NE, Eastern District.

23. See International Association of Chiefs of Police, *Survey*, 2.

24. Florida State Board of Health, *Annual Report*, 1956, 184–86; 1957, 203–5.

25. See ibid., 1961, 193; 1962, 216; 1963, 135 (translated from Spanish).

26. Chilean drug traffickers continued sending cocaine to the United States until the beginning of the 1970s, at times doing so in association with Cubans who lived in the United States. An important case in this respect was that of Oscar Squella-Avendaño, who hailed from the Chilean elite and owned a fleet of cargo planes. Squella-

Avendaño's gang, composed of Chileans and Cubans, was captured in the mid-1970s, after the Chilean had landed one of his planes, with two hundred pounds of cocaine in its hold, at the Miami International Airport. See *United States of America v. Marco Osorio, Andrés R. Rodríguez, Jorge Vazquez, Carlos Rojas, Rodolfo Quintanilla, Oscar Squella-Avendaño, and Raul de Maria*, no. 70-382-Cr-CF, RG21SE, 77 A0076, Box 17; *United States of America v. Marco Osorio, a.k.a. Jose Fernandez, Andrés R. Rodríguez, Jorge Vazquez, Carlos Rojas, Rodolfo Quintanilla, Oscar Squella-Avendaño, and Raul de Maria*, no. 70-572-Cr-CF, RG21SE, 830291, Box 14.

27. On the substantial number of drug trafficking cases in the Miami area that involved Americans, see *United States of America v. Nathaniel Chatman*, no. 11.610-M-Cr, RG21SE, Criminal Case Files, 1916–, Box 371; *United States of America v. John Beverly*, no. 11.707-M-Cr, RG21SE, Criminal Case Files, 1916–, Box 374; *United States of America v. Robert S. Hyman, alias Bobby Roman*, no. 11.468-M-Cr, RG21SE, Criminal Case Files, 1916–, Box 365; *United States of America v. Walter Hirnyk Jr.*, no. 11.696-M-Cr, RG21SE, Criminal Case Files, 1916–, Box 374; *United States of America v. John Doe Alias Pee Wee (True name: Ellis Lee Wallace)*, no. 11.619-M-Cr, RG21SE, Criminal Case Files, 1916–, Box 372; *United States of America v. Bernard O. Smith*, no. 11.717-M-Cr, RG21SE, Criminal Case Files, 1916–, Box 374; *United States of America v. George Hurd*, no. 11.961-M-Cr, RG21SE, Criminal Case Files, 1916, Box 383; *United States of America v. Ulysses Walker*, no. 11.964-M-Cr, RG21SE, Criminal Case Files, 1916–, Box 384; *United States of America v. Gladys Wallace*, no. 11.928-M-Cr, RG21SE, Criminal Case Files, 1916–, Box 382; *United States of America v. Charles Edward Grier*, no. 12.048-M-Cr, RG21SE, Criminal Case Files, 1916–, Box 400; *United States of America v. Joseph Vitale*, no. 12.060-M-Cr, RG21SE, Criminal Case Files, 1916–, Box 402; *United States of America v. Joseph Vitale*, no. 12.061-M-Cr, RG21SE, Criminal Case Files, 1916–, Box 403; *United States of America v. Eugene T. Pinder*, no. 12.065-M-Cr, RG21SE, Criminal Case Files, 1916–, Box 403; *United States of America v. David Frank Rossiter*, no. 12.106-M-Cr, RG21SE, Criminal Case Files, 1916–, Box 404; *United States of America v. James Oblesby*, no. 12.269-M-Cr, RG21SE, Criminal Case Files, 1916–, Box 412; *United States of America v. Gerald Milton Seidler*, no. 61-128, RG21SE, Criminal Case Files, 1916–, Box 404; *United States of America v. Sanford Ralph Abramson*, no. 53-62-M-Cr, RG21SE, Criminal Case Files, 1916–, Box 427; *United States of America v. Herbert Raymond Bridges*, no. 142-62-M-Cr, RG21SE, Criminal Case Files, 1916–, Box 431; *United States of America v. Al Levy*, no. 195-62-M-Cr, RG21SE, Criminal Case Files, 1916–, Box 435; *United States of America v. Arthur Curtis*, no. 311-62-M-Cr, RG21SE, Criminal Case Files, 1916–, Box 441; *United States of America v. Richard Greenfield*, no. 340-62-M-Cr, RG21SE, Criminal Case Files, 1916–, Box 443; *United States of America v. Wille B. Harris, alias Harris Goodblack*, no. 632-62-M-Cr, RG21SE, Criminal Case Files, 1916–, Box 462; *United States of America v. Robert Lee Cason*, no. 590-62-M-Cr, RG21SE, Criminal Case Files, 1916–, Box 461; *United States of America v. Martin L. Karp, Robert Smusz, alias Lefty, and Edward C. Delaney*, no. 63-58-Cr-EC, RG21SE, Criminal Case Files, 1916–, Box 467; *United States of America v. Marvin Roscher and Barry Landsman*, no. 63-112-Cr-EC, RG21SE, Criminal Case Files, 1916–, Box 470; *United States of America v. Anthony John Novello*, no. 64-172-Cr-CF, RG21SE, Criminal Case Files, 1916–; *United States of America*

v. Eddie Lee Kirkland, no. 63-206-Cr-EC, RG21SE, Criminal Case Files, 1916–, Box 471; *United States of America v. Jerome W. White*, no. 63-207-Cr-EC, RG21SE, Criminal Case Files, 1916–, Box 471; *United States of America v. Delfina Davis*, no. 63-216-Cr-EC, RG21SE, Criminal Case Files, 1916–, Box 471; *United States of America v. J. L. Jordan*, no. 63-274-Cr-EC, RG21SE, Criminal Case Files, 1916–, Box 476; *United States of America v. Phillip Anthony Roker*, no. 63-447-Cr-EC, RG21SE, Criminal Case Files, 1916–, Box 489; *United States of America v. Hyman Lesnick*, no. 63-642-Cr-CF, RG21SE, Criminal Case Files, 1916–; *United States of America v. Aceie Casey Pearman, alias 'TC,'* no. 64-309-Cr-DD, RG21SE, Criminal Case Files, 1916–, Box 525; *United States of America v. Sally Lin Holtzman and Edward Leonard Rapp*, no. 64-485-Cr-CF, RG21SE, Criminal Case Files, 1916–, Box 536; *United States of America v. Edward Mitchell, with Aliases*, no. 65-62-Cr-EC, RG21SE, Criminal Case Files, 1916–, Box 577; *United States of America v. Martin J. Matza and Candence Elizabeth Witlin*, no. 66-60-Cr-WM, RG21SE, Criminal Case Files, 1916–, Box 601; *United States of America v. William E. Adams and Kenneth Latimer*, no. 66-247-Cr-DD, RG21SE, 73A188, Box 610; *United States of America v. Arthur Franklin Dukeshire*, no. 67-159-Cr-CA, RG21SE, 73A188, Box 629; *United States of America v. Scott E. Harris, Armand Allen Rice, Blythe Lynn Vigo, and Ariel Nicolas Arenado*, no. 69-89-Cr-WM, RG21SE, 71A0075, Box 2.

28. See Musto and Korsmeyer, *Quest*, xv–xvii, 1–3.

Bibliography

Archives

Bogotá, Colombia
  Archivo General de la Nación
    Fondo Ministerio de Relaciones Exteriores
Camagüey, Cuba
  Archivo Histórico Provincial de Camagüey
    Índice del Fondo Juzgado de Instrucción del Partido Judicial de Camagüey
      (1899–1954)
College Park, Maryland
  U.S. National Archives and Records Administration
    Record Group 59, General Records of the Department of State
    Record Group 170, Records of the Drug Enforcement Administration
East Point–Ellenwood–Morrow, Georgia
  U.S. National Archives and Records Administration, Southeast Region
    Record Group 21, Records of the District Courts of the United States
Havana, Cuba
  Archivo Nacional de Cuba
    Fondo Banco Nacional de Cuba
    Fondo Chibás
    Fondo Donativos y Remisiones
    Fondo Grau
    Fondo Ministerio de Estado
    Fondo Ministerio de Relaciones Exteriores
    Fondo Presidios y Cárceles
    Fondo Secretaría de Estado
    Fondo Secretaría de la Presidencia
Miami, Florida
  Richter Library, University of Miami
    Archives and Special Collections Department
      Collection 341, Pan American World Airways
    Cuban Heritage Collection
      Collection 0124, Lyceum and Lawn Tennis Club, La Havana
  U.S. District Court
    Criminal Dockets

New York City
U.S. National Archives and Records Administration, Northeast Region
Record Group 21, Records of the District Courts of the United States

Official Documents

CUBA

Banco de Fomento Agrícola e Industrial de Cuba. *Memoria, 1951–1952.* Havana: Editorial Lex, 1952.
———. *Memoria, 1952–1953.* Havana: Editorial Lex, 1953.
———. *Memoria, 1953–1954.* Havana: Editorial Lex, 1954.
Havana. *Gaceta Oficial de la República de Cuba.*
Directorio Telefónico de la Habana, 1958.

GREAT BRITAIN

British Documents on Foreign Affairs: Reports and Papers from the Foreign Office Confidential Print. Part 2, series D, *Latin America, 1920–1924.* Vol. 3. Bethesda, Md.: University Publications of America, 1989.
British Documents on Foreign Affairs: Reports and Papers from the Foreign Office Confidential Print. Part 2, series D, *Latin America, May 1933–March 1934.* Vol. 10. Bethesda, Md.: University Publications of America, 1991.
British Documents on Foreign Affairs: Reports and Papers from the Foreign Office Confidential Print. Part 2, series D, *Latin America, March 1934–June 1934.* Vol. 11. Bethesda, Md.: University Publications of America, 1991.
British Documents on Foreign Affairs: Reports and Papers from the Foreign Office Confidential Print. Part 2, series D, *Latin America, May 1934–January 1935.* Vol. 12. Bethesda, Md.: University Publications of America, 1991.
British Documents on Foreign Affairs: Reports and Papers from the Foreign Office Confidential Print. Part 2, series D, *Latin America, January 1935–July 1935.* Vol. 13. Bethesda, Md.: University Publications of America, 1991.
British Documents on Foreign Affairs: Reports and Papers from the Foreign Office Confidential Print. Part 2, series D, *Latin America, February 1938–March 1939.* Vol. 19. Bethesda, Md.: University Publications of America, 1992.
British Documents on Foreign Affairs: Reports and Papers from the Foreign Office Confidential Print. Part 2, series D, *Latin America, March 1939–December 1939.* Vol. 20. Bethesda, Md.: University Publications of America, 1992.
British Documents on Foreign Affairs: Reports and Papers from the Foreign Office Confidential Print. Part 3, series D, *Latin America, January–December 1941.* Vol. 3. Bethesda, Md.: University Publications of America, 1998.
British Documents on Foreign Affairs: Reports and Papers from the Foreign Office Confidential Print. Part 3, series D, *Latin America, January–June 1943.* Vol. 6. Bethesda, Md.: University Publications of America, 1998.
British Documents on Foreign Affairs: Reports and Papers from the Foreign Office

Confidential Print. Part 4, series D, *Latin America, January–December 1947.* Vol. 3. Bethesda, Md.: University Publications of America, 2001.

British Documents on Foreign Affairs: Reports and Papers from the Foreign Office Confidential Print. Part 4, series D, *Latin America, January–December 1948.* Vol. 5. Bethesda, Md.: University Publications of America, 2002.

British Documents on Foreign Affairs: Reports and Papers from the Foreign Office Confidential Print. Part 4, series D, *Latin America, January–December 1949.* Vol. 7. Bethesda, Md.: University Publications of America, 2002.

LEAGUE OF NATIONS

Records of the Conference for the Limitation of the Manufacture of Narcotic Drugs. Vol. 1. Geneva: League of Nations, 1931.

UNITED STATES

Convention between the United States and Cuba: Prevention of Smuggling of Intoxicating Liquors. Treaty Series, no. 738. Washington, D.C.: U.S. Government Printing Office, 1926.

Convention between the United States and Cuba: To Suppress Smuggling. Treaty Series, no. 739. Washington, D.C.: U.S. Government Printing Office, 1926.

Convention between the United States and Denmark: Prevention of Smuggling in Intoxicating Liquors. Treaty Series, no. 693. Washington, D.C.: U.S. Government Printing Office, 1924.

Convention between the United States and Germany: Prevention of Smuggling in Intoxicating Liquors. Treaty Series, no. 694. Washington, D.C.: U.S. Government Printing Office, 1924.

Convention between the United States and Great Britain: Prevention of Smuggling in Intoxicating Liquors. Treaty Series, no. 685. Washington, D.C.: U.S. Government Printing Office, 1924.

Convention between the United States and Italy: Prevention of Smuggling in Intoxicating Liquors. Treaty Series, no. 702. Washington, D.C.: U.S. Government Printing Office, 1924.

Convention between the United States and Mexico: To Prevent Smuggling and for Certain Other Objects. Treaty Series, no. 732. Washington, D.C.: U.S. Government Printing Office, 1926.

Convention between the United States and the Netherlands: Prevention of Smuggling in Intoxicating Liquors. Treaty Series, no. 712. Washington, D.C.: U.S. Government Printing Office, 1925.

Convention between the United States and Norway: Prevention of Smuggling in Intoxicating Liquors. Treaty Series, no. 689. Washington, D.C.: U.S. Government Printing Office, 1924.

Convention between the United States and Panama: Prevention of Smuggling in Intoxicating Liquors. Treaty Series, no. 707. Washington, D.C.: U.S. Government Printing Office, 1925.

Convention between the United States and Sweden: Prevention of Smuggling in Intoxicating Liquors. Treaty Series, no. 698. Washington, D.C.: U.S. Government Printing Office, 1924.

Florida State Board of Health. *Annual Report.* Jacksonville: Board of Health, 1956, 1957, 1961, 1962, 1963.

International Association of Chiefs of Police, Field Operations Division. *A Survey Conducted for the Florida Bureau of Law Enforcement.* 1969.

U.S. Congress, House of Representatives. *Dominican Drug Trafficking: Hearing before the Select Committee on Narcotics Abuse and Control.* 103rd Cong., 1st sess., March 24, 1993. Washington, D.C.: U.S. Government Printing Office, 1979.

————. *The Emerging Drug Threat from Haiti: Hearing before the Subcommittee on Criminal Justice, Drug Policy, and Human Resources of the Committee on Government Reform.* 106th Cong., 2nd sess., April 12, 2000. Washington, D.C.: U.S. Government Printing Office, 2001.

————. *Guatemala and the Dominican Republic: Drug Corruption and Other Threats to Democratic Stability: Hearing before the Subcommittee on the Western Hemisphere of the Committee on International Relations.* 107th Cong., 2nd sess., October 10, 2002. Washington, D.C.: U.S. Government Printing Office, 2002.

————. *The Scope of Drug Abuse in Puerto Rico — Supply and Demand Reduction: Hearings before the Select Committee on Narcotic Control Abuse and Control.* 96th Cong., 1st sess., April 19, 20, and 21, 1979. Washington, D.C.: U.S. Government Printing Office, 1979.

U.S. Congress, Senate. *Drugs, Law Enforcement, and Foreign Policy: A Report prepared by the Subcommittee on Terrorism, Narcotics, and International Operations of the Committee on Foreign Relations.* Washington, D.C.: U.S. Government Printing Office, 1989.

————. *Haitian Narcotics Activities: Hearing before the Caucus on International Narcotics Control of the United States Senate.* 100th Cong., May 21, 1988. Washington, D.C.: U.S. Government Printing Office, 1989.

————. *Investigation of Organized Crime in Interstate Commerce: Hearings before a Special Committee to Investigate Organized Crime in Interstate Commerce.* Part 1, *Florida.* Washington, D.C.: U.S. Government Printing Office, 1950.

————. *Investigation of Organized Crime in Interstate Commerce: Hearings before a Special Committee to Investigate Organized Crime in Interstate Commerce.* Part 1-a, *Florida.* Washington, D.C.: U.S. Government Printing Office, 1951.

————. *Investigation of Organized Crime in Interstate Commerce: Hearings before a Special Committee to Investigate Organized Crime in Interstate Commerce.* Part 14, *Narcotics.* Washington, D.C.: U.S. Government Printing Office, 1951.

U.S. Department of State. *Foreign Relations of the United States, 1952–1954.* Vol. 4, *The American Republics.* Washington, D.C.: U.S. Government Printing Office, 1952–54.

————. *Foreign Relations of the United States, 1934.* Vol. 5, *The American Republics.* Washington, D.C.: U.S. Government Printing Office, 1934.

————. *Foreign Relations of the United States, 1946.* Vol. 11, *The American Republics.* Washington, D.C.: U.S. Government Printing Office, 1946.

——. *Foreign Relations of the United States, 1947.* Vol. 8, *The American Republics.* Washington, D.C.: U.S. Government Printing Office, 1947.

——. *Foreign Relations of the United States, 1948.* Vol. 9, *The Western Hemisphere.* Washington, D.C.: U.S. Government Printing Office, 1948.

——. *Foreign Relations of the United States, 1950.* Vol. 2, *The United Nations; the Western Hemisphere.* Washington, D.C.: U.S. Government Printing Office, 1950.

——. *Foreign Relations of the United States, 1958–1960.* Vol. 6, *Cuba.* Washington, D.C.: U.S. Government Printing Office, 1958–60.

——. *Foreign Relations of the United States, 1961–1963.* Vol. 10, *Cuba.* Washington, D.C.: U.S. Government Printing Office, 1961–63.

——. *Papers Relating to the Foreign Relations of the United States, 1902.* Washington, D.C.: U.S. Government Printing Office, 1902.

——. *Papers Relating to the Foreign Relations of the United States, 1915.* Washington, D.C.: U.S. Government Printing Office, 1915.

U.S. General Accounting Office. 15391 GAO Documents, OSI-95-6R; B-259592, microfiche.

U.S. Treasury Department, Federal Bureau of Narcotics. *Traffic in Opium and Other Dangerous Drugs for the Year Ended December 31, 1929.* Washington, D.C.: U.S. Government Printing Office, 1930.

——. *Traffic in Opium and Other Dangerous Drugs for the Year Ended December 31, 1946.* Washington, D.C.: U.S. Government Printing Office, 1947.

——. *Traffic in Opium and Other Dangerous Drugs for the Year Ended December 31, 1947.* Washington, D.C.: U.S. Government Printing Office, 1948.

——. *Traffic in Opium and Other Dangerous Drugs for the Year Ended December 31, 1948.* Washington, D.C.: U.S. Government Printing Office, 1949.

——. *Traffic in Opium and Other Dangerous Drugs for the Year Ended December 31, 1949.* Washington, D.C.: U.S. Government Printing Office, 1950.

——. *Traffic in Opium and Other Dangerous Drugs for the Year Ended December 31, 1950.* Washington, D.C.: U.S. Government Printing Office, 1951.

——. *Traffic in Opium and Other Dangerous Drugs for the Year Ended December 31, 1951.* Washington, D.C.: U.S. Government Printing Office, 1952.

——. *Traffic in Opium and Other Dangerous Drugs for the Year Ended December 31, 1955.* Washington, D.C.: U.S. Government Printing Office, 1956.

——. *Traffic in Opium and Other Dangerous Drugs for the Year Ended December 31, 1957.* Washington, D.C.: U.S. Government Printing Office, 1958.

Newspapers, Magazines, and Bulletins

Bohemia (Havana)
Diario de la Marina (Havana)
El Mundo (Havana)
Havana Post
Life (Chicago)
Miami Herald

New York Times
Policía Secreta Nacional (Havana)
Time (Chicago)
United Nations Bulletin (New York)
United Nations Weekly Bulletin (New York)
United Nations Review (New York)
Washington Post

Other Works

Acker, Caroline Jean. *Creating the American Junkie: Addiction Research in the Classic Era of Narcotic Control*. Baltimore: Johns Hopkins University Press, 2002.

———. "From All Purpose Anodyne to Marker of Deviance: Physicians' Attitudes towards Opiates in the U.S. from 1890 to 1940." In *Drugs and Narcotics in History*, edited by Roy Porter and Mikulás Teich, 114–32. Cambridge: Cambridge University Press, 1995.

Adames, Fausto Rosario. *Droga y política en República Dominicana: El reinado de Vincho Castillo*. Santo Domingo: Impresos Vargas, 1998.

Agnew, Derek. *Undercover Agent — Narcotics*. London: Corgi, 1961.

Aguilar, Luis E. *Cuba: Conciencias y revolución (El proceso de una reflexión sobre el problema cubano)*. Miami: Ediciones Universal, 1972.

———. *Cuba 1933: Prologue to Revolution*. Ithaca: Cornell University Press, 1972.

Aguilar-León, "La 'década trágica.'" In *La Habana 1952–1961: El final de un mundo, el principio de una ilusión*, edited by Jacobo Machover, 67–83. Madrid: Alianza Editorial, 1995.

Alavez Martín, Elena. *La ortodoxia en el ideario americano*. Havana: Editorial de Ciencias Sociales, 2002.

Alejandro, Ramón. "Primicias del delito sexual." In *La Habana 1952–1961: El final de un mundo, el principio de una ilusión*, edited by Jacobo Machover, 50–60. Madrid: Alianza Editorial, 1995.

Allen, Christian M. *An Industrial Geography of Cocaine*. New York: Routledge, 2005.

Allen, Frederick Lewis. *Only Yesterday: An Informal History of the 1920s*. 1931; New York: Harper and Row, 1964.

Álvarez Estévez, Rolando. *Huellas francesas en el occidente de Cuba (siglos XVI al XIX)*. Havana: Ediciones José Martí, 2001.

Álvarez Estévez, Rolando, and Marta Guzmán Pascual. *Alemanes en Cuba (siglos XVII al XIX)*. Havana: Editorial de Ciencias Sociales, 2004.

———. *Japoneses en Cuba*. Havana: Fundación Fernando Ortiz, 2002.

Ambrose, Stephen E. *Eisenhower: Soldier and President*. New York: Touchstone, 1991.

Ameringer, Charles D. *The Caribbean Legion: Patriots, Politicians, Soldiers of Fortune, 1946–1950*. University Park: Pennsylvania State University Press, 1996.

———. *The Cuban Democratic Experience: The Auténtico Years, 1944–1952*. Gainesville: University Press of Florida, 2000.

Anderson, Jack, and Fred Blumenthal. *The Kefauver Story*. New York: Dial, 1956.

Anslinger, Harry J. *The Murderers: The Story of the Narcotic Gangs*. London: Barker, 1962.

———. *The Protectors: Narcotics Agents, Citizens, and Officials against Organized Crime in America*. New York: Farrar, Straus, 1964.

Anslinger, Harry J., and William F. Tompkins. *The Traffic in Narcotics*. New York: Funk and Wagnalls, 1953.

Antón, Alex, and Roger E. Hernández. *Cubans in America: A Vibrant History of a People in Exile*. New York: Kensington, 2002.

Arango Jaramillo, Mario. *Impacto del narcotráfico en Antioquia*. Medellín: Editorial J. M. Arango, 1988.

Arango Jaramillo, Mario, and Jorge Child. *Coca-Coca: Historia, manejo político, y mafia de la cocaína*. N.p.: Editorial Dos Mundos, 1986.

Arango Mejía, Gabriel. *Genealogías de Antioquia y Caldas*. 2 vols. 1942; Medellín: Litoarte, 1993.

Arboleya, Jesús. *La contrarevolución cubana*. Havana: Editorial de Ciencias Sociales, 1997.

Argote-Freyre, Frank. "Fulgencio Batista: From Revolutionary to Strongman." Ph.D. diss., State University of New Jersey, 2004.

Arias Fernández, Francisco. *Cuba contra el narcotráfico: De víctimas a centinelas*. Havana: Editora Política, 2001.

Astorga, Luis. "Cocaine in Mexico: A Prelude to 'Los Narcos.'" In *Cocaine: Global Histories*, edited by Paul Gootenberg, 183–91. London: Routledge, 1999.

———. *Drogas sin fronteras*. Mexico City: Editorial Grijalbo, 2003.

Attard-Maraninchi, Marie-Françoise. *Le Panier, village corse a Marseille*. Paris: Éditions Autrement, 1997.

Ayala, César J. *American Sugar Kingdom: The Plantation Economy of the Spanish Caribbean, 1898–1934*. Chapel Hill: University of North Carolina Press, 1999.

Balsamo, William, and George Carpozi Jr. *Crime Incorporated or Under the Clock: The Inside Story of the Mafia's First Hundred Years*. Far Hills, N.J.: New Horizon, 1996.

Bardach, Ann Louise. *Cuba Confidential: Love and Vengeance in Miami and Havana*. New York: Random House, 2002.

Barnet, Miguel. *Gallego*. 1983; Havana: Editorial Letras Cubanas, 1988.

———. *La vida real*. 1986; Havana: Editorial Letras Cubanas, 2003.

Barroso, Manuel. "Toxicomanía." *Policía Secreta Nacional* 2, no. 6 (1938): 14–17.

Batista, Fulgencio. *Piedras y leyes*. Mexico City: Ediciones Botas, 1961.

Beals, Carleton. *The Crime of Cuba*. 1933; New York: Arno and the New York Times, 1970.

Bell, Daniel. *The End of Ideology: On the Exhaustion of Political Ideas in the Fifties*. Glencoe, Ill.: Free Press, 1960.

Bender, Thomas, ed. *Rethinking American History in a Global Age*. Berkeley: University of California Press, 2002.

Benedetti, Héctor Angel, ed. *Las mejores letras de tango: Antología de doscientas cincuenta letras, cada una con su historia*. Buenos Aires: Planeta, 2000.

Benítez, Fernando. *La batalla de Cuba*. Mexico City: Ediciones Era, 1960.

Benjamin, Jules R. *The United States and the Origins of the Cuban Revolution: An Empire of Liberty in an Age of National Liberation*. Princeton: Princeton University Press, 1990.

Bergreen, Laurence. *Capone: The Man and the Era*. New York: Simon and Schuster, 1995.

Berridge, Virginia. *Opium and the People: Opiate Use and Drug Control Policy in Nineteenth and Early Twentieth Century England*. 1981; London: Free Association Books, 1999.

Bissell, Richard M., Jr. *Reflections of a Cold Warrior: From Yalta to the Bay of Pigs*. New Haven: Yale University Press, 1996.

Bohning, Don. *The Castro Obsession: U.S. Covert Operations against Cuba, 1959–1965*. Washington, D.C.: Potomac, 2005.

Bonsal, Philip W. *Cuba, Castro, and the United States*. Pittsburgh: University of Pittsburgh Press, 1971.

Botello, Santiago, and Mauricio Angulo. *Conexión Habana: Una peligrosa infiltración en las mafias cubanas*. Madrid: Ediciones Temas de Hoy, 2005.

Brook, Timothy, and Bob Tadashi Wakabayashi. "Introduction: Opium's History in China." In *Opium Regimes: China, Britain, and Japan, 1839–1952*, edited by Timothy Brook and Bob Tadashi Wakabayashi, 1–27. Berkeley: University of California Press, 2000.

Buajasán Marrawi, José, and José Luis Méndez Méndez. *La República de Miami*. Havana: Editorial de Ciencias Sociales, 2003.

Buch Rodríguez, Luis M., and Reinaldo Suárez Suárez. *Otros pasos del gobierno revolucionario cubano: El fin de la luna de miel*. Havana: Editorial de Ciencias Sociales, 2002.

Bullington, Bruce. "A Smugglers' Paradise: Cocaine Trafficking through the Bahamas." *Crime, Law, and Social Change* 16, no. 1 (1991): 59–83.

Bundy, William. *A Tangled Web: The Making of Foreign Policy in the Nixon Presidency*. New York: Hill and Wang, 1999.

Bunge, César A. *Perón y yo: Lo que Perón no dijo*. Buenos Aires: Biblioteca del Muelle, 2000.

Burnham, John C. *Bad Habits: Drinking, Smoking, Taking Drugs, Gambling, Sexual Misbehavior, and Swearing in American History*. New York: New York University Press, 1993.

Busquet, Raoul, and Constant Vautravers. *Histoire de Marseille*. 1945; Marseille: Éditions Robert Laffont/Éditions Jeanne Laffite, 1998.

Caballero, Armando O. "La droga asesina." *Policía Secreta Nacional* 10, no. 4 (1942): 182–84.

Cabrera Déniz, Gregorio J. *Canarios en Cuba: Un capítulo en la historia del archipiélago (1875–1931)*. Las Palmas de Gran Canaria: Ediciones del Cabildo Insular de Gran Canaria, 1996.

Cabrera Infante, Guillermo. *Mea Cuba*. 1992; Madrid: Alfaguara, 1999.

Calvo Ospina, Hernando. *Ron Bacardí: La guerra oculta*. Havana: Casa Editora Abril, 2000.

Cantón Navarro, José. *Historia de Cuba: El desafío del yugo y la estrella*. Havana: Editorial SI-MAR, 2001.

Carbajo, Antonio. *Recuerdo de Camagüey Cuba*. Miami Springs: Language Research Press, 1975.

Cardelle y Penichet, José. "Contribución al estudio de la jerga de los marihuanómanos y expendedores de marihuana en Cuba." *Policía Secreta Nacional* 2, no. 3 (1938): 7–20.

Cardiel Marín, Rosario. "La migración china en el norte de Baja California, 1877–1949." In *Destino México: Un estudio de las migraciones asiáticas a México, siglos XIX y XX*, coordinated by María Elena Ota Mishima, 189–254. Mexico City: El Colegio de México, 1997.

Cardona Gutiérrez, Ramiro, and Sara Rubiano de Velásquez, eds. *El éxodo de colombianos: Un estudio de la corriente migratoria a los Estados Unidos y un intento para propiciar su retorno*. Bogotá: Ediciones Tercer Mundo, 1980.

Carrillo, Justo. *A Cuba le tocó perder*. Miami: Ediciones Universal, 1993.

Carrizosa Argáez, Enrique. *Linajes y bibliografías de los gobernantes de nuestra nación, 1830–1990*. Bogotá: Instituto Colombiano de Cultura Hispánica, 1990.

Casuso, Teresa. *Cuba and Castro*. New York: Random House, 1961.

Centro de Investigaciones Históricas de la Seguridad del Estado. *Operación Mangosta: Fracaso de una invasión secreta*. CD. Havana: Minint, n.d.

Cepero, Eloy G. *Cuba, 1902–1962: Un viaje a través de postales/A Journey through Postcards*. Miami: AC Graphics, 2002.

Chang, Ching Chieh. "The Chinese in Latin America: A Preliminary Geographical Survey with Special Reference to Cuba and Jamaica." Ph.D. diss., University of Maryland, 1956.

Charbonneau, Jean-Pierre. *The Canadian Connection*. Ottawa: Optimum, 1976.

Chevannes, Barry. *Background to Drug Use in Jamaica*. Working Paper no. 34. Kingston, Jamaica: Institute of Social and Economic Research, University of West Indies, 1988.

Chibás, Eduardo. "El último aldabonazo." In *In Memoriam: Ensayo biográfico e iconográfico del líder del decoro patrio*, edited by Raúl Quintana and Cristóbal Zamora, 35. Havana: Tipografía Ponciano, 1951.

CIA Targets Fidel: Secret 1967 CIA Inspector General's Report on Plots to Assassinate Fidel Castro. Melbourne, Australia: Ocean Press, 1996.

Cirules, Enrique. *Conversación con el último norteamericano*. Havana: Editorial Letras Cubanas, 1988.

———. *El imperio de La Habana*. 1993; Havana: Editorial Letras Cubanas, 1999.

———. *La mafia en Cuba*. CD. Havana: Instituto Cubano del Libro, 2001.

———. *The Mafia in Havana: A Caribbean Mob Story*. New York: Ocean Press, 2004.

———. "La mafia norteamericana en Cuba (I): El imperio de La Habana." *Bohemia*, 4 October 1991, 4–7.

———. "La mafia norteamericana en Cuba (II): Operaciones y fraudes." *Bohemia*, 11 October 1991, 15–17.

———. "La mafia norteamericana en Cuba (III): Los negocios de Don Amleto." *Bohemia*, 18 October 1991, 13–17.

———. "La mafia norteamericana en Cuba (IV, final): Trafficante, la era de la cocaína." *Bohemia*, 25 October 1991, 14–17.

———. *La vida secreta de Meyer Lansky en La Habana*. Havana: Editorial de Ciencias Sociales, 2004.

Clark, Sydney. *All the Best in Cuba*. New York: Dodd, Mead, 1946.

Clerc, Jean-Pierre. "Una democracia dos veces asesinada." In *La Habana 1952–1961: El final de un mundo, el principio de una ilusión*, edited by Jacobo Machover, 84–98. Madrid: Alianza Editorial, 1995.

Coltman, Leycester. *The Real Fidel Castro*. New Haven: Yale University Press, 2003.

Comisión Económica para América Latina y el Caribe. *La economía cubana: Reformas estructurales y desempeño en los noventa*. 1997; Mexico City: Comisión Económica para América Latina y el Caribe/Agencia Sueca de Cooperación Internacional para el Desarrollo/Fondo de Cultura Económica, 2000.

Commission on Cuban Affairs. *Problems of the New Cuba*. New York: Foreign Policy Association, 1935.

Conde, Yvonne M. *Operation Pedro Pan: The Untold Exodus of 14,048 Cuban Children*. New York: Routledge, 1999.

Conte Agüero, Luis. *Eduardo Chibás el adalid de Cuba*. 1955; Miami: La Moderna Poesía, 1987.

Corbitt, Duvon Clough. *A Study of the Chinese in Cuba, 1847–1947*. Wilmore, Ky.: Asbury College, 1971.

Costa, Octavio R. *Imagen y trayectoria del cubano en la historia: La República (1902–1959)*. Miami: Ediciones Universal, 1998.

Cotler, Julio. *Drogas y política en el Perú: La conexión norteamericana*. Lima: Instituto de Estudios Peruanos, 1999.

Courtwright, David T. *Dark Paradise: A History of Opiate Addiction in America*. 1982; Cambridge: Harvard University Press, 2001.

———. *Forces of Habit: Drugs and the Making of the Modern World*. Cambridge: Harvard University Press, 2001.

———. *Violent Land: Single Men and Social Disorder from the Frontier to the Inner City*. Cambridge: Harvard University Press, 1996.

Courtwright, David T., Herman Joseph, and Don Des Jarlais. *Addicts Who Survived: An Oral History of Narcotic Use in America, 1923–1965*. Knoxville: University of Tennessee Press, 1989.

Coyula, Mario, ed. *La Habana que va conmigo*. Havana: Editorial Letras Cubanas, 2002.

Crespo Villate, Mercedes. *Legación cubana en China, 1904–1959: Primeros consulados diplomáticos cubanos y vivencias históricas con la nación asiática*. Havana: Editorial SI-MAR, 2004.

Cruz-Taura, Graciella. "The Impact of the Castro Revolution on Cuban Historiography." Ph.D. diss., University of Miami, 1978.

Curti, Segundo. "La Habana, una de las grandes ciudades del orbe." In *La Habana que va conmigo*, edited by Mario Coyula, 109–37. Havana: Editorial Letras Cubanas, 2002.

Dallek, Robert. *An Unfinished Life: John F. Kennedy, 1917–1963*. Boston: Little, Brown, 2003.

Davenport-Hines, Richard. *La búsqueda del olvido: Historia global de las drogas, 1500–2000*. Madrid: Turner Publications/Fondo de Cultura Económica, 2003.

Davis, John A. *Mafia Dynasty: The Rise and Fall of the Gambino Crime Family*. New York: Harper Paperbacks, 1994.

De Arce, Luis A. *La vagancia: El juego*. Havana: Editorial Librería Selecta, 1952.

De Castroverde, Waldo. *Que la patria se sienta orgullosa: Memorias de una lucha sin fin*. Miami: Ediciones Universal, 1999.

Deere, Carmen Diana. "Here Come the Yankees! The Rise and Decline of United States Colonies in Cuba, 1898–1930." *Hispanic American Historical Review* 78, no. 4 (1998): 729–65.

Deitche, Scott M. *Cigar City Mafia: A Complete History of the Tampa Underworld*. Fort Lee, N.J.: Barricade, 2004.

De la Cruz Ochoa, Ramón. *Crimen organizado: Tráfico de drogas, lavado de dinero y terrorismo*. Havana: Editorial de Ciencias Sociales, 2004.

De la Fuente, Alejandro. *A Nation for All: Race, Inequality, and Politics in Twentieth-Century Cuba*. Chapel Hill: University of North Carolina Press, 2001.

De la Osa, Enrique. *En Cuba: Primer tiempo, 1943–1946*. 1990; Havana: Editorial de Ciencias Sociales, 2002.

De la Torre Mulhare, Mirta. "Sexual Ideology in Pre-Castro Cuba: A Cultural Analysis." Ph.D. diss., University of Pittsburgh, 1969.

De la Torriente Brau, Pablo. *Testimonios y reportajes*. Havana: Centro Cultural Pablo de la Torriente Brau, 2001.

Denton, Sally, and Roger Morris. *The Money and the Power: The Making of Las Vegas and Its Hold on America, 1947–2000*. New York: Knopf, 2001.

De Palma, Anthony. *The Man Who Invented Fidel: Castro, Cuba, and Herbert L. Matthews of the "New York Times."* New York: Public Affairs, 2006.

De Paz Sánchez, Manuel. *Zona Rebelde: La diplomacia española ante la revolución cubana (1957–1960)*. Tenerife: Centro de la Cultura Popular Canaria, 1997.

Desch, Michael C., Jorge I. Domínguez, and Andrés Serbin. *From Pirates to Drug Lords: The Post–Cold War Caribbean Security Environment*. Albany: State University of New York Press, 1998.

Díaz-Briquets, Sergio, and Jorge Pérez-López. *Corruption in Cuba: Castro and Beyond*. Austin: University of Texas Press, 2006.

Díaz Martínez, Yolanda. "Sociedad, violencia, y criminalidad masculina en La Habana de finales del siglo XIX: Aproximaciones a una realidad." In *La sociedad cubana en los albores de la República*, edited by Mildred de la Torre Molina et al., 49–89. Havana: Editorial de Ciencias Sociales, 2002.

Dikötter, Frank, Lars Laamann, and Zhou Xun. *Narcotic Culture: A History of Drugs in China*. Chicago: University of Chicago Press, 2004.

Domínguez, Jorge I. "Cuba since 1959." In *The Cambridge History of Latin America*, edited by Leslie Bethell, 7:457–508. Cambridge: Cambridge University Press, 1990.

Donadío, Alberto. *El Uñilargo: La corrupción en el régimen de Rojas Pinilla*. Medellín: Hombre Nuevo Editores, 2003.

Douglass, Joseph D. *Red Cocaine: The Drugging of America*. Atlanta: Clarion House, 1990.

Dubois, Jules. *Fidel Castro: Rebel, Liberator, or Dictator?* Indianapolis: Bobbs-Merrill, 1959.

Dubro, James, and Robin F. Rowland. *King of the Mob: Rocco Perri and the Women Who Ran His Rackets*. Markham, Ont.: Viking, 1987.

Dumur, Jean A. *Cuba*. Lausanne: Éditions Rencontre, 1962.

Dye, Alan. *Cuban Sugar in the Age of Mass Production: Technology and the Economics of the Sugar Central, 1899–1929*. Stanford: Stanford University Press, 1998.

Eire, Carlos. *Waiting for Snow in Havana: Confessions of a Cuban Boy*. New York: Free Press, 2003.

Eisenberg, Dennis, Uri Dan, and Eli Landau. *Meyer Lansky: Mogul of the Mob*. New York: Paddington, 1979.

Elizalde, Rosa Miriam. *Flores desechables: Prostitución en Cuba*. Havana: Ediciones Abril, 1996.

Elliston, Jon, ed. *Psywar on Cuba: The Declassified History of U.S. Anti-Castro Propaganda*. Melbourne, Australia: Ocean Press, 1999.

Ely, Roland T. *Cuando reinaba su majestad el azúcar*. Buenos Aires: Editorial Sudamericana, 1963.

Escalante Font, Fabián. *La guerra secreta: Acción ejecutiva*. Havana: Editorial de Ciencias Sociales, 2003.

Escohotado, Antonio. *Historia de las drogas*. Vol. 2. Madrid: Alianza Editorial, 1998.

Falcoff, Mark. *Cuba, the Morning After: Confronting Castro's Legacy*. Washington, D.C.: American Enterprise Policy Institute Press, 2003.

Farber, Samuel. *The Origins of the Cuban Revolution Reconsidered*. Chapel Hill: University of North Carolina Press, 2006.

Farr, Jory. *Rites of Rhythm: The Music of Cuba*. New York: Harper Collins, 2003.

Feder, Sid, and Joachim Joesten. *The Luciano Story*. 1954; New York: Da Capo, 1994.

Fergusson, Erna. *Cuba*. New York: Knopf, 1946.

Fermor, Patrick Leigh. "Havana Carnival, 1949." In *Travelers' Tales of Old Havana*, edited by John Jenkins, 150–57. Melbourne, Australia: Ocean Press, 2002.

Fernández, Damián J. *Cuba and the Politics of Passion*. Austin: University of Texas Press, 2000.

———. Introduction to *Cuba Transnational*, edited by Damián Fernández, xiii–xviii. Gainesville: University Press of Florida, 2005.

Fernández, Frank. *Cuban Anarchism: The History of a Movement*. Tucson: See Sharp, 2001.

Fernández Barrios, Flor. *Blessed by Thunder: Memoir of a Cuban Girlhood*. Seattle: Seal, 1999.

Fernández Miranda, Roberto. *Mis Relaciones con el General Batista*. Miami: Ediciones Universal, 1999.

Fernández Robaina, Tomás. *Historias de mujeres públicas*. Havana: Editorial Letras Cubanas, 1998.

Fischer, David Hackett. *Albion's Seed: Four British Folkways in America*. New York: Oxford University Press, 1989.

Fisher, M. F. K. *A Considerable Town*. 1964; New York: Knopf, 1978.

Forst, Donald, comp. *The Heroin Trail*. New York: Signet, 1974.

Frank, Waldo. *Cuba: Prophetic Island*. New York: Marzani and Munsell, 1961.

Franqui, Carlos. *Camilo Cienfuegos*. Barcelona: Seix Barral, 2001.

Frattini, Eric. *Mafia, S.A.: 100 años de Cosa Nostra*. Madrid: Espasa Calpe, 2002.

Freire, Joaquín. *Historia de los municipios de Cuba*. Miami: La Moderna Poesía, 1985.

Fredrickson, George M. *The Comparative Imagination: On the History of Racism, Nationalism, and Social Movements*. Berkeley: University of California Press, 2000.

Friman, H. Richard. *NarcoDiplomacy: Exporting the U.S. War on Drugs*. Ithaca: Cornell University Press, 1996.

Fuentes, Norberto. *Narcotráfico y tareas revolucionarias: El concepto cubano*. Miami: Ediciones Universal, 2002.

Fursenko, Aleksandr, and Timothy Naftali. *"One Hell of a Gamble": Khrushchev, Castro, and Kennedy, 1958–1964*. New York: Norton, 1997.

Gagliano, Joseph. *Coca Prohibition in Peru: The Historical Debates*. Tucson: University of Arizona Press, 1994.

Galván Tudela, J. Alberto, ed. *Canarios en Cuba: Una mirada desde la antropología*. Santa Cruz de Tenerife: Organismo Autónomo de Museos y Centros del Cabildo de Tenerife/Consejería de Presidencia y Relaciones Institucionales del Gobierno de Canarias/Área de Desarrollo Económico, Industria, Transporte y Comercio del Cabildo de Tenerife, 1997.

Galvis, Silvia, and Alberto Donadío. *Colombia Nazi, 1939–1945*. Bogotá: Planeta, 1986.

García, Cristina. *Monkey Hunting*. New York: Knopf, 2003.

García, María Cristina. *Havana USA: Cuban Exiles and Cuban Americans in South Florida, 1959–1994*. Berkeley: University of California Press, 1996.

García Álvarez, Alejandro. *La gran burguesía comercial en Cuba, 1899–1920*. Havana: Editorial de Ciencias Sociales, 1990.

García-Pérez, Gladys Marel. *Insurrection and Revolution: Armed Struggle in Cuba, 1933–1945*. Boulder, Colo.: Rienner, 1998.

Gellman, Irwin F. *Roosevelt and Batista: Good Neighbor Diplomacy in Cuba, 1933–1945*. Albuquerque: University of New Mexico Press, 1973.

Geyer, Georgie Anne. *Guerrilla Prince: The Untold Story of Fidel Castro*. Boston: Little, Brown, 1991.

Gil Carballo, Antonio. *Expendedores y viciosos*. Havana: Propiedad de Rogelio A. Pujol, 1937.

Gimbel, Wendy. *Havana Dreams: A Story of a Cuban Family.* New York: Vintage, 1999.

Gleijeses, Piero. *Conflicting Missions: Havana, Washington, and Africa, 1959–1976.* Chapel Hill: University of North Carolina Press, 2002.

Glinn, Burt. *Havana: The Revolutionary Moment/La Habana: El momento revolucionario.* New York: Umbrage, 2001.

Goldfard, Ronald. *Perfect Villains, Imperfect Heroes: Robert F. Kennedy's War against Organized Crime.* 1995; Sterling, Va.: Capital, 2002.

González, Emilio T. *The Cuban Connection: Drug Trafficking and the Castro Regime.* Cuban Studies Association, Occasional Paper Series, vol. 2, no. 6. Miami: University of Miami, 1997.

González, Reynaldo. *La Fiesta de los Tiburones.* Havana: Editorial de Ciencias Sociales, 2001.

González Echevarría, Roberto. *The Pride of Havana: A History of Cuban Baseball.* New York: Oxford University Press, 2001.

Gootenberg, Paul. "Between Coca and Cocaine: A Century or More of U.S.-Peruvian Drug Paradoxes, 1860–1980." *Hispanic American Historical Review* 83, no. 1 (2003): 119–50.

———. "Cocaine in Chains: The Rise and Demise of a Global Commodity, 1860–1950." In *From Silver to Cocaine: Latin American Commodity Chains and the Building of a World Economy, 1500–2000,* edited by Steven Topik, Carlos Marichal, and Zephyr Frank, 321–51. Durham: Duke University Press, 2006.

———. "Reluctance or Resistance?: Constructing Cocaine (Prohibitions) in Peru, 1910–50." In *Cocaine: Global Histories,* edited by Paul Gootenberg, 46–79. London: Routledge, 1999.

———. "Secret Ingredients: The Politics of Coca in U.S.-Peruvian Relations, 1915–65." *Journal of Latin American Studies* 36, no. 2 (2004): 233–65.

———, ed. *Cocaine: Global Histories.* London: Routledge, 1999.

Gordon, Colin. *New Deals: Business, Labor, and Politics in America, 1920–1935.* Cambridge: Cambridge University Press, 1994.

Gorman, Joseph Bruce. *Kefauver: A Political Biography.* New York: Oxford University Press, 1971.

Gosch, Martin A., and Richard Hammer. *The Last Testament of Lucky Luciano.* Boston: Little, Brown, 1975.

Gott, Richard. *Cuba: A New History.* New Haven: Yale University Press, 2004.

Grau Alsina, Ramón, and Valerie Ridderhoff. *Mongo Grau: Cuba desde 1930.* Madrid: Agualarga Editores, n.d.

Greene, Graham. *Our Man in Havana.* 1958; New York: Penguin, 1971.

Grenier, Guillermo J., and Lisandro Pérez. *The Legacy of Exile: Cubans in the United States.* Boston: Allyn and Bacon, 2003.

Griffith, Ivelaw L. *Drugs and Security in the Caribbean: Sovereignty under Siege.* University Park: Pennsylvania State University Press, 1997.

———. "The Geography of Drug Trafficking in the Caribbean." In *From Pirates to Drug Lords: The Post–Cold War Caribbean Security Environment,* edited by Michael C. Desch, Jorge I. Domínguez, and Andrés Serbin, 97–119. Albany: State University of New York Press, 1998.

———, ed. *The Political Economy of Drugs in the Caribbean*. New York: Palgrave, 2000.

Guanche, Jesús. *Componentes étnicos de la nación cubana*. Havana: Fundación Fernando Ortiz/Ediciones Unión, 1996.

Guanche, Julio César. *La imaginación contra la norma: Ocho enfoques sobre la República de 1902*. Havana: Centro Cultural Pablo de la Torriente Brau, 2004.

Guerra y Sánchez, Ramiro. *Manual de historia de Cuba desde su descubrimiento hasta 1868*. Havana: Editorial de Ciencias Sociales/Instituto Cubano del Libro, 1971.

———. *Sugar and Society in the Caribbean: An Economic History of Cuban Agriculture*. New Haven: Yale University Press, 1964.

Guy, Donna J. *Sex and Danger in Buenos Aires: Prostitution, Family, and Nation in Argentina*. Lincoln: University of Nebraska Press, 1991.

Halberstam, David. *The Fifties*. New York: Villard, 1993.

Ham Chande, Roberto. "La Migración china hacia México a través del registro nacional de extranjeros." In *Destino México: Un estudio de las migraciones asiáticas a México, siglos XIX y XX*, coordinated by María Elena Ota Mishima, 167–88. Mexico City: El Colegio de México, 1997.

Hanes, W. Travis, and Frank Sanello. *The Opium Wars: The Addiction of One Empire and the Corruption of Another*. Naperville, Ill.: Sourcebooks, 2002.

Helg, Aline. *Lo que nos corresponde: La lucha de los negros y mulatos por la igualdad en Cuba, 1886–1912*. Havana: Imagen Contemporánea, 2000.

Hemingway, Ernest. *To Have and Have Not*. 1937; New York: Scribner, 1996.

Henríquez, Eusebio. *Farmacodependencia y narcotráfico en República Dominicana: Factores culturales, sociales y económicos*. Santo Domingo: Taller, 1990.

Hermer, Consuelo, and Marjorie May. *Havana Mañana: A Guide to Cuba and the Cubans*. New York: Random House, 1941.

Hijuelos, Oscar. *A Simple Habana Melody (From When the Word Was Good)*. New York: Collins, 2002.

Hill, Herbert. "Anti-Oriental Agitation and the Rise of Working Class Racism." *Society* 10, no. 2 (1973): 43–48, 50–54.

Himmelstein, Jerome L. *The Strange Career of Marihuana, Politics, and Ideology of Drug Control in America*. Westport, Conn.: Greenwood, 1983.

Hinckle, Warren, and William Turner. *Deadly Secrets: The CIA-Mafia War against Castro and the Assassination of J.F.K.* New York: Thunder's Mouth, 1993.

Hu-DeHart, Evelyn. "Coolies on the Plantations: Opium and Social Control." Paper presented at the Conference of the International Society for the Study of the Chinese Overseas, University of Copenhagen, 2004.

Ibarra Guitart, Jorge. *Sociedad de Amigos de la República: Historia de una mediación, 1952–1958*. Havana: Editorial de Ciencias Sociales, 2003.

International Bank for Reconstruction and Development. *Report on Cuba*. Washington, D.C.: International Bank for Reconstruction and Development, 1951.

Jankowski, Paul. *Communism and Collaboration: Simon Sabiani and Politics in Marseille, 1919–1944.* New Haven: Yale University Press, 1989.

Jay, Mike. *Emperors of Dreams: Drugs in the Nineteenth Century.* Sawtry, England: Dedalus, 2000.

Jenkins, John, ed. *Travelers' Tales of Old Cuba.* Melbourne, Australia: Ocean Press, 2002.

Jenks, Leland H. *Our Cuban Colony: A Study in Sugar.* New York: Vanguard, 1928.

Jiménez, Guillermo. *Las empresas de Cuba, 1958.* Miami: Ediciones Universal, 2000.

Jiménez Pastrana, Juan. *Los chinos en las luchas por la liberación cubana (1847–1930).* Havana: Instituto de Historia, 1963.

Jonnes, Jill. *Hep-Cats, Narcs, and Pipe Dreams: A History of America's Romance with Illegal Drugs.* New York: Scribner, 1996.

Jorrín, Enrique. "Espíritu Burlón." In *La música cubana en Colombia y la música colombiana en Cuba,* compiled by José Portaccio Fontalvo, 78. Bogotá: Disformas Triviño, 2003.

Kavieff, Paul R. *The Purple Gang: Organized Crime in Detroit, 1910–1945.* Fort Lee, N.J.: Barricade, 2000.

Kefauver, Estes. *Crime in America.* London: Gollancz, 1952.

Kennedy, Robert F. *The Enemy Within: The McClellan Committee Crusade against Jimmy Hoffa and Corrupt Labor Unions.* 1960; New York: Da Capo, 1994.

Kinder, Douglas Clark. "Bureaucratic Cold Warrior: Harry J. Anslinger and Illicit Narcotics Traffic." *Pacific Historical Review* 50, no. 2 (1981): 169–91.

Knight, Franklin W. *The Caribbean: The Genesis of a Fragmented Nationalism.* New York: Oxford University Press, 1990.

———. *Slave Society in Cuba during the Nineteenth Century.* Madison: University of Wisconsin Press, 1990.

Kohn, Marek. *Dope Girls: The Birth of the British Drug Underground.* 1992; London: Granta, 2001.

Kolko, Gabriel. *Main Currents in Modern American History.* 1976; New York: Pantheon, 1984.

Kornbluh, Peter, ed. *Bay of Pigs Declassified: The Secret CIA Report on the Invasion of Cuba.* New York: New Press, 1998.

Krauze, Enrique. *La presidencia imperial: Ascenso y caída del sistema político mexicano (1940–1996).* 1997; Mexico City: Fábula Tusquets Editores, 2004.

Kwong, Meter, and Dušanka Miščević. *Chinese America: The Untold Story of America's Oldest New Community.* New York: New Press, 2005.

Lacey, Robert. *Little Man: Meyer Lansky and the Gangster Life.* Boston: Little, Brown, 1991.

Lam, Rafael. *Tropicana: Un paraíso bajo las estrellas.* Havana: Editorial José Martí, 1997.

Latour, José. *Havana World Series.* New York: Grove, 2003.

Lawrenson, Helen. *Latins Are Still Lousy Lovers.* London: Hale, 1970.

Lazo, Mario. *Dagger in the Heart: American Policy Failures in Cuba.* New York: Funk and Wagnalls, 1970.

Leff, Nathaniel H. "Economic Development through Bureaucratic Corruption." In *Political Corruption: Concepts and Contexts*, edited by Arnold J. Heidenheimer and Michael Johnston, 307–20. New Brunswick, N.J.: Transaction, 2002.

Lema, Ana María. "The Coca Debate and Yungas Landowners during the First Half of the 20th Century." In *Coca, Cocaine, and the Bolivian Reality*, compiled by Madeline Barbara Léons and Harry Sanabria, 99–115. Albany: State University of New York Press, 1997.

Lemogodeuc, Jean-Marie. "Orígenes, Ciclón, Lunes: Una literatura en ebullición." In *La Habana 1952–1961: El final de un mundo, el principio de una ilusión*, edited by Jacobo Machover, 145–58. Madrid: Alianza Editorial, 1995.

Le Riverend, Julio. *La Habana, espacio y vida*. Madrid: Editorial MAPFRE, 1992.

———. *Historia económica de Cuba*. Havana: Editorial de Ciencias Sociales, 1985.

———. *La República: Dependencia y revolución*. 1966; Havana: Editorial de Ciencias Sociales, 2001.

Leuchtenburg, William E. *Franklin D. Roosevelt and the New Deal, 1932–1940*. New York: Harper Colophon, 1963.

Levi, Vicki Gold, and Steven Heller. *Cuba Style: Graphics from the Golden Age of Design*. New York: Princeton Architectural, 2002.

Levine, Robert M. *Brazilian Legacies*. New York: Sharpe, 1997.

———. *Tropical Diaspora: The Jewish Experience in Cuba*. Gainesville: University of Florida Press, 1993.

Lewis, Oscar, Ruth M. Lewis, and Susan M. Ridgon. *Four Men: Living the Revolution: An Oral History of Contemporary Cuba*. Urbana: University of Illinois Press, 1977.

"Líbano." In *Gran Enciclopedia del Mundo*, 11:974–78. 1948; Bilbao: Durvan, 1967.

Lino Gato, Diego. "Origen de los vicios." *Policía Secreta Nacional* 13, no. 5 (1944): 204–5.

López-Fresquet, Rufo. *My Fourteen Months with Castro*. Cleveland: World, 1966.

López Leiva, Francisco. *El bandolerismo en Cuba (contribución al estudio de esta plaga social)*. Havana: Imprenta El Siglo XX, 1930.

Lorenz, Marita, and Ted Schwarz. *Marita: One Woman's Extraordinary Tale of Love and Espionage from Castro to Kennedy*. New York: Thunder's Mouth, 1993.

Lowinger, Rosa, and Ofelia Fox. *Tropicana Nights: The Life and Times of the Legendary Cuban Nightclub*. Orlando, Fla.: Harcourt, 2005.

Luis, William. *Culture and Customs of Cuba*. Westport, Conn.: Greenwood, 2001.

Lumsden, Ian. *Machos, Maricones, and Gays: Cuba and Homosexuality*. Philadelphia: Temple University Press, 1996.

Lundberg, Ferdinand. *The Rich and the Super-Rich: A Study in the Power of Money Today*. New York: Stuart, 1968.

Macaulay, Neill. *A Rebel in Cuba: An American's Memoir*. 1970; Micanopy, Fla.: Wacahoota, 1999.

Machover, Jacobo. "Memoria de La Habana desaparecida." In *La Habana 1952–1961: El final de un mundo, el principio de una ilusión*, edited by Jacobo Machover, 17–25. Madrid: Alianza Editorial, 1995.

Mallory, Walter H., and Joseph Barber, eds. *Political Handbook of the World: Parlia-*

ments, Parties, and Press as of January 1, 1953. New York: Harper/Council on Foreign Relations, 1953.

Maluquer de Motes, Jordi. "La inmigración española en Cuba: Elementos de un debate histórico." In *Cuba la perla de las Antillas: Actas de las I Jornadas sobre "Cuba y su Historia,"* edited by Consuelo Naranjo Orovio and Tomás Mallo Gutiérrez, 137–47. Madrid: Ediciones Doce Calles/Consejo Superior de Investigaciones Científicas, 1994.

———. *Nación e inmigración: Los españoles en Cuba (ss. XIX y XX)*. Barcelona: Ediciones Júcar/Fundación Archivo de Indianos, 1992.

Marconi Braga, Michael. "To Relieve the Misery: Sugar Mill Workers and the 1933 Cuban Revolution." In *Workers' Control in Latin America, 1930–1979*, edited by Jonathan C. Brown, 16–44. Chapel Hill: University of North Carolina Press, 1997.

Marino, Giuseppe Carlo. *Historia de la mafia: Un poder en las sombras*. Barcelona: Vergara, 2002.

———. *Los Padrinos y las nefastas virtudes del puro poder*. Barcelona: Javier Vergara Editor, 2004.

Marrero, Leví. *Geografía de Cuba*. Miami: La Moderna Poesía, 1981.

Martínez-Fernández, Luis. "Prío Socarrás, Carlos (1903–1977)." In *Encyclopedia of Cuba: People, History, Culture*, edited by Luis Martínez-Fernández, D. H. Figueredo, Louis A. Pérez Jr., and Luis González, 2:182–83. Westport, Conn.: Greenwood, 2003.

Mascarós, Julio César. *Historia de la banca en Cuba (1492–2000)*. Havana: Editorial de Ciencias Sociales, 2004.

Mason, Philip P. *Rum Running and the Roaring Twenties: Prohibition on the Michigan-Ontario Waterway*. Detroit: Wayne State University Press, 1995.

Masterson, Daniel M., and Sayaka Funada-Classen. *The Japanese in Latin America*. Champaign: University of Illinois Press, 2004.

Masud-Piloto, Felix Roberto. *From Welcomed Exiles to Illegal Immigrants: Cuban Migration to the U.S., 1959–1995*. Lanham, Md.: Rowman and Littlefield, 1996.

Matos, Huber. *Cómo llegó la noche*. Barcelona: Tusquets Editores, 2002.

Matthews, Herbert L. *Cuba*. New York: Macmillan, 1964.

McAvoy, Muriel. *Sugar Baron: Manuel Rionda and the Fortunes of Pre-Castro Cuba*. Gainesville: University Press of Florida, 2003.

McCarthy, Kevin M. *Aviation in Florida*. Sarasota: Pineapple, 2003.

McClellan, John L. *Crime without Punishment*. New York: Fuell, Sloan, and Pearce, 1962.

McCoy, Alfred W. *The Politics of Heroin: CIA Complicity in the Global Drug Trade*. New York: Hill, 1991.

McGerr, Michael. "The Price of the 'New Transnational History.'" *American Historical Review* 96, no. 4 (1991): 1056–67.

Menéndez Paredes, Rigoberto. *Componentes Árabes en la cultura cubana*. Havana: Ediciones Boloña, 1999.

Mesa-Lago, Carmelo. *The Economy of Socialist Cuba: A Two-Decade Appraisal*. Albuquerque: University of New Mexico Press, 1981.

Messick, Hank. *Of Grass and Snow: The Secret Criminal Elite.* Englewood Cliffs, N.J.: Prentice Hall, 1979.

Meyer, Kathryn, and Terry Parssinen. *Webs of Smoke: Smugglers, Warlords, Spies, and the History of the International Drug Trade.* Lanham, Md.: Rowman and Littlefield, 1998.

Meyers, Fred I. *The Gilmore: Manual azucarero de Cuba; Cuba Sugar Manual, 1959.* New Orleans: Gilmore, 1959.

Montaner, Carlos Alberto. *Cuba: Un siglo de doloroso aprendizaje.* Miami: Brickell, 2002.

———. *Viaje al corazón de Cuba.* Barcelona: Plaza y Janés, 1999.

Moore, Robin D. *Nationalizing Blackness: Afrocubanismo and Artistic Revolution in Havana, 1920–1940.* Pittsburgh: University of Pittsburgh Press, 1997.

Moreno Fraginals, Manuel. *Cuba/España, España/Cuba.* 1995; Barcelona: Crítica, 2002.

———. *La historia como arma y otros estudios sobre esclavos, ingenios, y plantaciones.* Barcelona: Crítica, 1983.

———. *El ingenio: Complejo económico social cubano del azúcar.* 1964; Barcelona: Crítica, 2001.

Morgan, H. Wayne. *Drugs in America: A Social History, 1800–1980.* Syracuse: Syracuse University Press, 1981.

Mormino, Gary R. *Land of Sunshine, State of Dreams: A Social History of Modern Florida.* Gainesville: University Press of Florida, 2005.

Mormino, Gary R., and George E. Pozzetta. *The Immigrant World of Ybor City: Italians and Their Latin Neighbors in Tampa, 1885–1985.* Gainesville: University Press of Florida, 1998.

Moscow, Alvin. *Merchants of Heroin: An In-Depth Portrayal of Business in the Underworld.* New York: Dial, 1968.

Moya, José C. *Cousins and Strangers: Spanish Immigrants in Buenos Aires, 1850–1930.* Berkeley: University of California Press, 1998.

———. "Spanish Emigration to Cuba and Argentina." In *Mass Migration to Modern Latin America*, edited by Samuel L. Bailey and Eduardo José Míguez, 9–28. Wilmington, Del.: Scholarly Resources, 2003.

Munn, Michael. *The Hollywood Connection: The True Story of Organized Crime in Hollywood.* London: Robson, 1993.

Musto, David F. *The American Disease: Origins of Narcotic Control.* 1973; New York: Oxford University Press, 1999.

———, ed. *Drugs in America: A Documentary History.* New York: New York University Press, 2002.

———, ed. *One Hundred Years of Heroin.* Westport, Conn.: Auburn House, 2002.

Musto, David F., and Pamela Korsmeyer. *The Quest for Drug Control: Politics and Federal Policy in a Period of Increasing Substance Abuse, 1963–1981.* New Haven: Yale University press, 2002.

Nadelmann, Ethan A. *The Internationalization of U.S. Criminal Law Enforcement.* University Park: Pennsylvania State University Press, 1993.

Naím, Moisés. *Illicit: How Smugglers, Traffickers, and Copycats Are Hijacking the Global Economy*. New York: Doubleday, 2005.

Naranjo Orovio, Consuelo. *Cuba vista por el emigrante español a la isla, 1900–1959*. Madrid: Consejo Superior de Investigaciones Científicas, 1987.

———. *Del campo a la bodega: Recuerdos de Gallegos en Cuba (siglo XX)*. La Coruña: Ediciós do Castro, 1988.

———. "Immigration (Twentieth Century)." In *Encyclopedia of Cuba: People, History, Culture*, edited by Luis Martínez-Fernández, D. H. Figueredo, and Louis A. Pérez Jr., 1:159–61. Westport, Conn.: Greenwood, 2003.

———. "La población española en Cuba, 1880–1953." In *Cuba la perla de las Antillas: Actas de las I Jornadas sobre "Cuba y su Historia,"* edited by Consuelo Naranjo Orovio and Tomás Mallo Gutiérrez, 121–36. Madrid: Ediciones Doce Calles/Consejo Superior de Investigaciones Científicas, 1994.

Nelli, Humbert S. *The Business of Crime: Italians and Syndicate Crime in the United States*. 1976; Chicago: University of Chicago Press, 1981.

Niblo, Stephen R. *Mexico in the 1940s: Modernity, Politics, and Corruption*. Wilmington, Del.: Scholarly Resources, 1999.

Núñez, Pastorita. "Nací en el barrio de los guapos, de los náñigos y de los revolucionarios verdaderos." In *La Habana que va conmigo*, edited by Mario Coyula, 180–99. Havana: Editorial Letras Cubanas, 2002.

Núñez Jiménez, Antonio. *En marcha con Fidel, 1959*. 1982; Havana: Editorial de Ciencias Sociales, 2002.

O'Brien, Thomas F. *The Revolutionary Mission: American Enterprise in Latin America, 1900–1945*. Cambridge: Cambridge University Press, 1996.

Ogle, Maureen. *Key West: History of an Island of Dreams*. Gainesville: University Press of Florida, 2003.

Orejuela Martínez, Adriana. *El son no se fue de Cuba: Claves para una historia, 1959–1973*. Bogotá: Ediciones Arte Cultura y Sociedad, 2004.

Ortiz, Fernando. *Los negros curros*. 1986; Havana: Editorial de Ciencias Sociales, 1995.

———. *Los negros esclavos*. 1916; Havana: Editorial de Ciencias Sociales, 1996.

Padula, Alfred L. "The Fall of the Bourgeoisie: Cuba, 1959–1961." Ph.D. diss., University of New Mexico, 1974.

Pardo Llada, José. *Fidel y el "Ché."* Barcelona: Plaza y Janés, 1988.

Paterson, Thomas G. *Contesting Castro: The United States and the Triumph of the Cuban Revolution*. New York: Oxford University Press, 1994.

Pavia, Peter. *The Cuba Project: Castro, Kennedy, Dirty Business, Double Dealing, and the FBI's Tamale Squad*. New York: Palgrave Macmillan, 2006.

Peláez Huerta, Antonio Ramón. *Imágenes de La Habana Antigua*. Madrid: Agularga Editores, n.d.

Pérez, Juan de Dios. *El juego, factor de disolución ciudadana*. Havana: Editorial La Verdad, 1952.

Pérez, Lisandro. "Cuban Miami." In *Miami Now! Immigration, Ethnicity, and Social Change*, edited by Guillermo J. Grenier and Alex Stepick III, 83–108. Gainesville: University Press of Florida, 1993.

Pérez, Louis A., Jr. *Cuba: Between Reform and Revolution*. New York: Oxford University Press, 1988.

———. *Cuba and the United States: Ties of Singular Intimacy*. Athens: University of Georgia Press, 1997.

———. "Cuba, c. 1930–1959." In *The Cambridge History of Latin America*, edited by Leslie Bethell, 7:419–55. Cambridge: Cambridge University Press, 1990.

———. *Cuba under the Platt Amendment, 1902–1934*. Pittsburgh: University of Pittsburgh Press, 1986.

———. *Essays on Cuban History: Historiography and Research*. Gainesville: University Press of Florida, 1995.

———. *On Becoming Cuban: Identity, Nationality, and Culture*. Chapel Hill: University of North Carolina Press, 1999.

———. *To Die in Cuba: Suicide and Society*. Chapel Hill: University of North Carolina Press, 2005.

———. "We Are the World: Internationalizing the National, Nationalizing the International." *Journal of American History* 89, no. 2 (2002): 558–66.

———, ed. *Slaves, Sugar, and Colonial Society: Travel Accounts of Cuba, 1801–1899*. Wilmington, Del.: Scholarly Resources, 1992.

Pérez, Louis A., Jr., and Rebecca J. Scott, eds. *The Archives of Cuba/Los archivos de Cuba*. Pittsburgh: University of Pittsburgh Press, 2003.

Pérez, Orlando J. "Drugs and Post-Intervention Political Economy in Haiti and Panama." In *The Political Economy of Drugs in the Caribbean*, edited by Ivelaw L. Griffith, 138–61. New York: Palgrave, 2000.

Pérez de la Riva, Juan. "El viaje a Cuba de los culíes chinos." In *Contribución a la historia de la gente sin historia*, edited by Pedro Deschamps Chapeaux and Juan Pérez de la Riva, 191–213. Havana: Editorial de Ciencias Sociales, 1974.

Pérez Rubio, Dania. *Hotel Nacional de Cuba: El hotel de mis sueños*. Havana: Editorial José Martí, 1999.

Pérez-Stable, Marifeli. *The Cuban Revolution: Origins, Course, and Legacy*. New York: Oxford University Press, 1999.

Phillips, Ruby Hart. *Cuba: Island of Paradox*. New York: McDowell, Obolensky, 1959.

———. *The Cuban Dilemma*. New York: Obolensky, 1962.

Piccato, Pablo. *City of Suspects: Crime in Mexico City, 1900–1931*. Durham: Duke University Press, 2001.

Pino Santos, Oscar. *Los años 50: En una Cuba que algunos añoran, otros no quieren ni recordar y los más desconocen*. Havana: Instituto Cubano del Libro, 2001.

———. *El asalto a Cuba por la oligarquía financiera yanqui*. Buenos Aires: Editorial Universitaria de Buenos Aires, 1974.

Pogolotti, Marcelo. *La República de Cuba a través de sus escritores*. Havana: Editorial Letras Cubanas, 2002.

Portell-Vilá, Herminio. *Nueva historia de la República de Cuba (1898–1979)*. 1986; Miami: La Moderna Poesía, 1996.

Porter, Roy, and Mikulás Teich, eds. *Drugs and Narcotics in History*. Cambridge: Cambridge University Press, 1995.

Prada, Pedro. *La secretaria de la República*. Havana: Editorial de Ciencias Sociales, 2001.

Puebla, Carlos. "Y en eso llegó Fidel." Kubamusika, CD no. 2, *Crónicas de la Revolución Cubana*.

Quirk, Robert E. *Fidel Castro*. New York: Norton, 1993.

Quiza Moreno, Ricardo. "Fernando Ortiz y su hampa afrocubana." In *Diez nuevas miradas de historia de Cuba*, compiled by José A. Piqueras Arenas, 227–45. Castelló de la Plana: Publicaciones de la Universitat Jaime I, 1998.

Rabe, Stephen G. *Eisenhower and Latin America: The Foreign Policy of Anticommunism*. Chapel Hill: University of North Carolina Press, 1988.

———. *The Most Dangerous Area in the World: John F. Kennedy Confronts Communist Revolution in Latin America*. Chapel Hill: University of North Carolina Press, 1999.

Ragano, Frank, and Selwyn Raab. *Mob Lawyer*. New York: Scribner's, 1994.

Raimundo, Daniel Efraín. *Habla el Coronel Orlando Piedra*. Miami: Ediciones Universal, 1994.

Ramonet, Ignacio. *Fidel Castro: Biografía a dos voces*. Bogotá: Editorial Random House Mondadori, 2006.

Recio, Gabriela. "Drugs and Alcohol: U.S. Prohibition and the Origins of the Drug Trade in Mexico, 1910–1930." *Journal of Latin American Studies* 34, no. 1 (2002): 21–42.

Repetto, Thomas. *American Mafia: A History of Its Rise to Power*. New York: Holt, 2004.

Rieff, David. *The Exile: Cuba in the Heart of Miami*. New York: Touchstone, 1993.

Roberts, W. Adolphe. *Havana: The Portrait of a City*. New York: Coward-McCann, 1953.

Rodgers, Daniel T. "Exceptionalism." In *Imagined Histories: American Historians Interpret the Past*, edited by Anthony Molho and Gordon S. Wood, 21–40. Princeton: Princeton University Press, 1998.

Rogers, William W. "Fortune and Misfortune: The Paradoxical Twenties." In *The New History of Florida*, edited by Michael Gannon, 287–303. Gainesville: University Press of Florida, 1996.

———. "The Great Depression." In *The New History of Florida*, edited by Michael Gannon, 304–22. Gainesville: University Press of Florida, 1996.

Rodríguez, Eduardo Luis. *La Habana: Arquitectura del siglo XX*. Barcelona: Blume, 1998.

Rodríguez, Jorge L., and Diana Rodríguez. *En alas cubanas*. Miami: Tagle, 2002.

Rodríguez-Luis, Julio. *Memoria de Cuba*. Miami: Ediciones Universal, 2001.

Rodríguez Mesa, Gonzalo. *El proceso de industrialización de la economía cubana*. Havana: Editorial de Ciencias Sociales, 1985.

Rodríguez Zahar, León. *Líbano, espejo del Medio Oriente: Comunidad, confesión y estado, siglos VII–XXI*. Mexico City: El Colegio de México, 2004.

Roig de Leuchsenring, Emilio. *Males y vicios de la Cuba republicana: Sus causas y remedios*. Havana: Oficina del Historiador de la Ciudad, 1959.

Román, Daniel. *Así era Cuba*. Miami: Ediciones Universal, 1994.

Rothchild, John. *Up for Grabs: A Trip through Time and Space in the Sunshine State*. Gainesville: University Press of Florida, 2000.

Rousseau González, Isel, ed. *La sociedad neocolonial cubana: Corrientes ideológicas y partidos políticos/colectivo de autores*. Havana: Editorial de Ciencias Sociales, 1984.

Ruiz, Raúl R., and Martha Lim Kim. *Coreanos en Cuba*. Havana: Fundación Fernando Ortiz, 2000.

Russo, Gus. *Live by the Sword: The Secret War against Castro and the Death of JFK*. Baltimore: Bancroft, 1998.

———. *The Outfit: The Role of Chicago's Underworld in the Shaping of Modern America*. New York: Bloomsbury, 2001.

Ryan, Alan, ed. *The Reader's Companion to Cuba*. San Diego: Harcourt Brace, 1997.

Saco, José Antonio. *La vagancia en Cuba*. 1832; Havana: Publicaciones del Ministerio de Educación, 1946.

Sáenz Rovner, Eduardo. "Elites, estado, y política económica en Colombia durante el segundo tercio del siglo XX." *Análisis Político* 32 (1997): 66–79.

———. *La ofensiva empresarial: Industriales, políticos, y violencia en los años 40 en Colombia*. Bogotá: Tercer Mundo Editores/Ediciones Uniandes, 1992.

———. "La prehistoria del narcotráfico en Colombia: Serie documental: Desde la Gran Depresión hasta la Revolución Cubana." *INNOVAR, revista de ciencias administrativas y sociales* 8 (1996): 65–92.

———. "La prehistoria del narcotráfico en Colombia: Temores norteamericanos y realidades colombianas durante la primera mitad del siglo XX." In *La crisis sociopolítica colombiana: Un análisis no coyuntural de la coyuntura*, compiled by Luz Gabriela Arango, 190–212. Bogotá: CES Facultad de Ciencias Humanas-Universidad Nacional de Colombia/Fundación Social, 1997.

Salas, Luis. *Social Control and Deviance in Cuba*. New York: Praeger, 1979.

Sánchez-Albornoz, Nicolás. *The Population of Latin America: A History*. Berkeley: University of California Press, 1974.

Sann, Paul. *The Lawless Decade: A Pictorial History of a Great American Transition, from the World War I Armistice and Prohibition to Repeal and the New Deal*. New York: Bonanza, 1957.

Scarpaci, Joseph L., Roberto Segre, and Mario Coyula. *Havana: Two Faces of the Antillean Metropolis*. Chapel Hill: University of North Carolina Press, 2002.

Schwartz, Rosalie. *Pleasure Island: Tourism and Temptation in Cuba*. Lincoln: University of Nebraska Press, 1997.

Scott, Rebecca J. *Slave Emancipation in Cuba: The Transition to Free Labor, 1860–1899*. 1985; Pittsburgh: University of Pittsburgh Press, 2000.

Serpa, Enrique. *Contrabando*. 1938; Havana: Editorial Arte y Literatura, 1975.

Shelton, Raúl M. *Cuba y su cultura*. Miami: Ediciones Universal, 1993.

Sifrakis, Carl. *The Mafia Encyclopedia*. New York: Checkmark, 1999.

Siragusa, Charles. *The Trail of the Poppy: Behind the Mask of the Mafia*. Englewood Cliffs, N.J.: Prentice Hall, 1966.

Skierka, Volker. *Fidel Castro: A Biography*. 2000; Cambridge: Polity, 2004.

Sloan, Irving J. *Our Violent Past: An American Chronicle.* New York: Random House, 1970.

Smallman, Shawn C. *Fear and Memory in the Brazilian Army and Society, 1889–1954.* Chapel Hill: University of North Carolina Press, 2002.

Smith, Earl E. T. *The Fourth Floor: An Account of the Castro Communist Revolution.* 1962; Washington, D.C.: U.S. Cuba Press, 2000.

Smith, Frederick H. *Caribbean Rum: A Social and Economic History.* Gainesville: University Press of Florida, 2005.

Smith, Lois M., and Alfred Padula. *Sex and Revolution: Women in Socialist Cuba.* New York: Oxford University Press, 1996.

Smith, Robert F. *The United States and Cuba: Business and Diplomacy, 1917–1960.* New Haven, Conn.: College and University Press, 1960.

Smith, Wayne S. *The Closest of Enemies: A Personal and Diplomatic Account of U.S.-Cuban Relations since 1957.* New York: Norton, 1987.

Sobrado López, José. *El vicio de la droga en Cuba.* Havana: Editorial Guerrero, 1943.

Soler Martínez, Rafael R. *Los españoles en el movimiento obrero oriental.* Havana: Colección Santiago de Cuba, 1994.

Sondern, Frederic. *Brotherhood of Evil: The Mafia.* New York: Farrar, Straus, and Cudahy, 1959.

Spillane, Joseph F. *Cocaine: From Medical Marvel to Modern Menace in the United States, 1884–1920.* Baltimore: Johns Hopkins University Press, 2000.

Stoner, K. Lynn. *From the House to the Streets: The Cuban Woman's Movement for Legal Reform, 1898–1940.* Durham: Duke University Press, 1991.

Streatfeild, Dominic. *Cocaine: An Unauthorized Biography.* New York: St. Martin's, 2001.

Suárez Rivas, Eduardo. *Un pueblo crucificado.* Coral Gables, Fla.: Service FOCET, 1964.

Suárez Suárez, Reinaldo. *Un insurreccional en dos épocas: Con Antonio Guiteras y con Fidel Castro.* Havana: Editorial de Ciencias Sociales, 2001.

Sublette, Ned. *Cuba and Its Music: From the First Drums to the Mambo.* Chicago: Chicago Review Press, 2004.

Suchlicki, Jaime. *Cuba from Columbus to Castro and Beyond.* Washington, D.C.: Brassey's, 2002.

———. *Historical Dictionary of Cuba.* Lanham, Md.: Scarecrow, 2001.

———. *University Students and Revolution in Cuba, 1920–1968.* Coral Gables, Fla.: University of Miami Press, 1969.

Summers, Anthony, and Robbyn Swan. *The Arrogance of Power: The Secret World of Richard Nixon.* New York: Viking, 2000.

———. *Sinatra: The Life.* New York: Knopf, 2005.

Sweig, Julia E. *Inside the Cuban Revolution: Fidel Castro and the Urban Underground.* Cambridge: Harvard University Press, 2002.

Szulc, Tad. *Fidel: A Critical Portrait.* 1986; New York: Post Road Press, 2000.

Tamames Henderson, Marco Antonio. *De la Plaza de Armas al Parque Agramonte: Iconografía, símbolos, y significados.* Camagüey: Editorial Acana, 2003.

Temime, Émile. *Histoire de Marseille de la Révolution à nos tours*. Paris: Perrin, 1999.

Temime, Émile, and Natalie Deguigné. *Le camp du Grand Arénas: Marseille, 1944–1966*. Paris: Éditions Autrement, 2001.

Thomas, Hugh. *Cuba; or, The Pursuit of Freedom*. 1971; New York: Da Capo, 1998.

Thoumi, Francisco E. *Economía política y narcotráfico*. Bogotá: Tercer Mundo Editores, 1994.

———. *Illegal Drugs, Economy, and Society in the Andes*. Washington, D.C.: Woodrow Wilson Center Press, 2003.

———. *Ventajas competitivas ilegales, el desarrollo de la industria de drogas ilegales y el fracaso de las políticas contra las drogas en Afganistán y Colombia*. Borradores de Investigación, no. 1. Bogotá: Facultad de Economía, Centro de Estudios y Observatorio de Drogas y Delito, Universidad del Rosario, 2005.

Topik, Steven, Carlos Marichal, and Zephyr Frank, eds. *From Silver to Cocaine: Latin American Commodity Chains and the Building of a World Economy, 1500–2000*. Durham: Duke University Press, 2006.

Tovar Pinzón, Hermes. *Colombia: Droga, economía, guerra y paz*. Bogotá: Planeta Colombiana, 1999.

Tracy, Sarah W., and Carolina Jean Acker, comps. *Altering American Consciousness: The History of Alcohol and Drug Abuse in the United States, 1800–2000*. Amherst: University of Massachusetts Press, 2004.

Trocki, Carl A. *Opium, Empire and the Global Political Economy: A Study of the Asian Opium Trade, 1750–1950*. London: Routledge, 1999.

Tully, Andrew. *Treasury Agent: The Inside Story*. New York: Simon and Schuster, 1958.

Turkus, Burton B., and Sid Feder. *Murder, Inc.: The Story of the Syndicate*. 1951; New York: Da Capo, 1992.

Tyrrell, Ian. "American Exceptionalism in an Age of International History." *American Historical Review* 96, no. 4 (1991): 1031–55.

Valdés-Dapena, Jacinto. *Operación Mangosta: Preludio de la invasión directa a Cuba*. Havana: Editorial Capitán San Luis, 2002.

Valentine, Douglas. *The Strength of the Wolf: The Secret History of America's War on Drugs*. London: Verso, 2004.

Valle, Amir. *Jineteras*. Bogotá: Editorial Planeta Colombiana, 2006.

Vallina Mendoza, René. *Disparos de esperanza: Apuntes para la lucha clandestina en Camagüey, 1955–1959*. Camagüey: Editorial Acana, 2001.

Velásquez Mainardi, Miguel Angel. *El narcotráfico y el lavado de dólares en República Dominicana*. Santo Domingo: Editorial Corripio, 1992.

Vélez, Francisco José. *Geografía médico-sanitaria del término municipal del Mariel*. Havana: Imprenta Pérez Sierra, 1927.

———. *Páginas de la historia del Mariel*. Havana: Imprenta Marón, 1960.

Verrill, A. Hyatt. "Treasure Island, 1931." In *Travelers' Tales of Old Cuba*, edited by John Jenkins, 133–37. Melbourne, Australia: Ocean Books, 2002.

Vignier, Alonso G., and Guillermo Alonso. *La corrupción política y administrativa en Cuba: 1944–1952*. Havana: Editorial de Ciencias Sociales, 1973.

Vizzini, Sal, Oscar Fraley, and Marshall Smith. *Vizzini: The Secret Lives of America's Most Successful Undercover Agent.* New York: Arbor House, 1972.

Waldron, Lamar, with Thom Hartmann. *Ultimate Sacrifice: John and Robert Kennedy, the Plan for a Coup in Cuba and the Murder of JFK.* New York: Carroll and Graf, 2005.

Walker Evans: Cuba. Los Angeles: J. Paul Getty Museum, n.d.

Walker, Phyllis Greene. "National Security." In *Cuba: A Country Study,* 4th ed., edited by Rex A. Hudson, 283–364. Washington, D.C.: Federal Research Division, Library of Congress, 2002.

Walker, William O., III. "Drug Control and the Issue of Culture in American Foreign Relations." *Diplomatic History* 12, no. 4 (1988): 365–82.

———. *Drug Control in the Americas.* 1981; Albuquerque: University of New Mexico Press, 1989.

———. *Opium and Foreign Policy: The Anglo American Search for Order in Asia, 1912–1954.* Chapel Hill: University of North Carolina Press, 1991.

———, ed. *Drugs in the Western Hemisphere: An Odyssey of Cultures in Conflict.* Wilmington, Del.: Scholarly Resources, 1996.

Wall, Joseph Frazier. *Alfred I. du Pont: The Man and His Family.* New York: Oxford University Press, 1990.

Weyl, Nathaniel. *Red Star over Cuba: The Russian Assault on the Western Hemisphere.* New York: Devin-Adair, 1961.

Whitehead, Laurence. "High-Level Political Corruption in Latin America: A 'Transitional' Phenomenon." In *Combating Corruption in Latin America,* edited by Joseph S. Tulchin and Ralph H. Espach, 107–29. Washington, D.C.: Woodrow Wilson Center Press, 2000.

Whitney, Robert. *State and Revolution in Cuba: Mass Mobilization and Political Change, 1920–1940.* Chapel Hill: University of North Carolina Press, 2001.

Yongming, Zhou. *Anti-Drug Crusades in Twentieth-Century China: Nationalism, History, and State Building.* Lanham, Md.: Rowman and Littlefield, 1999.

Zaitch, Damián. *Trafficking Cocaine: Colombian Drug Entrepreneurs in the Netherlands.* The Hague: Kluwer Law International, 2002.

Zanetti, Oscar. *Los cautivos de la reciprocidad.* Havana: Editorial de Ciencias Sociales, 2003.

Zanetti, Oscar, and Alejandro García. *Sugar and Railroads: A Cuban History, 1837–1959.* Chapel Hill: University of North Carolina Press, 1987

Index

ABC, 31, 33

Acosta Carrasco, Rubén, 137

Additional Extradition Treaty, 23–24

Aga Khan, 108

Agricultural colonies in Cuba, 4

Agriculture, postrevolutionary reforms, 132

Aguilar, Luis E., 126

Air travel industry, 5, 12, 20, 66, 69, 111, 118

Alarcón, Enrique, 100

Albertini, Dominique, 110

Alberto Montaner, Carlos, 60

Alcohol smuggling, 2, 18–26. *See also* Prohibition

Alekseev, Alexandr, 133

Alemán, José Manuel, 60

Alfonso, Juan Manuel, 68

Allen, Christian M., 6, 156 (n. 68)

Almejeiras, Efigenio, 135

Alonso-Pujol, Guillermo, 87

Alsina, Paulina, 66, 67

Álvarez, Epifanio, 40

Álvarez, Inocente, 63

Álvarez Digat, Ernesto, 42

American Society of Travel Agents (ASTA), 130

Anastasia, Albert, 140

Andean countries, 11, 95–101, 107, 117, 120, 136

Aníbal Pérez, Juan, 101

Anslinger, Harry J.: policies and management style, 8; on effects of marijuana use, 39; Palacios Planas letter to, 61–62; Luciano investigation and, 67–68, 71–72; Kefauver investigation, involvement in, 81–82; Peru's drug trafficking, negotiations to close, 96; embargo on export of legal drugs and, 99–100; Batista administration, relations with, 113; Cuban antinarcotics efforts, positive response to, 119, 137; Gaffney report to, 121; on deportation of mafia in Cuba, 135; anticommunist scare tactics used by, 138, 141; Castro administration, relations with, 138, 141, 144, 145; Trafficante accusations and, 139; Giordano replaces, 145; Japan accused of drug trafficking and, 204 (n. 93)

Antinori crime family, 68

Arce Valdés, Roberto (Papagayo), 116

Argentina, 2, 20, 100

Arias Cruz, Virginia, 118

Arias Fernández, Francisco, 10

Arias Izouzu, Manuel, 118

Arms trafficking, 100, 111

Astorga, Luis, 12

Australia, 115

Bahamas, 18

Balarezo, Eduardo, 96

Bank for Economic and Social Development (BANDES), 92–93

Banking system, 92–93

Barnet, Miguel, 96

Baron, Charles, 124

Barroso, Manuel, 53

Batista, Fulgencio: Mendieta supported by, 32, 34; 1934 bomb attacks and, 34; power of, 37; overthrow plot against,

58; corrupt practices of, 60, 67, 113–14; Prío overthrow and, 77–78; Lansky (Meyer) and, 89, 90; BANDES and, 93; Mondolini deportation, 109; departs Cuba, 123

Batista administration: drug trafficking and, 9–10, 113–22, 148; corruption in, 10, 58–60, 83, 113; U.S. relations, 58–59, 78, 178 (n. 29); League of Nations convention compliance, 62–63; gambling under, 83, 87, 89–90; elites opposition to, 128

Bay of Pigs invasion, 143
Beals, Carleton, 86
Beaulac, Willard, 78
Beers, Wilson, 59, 63, 64
Beirut, 106
Belt, Guillermo, 68, 69
Bengochea, Victoriano, 41
Benítez, Fernando, 126
Benítez, Manuel, 59
Benjamin, Jules R., 60
Bergreen, Laurence, 83
Betancourt, Ernesto, 123
Betancourt, Rómula, 77
Bistoni, Ansan Albert, 109–10, 147
Boggs Act, 115
Bolita, 82, 83, 84
Bolivia, cocaine production and trafficking, 97–98, 107, 117, 120, 136
Bonsal, Philip, 130, 131, 132–33
Borroto Díaz, Ricardo, 136
Bosch, José M., 128
Bosch-Bacardí clan, 128
Bowman, John, 19
Braden, Spruille, 58–59, 62
Brook, Timothy, 11
Brun D'Avoglio, Luis, 99
Buenos Aires, 20

Cadena, Guillermo, 100
Caja de Retiro del Sindicato Gastronómico (Food Workers Union Pension Fund), 92

Calixto García Hospital, 51
Camagüey, Cuba, 3, 21, 110–12
Cammarata, Frank, 139
Campa, Miguel A., 114
Camp Columbia, 34, 66, 69, 77, 136
Camp Libertad, 136
Camp Triscornia, 4–5, 69
Canada, 2, 107–10
Canadian-U.S. relations, 18–19, 21, 147–48
Cañal, Angelito, 63
Canary Islands, 4
Cañas Perdomo, A., 37
Cantú, Esteban, 54
Capestany, Manuel, 70
Capone, Ralph, 67
Capone crime syndicate, 19
Carbone, Paul. *See* Venture, Paul
Caribbean islands, 12
Caribbean Legion, 77
Casino de la Playa, 86
Casinos: government subsidization of, 8, 85–86, 90; growth in, elements contributing to, 13; Kefauver investigation of U.S., 82; U.S. employees in, 82, 90; U.S. opposition to, 85–86; honest, 90, 91; revenue from, 93; 1959 destruction of, 123; after the revolution, 123–25. *See also* Gambling
Castro, Fidel: reform campaigns, 9; corruption accusations made by, 76, 113–14; Operacíon Matrimonio, 125–26; compared to Christ, 126–27; elite support for, 128; mafia and, 133, 135, 141, 143; assassination of, U.S. plans for, 133, 143–44; U.S. media attacks on, 140–41, 144; Prío's support for, 177 (n. 14)
Castro, Raúl, 125–26, 130, 132–33
Castro administration: revisionist historiography of, 10–11; gambling and casino industry policy, 93, 123–25; tourism policy, 124, 126, 128–30; political arrests and executions, 130–31; diplomatic recognition of, 131–32; U.S. plans to overthrow, 133, 143; drug traffickers

arrest and prosecution by, 135–40; hotels, nationalization of, 140; U.S. disinformation campaign against, 141–45; bombing of, plans for, 193 (n. 51)

Castroverde, Jorge A., 127–28

Catalanotti, Giuseppe, 120

Cavanese, Pierre. *See* Di Giorgio, Giuseppe

Cellini, Dino, 138

Central Intelligence Agency (CIA), 105, 133, 143, 179 (n. 29)

Céspedes, Carlos Manuel de, 31, 86

Chibás, Eduardo, 76, 88, 89–90, 113–14, 175 (n. 35)

Chile, 95, 98–100

China: revolutionary policy and revisionist historiography, 10–11; opium use and production in, 45–46, 144–45; migration from, 46–50, 54, 55–56; treaty to end human trafficking and, 47; relations with Cuba, 47, 133; drug trafficking, U.S. accusations of, 144–45; heroin production and trafficking by, 145; antidrug policy, 145–46

Chinese associations, 51–52, 55

Chinese immigrants: opium use by, 2, 38, 43, 47, 48, 50–51, 54, 56, 110, 117; trafficking of, 28–29, 46–47; assimilation of, 43, 46, 50, 56; business ownership by, 47–48, 50; prejudice against, 48–49, 53–54, 55; crime and, 51–52; restrictions on, 52–53; in Mexico, 54; gambling traditions, 85. *See also* Immigrants

Cienfuegos, Cuba, 3

Cigarette smuggling, 26, 28, 59, 106, 107

Cipriano de Mosquera, Tomás, 1

Cirules, Enrique, 8, 10, 12, 93, 179 (n. 29)

Ciudad Juárez distillery, 18

Club Tropicana, 138

Cocaine: ethnicity and class distinctions in users of, 2, 9, 38; Prío report on, 75; seizures of, 95–96, 97, 98, 118–20

Cocaine production and trafficking:

Andean countries and, 2, 95–101, 107, 117, 120, 136, 150; World War II and, 58; government protections and, 63; couriers for, 111, 118; United States and, 122, 149; Mexico and, 148. *See also* Drug traffickers; Drug trafficking

Coca leaf production, 95, 97

Cold War, 8

Colombia, 2, 70, 100–101, 141, 149–50

Communications industry, 5

Communism, 8, 138, 141

Compañía de Fomento del Turismo casino project, 85–86

Congress of Latin American Tourist Organizations, 130

Contrabando (Serpa), 22, 23

Corruption: Batista administration and, 10, 58–60, 67, 103; Follmer report on, 57–58; U.S. residents in Cuba and, 59; Prío administration and, 60, 75–79, 87; Grau administration and, 60, 114; World War II and post–World War II eras and, 60–61, 66–67; Castro's accusations of, 113–14

Corsican drug dealers, 105–6, 108–11, 147

Costello, Frank, 66, 71

Cotrone, Giuseppe, 110

Cotrone, Vincent, 110

Courtwright, David T., 8

Crime, 39–40, 51–52, 82, 150

Crime Commission of Greater Miami, 82

Croce, Jean Baptiste, 109–10, 147

Cros, Raúl, 136

Cuba, prerevolutionary: economic growth and social fluidity in, 2–5, 19–21, 60, 92; immigration's impact on society in, 3–5; wars of independence, 5, 47; population, 10; prostitution in, 10, 126; Prohibition and, 19–21; tourism promotion, 21; political instability in 1930s, 31–35; U.S. workers in, corrupt practices of, 59; drug seizures and, 63, 75, 118–20; banking system reorganization post–World War II, 92. *See also specific administrations*

Cubana de Aviación, 111

Cuban Bank for Agricultural and Industrial Development (BANFAIC), 92–93

Cuban Revolution (1959), 121, 123–33

Cuban Revolutionary Party (Auténticos), 59

Curbelo, Carlos Aulet, 118

Cusack, John, 110–11, 122

De Castroverde, Jorge A., 115, 136

De Gaulle, Charles, 106

De la Carrera, Antonio, 136

Democratic Party (United States), 82–83

Dempsey, Jack, 66

Denmark, 23

Dewey, John, 26

Dewey, Thomas E., 65

Díaz Lanz, Pedro Luis, 130

Díaz Lorenzo, Adolfo, 136

Di Giorgio, Giuseppe (Pierre Cavanese), 138

Dillon, Joseph H., 135–36

Di Marco, Carmen, 98

Directorio Central de las Sociedades de la Raza de Color (Central Board of Associations of Colored People), 46–47

Dolz, Ricardo, 86

Dominican Republic, 12, 77

Dorticós, Osvaldo, 130

Drug traffickers: couriers for, 2, 35, 36, 59, 96, 104, 111, 118, 121, 149, 150; gender, ethnicity, and class distinctions and, 6, 38, 76, 105, 120, 122; economic and political power of, 8; government protection of, 9, 63; immigrants as, 11–12, 40–43, 51, 54, 96, 150–51; deportation/extradition and, 109, 120, 135–40, 147–48; refuge in Cuba for, 121–22, 148; execution of, 138

—arrest and prosecution of: in Cuba, 2, 38, 41–42, 63, 109, 111, 113, 115–22, 135–40; gender, ethnicity, and class distinctions and, 9, 38, 122; FBN undercover operations, 40–41, 101, 108; avoiding, techniques for, 41–42; Andean countries, 96, 97–98, 101; French, 106, 109; denial of bail benefit, 115, 136; U.S., 115, 141–42, 148–49; Middle Eastern, 117–18; FBN advice to Castro regarding, 135; Cuban refugees, 141–42; in Canada, 147–48

Drug trafficking: culture's defining role in, 11; League of Nations convention on narcotics and, 37–38, 62–63; World War II narcotics availability and, 55, 58, 95, 104; in fiction, 96; postrevolutionary Cuba and, 135–40; refugees to United States arrested for, 141–42. *See also specific countries; specific drugs*

—prerevolutionary: transshipment points, 2–3, 12, 96–99, 104, 110–12, 120–21; growth in, elements of, 5–7, 12–13, 35–43, 121; mafia and, 7–8, 115–16; genocide of dominant class and, 8–10; government suppression of, 23–24, 38, 40–41; decline in, government reports on, 37; by U.S. workers, 59; Palacios Planas letter on, 61–62; Prío administration and, 75–79; Batista administration and, 113–22

Drug use/users: U.S. politics of reform and, 8–9; treatment facilities for, 50, 51, 63; World War II and post–World War II eras and, 55, 61, 65, 95, 104; increases in, government reports on, 61–62, 75–76; Marseille statistics on, 106; revolution and, 127–28

Dulles, Allen, 131

Du Pont, Irénée, 26

Du Pont, Pierre, 26

Echavarría Olózaga family, 1

Economy: growth of, 2–5, 21, 60; tourism and, 19–21, 89–93, 124, 126, 128–30;

Machado policy of self-sufficiency, 24; BANFAIC stabilization of, 92; foreign investment in, 92. *See also* Sugar industry
Ecuador, 2, 100–101, 120
Egypt, 107
Eisenhower, Dwight D., 131–32
Elías Calles, Plutarco, 55
Embargo on export of legal drugs, 57, 68, 70, 99–100
Emerald smuggling, 150
Esmori y Rodríguez, Rafael, 41
Espíritu Burlón (song), 89
Estévez Infante, Miguel, 41
Estrada Palma, Tomás, 52–53

Federal Bureau of Narcotics (FBN): combating Communism, 8; Follmer report on narcotics smuggling and, 36–37, 57–58; undercover operations, 40–41, 101; diversion of legal drugs investigation, 57–58; Luciano investigation, 67–68, 71–72; Prío Socarrás (Francisco) surveillance, 78; Kefauver investigation, involvement in, 81; seizure of narcotics by, 95, 108; Mondolini investigation, 110–11; Batista's cooperation with, 113; training provided by, 115; Cuba relations, Castro administration, 135–40; China accused of drug trafficking by, 145; opium production in Cuba, report on, 145; Mexico, cooperation with, 148; Lindesmith investigation, 156 (n. 44)
Femeniar Lores, Francisco, 118
Fernández, Damián J., 7
Fernández, Manuel, 41
Fernández Miranda, Roberto, 91, 123
Fernández Trujillo, Jorge, 120
Fernández Trujillo, José, 120
Fernández y Batista, Marta, 91
Fernández y Fernández, José Antonio (El Gallego), 41–43
Fernández y Fernández, Mario, 136, 138

Ferrara, Orestes, 24, 85
Florida, 10, 18, 20–21, 28, 59, 82, 83, 85, 150–51
Follmer, Claude, 36, 57–58, 61
Ford, Henry, 17
Fox, Martín, 91, 128
France, 3, 103–12, 147
Frank, Waldo, 89
Franqui, Carlos, 126

Gaffney, George H., 121
Galante, Carmine, 135
Gallegos, Rómula, 77
Gambling: economic growth and, 3–5, 89–93; drug trafficking, effect on, 13; financial advantages to government officials and, 59, 86; mafia investment in, 67, 82, 83, 89, 90–93, 110, 125; popularity of, 83–86; in fiction, 84; ethnicity and social class, relationship to, 84, 85, 86–87; criticism of, 84, 87–88; tradition of, 84, 88; prerevolutionary government attempts to suppress, 84–85; postrevolutionary government attempts to suppress, 84–85, 123–25; immigrant traditions assimilated, 85. *See also* Casinos
García Menocal, Mario, 86
García y García, Alvaro, 40
Gardner, Winthrop, 59
Genovese, Vito, 115–16
Germany, 23, 71
Gil Carballo, Antonio, 36, 50, 51, 53, 63
Giordano, Henry L., 145
Gompers, Samuel, 49
González, Angel, 58
González, Miguel Angel, 98
González Aguilera, Luis, 120, 149
González Hernández, Miguel Angel, 118
González Lastra, Miguel Angel, 118
González López, Jorge, 118
Gootenberg, Paul, 12
Gordon, Larry, 37
Grace Line ships, 96, 99

Graham, Walter, 138
Gran Casino Nacional, 86–87
Granma, 177 (n. 14)
Grau administration, 32–33, 60, 62–63, 66, 69–70, 77, 114
Grau San Martín, Francisco, 66
Grau San Martín, Ramón, 32–33, 59, 60, 67, 69, 175 (n. 35)
Graziani, Lucien Gabriel, 110
Great Britain: U.S. relations with, 18, 23, 99–100; social norms and restrictions and, 19–20; Spanish relations with, 22; opium trade in China and, 45; Chinese migration to, 49; Cuban relations with, 58, 76–77, 131; drug traffickers, sentences imposed on, 115
Great Depression, 2, 24, 26, 27
Greece, 107
Griffith, Ivelaw L., 12
Güel, Dario, 120
Guerra, Pablo, 141
Guerra y Sánchez, Ramiro, 22
Guevara, Ernesto (Ché), 125–26, 130
Guiteras Holmes, Antonio, 33, 34
Gurfein, Murry I., 65
Gutiérrez, Gustavo, 23–24

Haffenden, Charles R., 65
Haiti, 3, 12, 28
Harb, Rames, 98
Hashish, 107
Havana: immigrant populations in, 3–4; Prohibition's economic effect in, 19–21; 1934 bomb attacks in, 33–35; drug availability in, 42; Chinese community in, 47–48, 50–52
Havana Hilton, 92
Heath, Dwight B., 8
Hemingway, Ernest, 22
Henrich, Freddy, 98
Hernández Márquez, César, 40
Heroin production and trafficking, 103–12, 115–16, 122, 145, 149. *See also* Drug traffickers; Drug trafficking

Herrán, Pedro Alcántara, 1
Herrán Olózaga, Rafael, 1, 149
Herrán Olózaga, Tomás, 1, 149
Herrera, Benito, 63, 67, 70
Hevia, Carlos, 32
Hill, Robert C., 132
Hill, Virginia, 67
Hilton, Conrad, 91
Hogan, Joseph John, 138
Homosexuality, repression of, 125
Honduras, 25
Horse racing, 82
Hotel Capri, 90–91
Hotel industry: Prohibition's effect on, 19; mafia control of, 90–93, 140; foreign investment in, 92; government subsidies for, 92–93, 140; 1959 riots and, 123; postrevolutionary nationalization of, 140
Hotel Nacional, 90–91
Hotel Riviera, 90, 92–93, 138, 140
Human trafficking, 28–29, 46–47, 106

Ibáñez de Sánchez, Blanca, 78, 98, 120, 149
Ibrahim, Ismail Towfie, 40
Immigrants: as drug traffickers, 11–12, 40–43, 51, 96, 150–51; trafficking of, 28–29, 46–47; statistics concerning, 46, 50. *See also* Chinese immigrants; Migration
Immigration, Machado campaign against, 52
India, 110
Industrial growth, prerevolutionary, 3
Inter-American Conference for Democracy and Freedom, 77
Internal Revenue Service, 81
Interpol (International Criminal Police Organization), 115
Iran, 107, 108
Isle of Pines, 3–4
Italy, 23, 65, 70–73, 104–5, 120

Jamaica, 12, 28
Japan, 2, 4, 145
Java, 95
Johnson, Frank, 41
Johnston, William, 116, 117, 118–21
Jordán Pereira, Octavio (El Cubano Loco), 42
Joven Cuba, 33, 34

Kansas City, 57
Kefauver Committee, 81–83
Kennedy, John F., 143
Kennedy, Robert F., 143
Kuchilán, Mario, 77

Lansky, Jake, 83, 138
Lansky, Meyer: Luciano and, 66, 67, 89; casino ownership and, 82; gambling in Cuba, involvement in, 83, 89–93; BANDES program and, 92–93; departs Cuba, 124, 138; deportation of, 135, 138; Anastasia assassination and, 140; investment losses of, 140; U.S. charges against, 183 (n. 90)
La Paz, Bolivia, 97–98
Law of agrarian reform, 132
Lazareto del Mariel, El, 50, 51, 63
League of Nations convention on narcotics, 37–38, 62–63
Lebanon, 106–7, 117
Lee, Reginald, 103
Le Havre, France, 107
Lemes García, Jorge Juan, 98
Le Riverend, Julio, 178 (n. 29)
Levine, Samuel, 101
Lima, Peru, 97
Lindesmith, Alfred R., 156 (n. 44)
Literacy rates, prerevolutionary, 2–3
Loan sharks, 82
London, 19–20
López Leiva, Francisco, 53
Lo Piccolo, Joseph, 138
Lottery gambling, 84–85, 86–89
Louza, José, 40

Lozada y González, Manuel, 41
Lozano, Guillermo, 100–101
Luciano, Salvatore (Lucky), 65–73, 89, 92
Lyceum and Lawn Tennis Club, 87, 127

Machado, Gerardo, 23, 33
Machado administration, 23–24, 31, 52, 86
Mafia
—in Cuba: drug trade and, 8, 13; 1946 Christmas meeting, 67; deportation of, 69–70, 135–40; casino gambling, control of, 89, 90–93, 110, 125, 140; postrevolutionary policy on, 93, 123–24; Castro and, 133, 135, 141, 143
—in United States: alcohol smuggling and, 18–19; Kefauver Committee investigations into, 81–83; gambling business of, 82; political machines protecting, 82; and ethnicity and class distinctions, 83; drug trade and, 115–16, 183 (n. 90); Anastasia assassination, 140. See also specific members
Mafia special-services, 179 (n. 29)
Mañach, Jorge, 62
Marijuana: ethnicity and class distinctions in users of, 2, 9, 38, 39, 63; production and trafficking of, 38, 63, 107, 116, 137–38, 150; crime tied to use of, 39–40; U.S. and Cuban campaigns against, 39–40; arrest and prosecution for trafficking in, 63, 107, 122, 137–38; Prío report on, 75; seizures of, 75, 116–20, 137; postrevolutionary policy on, 125, 137–38. See also Drug traffickers; Drug trafficking
Marijuana Tax Act, 39
Marriage, Castro's policy on, 125–26
Marseille, France, 103–5, 110
Marshall, George, 68
Martí, José, 23
Martin, Frank, 120
Martínez, Sáenz, 32
Martínez Arenas, Abelardo, 136

Martínez del Rey, Abelardo (El Teniente), 42

Martínez Minanoz, Khossee Kholian, 117

Martínez Rodríguez del Rey, Abelardo (El Teniente), 97, 98, 100, 101, 118, 119, 136–37

Martínez Rodríguez del Rey, Jorge (El Bacardi), 98, 119, 136–37

Martínez Swett, Luis, 101

Maruiz, Benedicto, 41

Matos, Huber, 130

Matthews, Herbert L., 125

Mederos de González, Elena, 127

Melvis, 120

Mencken, H. L., 19

Méndez, Oscar, 100

Méndez Marfa, Manuel (Manolín), 98, 118

Méndez Pérez, Oscar, 118

Mendieta, Carlos, 32–34, 38–39

Mera, Abel, 118

Mesa, Rodríguez, 179 (n. 29)

Mexico: North American investment in, 2; tradition and culture of drug use in, 11; Prohibition and, 18; U.S. relations, 21, 68; Chinese immigrants in, 54–55; narcotics trafficking, 54–55, 104, 147, 148

Meyer, Kathryn, 7, 12

Miami, 21, 121, 141–42

Migration, 3–7, 19. See also Immigrants

Miller, Edward G., 78

Minas, Steve, 136

Minaudo, Onofrio, 120

Miró Cardona, José, 124

Moms, Jesús (Orejitas), 100–101

Mondolini, Paul Damien, 108–11, 147

Montgomery, Ruth, 140

Moreno Fraginals, Manuel, 22, 46, 50

Morphine, 63, 75

Moubarak, José Flaifel (Pepe el Cubano), 117–18

Munroe, William (Butch), 110

Musto, David, 8

Myers, David. See Simpson, Dave

Narcotic Control Act (United States), 115

Narcotics: defined, 14; League of Nations convention on, 37–38, 62–63; World War II availability of, 55, 95, 104. See also specific narcotics

National Prohibition Act, 18, 36

Navarro, Cantón, 179 (n. 29)

Nelli, Humbert S., 11

Netherlands, 23

Nicaragua, 149

Nixon, Richard M., 133

Nogueira, Pedro, 68

North America. See specific countries

North Korea, 145

Norway, 23

Nuevitas, Cuba, 110, 111

Numbers racket. See Bolita

Oil industry, 133

Olivera, J. Ray, 78

Operacíon Matrimonio, 125–26

Operation Mongoose, 143

Opium production and trafficking: FBN undercover operations and, 41; shipping industry and, 41–42; Great Britain and, 45; in Mexico, 54–55; World War II and, 55; in Andean countries, 56, 98–99; in France, 103–4; in Cuba, 110, 145; ECOSOC protocol, 114; seizures from, 117–18; China-to-Cuba connection, 144–45. See also Drug traffickers; Drug trafficking

Opium use: Chinese in Cuba and, 2, 38, 43, 47, 48, 50–51, 54, 56, 110, 117; ethnicity and class distinctions in, 9, 50; United States and, 46, 48–49; non-Chinese, 48–49, 51; Prío report on, 75

Opium Wars, 45

Organized crime. See Mafia

Ormento, John, 135

Orsini, Joseph. *See* Venture, Paul
Orthodox Party, 114
Ortiz, Fernando, 20, 54, 84

Palacios Planas, Eduardo, 57, 61
Palma y Romay, Ramón de, 84
Panama, 23
Pan American Airways, 20–21, 111
Paroutian, Antranik (André), 110, 148
Parssinen, Terry, 7, 12
Pascua en San Marcos, La (Palma y
    Romay), 84
Patrizi, Joseph, 110
Pedraza, José A., 58
Peña y Rodríguez, José Francisco
    (Tomás) de la, 41
Pequeño, Alfredo, 67
Perdomo Oviedo, Pedro, 118
Pérez, Louis A., Jr., 10, 19, 32, 60, 93
Pérez Carballo, Germán, 118
Pérez Dámera, Genovevo, 66, 76
Pérez Fernández, José Gabriel, 117–18
Perón, Juan Domingo, 100
Pertierra, Indalecio, 66
Peru, 55–56, 95–97, 107, 117, 136
Piedra, Orlando, 109, 118–20
Piedra, Osvaldo, 193 (n. 51)
Pino Santos, Oscar, 179 (n. 29)
Platt Amendment, 33
P.M. (Pasado Meridiano) (film), 125
Portell-Vilá, Herminio, 67
Portugal, 45
Prío administration: corruption in, 60,
    76, 79, 87, 114; drug trafficking and,
    75–79; Batista overthrow of, 77; demo-
    cratic movements support, 77
Prío Socarrás, Antonia, 76
Prío Socarrás, Carlos: corrupt practices
    of, 60, 76; Luciano and, 66, 69; elec-
    tion of, 73; drug use by, 73, 78–79, 121;
    guerrilla struggle supported by, 128
Prío Socarrás, Francisco, 70, 78
"Program of Covert Action against the
    Castro Regime" (CIA), 133

Prohibition, 2, 9, 17–27, 82
Prostitution, 10, 98–99, 126
Puebla, Carlos, 127
Puerto Rico, 21, 149
Purple Gang, 19

Quiñones Campos, José, 41

Raft, George, 91
Railroad industry, 21, 46, 54
Rakusin, Samuel L., 40–41
Ramos, Domingo F., 37
Recio, Alberto, 62
Recio, Gabriela, 55
Reformism, 8–9
Regalado Falcón, Apolonio, 118
Religious organizations opposed to gam-
    bling, 87
Rivard, Lucien, 109–11, 138–39, 147–48
Rodriguez Téllez, Carlos, 100
Rodríguez Yzuaga, Pastor, 118
Roig de Leuchsenring, Emilio, 88
Roosevelt, Franklin D., 26, 31, 39, 58
Roosevelt (Franklin D.) administration,
    24, 27
Rothman, Norman, 110, 111
Rum Treaty, 23–24

Sabiani, Simon, 105
Saco, José Antonio, 84
Saint Pierre (Champagne island), 25
Salas Fonseca, José, 118
Sans Souci nightclub, 90–91
Santiago de Cuba, 4, 21
Saucedo, Celina, 137
Saucedo, Enrique, 137
Schwartz, Rosalie, 12
Serpa, Enrique, 22, 23
Shehab, Farid, 107
Shipping industry: improvements after
    war of 1895–98, 5; drug trafficking
    and, 12, 35–36, 41–42, 76, 96, 107–8, 117;
    alcohol smuggling and, 20–22, 25–27
Siegel, Benjamin (Bugsy), 66, 67

Silesi, Joseph, 140
Simpson, Dave (David Myers), 40–41
Sinatra, Frank, 66, 67
Siragusa, Charles, 106, 136, 138, 140,
    141–42, 144–45
Slave labor, 46–47
Slave trade, 106
Smathers, George, 143
Smith, Earl E. T., 91, 131
Smuggling: alcohol, 2, 18–26; tourists
    and, 20–21; shipping industry and,
    20–22, 25–27; history in Cuba, 22–23;
    U.S. negotiations to end, 23–25; ciga-
    rette, 26, 28, 59, 106, 107; contraband
    other than liquor, 26, 106; tax eva-
    sion through, 27; U.S. operations for,
    27–28; government suppression of, 28;
    human trafficking and, 28–29, 46–47,
    106; arms trafficking and, 101, 111;
    Marseille and, 106; emerald, 150
Sobrado López, José, 38, 39, 63
Social welfare, 2–3, 87, 126
South Korea, 145
Soviet Union, 133
Spain, 3–5, 22, 28, 41, 147
Spanish-American War, 21
Spechar, Mario, 98
Spirito, François L., 105
Stevenson, Adlai, 82–83
Suárez, José, 120
Suárez Rivas, Eduardo, 66
Suárez Rivas, José, 69, 92
Sugar industry: 1930s political instability,
    effect on, 2, 31; economy of, 2, 90; im-
    migrant labor and, 3, 28–29, 46–47, 56;
    immigrant investment in, 5; U.S. trade
    relations and, 24, 27, 69–70, 133; 1958
    sabotage campaign and, 121; after the
    revolution, 128, 132. *See also* Economy
Sweden, 23
Syria, 107, 117

Taiwan, 145
Tarafa, Cuba, 110

Ten Years' War (1868–78), 5, 47
Thoumi, Francisco, 6, 7
Tiempo viejos, 20
Tobacco industry, 18
To Have and Have Not (Hemingway),
    22
Torbay, Joffre, 100
Toudayan, Edouard, 147
Tourine, Charles, Jr., 98, 138–39
Tourine, Charles, Sr., 98
Tourist industry: Reformism and, 9;
    post–World War II, 10; Prohibition
    and, 19–21; prerevolutionary pro-
    motions, 21; Batista administration
    and, 89; Chibás support of, 89–90;
    gambling and, 89–93; BANFAIC pro-
    motion of, 92; foreign investment in,
    92; government subsidization of, 92;
    Florida, 121; after the revolution, 124,
    126, 128–30
Trafficante, Santo, Jr., 83, 90–91, 139–40
Tropicana, 59, 90–91, 128
Trujillo, Rafael Leonidas, 77
Turkey, 36, 106–7
26 July Movement, 121, 123

United Nations Commission on Narcotic
    Drugs, 138
United Nations Economic and Social
    Council (ECOSOC) meeting, 114
United States: sugar demand in, 2; Prohi-
    bition, 2, 9, 17–27, 82; Cuba compared
    to, 3, 48, 50; migration to Cuba and,
    3–4, 19; Progressive Era reformism,
    8–9; trafficking in illegal immigrants
    and, 28; drug use in, 39, 46, 48–49, 151;
    immigrants in, 48–49, 96–97, 141–42,
    150–51; drug trafficking in, 55, 96–97,
    122, 141–42, 148, 150–51; organized
    crime investigations, 81–83; gambling
    in, 82; employees in Cuba, 82, 90; drug
    seizures in, 95–96, 97, 98, 107–8; drug
    traffickers, deportation of, 120; Cuban
    refugees in, 135, 141–42; Prío over-

throw and, 178 (n. 29). *See also specific states*

U.S.-Cuban drug diplomacy: deportation/extradition of drug traffickers and, 21–22, 135–40; embargo on export of legal drugs and, 57, 68, 70; Luciano in, 64, 67–70; Corsican drug traffickers and, 108–11; antinarcotics efforts recognized by FBN, 118–19, 137; Castro administration and, 135–46

U.S.–Cuban relations

—prerevolution: financial, direct investment, 5; occupation by U.S. forces and, 21, 33; smuggling, treaties agreeing to end, 23–25; trade relations and, 24, 27, 69–70; Grau administration and, 32–33, 69; Mendieta administration and, 33; corruption in Cuba, report criticizing, 58–59; Batista administration and, 58–59, 78, 113

—postrevolution: normalization of, 131–32; U.S. business interests and, 132, 133, 140; *La Coubre* explosion and, 132–33; embargo of goods and, 133; severing of, 133; U.S. overthrow plans and, 133, 143; mafia, deportation of, 135–40; refugees arrested on drug charges, 141–42; disinformation campaign and, 141–44

U.S. foreign relations: with Canada, 18–19, 21, 147–48; with Great Britain, 23, 99–100; smuggling, treaties agreeing to end, 23–25; embargo on export of legal drugs and, 57, 68, 70, 99–100; with Mexico, 68; Italy, 70–73, 105; with Chile, 99–100; with France, 106

University of Havana strike, 34
Urban warfare, 31, 33
Urigen Bravo, Miguel, 141
Urrutia, Manuel, 124–25, 136
Uruguay, 2

Vaccaro, Sarro, 40
Valentine, Douglas, 12
Valle, Amir, 10
Valparaíso, Chile, 98–99
Venezuela, 77
Venture, Paul (Paul Carbone), 105
Vera Serafín, Aldo, 136
Vida real, La (Barnet), 96
Vizzini, Salvatore, 110–11, 120

Wakabayashi, Bob Tadashi, 11
Walker, William O., 11, 12
War of 1895–98, 5
Wealth gap, 3
Welles, Sumner, 31
White, George H., 101
Whitney, Robert, 32
Woman's Christian Temperance Union, 17
Wood, Leonard, 4
World War I and post–World War I eras, 17–18, 60
World War II and post–World War II eras, 55, 65, 95, 104

Yapur, Nicolás Flaifel, 117
Yugoslavia, 107

Zappoli, Salvatore, 37